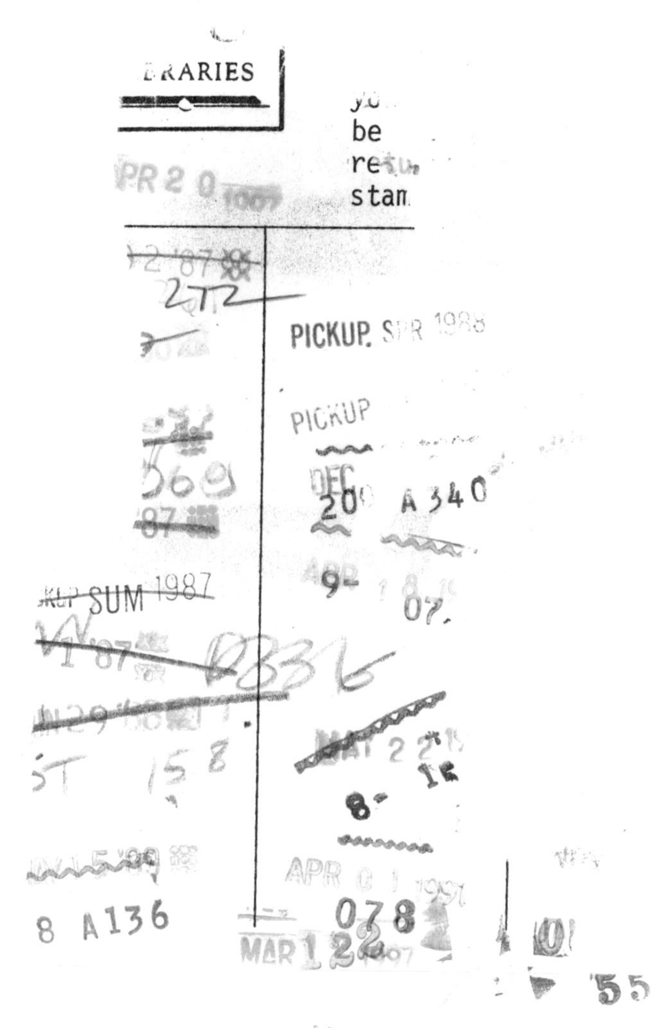

D. Stanley Eitzen
Professor of Sociology
Colorado State University

George H. Sage
Professor of Physical Education
University of Northern Colorado

Sociology of American Sport

Wm. C. Brown Company Publishers
Dubuque, Iowa

Consulting Editor

Aileene Lockhart
Texas Woman's University

Library of Congress Catalog Card Number: 77-89751

ISBN 0—697—07146—4

Printed in the United States of America

Contents

Preface vii

1 **The Sociological Analysis of Sport in Society** 1
The Discipline of Sociology 1
Sport as a Microcosm of American Society 14
Summary 19

2 **Social and Cultural Sources for the Rise of Sport in America** 25
The Transformation of American Sport 25
The Technological Revolution and Sport 30
Industrialization, Urbanization, and Sport 41
Cultural Forces for the Rise of Sport 49
Summary 54

3 **Sport and American Values** 59
The American Value System 59
Societal Values and Sport 65
Summary 74

4 **Sport and American Education** 79
The Role of Sport in Secondary Schools 80
The Consequences of Sport for Schools, Communities, and Individuals 86
Problems, Dilemmas, and Controversies 93
Summary 104

5 **Sport and Religion** 111
Religion and Society 112
The Changing Relationship of Sport and Religion 114
Religion Uses Sport 121
Sport Uses Religion 128
Summary 137

6 **Sport and the Polity** 143
The Political Uses of Sport 145

The Political Attitudes of Coaches and Athletes 155
Summary 162

7 **Sport and the Economy** 169
The Interrelationship of Sport and the Economy 169
The Economics of "Corporate Sport" 179
Summary 202

8 **Sport, Social Stratification, and Social Mobility** 209
Social Class and Sport 209
Social Mobility and Sport 219
Summary 230

9 **Racism in Sport** 235
The History of Black Involvement in Sport 235
Black Dominance in Sport 239
Racial Discrimination in Sport 244
Summary 255

10 **Females in American Sport: Continuity and Change** 261
Social Sources of Sexism in Sport 262
Consequences of Sexism for Females in Sport 269
Women's Liberation Movement and Sport 281
Summary 283

11 **Contemporary Trends and the Future of Sport in America** 289
Trends in Population 289
Trends of Industry and Technology 291
The American Economy 301
Future Trends for Minorities in American Sport 308
Trends in American Values 310
Summary 320

Index 325

Preface

Sport takes place in social settings and has a profound influence on the social life of large numbers of Americans of all ages, but the study of sport from a sociological perspective has not been prominent until quite recently. However, academic fashions are changing and in the past decade the tools of sociology—its theories and methods—have been increasingly employed in the service of studying sport. As a consequence, a cumulative and systematic body of knowledge is beginning to take form. The literature has grown rapidly through books, beginning with anthologies and culminating in full-blown texts and periodicals, such as the *International Review of Sport Sociology,* which began publication in 1966, and, more recently, the *Review of Sport and Leisure* and the *Journal of Sport and Social Issues.* Also, several international conferences on sport sociology have stimulated worldwide sociological study of sport, and this subject has had a prominent place in the convention programs of the American Association for Health, Physical Education, and Recreation, as well as national and regional meetings of sociology associations. Finally, sport sociology classes are now commonly offered by sociology and physical education departments throughout the nation.

Three goals guided our efforts in writing this book. In the analysis of the American sport structure, we hope to have the reader better understand sport and also to implicitly incorporate the sociological perspective in his or her repertoire for understanding other parts of the social world.

The second goal is to impress on our colleagues in sociology and physical education the importance of including the sociology of sport as a legitimate subfield in each of the two disciplines. We hope that this book will infuse physical educators with the viability of social forces in sports activities and organizations. While the mechanical and physiological factors of movement are important, the social milieu in which participation is embedded is crucial with respect to who participates, when, where, and the consequences of such participation. Sport involvement is more than making use of the levers of the body and using strength and endurance to achieve the objective. To sociologists, our message is that sport is a social activity worthy of serious inquiry. It is a substantive topic as worthy of sociologists' attention as such standard specialities as the family, religion, and politics. Not only is sport a microcosm of the larger society but sports phenomena also offer a fertile field to test sociological theories.

Our final goal is to make the reader aware of the positive and negative consequences of the way sport is organized in American society. We are concerned about some of the trends in sport, especially the move away from athlete-oriented activities toward the impersonality of what we term "corporate sport." We are committed to moving sport and society in a more humane direction and this requires, as a first step, a thorough understanding of the principles that underlie the social structures and processes that create, sustain, and transform the social organizations within the institution of sport.

In chapter 1 we describe the focus of sociology as a discipline and identify the different analytic levels employed by sociologists. We then show how sport provides an ideal setting for utilizing certain sociological instruments and methodologies, and affords a setting for testing sociological theories.

The phenomenon of sport represents one of the most pervasive social institutions in the United States, and in chapter 2 we discuss the relationship between the technological, industrial, and urban development and the rise of organized sport.

The major theme of this volume is that sport is a microcosm of American society. Salient American social values are identified in chapter 3, and we discuss how sport reflects and reinforces the core values, beliefs, and ideologies of the society.

Sport and education are inexorably intertwined in American society. In chapter 4, we examine the social sources responsible for the promotion of these programs and the consequences of school sports programs on the academic environment.

In chapter 5, we examine the relationship of one of the oldest universal social institutions—religion—and one of the newest—sport. We trace the changing relations between the two institutions, and show how contemporary sport has many of the characteristics of religion. We also describe how religious agents and agencies use sport to promote religion and show how athletes employ magico-religious rituals, taboos, and fetishes in the hopes of enhancing their performance.

While the sport establishment publicly disavows any relationship between politics and sport, the fact is that the two are closely related. In chapter 6, we discuss the close ties and show that there are several characteristics inherent in both institutions that serve to guarantee this strong relationship.

Economic factors play an overriding role in much of contemporary organized sport. Not only has the growth of the American economy and the emergence of unprecedented affluence, especially in the past two decades, had an impact on sports, but the enormous increase of interest in sport has had a dramatic economic impact. Chapter 7 describes the multidimensional aspects of economic considerations on sport.

Sport is typically assumed to be an egalitarian and meritocratic institution. In chapter 8, we examine the truth of these two assumptions and show that they are largely myths.

Systematic and pervasive discrimination against blacks has been a historical feature of American society, but many Americans have believed that sport has been free of racism. Chapter 9 documents the historical and contemporary facts that illustrate that sport has had and still has many of the same racial problems of the larger society.

The theme of chapter 10 is that the world of sport has been the exclusive domain of males and that social-cultural forces have combined to virtually exclude female sport involvement. We discuss how changing attitudes toward sex roles are now giving girls and women opportunities in sport previously denied them.

In the final chapter, chapter 11, we speculate on the future of American sport. Our basic theme in this chapter is that since sport reflects American society as the society changes, sport will also undoubtedly undergo some transformation. We discuss several current trends and possible future changes in American society and discuss how each will be manifested in sport changes.

The development of this volume has been a coordinated effort by both authors in that we have made contributions of one kind or another to each of the chapters. However, to expedite the writing of the chapters, a division of labor was necessary. Eitzen is primarily responsible for the chapters dealing with the sociological analysis of sport, sport and American values, sport and education, politics, economics, social stratification, and racism; while Sage is primarily responsible for the chapters on the rise of American sport, sport and religion, females in sport, and the future of sport. We had the advantage of having several conscientious reviewers who made a number of useful suggestions on the original manuscript. Most of the suggestions were incorporated into the revised manuscript; some were not. The weaknesses that remain are shared by the authors.

We feel that our sports backgrounds and academic interests harmonize in such a way that we form a unique "team" for writing a book on sport sociology. Both of us are former high school and collegiate athletes. Eitzen has coached on the high school level and been involved in various capacities in youth sports programs; Sage has coached at the youth, high school, and college levels. We have conducted considerable research and published widely in sport sociology. Eitzen is well known in sociology for his studies of racism in sport and his analyses of the social organization of sport. Sage is known for his studies of coaches and his successful anthology, *Sport and American Society*. Although Sage is a physical educator and Eitzen a sociologist, our approach to the sociology of sport is remarkably similar.

This book began as a joint venture by Eitzen, Norman Yetman, and George Ritzer while they were colleagues at the University of Kansas. But when Eitzen left for Colorado State University and Ritzer for the University of Maryland, the project stalled and eventually died. After a dormant period, George Sage entered the project as a coauthor with Eitzen. Although the final product is a blend of Eitzen and Sage, the influence of Yetman and Ritzer remain. Ritzer was instrumental in developing the overall structure of the book and the organization of each chapter. Yetman's important contributions were the writing of the initial draft of the economics chapter and his research with Eitzen that provided the material for approximately one-half of the chapter on minority groups. Our thanks to these friends and colleagues.

The Sociological Analysis of Sport in Society 1

The subject of this book is sport, an extraordinarily pervasive social phenomenon in American society. The sociological perspective is the analytical approach that we will use to examine this very important human activity. We must begin, then, with an introduction to the discipline of sociology.

The Discipline of Sociology

Sociology is the scientific discipline that describes and explains human social organization. The size of a human group under study can range from a couple to a church, a corporation, a community, or a society. The sociologist is interested in the patterns that emerge whenever people interact over periods of time. Although groups may differ in size and purpose, there are similarities in structure and in the processes that create, sustain, and transform the structure. In other words, although one group may exist to knit quilts for charity while another has the goal of winning football games, they will be alike in many important ways. We know, for example, that through recurrent interaction certain characteristics emerge: (1) a division of labor; (2) a hierarchical structure of ranks, i.e., differences in power, prestige, and rewards; (3) rules; (4) punishments for the violations of rules; (5) criteria for the evaluation of things, people, ideas, and behavior; (6) symbols with special meanings (specialized language such as nicknames, gestures, or objects); and (7) member cooperation to achieve group goals.[1]

Sociologists are not only interested in the underlying order of social life, but also in the principles that explain human behavior. Sociology is joined in this quest by other disciplines, especially biology and psychology. Biological explanations for human behavior focus on the structure (potential and limitations) of the human body and the innate drives (hunger, thirst, sex, and comfort) that constrain us. *Sociobiology,* by Edward Wilson, for example, provides the controversial but forceful argument that human genetic heritage explains much behavior, from the way human life is ordered in groups to the prevalence of violence.[2]

Psychological explanations for human behavior are also prevalent. Scientists and laymen alike are prone to explain behavior using assumptions about the psyches of individuals. Psychologists are helpful in explaining why, for example, particular individuals may be violent, self-destructive, criminal, humanitarian, saintly, prejudiced, poor, alcoholics, or failures.

However, biological and psychological explanations are only partially useful because they focus exclusively on the individual. The sociological approach, in contrast, stresses those factors external to the individual. These might be social conditions in the community or society such as the rate of unemployment, the degree of inflation, the amount of leisure time, the extent of urban blight, the restricted opportunities for minority groups, or the distribution of power. An extremely important external source of human behavior is the meanings that the members of a social organization share. We call these shared meanings "culture." Under this rubric are included the standards to evaluate behavior, ideology, customs, expectations for persons occupying various positions, and rules—all of which limit the choices of individuals regardless of their biological heritage or their psychological proclivities. A final external source of control is one's social location. Each individual in society is, because of his or her wealth, occupation, education, religion, racial and ethnic heritage, and family background, ranked by others and by oneself. One's placement in this complex hierarchy exerts pressures, subtle and blatant, on people to behave in prescribed ways.

Because sociology is typically superseded by psychological explanations, the goal of this book is to provide a purely sociological analysis and explanation of sport in American society. Such an inquiry, it is hoped, will not only be interesting and insightful but will introduce the reader to a new and meaningful way to understand the social world—and the phenomenon of sport.

Assumptions of the Sociological Perspective

We have seen that human behavior is examined through different disciplinary lenses and that each makes important contributions to knowledge. Of the disciplines focusing on human behavior, sociology is commonly the least understood. The implicit goal of this book is to introduce you to the sociological ways of perceiving and interpreting the role of sport in American society. Let's begin by enumerating the assumptions of the sociological approach that provide the foundation for this unique way of viewing the world.[3]

Individuals Are, by Their Nature, Social Beings

There are two fundamental reasons for this assumption. First, children enter the world totally dependent on others for their survival. This initial period of dependence means, in effect, that each of us is immersed in social groups from birth. A second basis for the social nature of human beings is that throughout history people have found it advantageous to cooperate with others (for defense, for material comforts, to overcome the perils of nature, and to improve technology).

Individuals Are Socially Determined

This essential assumption stems from the first, that humans are social beings. Individuals are products of their social environments for several reasons. During infancy, the child is at the mercy of others, especially parents. These persons can shape the infant's potential behaviors in an infinite variety of ways depending on their proclivities and those of the society. Parents will have a profound impact on that child's way of thinking about himself/herself and about others; they will transmit religious views, parental attitudes, and how other groups are to be rated. The child will be punished for certain behaviors and rewarded for others. Whether that child becomes a bigot or integrationist, traditionalist or innovator, saint or sinner, athlete or nonathlete, depends in large measure on the parents, siblings, and others who interact with him/her.

Parents may transmit to their offspring some idiosyncratic beliefs and behaviors, but most significantly they act as cultural agents, transferring the ways of the society to their children. As a consequence, the child is not only born into a family but also into a society. That society thus shapes personality characteristics and perceptions of the individual. Berger has summarized the impact of this:

> Society not only controls our movements, but shapes our identity, our thoughts and our emotions. The structures of society become the structures of our own consciousness. Society does not stop at the surface of our skins. Society penetrates us as much as it envelops us.[4]

The individual's identity is socially bestowed and is shaped by the way he/she is accepted, rejected, and/or defined by others. Whether an individual is attractive or plain, witty or dull, worthy or unworthy depends on the values of society and the groups in which the individual is immersed. Although the genes determine one's physical characteristics, the social environment, especially social location, determines how those characteristics will be evaluated.

By suggesting that people are socially determined is another way of saying that they are, in many ways, puppets dependent on and manipulated by social forces. A major function of sociology is to identify the social forces that affect us so greatly. Freedom, as McGee has pointed out, can only come from a recognition of these unseen forces:

> Freedom consists in knowing what these forces are and how they work so that we have the option of saying no to the impact of their operation. For example, if we grow up in a racist society, we will be racists unless we learn what racism is and how it works and then choose to refuse its impact. In order to do so, however, we must recognize that it is there in the first place. People often are puppets, blindly danced by strings of which they are unaware and over which they are not free to exercise control. A major function of sociology is that it permits us to recognize the forces operative on us and to untie the puppet strings which bind us, thereby giving us the option to be free.[5]

So, one task of sociology is to learn, among other things, what racism and sexism are and to determine how they work. But, this is often difficult because we typically do not recognize their existence—because social forces may have prompted us to believe and behave in racist and sexist ways.

To say that we are puppets is really too strong, however. This assumption is not meant to imply a total social determinism. The metaphor is used to convey the idea that much of who we are and what we do is a product of our social environment. But, there are nonconformists, deviants, and innovators. Society is not a rigid, static entity composed of robots. While the members of society are shaped by their social environment, they also change that environment. Human beings are the *shapers* of society as well as the *shapees.* This is the third assumption of the sociological approach.

Individuals Create, Sustain, and Change the Social Forms Within Which They Conduct Their Lives

While humans are largely puppets of their society, they are also puppeteers. In brief, the argument is that social groups of all sizes and types (families, peer groups, work groups, corporations, communities, and societies) are made by humans. What interacting persons create becomes a source of control over them (i.e., they become puppets of their own creation). But the continuous interaction of the group's members also changes the group.[6]

Three important implications stem from this assumption that groups are created by persons in interaction. First, the created social forms have a certain momentum of their own that defies change. The ways of doing and thinking common to the group are "natural" and "right." Although man-made, the group's expectations and structures take on a sacred quality—the sanctity of tradition—that constrains behavior in socially prescribed ways.

A second implication is that social arrangements, because they are a result of social activity, are imperfect. Slavery benefited some segments of society by taking advantage of others. A competitive free enterprise system creates "winners" and "losers." The wonders of technology make worldwide transportation and communication easy and relatively inexpensive, but they also create pollution and the waste of natural resources. These examples show that there are positive and negative consequences emanating from human organization. A final implication is that individuals through collective action are capable of changing the structure of society and even the course of history.[7]

Problems with the Sociological Perspective

Sociology is not a comfortable discipline and therefore will not appeal to everyone. To look behind the "closed doors" of social life is fraught with danger. The astute observer of society must ask such questions as: How does it really work? Who really has the power? Who benefits under the existing social arrangements, and who does not? To ask such questions means that the inquirer is interested in looking beyond the commonly accepted "official" definitions. As Berger has put it, "[the] sociological perspective involves a process of 'seeing through' the facades of social structures."[8] The underlying assumption of the sociologist is that things are *not* as they seem. Is big-time college football educational? Does sport build character? Is professional sport free of racism? Is sport a mobility escalator? To make such queries is to question existing myths, stereotypes, and official dogma. The critical examination of society tends to demystify and demythologize. It sensitizes the individual to the inconsistencies present in society.

The sociological assumption providing the basis for this critical stance is that the social world is made by people—and therefore not sacred. The economic system, the law, ideology, the way power is distributed, and the institution of sport are all created and sustained by people. As a consequence, they can be changed by people. But, if the change is to correct imperfections, then we must truly understand how social phenomena work. The central task of this book is to aid in such an understanding of sport in American society.

The sociological perspective is also discomforting to many because the understanding of the constraints of society is liberating. Traditional sex roles, for example, are no longer "sacred" for many persons. But, while this is liberating from the constraints of tradition, it is also freedom from the protection that custom provides. The robotlike acceptance of tradition is comfortable because it frees us from choice (and therefore blame) and from ambiguity. So, the understanding of society is a two-edged sword, freeing us, but also increasing the probability of frustration, anger, and alienation.

A final source of discomfort is that the behavior of the subjects is not always certain. Prediction is not always accurate because people can choose between options, and they can be persuaded by rational and irrational factors. The result is that if sociologists know the social conditions, they can only predict the consequences in terms of probabilities. On the other hand, chemists know exactly what will occur if a certain measure of one chemical element is mixed with a precise amount of another in a test tube. Or, civil engineers armed with the knowledge of rock formations, type of soils, wind currents, and temperature extremes know exactly what specifications are needed in building a dam in a certain place. They could not, however, if the foundation and building materials kept shifting. That is the problem—and the source of excitement—for the sociologist. Social life is highly complex, and its study is beset by change and uncertainties. Although the goal is to reduce the margin of error, its complete elimination is impossible as long as humans are not robots.

Units of Sociological Analysis

We have seen that sociologists are interested in social organizations and how social forces operate to channel human behavior. The scope ranges from individuals sharing common social characteristics, to small groups, to society.

The Social Psychological Approach

Some sociologists focus on human behavior rather than social organizations. They direct their research to finding under what social circumstances people behave in predictable ways. We know, for example, that the social group has great power over its members. One classic study of conformity by Solomon Asch shows dramatically how we tend to give in to group pressure.[9] Asch asked the subjects of an experiment to compare the length of lines on cards. The subjects were asked one at a time to identify verbally the longest line. All the subjects but one were confederates of the experimenter, coached to give the same wrong answer, thereby placing the lone subject in the awkward position of contradicting the evidence of his senses. Each experiment consisted of 18 trials, with the confederates giving wrong responses on 12 and correct ones on 6. For the 50 test subjects going through this ordeal, the average number of times they went along with the majority with incorrect judgments was 3.84. While 13 of the 50 were independent and gave responses in accord with their perceptions, 37 (74 percent) caved in to the group pressure at least once (12 did eight or more times). In other experiments where the confederates were not unanimous in their responses, the test subjects were freed from the overwhelming group pressure and generally had confidence enough in their perceptions to give the correct answer.

Social psychological research has been popular among sport sociologists. Typically, they have compared athletes and nonathletes on a number of dependent variables. The assumption is that the athletic experience makes a difference in political and religious attitudes, in values, psychological attributes, and "character."

The Micro Level

Here, the emphasis is on the structure of relatively small groups (e.g., friendship groups, the family and organized groups like the Friday Night Poker Club, the Nazarene Church, the African Violet Society, and the Pretty Prairie High School football team). Some of the research questions of interest at this level are: What are the principles underlying group formation, stability, and change? What are the most effective forms of organization to accomplish group goals? Under what conditions is member cooperation maximized? Under what conditions is member behavior least predictable?

Sport teams are especially useful research settings in which to test theories about social organization. Since this is the most common form of research in the sociology of sport, let's look at some representative studies.

The Study of Organizational Goal Attainment. Sports teams have specific goals, and the members are in agreement on the goals. They have a single objective that overrides all other considerations—they are organized to win games.[10] Not only is the goal of an athletic team clear, but there is also a convenient and accurate measure of that goal—the winning percentage for the season. Another important advantage of using teams for organizational research is that they are amenable to comparative studies. They provide hundreds of organizational units similar on several relevant dimensions. They are exactly the same size, they must abide by the same rules, they have a relatively common means of recruitment and training of personnel, and they have a similar social structure (hierarchy of roles, communication networks, social control). By controlling all of these variables (i.e., keeping them constant), one can determine under what other social conditions is goal attainment enhanced in social organizations. For example, Eitzen conducted a study of 288 high school basketball teams and found that the homogeneity of background characteristics of team members (religion, socioeconomic status, and neighborhood background) was positively related to team success. His explanation for this relationship was that heterogeneity of players increased the likelihood of cliques within the team, which reduced cohesion and ultimately resulted in poor team performance.[11]

The Study of Leadership. What is the effect on organizational goal attainment when there is a change in management? There are three possible consequences of a change in key leadership roles: the effectiveness of an organization may increase, decrease, or remain relatively the same. When Alvin Gouldner described leadership change in a gypsum mine, he showed a decline in organizational effectiveness as the new and more bureaucratically oriented manager introduced different rules, made new interpretations, and invoked more negative sanctions than his predecessor.[12] While instructive, this study was only of a single case and therefore in need of replication many times over. Oscar Grusky studied the effects of managerial change in major league baseball and confirmed Gouldner's finding. Grusky found a negative relationship between the rate of managerial change and organizational effectiveness—i.e., the greater the turnover in leadership, the poorer the organizational performance.[13] Eitzen and Yetman extended Grusky's work by looking at many more leadership changes—657 changes on 129 college basketball teams rather than 135 on 16 professional baseball teams.[14] They found, first, that in the short run, coaching changes have no effect on winning if the record of the previous coach is taken into account. Poor performance leads to a change in coaches (ritual scapegoating) as does good performance because coaches are upwardly mobile. But, subsequent performance after a coaching change appears to depend on whether the new coach took over a winning or losing team.

Since the same thing happens when the winning percentages in adjacent years are compared with no coaching change (2,114 comparisons), the conclusion of the authors was that when team success of the preceding year is taken into account, a coaching change has the same impact as if no coaching change had occurred.

Majority-Minority Relations. Grusky's theoretical propositions that organizational leadership tends to be recruited from "high interactor" (central) positions within the organization has led to an interesting extension into the field of majority-minority relations by Loy and McElvogue.[15] They derived the following micro theory, combining the insights of Grusky and Blalock:[16] (1) discrimination is directly related to intimate personal contact; (2) intimate personal contact is directly related to social interaction; (3) social interaction is directly related to organizational centrality; and (4) discrimination is directly related to centrality. They examined the racial distribution by playing positions in both football and basketball and found very strong evidence that blacks were found disproportionately in the noncentral positions. We will examine this study in detail in chapter 9.

Competition and Cooperation. The special subject matter of sociology is social interaction. Two forms that interaction may take are competition and cooperation. These processes need to be understood better for theoretical and practical reasons. Sport provides innumerable instances where both of those processes occur, separately and simultaneously. On the one hand, sports contests are instances of institutionalized conflict.[17] Therefore, they serve to control undesirable aggression and violence in socially acceptable channels.[18] On the other hand, sports teams require cooperation to be effective. An important question, some would say the central question, in sociology is what facilitates group cohesion? Under what conditions do members pull together and when do they pull apart? The leadership of sports teams (coaches, managers, athletic directors) spend a good deal of their time working to build group unity. Some are successful while others are not. Is it a matter of charisma, authoritarianism, homogeneity of personnel, winning, social control, or what?

The Macro Level

Small groups such as families, friendship groups, and sports teams illustrate nicely the process and components of social organization. But, each of these groups exists in a larger social setting—a context that is also structured—with norms, statuses, roles, and mechanisms of social control. These are the components of social structure that constrain social groups and the attitudes and behaviors of individuals, regardless of their group memberships.

Societal Norms. There are societal prescriptions for how one is to act and dress in given situations—e.g., at a football game, concert, restaurant, church, park, or classroom. In other words, norms are situational. Clearly, behavior considered appropriate for spectators at a football game (spontaneous screams of exuberance or despair, the open criticism of authority figures, and even the destruction of property) would be inexcusable behavior at a poetry reading. We know what is expected of us in these different situations. We also know how to act with members of the opposite sex, with elders, with social inferiors, and with equals. Thus, behavior in society is patterned. We know how to behave, and we can anticipate how others will behave. This allows interaction to occur smoothly.

Values. Bases for the norms, values are also part of society's culture. Values are the criteria used in evaluating objects, ideas, acts, feelings, or events as to their relative desirability, merit, or correctness. Since this is the topic of chapter 3, we will only state here that the members of society are taught explicitly and implicitly how to judge whether someone or something is good or bad, moral or immoral, appropriate or inappropriate. Americans, for example, know intuitively that winning (in school, in sports, in business, in life) is the highest goal. Americans not only value success, but they know precisely how to evaluate others and themselves on this critical dimension.

Status and Role at the Societal Level. Societies, like other social organizations, have social positions (statuses) and behavioral expectations (roles) for the occupants of these positions. There are family statuses (son or daughter, sibling, parent, husband, wife); age statuses (child, adolescent, adult, aged); sex statuses (male, female); racial statuses (black, chicano, Indian, white); and socioeconomic statuses (poor, middle class, wealthy). For each of these statuses there are societal constraints on behavior. To be a male or female in American society, for example, is to be constrained in a relatively rigid set of expectations (chapter 10 is devoted to a full discussion of this phenomenon). Similarly, blacks and other minorities, because of their minority status, have been expected to "know their place."

Social Institutions. One distinguishing characteristic of societies is the existence of a set of institutions. The popular usages of this term are imprecise and omit some important sociological considerations. An institution is *not* anything that is established and traditional (e.g., a janitor who has worked at the same school for forty-five years). An institution is *not* limited to specific organizations such as a school, a prison, or a hospital. An institution is much broader in scope and importance than a person, a custom, or a social organization. *Institutions are social arrangements that channel behavior in prescribed ways in the important areas of societal life.* They are interrelated sets of normative elements—norms, values, and role expectations—devised by the persons making up the society and passed on to succeeding generations to provide "permanent" solutions for crucial societal problems.

Institutions are cultural imperatives. They serve as regulatory agencies, channeling behavior in culturally prescribed ways.

> . . . institutions provide procedures through which human conduct is patterned, compelled to go, in grooves deemed desirable by society. And this trick is performed by making the grooves appear to the individual as the only possible ones.[19]

For example, a society instills in its members predetermined channels for marriage. Instead of allowing the sexual partners a whole host of options (e.g., polygyny, polyandry, group marriage), it is expected in American society that they will marry and set up a conjugal household. Although the actual options are many, the partners choose what society demands. In fact, they do not consider the other options as valid. The result is a patterned arrangement that regulates sexual behavior and insures a stable environment for the care of dependent children.

Institutions arise from the uncoordinated actions of multitudes of individuals over time. These actions, procedures, and rules evolve into a seemingly designed set of expectations because the consequences of these expectations provide solutions that help maintain social stability. The design is accidental, however; it is a product of cultural evolution.

All societies face problems in common. Although the variety of solutions is almost infinite, there is a functional similarity in their consequences—stability and maintenance of the system. The list below gives a number of common societal problems and the resulting institutions.

Societal Problems	**Institution**
Sexual regulation; maintenance of stable units that insure continued births and care of dependent children.	Family
Socialization of the newcomers to the society.	Education
Maintenance of order; the distribution of power.	Polity
Production and distribution of goods and services; ownership of property.	Economy

Societal Problems—*Continued*	Institution
Understanding the transcendental; the search for the meaning of life, death, and man's place in the world.	Religion
Understanding the physical and social realms of nature.	Science
Providing for physical and emotional health care.	Medicine

This partial list of institutions shows the type of societal problems for which solutions are continually sought. All societies, for instance, have some form of family, education, polity, economy, and religion. The variations on each of these themes found in societies is almost beyond imagination.[20]

Sport, too, is an institution.[21] If so, then what societal needs are served by sport? Several have been identified by various writers: (1) sport serves as a safety valve for both spectators and participants, dissipating excess energies, tensions, and hostile feelings in a socially acceptable way;[22] (2) athletes serve as role models, possessing the proper mental and physical traits to be emulated by the other members of society; and (3) sport is a secular, quasi-religious institution using ritual and ceremony to reinforce the values of society, and thereby regulating behavior to the channels prescribed by custom.[23]

Institutions are, by definition, conservative. They provide the answers of custom and tradition to questions of societal survival. For this reason, any attack on an institution is met by violent opposition. This is surely true for sport, as Edwards has noted:

> If this characterization is correct, one would expect that any attack upon the institution of sport in a particular society would be widely interpreted (intuitively, if not explicitly) as an attack upon the fundamental way of life of that society as manifest by the value orientations it emphasizes through sport. Hence, an attack upon sport constitutes an attack upon the society itself.[24]

Institutions provide for the unity and stability crucial for the survival of society. While absolutely necessary, institutions in contemporary society are often outmoded, inefficient, and unresponsive to the incredibly swift changes brought about by technological advances, population shifts, changing attitudes, and increasing worldwide interdependence. Because institutions are made by men and women, they can therefore be changed by these same persons. We should be guided by the insight that while institutions appear to have the quality of being "sacred," they are not. They can be changed.

But, critical examination is imperative. Social scientists must look behind the facades. They must not accept the patterned ways as the only "correct" ways. This is in the American heritage—as found in the Declaration of Independence. As Skolnick and Currie have put it:

> Democratic conceptions of society have always held that institutions exist to serve man, and that, therefore, they must be accountable to men. Where they fail to meet the tests imposed on them, democratic theory holds that they ought to be changed. Authoritarian governments, religious regimes, and reformatories, among other social systems, hold the opposite: in case of misalignment between individuals or groups and the "system," the individuals and groups are to be changed or otherwise made unproblematic.[25]

This book will focus on sport at the societal level. We will describe how sport reinforces American values. We will analyze the reciprocal linkages with other institutions—sport and education, sport and religion, sport and politics, and sport and the economy. Although the level of analysis is macro, the research findings from social psychological and micro studies will be included whenever appropriate.

Research Perspectives by Sport Sociologists

The scholarly interest in sport is growing rapidly throughout the world.[26] Sport-oriented research by social scientists is being reported in sociological, psychological, and physical education journals in increasing numbers. But, the scientific study of sport remains a relatively untapped area. We continue to be guided by myths and commonsense interpretations.

There are two basic approaches to research in the field of sport sociology—normative and nonnormative.[27] The normative orientation is value-laden research done to prove a point. It starts with assumptions about the way things should be and searches for evidence that this is or is not the case. There are three types of normative research. The first type is found among sociologists in the Communist-bloc countries. Their research is directed toward finding ways that sport can be organized and employed to meet the goals of the state. Thus, sport sociology has a mission to contribute to the betterment of society.

Another type of normative research has been found primarily among physical educators in the United States and western Europe. Research is focused on the demonstration of sport in building character (learning the values of hard work, competition, fair play, and teamwork).

A third type of normative research has a muckraking function. The researcher assumes beforehand that something is wrong (by his or her values) and sets out to prove it. An example of this type is research directed at proving that racism prevails in sport.[28] An entire book on sport has been written from a Marxist perspective, which attempts to show how sports are instrumental in maintaining capitalism by promoting competitiveness, elitism, sexism, nationalism, militarism, and racism and thus keeping the international working class divided against itself.[29]

The nonnormative approach, in contrast to the above, is the scientific description and explanation of what is (not what ought to be). The basic tenet of this approach is that the researcher must be objective and therefore, value-neutral. Sport is neither *a priori* good nor *a priori* bad. The goals of sport are not accepted nor rejected.

This research goal of objectivity while laudable, is, in our view, difficult if not impossible to attain. How one does research, chooses the problem, interprets and uses the findings are all affected by conscious and unconscious attitudes.[30] This is, of course, not to say that the researcher should stop striving to be objective. It only recognizes the relative impossibility of the task in the social sciences. But, if sociology is a science, the task is to strive to be as objective as possible, thereby fulfilling the basic canons of science.

A very serious problem with the value-neutral approach is that it does not take sides. It takes the way things are as a given entity (not good or evil). Thus, research in the name of value-neutrality supports the status quo. If there is racism, sexism, and drug abuse in sport, and if the athlete is being abused, then it seems to us that one cannot remain neutral. We cannot remain morally indifferent to injustice.

Friedrichs has argued that sociologists have tended toward one of two images—priest or prophet. The priestly role is one of fulfilling the canons of sciences. The prophetic role, on the other hand, involves making value choices and commitments. The choices that the sociological prophet makes are oriented in the direction of social reform, of constructing a "better society."[31] This role is the one taken by Jack Scott, whose love of sport has led him to direct his scholarly endeavors to rehumanize sport by bringing it back to the athletes.[32]

The material in this book reflects the normative and the nonnormative—the priestly and the prophetic—perspectives. Our goal is twofold: (1) to report what is known about sport and society from social science research; and (2) to make the case for reform. As social scientists, we are obliged to be as scientific as possible (using rigorous scientific techniques, reporting all findings—whether they support our values or not). At the same time, however, we are committed to moving sport and society in a more humane direction.

To accomplish these goals, we will question established orthodoxies, demythologize sport,[33] and point out the gaps between values and actual practices. Our intention, then, is to combine a scientific stance with the muckraking role. The latter is important because it forces us to examine such social problems as drug usage in sports, the prevalence of racism and sexism in sports, illegal recruiting, the inhumane treatment of players by bureaucratic organizations and authoritarian coaches, and the perversion of the original goal of sport.[34] Only by a thorough examination of such problems along with the traditional areas of attention, will we realistically understand the world of sport and its reciprocal relationship with the larger society.

Sport as a Microcosm of American Society

The analyst of society is inundated with data. She or he is faced with the problems of sorting out the important from the less important and with discerning patterns of behavior and their meanings. He or she needs shortcuts to ease the task. To focus on one institution—sport—is, we believe, just such a technique for understanding the complexities of the larger society. It is an institution that provides scientific observers with a convenient laboratory within which to examine values, socialization, stratification, bureaucracy—to name a few structures and processes—that also exist at the societal level. The games people play, the degree of competitiveness, the types of rules, the constraints on the participants, which groups benefit and which do not under the existing arrangements, the rate and type of change, and the reward system in sport provide us with a microcosm of the society in which it is embedded.[35]

Let's assume an astute sociologist from another society visited the United States with the intent to understand American values, the system of social control, the division of labor, and the system of stratification. Although he/she could find the answers by careful study and observation of any single institution (i.e., religion, education, polity, economy, or family), an attention on sport would also provide answers. If so, what would that sociologist find? It would not take long to discern the following qualities in sport that are also present in the larger society:

A High Degree of Competitiveness

Competition is ubiquitous in American society. Americans demand winners. In sports (for children and adults), winning is the ultimate goal, not pleasure in the activity. The adulation given winners is fantastic even if the wins are the result of questionable methods.

A Tremendous Emphasis on Materialism

The examples of the value Americans place on materialism are blatant in sports—e.g., players signing multimillion dollar contracts, golfers playing for weekly first place of $40,000 or more, the U.S. Olympic Committee with a stock portfolio in excess of $5 million, teams being moved to more economically fertile climates, and a football star receiving $10,000 to shave his mustache for advertising purposes.

The Pervasiveness of Racism
Racist attitudes and actions affect the play, position, number of starters, and futures of minority group members in American sport.

Individuals Dominated by Bureaucracies
These conservative organizations, through their desire to perpetuate themselves, curtail innovations and deflect activities away from the wishes of individuals—and the original intent of these organizations.

The Unequal Distribution of Power of Organizations
The structure of sport in America is such that power is in the hands of the wealthy (boards of regents, corporate boards of directors, the media, wealthy entrepreneurs, the boards of governors of the Amateur Athletic Union [AAU], U.S. Olympic Committee, and the National Collegiate Athletic Association [NCAA]). Evidence of the power of these individuals is seen in the antitrust exemption allowed them by Congress in dealing with athletes, tax breaks, and the concessions by communities to entice professional sports franchises to locate there—and, incidentally, benefit the wealthy of that community.

The Use of Conflict to Change Unequal Power Relationships
Conflict (strikes, boycotts, demonstrations) is used by the less powerful (blacks, women, athletes) to gain advantage in sport and in society.

The Pervasiveness of Sport

Social scientists are especially interested in sport because this phenomenon is so pervasive in American society; it is *not* a trivial aspect of American life. On the contrary, it is particularly important in an increasingly leisure-oriented society. Millions of Americans are vitally interested in sport. It consumes much of their conversation, reading material, leisure activity, and discretionary spending. Over one-tenth of the *World Almanac* is annually devoted to sports. In fact, sports receive more coverage in the almanac than politics, business, or science. The sports section is, for many, the most closely examined part of the daily newspaper; for millions of Americans it is the *only* news of vital concern. Newspapers, in turn, devote more space to sports than to a variety of other items, including business news, which should be of central importance in a capitalist economy. Evidence for the American sportmania is seen in the amount of television time devoted to it (1,250 hours in 1976 on national networks for an average of 24 hours per week), sometimes preempting regular programming and thereby even affecting family interaction patterns. Approximately 393 million persons watched the seven games of the 1975 World Series, with 76 million watching the final game.

Attendance figures (table 1-1) show further the tremendous and increasing interest of Americans in sport. A Gallup poll taken in 1972 found that about 70 million Americans attended at least one football game at the high school level or higher in one year, 63 million watched baseball in person, and 44 million attended a basketball game.[36]

But what of participation? Over two million high school and college students engage in sport on an interschool basis. Many millions more participate on intramural teams, work teams, town teams, church teams, junior high school teams, grade school teams, little league (in hockey, baseball, basketball, football, and soccer), YMCA, YWCA, YMHA, etc. A Nielsen survey in 1974 found that 52 percent of the sample swam at least occasionally for recreation purposes. Other activities were less popular but were engaged in by millions of Americans (see table 1-2). With the amount of leisure time and the level of affluence increasing for Americans, we can only assume that the participation in sports and the attendance at and interest in sports will increase.

All of these data demonstrate that American social life is infused with sport. As Boyle has put it:

> Sport permeates any number of levels of contemporary society, and it touches upon and deeply influences such disparate elements as status, race relations, business life, automobile design, clothing styles, the concept of the hero, language, and ethical values.[37]

Put another way, this time by the editors of the *Christian Century,* who justified a special issue on sport by saying:

> . . . it is because sports are so much more than simple amusements that they deserve serious attention. Sports claim high priorities in the budgets of families, schools, cities, and the media. Emotional and ethical styles, both individualistic and collective, are shaped in athletic arenas.[38]

Though an important component of American society worthy of serious sociological analysis, all too often sport has been relegated to popular commentators because academics have tended to ignore it as a frivolous activity.[39] We hope to demonstrate throughout this book that sport merits scientific and critical analysis. We intend to use the tools of modern sociology to analyze the role of sport in American society.

Levels of Sport

One final task remains for the first chapter. We need to establish at the outset the subject matter of this book. Our object of study is sport, which we define as any com-

Table 1-1. Spectators at Major Sports Events.

Sport	Year 1965	1974	Percentage Increase
Horse Racing	40,737,000	48,824,000	20%
Auto Racing	39,000,000	47,500,000	22%
College Football	24,683,000	31,235,000	27%
Major League Baseball	23,437,000	30,630,000	31%
Harness Racing	26,899,000	29,976,000	11%
College Basketball	16,384,000	24,630,000	50%
Dog Racing	10,865,000	16,274,000	50%
Professional Hockey	2,823,000	12,006,000	325%
Minor League Baseball	10,194,000	11,032,000	8%
Professional Football	6,956,000	10,236,000	47%
Professional Basketball	2,356,000	8,229,000	249%
Professional Boxing	1,743,000	2,675,000	53%

Source: *U.S. News and World Report* (September 8, 1975), p. 46.

Table 1-2. Participation in Play, Games, and Sports: 1974.

Activity	Estimate Number
Swimming	107,191,000
Bicycling	65,613,000
Fishing	61,263,000
Camping	54,435,000
Bowling	38,218,000
Table Tennis	33,501,000
Pool and Billiards	32,920,000
Boating	32,629,000
Softball	26,362,000
Ice Skating	24,875,000
Tennis	20,000,000

Source: Data gathered by A.C. Nielsen Company, reported in Neil Amdur, "Swimming Still Rates Top Participant Sport; Camping on Decrease," *New York Times* (March 24, 1974), p. L1, L5.

petitive physical activity that is guided by established rules.[40] The first of the three characteristics of sport—competition—involves the attempt to defeat an opponent. This "opponent" may be a mountain, a record, an individual, or a team. The second ingredient involves physical activity. One attempts to defeat an opponent through physical abilities such as strength, speed, stamina, or accuracy. Of course, the outcome is also determined by the employment of strategy as well as chance. The final characteristic of sport—rules—distinguishes it from more playful and spontaneous activities. The scope, rigidity, and enforcement of the rules, however, vary by type and level of sport, as we shall see shortly.

Our definition of sport is not very adequate because it is too broad. A pickup game of basketball and a game in the National Basketball Association are examples of two related but at the same time very different activities that fall under our definition of sport.[41] In the same way, an improvised game of one-on-one is sport. So is professional football. In this latter case, it has been argued that professional football is not sport because of the big business aspects or because it is more like work than play for the participants. Therefore, there is a need to differentiate among several levels of sport—"informal sport," "organized sport," and "corporate sport."[42]

Informal Sport

This type of sport involves playful, physical activity primarily for the enjoyment of participants. A touch football game, a neighborhood basketball game, a game of workup (baseball) are examples of this type of sport. In each of these examples, some rules guide the competition. These rules are determined by the participants (not a regulatory body).

Organized Sport

The presence of a rudimentary organization distinguishes "organized sport" from "informal sport." There are formal teams, leagues, codified rules, and related organizations. These exist primarily for the benefit of the players, working for fair competition, providing equipment, officials, scheduling rulings in disputed cases, and opportunities for persons to participate. YMCA leagues, city leagues, little league programs, interscholastic teams and leagues, low pressure college teams and leagues are examples of "organized sport" that have not lost the original purposes of the activity and not become too organized.[43]

Corporate Sport

This level of sport has elements of "informal sport" and "organized sport," but it has been modified by economics and politics. In Gilbert's words, "[corporate sport]" is a corrupted, institutionalized version of sport."[44] Here, we have sport as spectacle; sport as big business; sport as an extension of power politics. The pleasure in the activity for the participants has been lost in favor of pleasure for fans, owners, alumni, and other powerful groups.

Whereas sports organizations at the "organized sport" level devote their energies to preserving the activities in the participants' interest, organizations in the "corporate sport" stage have enormous power (often a monopoly). As their power increases, they devote less and less of their energies to satisfying the needs for which they were created. They become more interested in perpetuating the organization through public relations, making profits, monopolizing the media, crushing opposing organizations (e.g., AAU vs. NCAA, NBA vs. ABA), or merging with competing leagues to limit opposition and control player salaries, and reducing risk by being inflexible and noninnovative. Professional sports leagues, big-time college athletics governed by the NCAA, and the International Olympic Committee are examples of the bureaucracies that characterize "corporate sport" and subvert the pleasure of participating for the sake of the activity itself.[45]

The reader will have noted that these three levels of sport can be placed on a continuum from play to work. As one moves from "informal sport" to "corporate sport," the activities become more organized with a subsequent loss of autonomy and pleasure by athletes. Since "corporate sport" dominates sport in America today, we will focus on that level in this book. But, since that level is but an extension of the "organized sport" level, we will at times direct our attention there as well.

Summary

The perspective, concepts, and procedures of sociology are used in this book to describe and explain the institution of sport in American society. The subject matter of sociology is social organization. Sport involves different types of social organizations, such as teams and leagues. These organizations, in turn, are part of larger social organizations like schools, communities, international associations, and the society. The task of this book is to understand the principles that underlie the structures and processes that create, sustain, and transform these social organizations. This undertaking requires, most importantly, that the observer examine the social arrangements of sport from a critical stance. Some sample questions that must direct the serious investigator are: How does the organization really work? Who really has the power? And, who benefits and who does not?

The two fundamental themes of this book are introduced in this chapter. The first is that sport is a microcosm of society. Understanding the way sport is organized, the types of games people play, the degree of emphasis on competition, the compensation of the participants, and the enforcement of the rules are shorthand ways of understanding the complexities of the larger society in which sport is embedded. The converse is true also. The understanding of the values of society, the type of economy, and the treatment of minority groups, to name a few, provide important bases for the organization of sport.

The second theme is that the prevailing form of sport—the corporate level—has corrupted the original intentions of sport. Instead of player-oriented physical competition (informal sport), sport has become a spectacle, big business, and an extension of power politics. Play has become work. Spontaneity has been superseded by bureaucracy. The goal of pleasure in the physical activity has been replaced by extrinsic rewards, especially money.

Notes

1. See Muzafer Sherif and Carolyn W. Sherif, *Groups in Harmony and Tension* (New York: Octagon Books, 1966); William F. Whyte, *Street Corner Society* (Chicago: The University of Chicago Press, 1943); and Elliot Liebow, *Tally's Corner: A Study of Negro Street Corner Men* (Boston: Little, Brown, 1967). Illustrations of this process can also be found in classics, such as, William Golding, *The Lord of the Flies* (London: Faber and Faber, 1954); and George Orwell, *Animal Farm* (New York: Harcourt, Brace, 1946).
2. Edward O. Wilson, *Sociobiology: The New Synthesis* (Cambridge, Mass.: Belnap Press, 1975). This book has caused a good deal of controversy in the biological and social sciences; see especially the reviews of this book in *American Journal of Sociology* 82 (November, 1976), pp. 692-706; *Contemporary Sociology: A Journal of Reviews* 5 (November, 1976), pp. 727-737; and Richard Currier, "Sociobiology: The New Heresy," *Human Behavior* 5 (November, 1976), pp. 16-22.
3. For an elaboration on the discipline of sociology and the sociological perspective, see D. Stanley Eitzen, *In Conflict and Order: Understanding Society* (Boston: Allyn and Bacon, 1978, chapters 1-2); Robert Perrucci, Dean D. Knudsen, and Russell R. Hamby, *Sociology: Basic Structures and Processes* (Dubuque, Ia.: Wm. C. Brown Co. Publishers, 1977, chapters 1-3); and Peter L. Berger, *Invitation to Sociology: A Humanistic Perspective* (Garden City, N.Y.: Doubleday Anchor Books, 1963).
4. Berger, *Invitation to Sociology,* p. 121.
5. Reece McGee, *Points of Departure: Basic Concepts in Sociology* (Hinsdale, Ill.: The Dryden Press, 1975), pp. x-xi.
6. Marvin E. Olsen, *The Process of Social Organization* (New York: Holt, Rinehart and Winston, 1968).
7. See Charles H. Anderson, *Toward a New Sociology,* rev. ed. (Homewood, Ill.: Dorsey, 1974), p. 3. See also Karl Marx, *Communist Manifesto,* ed. J. H. Laski (New York: Pantheon, 1967).
8. Berger, *Invitation to Sociology,* p. 31.
9. Solomon E. Asch, "Effects of Group Pressure Upon the Modification and Distortion of Judgments," *Readings in Social Psychology,* 3rd ed., ed. Eleanor E. Maccoby, Theodore M. Newcomb, and Eugene L. Hartley (New York: Holt, Rinehart and Winston, 1958), pp. 174-183.
10. Of course, athletic teams and their members may have other goals as well—e.g., physical fitness, personal aggrandizement, and the "building of character." Such goals, however, will generally be secondary to the primary goal of winning games.
11. D. Stanley Eitzen, "The Effect of Group Structure on the Success of Athletic Teams," *International Review of Sport Sociology* 8 (1973), pp. 7-17.
12. Alvin W. Gouldner, *Patterns of Industrial Bureaucracy* (Glencoe, Ill.: The Free Press, 1954).

13. Oscar Grusky, "Managerial Succession and Organizational Effectiveness," *American Journal of Sociology* 69 (1963), pp. 21-31. See also William A. Gamson and Norman A. Scotch, "Scapegoating in Baseball," *American Journal of Sociology* 60 (1964), pp. 69-72.
14. D. Stanley Eitzen and Norman R. Yetman, "Managerial Change, Longevity and Organizational Effectiveness," *Administrative Science Quarterly* 17 (March, 1972), pp. 110-116. For other studies of leadership change on athletic teams, see Oscar Grusky, "The Effects of Formal Structure on Managerial Recruitment: A Study of Baseball Organization," *Sociometry* 26 (September, 1963), pp. 345-353; and John W. Loy, Jr. and John N. Sage, "The Effects of Formal Structure on Organizational Leadership: An Investigation of Interscholastic Baseball Teams," *Contemporary Psychology of Sport,* ed. Gerald S. Kenyon (Chicago: The Athletic Institute, 1970), pp. 363-373.
15. John W. Loy, Jr. and Joseph F. McElvogue, "Racial Segregation in American Sport," *International Review of Sport Sociology* 5 (1971), pp. 5-24. For a thorough review of the theory and research on centrality in sports teams see John W. Loy, Jr., James E. Curtis, and John N. Sage, "Career Contingencies of Positional Placement in the Formal Structure of Sport Organizations," *Exercise and Sport Science Reviews* 6 (1978).
16. Herbert Blalock, Jr., "Occupational Discrimination: Some Theoretical Propositions," *Social Problems* 9 (Winter, 1962), pp. 240-247. For an interesting theoretical study using integrated basketball teams to test how intergroup tensions can be reduced, see McKee McClendon and D. Stanley Eitzen, "Interracial Contact on Collegiate Basketball Teams: A Test of Sherif's Theory of Superordinate Goals," *Social Science Quarterly* 55 (March, 1955), pp. 960-966.
17. See Gunther Luschen, "Cooperation, Association and Context," *International Journal of Conflict Resolution* 14 (1970), pp. 21-34.
18. See John Paul Scott, "Sport and Aggression," *Contemporary Psychology of Sport,* ed. Gerald S. Kenyon (Chicago: The Athletic Institution, 1970), pp. 11-24, and the five papers that follow and react to it, pp. 25-41. See also Frederick C. Hatfield, "Some Factors Precipitating Player Violence: A Preliminary Report," *Sport Sociology Bulletin* 2 (Spring, 1973), pp. 3-5; and especially Richard Sipes, "War, Sports and Aggression: An Empirical Test of Two Rival Theories," *American Anthropologist* 75 (February, 1973), pp. 64-83.
19. Berger, *Invitation to Sociology,* p. 87.
20. The discussion on institutions is taken from D. Stanley Eitzen, *Social Structure and Social Problems in American Society* (Boston: Allyn and Bacon, 1974), pp. 221-222.
21. See Harry Edwards, *Sociology of Sport* (Homewood, Ill.: Dorsey, 1973), pp. 84-130.
22. See Sipes, "War, Sports and Aggression: An Empirical Test of Two Rival Theories," pp. 64-86.
23. Edwards, *Sociology of Sport,* p. 90.
24. Ibid.
25. Jerome H. Skolnick and Elliott Currie, "Approaches to Social Problems," *Crisis in American Institutions,* ed. Jerome H. Skolnick and Elliott Currie (Boston: Little, Brown, 1970), p. 15.
26. For summary descriptions and bibliographies of the sociology of sport, see Eldon E. Snyder and Elmer Spreitzer, "Sociology of Sport: An Overview," *The Sociological Quarterly* 15 (Autumn, 1974), pp. 467-487; Gunther Luschen, "The Development and Scope of a Sociology of Sport," *American Corrective Therapy Journal* 29 (March-April, 1975), pp. 34-43; Gunther Luschen, "On Sociology of Sport—General Orientation and its Trends in the Literature," *The Scientific View of Sport,* ed. Ommo Grupe et al. (Heidelberg: Springer-Verlag Berlin, 1972), pp. 119-154; Merill J. Melnick, "A Critical Look at Sociology of Sport," *Quest,* monograph 24 (Summer, 1975), pp. 34-47; and Howard L. Nixon II, *Sport and Social Organization* (Indianapolis: Bobbs-Merrill, 1976).
27. See John W. Loy, Jr. and Gerald S. Kenyon, "Frames of Reference: Overview," *Sport, Culture and Society,* ed. John W. Loy, Jr. and Gerald S. Kenyon (New York: MacMillan, 1969), pp. 9-11.
28. For an example of this type of research, see Norman R. Yetman and D. Stanley Eitzen, "Black Americans in Sports: Unequal Opportunity for Equal Ability," *Civil Rights Digest* 5 (August, 1972), pp. 21-34.
29. Paul Hoch, *Rip Off the Big Game: The Exploitation of Sports by the Power Elite*

(Garden City, N.Y.: Doubleday Anchor Books, 1972).

30. While we have taken the position that value-neutrality is impossible in the social sciences, it is not a simple issue and one that has encouraged considerable debate. For a summary of various positions, see George Ritzer, *Sociology: A Multiple Paradigm Science* (Boston: Allyn and Bacon, 1974), chapter 1.

31. Robert W. Friedrichs, *A Sociology of Sociology* (New York: The Free Press, 1970).

32. See Jack Scott, *Athletics for Athletes* (Oakland, Cal.: Other Ways Book, 1969); Jack Scott, *The Athletic Revolution* (New York: The Free Press, 1971).

33. For an elaboration of the various sports myths, see Eldon E. Snyder and Elmer Spreitzer, "Basic Assumptions in the World of Sports," *Quest,* monograph 24 (Summer, 1975), pp. 3-9.

34. A strong case has been made for this muckraking approach by Melnick, "A Critical Look at Sociology of Sport, pp. 34-47.

35. For an elaboration of this term, see especially Robert H. Boyle, *Sport: Mirror of American Life* (Boston: Little, Brown, 1963); Gerald S. Kenyon, "Sport and Society: At Odds or in Concert," *Athletics in America,* ed. Arnold Flath (Corvallis, Ore.: Oregon State University Press, 1972), pp. 34-41; Scott, *The Athletic Revolution* ; and Edwards, *Sociology of Sport,* 1973.

36. George Gallup, "The Gallup Poll: America's Interest in Sports Scores a Record High Jump," *Baltimore Sun* (January 21, 1973), p. 18.

37. Boyle, *Sport: Mirror of American Life,* pp. 3-4.

38. "Stance," *The Christian Century* 89 (April 5, 1972), p. 383.

39. As late as 1968, the two leading sociological journals had published only six articles on sport. Recent events in sociology and physical education suggest that this neglect is over and that sport is now accepted as a legitimate field of inquiry by serious social scientists. In 1966, for instance, a journal, the *International Review of Sport Sociology,* was first published. The group behind this venture was a separate research committee within the International Sociological Association and the International Council of Sport and Physical Education—the International Committee for the Sociology of Sport. This international organization has sponsored international symposia and elicited the cooperation of scholars in sociology and physical education to do research in sport. In the United States, three journals of recent origin are devoted exclusively to the sociology of sport—*Journal of Sport and Social Issues* (1976), *Review of Sport & Leisure* (1976) and *Journal of Sport Behavior* (1978). Further evidence for the emergence of sport as a legitimate subdiscipline in sociology is seen in the establishment of a separate section devoted to the area at the annual meetings of the American Sociological Association. Regional sociological societies now typically also include such a section. Parallel occurrences are found within physical education. Most important was the recommendation of a national committee in 1972 that all departments offering physical education as a major provide the sociology of sport as a core element of the program. These events in both disciplines would appear to assure the future and the legitimacy of the sociology of sport.

40. For elaborate discussions on the differences among play, game, and sport, see Johan Huizinga, *Homo Ludens: A Study of the Play Element in Culture* (Boston: Beacon Press, 1955); Rogert Caillois, *Man, Play and Games* (London: Thames and Hudson, 1962); John W. Loy, Jr., "The Nature of Sport: A Definitional Effort," *Sport in the Socio-Cultural Process,* ed. M. Marie Hart (Dubuque, Ia.: Wm. C. Brown Co. Publishers, 1972), pp. 50-66; and Edwards, *Sociology of Sport,* pp. 43-61.

41. Pete Axthelm, *The City Game* (New York: Harper's Magazine Press Book, 1970). Axthelm neatly juxtaposes these two forms of sport as found in New York City basketball.

42. The first and last of these distinctions were first made by Bil Gilbert, "Gleanings from a Troubled Time," *Sports Illustrated* 37 (December 25, 1972), pp. 34-46. Many of the ideas that follow stem from his insights.

43. A strong case can be made that many little league programs have become too organized and have lost sight of the goal of fun through participation for the youth. If so, they belong in the "corporate sport" category. See John Underwood, "Taking the Fun Out of a Game," *Sports Illustrated* 43 (November 17,

1975), pp. 87-90, 95-96, 98; Robert Lipsyte, "Young Athletes: Who Is a Failure?" *New York Times* (March 14, 1976), p. 25; and Robin Roberts, "Strike Out Little League," *Newsweek* (July 21, 1975), p. 11.

44. Gilbert, "Gleanings from a Troubled Time," p. 34.

45. "Pseudo sport" is another activity that is often included as sport on the pages of American newspapers, but one that we would claim falls outside even our broad definition of sport. Professional wrestling, the roller derby, and the Harlem Globetrotters are examples of "pseudosport." Although athletes are involved in these activities and the activities involve physical prowess, the activities are *not* sport because they are not competitive. Although packaged as competition, these activities exist solely for spectator amusement.

Social and Cultural Sources for the Rise of Sport in America 2

One of the main themes of this book is that sport is a microcosm of American society, or, as Robert Boyle observed, sport is a mirror of American life.[1] The idea that the sports of a given society reflect the society is not limited to America; numerous social scientists have shown how play, games, and sports activities are related to the social system in which they are embedded.[2] It is also true that the sport forms in a particular society have evolved out of the social and cultural traditions of that particular group, and can only be fully understood (if at all) by an understanding of the social history of that society.

A review of the past helps to explain current conditions and may even provide a basis for the prediction of future events. Any study of social phenomena based solely on the present reveals a very incomplete picture of reality. Current social circumstances are related to events of the past, consequently sociologists use history to develop an understanding of a given form of social behavior, making the current form of that behavior more meaningful. Fundamental to the study of any social institution within a given society—politics, religion, education—is a study of a history of that social group. In the case of sport, the social heritage of America provides excellent clues to understanding sport in its present form. In this chapter, we shall briefly examine the changing social-cultural conditions of American society over the past 200 years and attempt to show how these conditions have affected and influenced American sports.

In the past two centuries, the United States has grown from a few widely scattered and disunited settlements located along the eastern seaboard of part of North America into perhaps the most modern and industrially advanced nation in the world. It has also become one of the most advanced nations in sports. Fostered by a variety of historical, social, and economic conditions, sport has become a major national pastime. From an agrarian society whose inhabitants had little time for games and sports, except for special occasions, America has developed into a nation of urbanites who watch ten to twenty hours of sports on television each weekend and almost consider it a duty to participate in some form of exercise or sport for recreation. To understand the conditions responsible for this transformation of sports in American society, we must examine the changing social-cultural nature of America since its beginnings.

The Transformation of American Sport

The Colonial Period

There were no organized participant or spectator sports during the colonial period of America. In the first place, colonial settlers actually had very little time or opportunity to engage in sports. The harsh circumstances of wresting a living from the environment necessitated continual work. A basic fact of life in the colonies was that if the settlers did not direct most of their efforts to work they could not hope to survive. A second force restricting sports involvement was the church. Religion was the most powerful social institution in the colonies. Puritanism was prominent in the New England colonies, while other Protestant religions dominated social life in the middle and southern colonies. All of these religious groups placed severe restrictions on games and sports activities, with the Puritans being the most extreme. Attacks were directed at almost every form of amusement: dancing for its carnality; football for its violence; maypoles for their paganism; and sports in general because they were often performed on the Sabbath. Moreover, these religious criticisms of games and sports were closely bound to the dislike for the "play" element in sports. Honest labor was the greatest service to God, and one's moral duty; thus any form of play or amusement took on the badge of time-wasting, and idleness, and was therefore defined as a vice.[3] According to Dulles, the strict regulations adopted "in detestation of idleness" prohibiting sports activities "represented a determination to promote industry and frugality; they also reflected the Puritan concept of the evil inherent in any frivolous waste of time."[4]

Legislation prohibiting a form of social behavior and the actual social customs and actions of a people rarely coincide. In the case of the colonies, religious and legal structures failed to eliminate the urge to play among the early Americans. Although they were rare and frequently done in defiance of local laws, sports such as horse racing, shooting matches, cockfights, footraces, and wrestling matches were engaged in throughout the colonies to break the monotony of life. Moreover, farm festivals in which barnraising, quilting bees, and corn-husking activities took place also provided occasional amusement and entertainment. In *Sports of Colonial Williamsburg,* William Ewing said that the three outstanding sports of colonial Williamsburg were horse racing, cock fighting, and dancing, with the most popular being horse racing.[5] Other recreations common to all of the colonies were those associated with the taverns. The tavern was a social center, primarily for drinking but for all manner of popular pastimes, such as cards, billiards, bowling, and rifle and pistol shooting.

On the frontier, religious strictures against sport were rather ineffective, but social gatherings were fewer. However, the frontiersmen enjoyed themselves with a variety of competitive events when they met at barbecues and camp meetings. They gambled on horse races, cock fights, and bear-baiting contests. The sports and games that marked these infrequent social gatherings were typically rough and brutal; two of the popular events were fist fighting until one man could not continue and wrestling in which eye gouging and bone breaking holds were permitted. Horse racing was the most universal sport on the frontier, for every owner of a horse was confident of its prowess and eager to match it against others. The other constant companion of the frontiersman, his rifle, also engendered a pride in marksmanship, and shooting matches were a common form of competition.[6]

The Early Republic

The winning of national independence and the creation of a new nation did not immediately change social conditions, so in the first few decades of the 19th century, Americans enjoyed essentially the same recreations and sport as they had during the colonial period. But, as Dulles has noted, "new winds were blowing. The turbulent, expansive years of the first half of the [19th] century were to usher in changes in recreation as far-reaching as those in any other department of the national life."[7] The major catalyst for the transformation of sports was a series of inventions in England in the late 18th century, which completely changed the means by which goods were produced. These inventions ushered in two of the most important developments in human history—the technological and industrial revolutions. Technological advances made possible the large-scale manufacturing characteristic of industrialization. Industry needed a plentiful supply of labor located near plants and factories, so population shifts from rural to urban areas completely changed population characteristics and needs. Urbanization created a need for new forms of participation sports and commercialized spectator sports, and industrialization gradually supplied the standard of living and the leisure time necessary to support broad-based forms of recreation and organized sports.

As the nation changed from a rural to urban population and from largely home trades and individualized occupations to a large-scale industrial mode of production, a growing interest emerged in spectator sports, especially rowing, prize fighting, footracing, and similar activities, but the sport that excited the interest of the most Americans was horse racing.[8] With its traditions going back to early colonial days, horse racing was the first of the popular spectator sports. Dulles summarized this trend:

> Crowds ranging from twenty to fifty thousand, made up of all members of society, were . . . turning out as early as the 1820s for widely heralded horse races, for the regattas held at cities along the Atlantic seaboard, and for the grueling five- and ten-mile races of the professional runners.[9]

The growing enthusiasm for sports is illustrated by the song "Camptown Races" published in 1850 by Stephen Foster, one of America's most famous composers. This was the first American song of enduring popularity composed around a sporting theme. The tune ends:

> "I'll bet my money on a da bob-tail nag, Somebody bet on da bay."

The transformation from occasional and informal sports to highly organized and commercial spectator sports was begun in the antebellum[10] period of the 19th century.

The Latter Nineteenth Century

The gathering storm of dissension over slavery eventually erupted into civil war in 1861. Although the war momentarily slowed the rise of sport, the stimulus it gave to manufacturing and industrial expansion served as the economic basis for the rapid advances of sports in the latter 19th century. Although a few sports had gained popular appeal in the first half of the 19th century, prior to the 1870s the country had virtually no organized sports as we know them today. But in the two decades of the '70s and '80s, no transformation in the recreational and sports scene was more startling than the sudden burgeoning of physical activities, which, according to Dulles, "almost overnight introduced millions of Americans to a phase of life shortly destined to become a major preoccupation among all classes."[11]

To go with the established interest in horse racing, yachting, and prize fighting, new sports gained popularity. Lawn tennis, croquet, golf, and polo were sports that were pioneered by the wealthy as games for "polite society." But none of these sports developed so rapidly as baseball and American football. From an informal children's game in the early 18th century, baseball rules had been codified in the 1840s and groups of upper-social-class men organized clubs, taking care to keep out lower-social-class persons who might wish to play the sport. The first of these baseball clubs, the Knickerbockers, of New York, was, according to Harold Seymour:

> . . . primarily a social club with distinctly exclusive flavor—somewhat similar to what country clubs represented in the 1920s and 1930s, before they became popular with the middle class in general. . . . To the Knickerbockers a ball game was a vehicle for genteel amateur recreation and polite social intercourse rather than a hard-fought contest for victory.[12]

The Civil War tended to wipe out this upper-class patronage of the game, and a broad-base of popularity existed in 1869 when the first professional baseball team was formed. This was followed in 1876 by the organization of the first major league, and baseball became firmly entrenched as the "national pastime" by the end of the century.

Intercollegiate athletics began in 1852 with a rowing match between Harvard and Yale, but it was not until the 1870s and 1880s that the spread of intercollegiate sports became an established part of higher education and contributed to the enthusiasm for athletic and sporting diversions. From a spectator standpoint, football became the most popular sport. During this era, football was a sport for the upper classes rather than the masses, since it largely reflected the interests of the college crowd; the pigskin game did nevertheless develop into a national sport by 1900.[13]

The Twentieth Century

The final three decades of the 19th century saw the rise of sports sweep over the country, but it was in the succeeding thirty years that the athletic spirit became a prominent part of the American social scene. The 1890s, the prosperous years before World War I, and the uproarious decade of the 1920s comprise an important epoch in the history of American sport. The growth of the city, the rising standard of living, and the extension of leisure time were important social forces that combined with numerous other conditions to promote the expansion of sport to an unprecedented extent. The wealthy were no longer the only people with the leisure and means to enjoy recreational pursuits. Working-class persons gradually obtained shorter working hours and higher wages, enabling them to spend large sums of money on entertainment, one form of which was sport. Thus, sport discarded much of its aristocratic trappings and rapidly emerged as a popular form of entertainment and recreation. A British observer of the American scene in 1905 wrote:

> . . . [Sport] occupies the minds not only of the youth at the universities, but also of their parents and of the general public. Baseball matches and football matches excite an interest greater than any other public events except the Presidential election, and that comes only once in four years. . . . The American love of excitement and love of competition has seized upon these games.[14]

No single event heralded the beginning of what has been designated as the era of modern sports, but the Roaring '20s acted as a bridge connecting the old pastimes to contemporary sport. Sport swept over the nation in the 1920s, seeming to be the most engrossing of all social interests; it became a "bandwagon" around which rallied students and alumni, business and transportation interests, advertising and amusement industries, cartoonists and artists, novelists, and sports columnists.[15] Indeed, the 1920s are still looked upon as sports' Golden Age. Some of America's most famous athletes rose to prominence during those years: Babe Ruth, the "Sultan of Swat"; Knute Rockne and the "Four Horsemen of Notre Dame"; Jack Dempsey, heavyweight boxing champion; Bill Tilden in tennis; Bobby Jones in golf. These are only a few of the persons who contributed to the growing popularity of sport.

From the '20s onward, sport has become a pervasive part of American national life, penetrating into every level of our educational system and into the programs of social agencies and private clubs. This became especially true of the business world, affecting "such varied areas of our economic system as finance, fashion, journalism, trade, transportation, communication, insurance, advertising, sporting goods manufacture, and those marginal enterprises which profit from expenditures incidental to sport."[16]

Two major developments in sports characterize the past twenty years: The colossal expansion of amateur and professional spectator sports and the boom in participant sports. Amateur sports, from youth sports to intercollegiate athletic programs, have multiplied at a bewildering pace in recent years. Baseball and football were once about the only sports sponsored in youth programs, but now there are over 25 nationally organized youth sports programs—from swimming to motor bicycling—and it is now possible for children as young as six years of age to win a national championship. The limited high school and collegiate programs featuring 3 or 4 sports for boys only have now been expanded to include 12 to 15 sports for both males and females. On-site spectator sports in the United States have gross paid admissions of over $500 million a year. Some $70 million admissions are paid to horse racing, $29 million each to professional baseball and college football, and about $11 million to professional football.[17] These figures are, of course, dwarfed by the number of people who watch televised sports events.

Participant sports, the second main development of the past generation, have been a product of increased leisure and income. The construction of sports facilities and the manufacture of sports equipment inexpensive enough for the large mass of working-class Americans have had an important impact on participant sport. Finally, the increasing sedentary life-style of persons in all socioeconomic strata, with the rise in diseases related to this life-style, has been a stimulus for mass participation in sport and exercise. A recent national poll reported that approximately one-half of the adult American population engaged in some form of exercise or sport each week.[18] The number of sports participants is impressive. Kando estimated that in a single year 100 million persons swim, almost 10 million play golf at least 15 times, 11 million water skied, and 7 million snow skied; and bowlers far outnumbered all but swimmers.[19] Other sports have their devotees as well. Even allowing for considerable margin of error, sports participation involves enormous numbers of Americans.

This section has provided a brief overview of the enormous change in the nature and form of sports in America over the past several centuries. But a chronicling of changes does not provide insights about the reasons behind this transformation of sport. We shall now examine in more detail the actual social-cultural events responsible for the changing structure and function of sport.

The Technological Revolution and Sport

One of the most significant forces to transform sports from the occasional village festivals to the highly organized sports of today was the technological revolution. Beginning in the early decades of the 19th century, technological advances made possible the large-scale manufacturing characteristic of industrialization. Through the application of technology—the practical application of science to industry—many kinds of machines, laborsaving devices,. and scientific processes have been invented or perfected. The influence of technological advances for sport is succinctly summarized by Betts:

> The technological revolution is not the sole determining factor in the rise of sport, but to ignore its influence would result only in a more or less superficial understanding of the history of one of the prominent social institutions of modern America.[20]

Transportation

One area in which technology has had its greatest impact is transportation. Travel of any kind was difficult in the colonial period. A distance that today takes hours to travel took more than the same number of days in colonial times. Modes of transportation were limited to foot, horse, and water. Roads, when they existed, were primitive and dangerous, and often blocked by almost impassable rivers.

The first notable technological breakthrough in transportation came in the early 19th century with the development of the steam engine. This invention and its use on boats made it possible to develop river traffic fully. The first successful steamboat in America, the *Clermont,* was built by Robert Fulton, and in 1807 it chugged 150 miles up the Hudson River from New York to Albany in about 30 hours. Steamboats stimulated the building of canals and the enlarging of rivers, opening new areas that had previously been isolated and cut off from commerce and trade.

The steamboat did not solve all the transportation problems; river transportation was no help to people who did not happen to live near large rivers. Furthermore, it was not a particularly fast means of movement, because the large steamers sometimes had to carefully thread their way through very narrow or shallow water. About the time that canal building reached its peak, a new form of transportation began to compete with river transportation. This was the railroad. In 1830, a 14-mile stretch of the Baltimore and Ohio Railroad was opened; railroad construction expanded rapidly, made up mostly of short lines connecting principal cities, and by 1840 there were nearly 3,000 miles of track in the United States. By 1860, there were more than 30,000 miles of railroad in the nation, and they carried about two-thirds of the internal trade of the country. But it was the decade just after the Civil War that witnessed the completion of a transcontinental line, in 1869; other lines followed in the latter decades of the 1800s.

The first significant impact of technological advances on 19th-century sports is found in the steamboats and railroads of the antebellum era. As one of the first products of the age of steam, steamboats served as carriers of thoroughbred horses to such horse racing centers as Vicksburg, Natchez, and New Orleans, all located along the Mississippi River. Crowds attending horse races or prizefights were frequently conveyed to the site of the event via steamboats. The riverboats on the Mississippi also served as carriers of racing or prizefight news up and down the valley.[21]

More important, though, to the development of organized sport was the railroad.

In the years preceding the Civil War, the widespread interest in thoroughbred and trotting races was in great part nurtured by railroad expansion as horses and crowds were transported from one locality to another. Similarly, participants and spectators for prize fights and footraces were commonly carried to the site of competition by railroads. Since prize fighting was outlawed in many cities and states, it frequently became necessary to schedule the fights where they would not be disrupted by the authorities. This meant that prize fighting took on the features of a traveling show, with the actual site of the fight being passed on by word-of-mouth.

The railroad played an instrumental role in staging the first intercollegiate athletic event, a rowing race between Harvard and Yale. According to Lewis, "The proposal for America's first intercollegiate contest came from a railroad superintendent who was willing to defray all expenses and include a two-week vacation for the participants, in exchange for the attention the events would focus on an area serviced by his company. . . ."[22] The offer was accepted and the Boston, Concord, and Montreal Railroad transported the participants and fans to New Hampshire's Lake Winnipesaukee for the event. In 1869, the first intercollegiate football game between Rutgers and Princeton was attended by students riding a train pulled by a "jerky little engine that steamed out of Princeton on the memorable morning of November 6, 1869."[23] Throughout the final decades of the 19th century railroad transportation was an important factor in the growth of intercollegiate sports. Betts noted: "Intercollegiate athletics depended on railroad service for carrying teams and supporters to football, baseball, and rowing, as well as track and field contests."[24]

The fledgling major league baseball clubs made use of the rapidly expanding railroad network in the 1870s "and the organization of the National League in 1876 was only possible with the continued development of connecting lines."[25] As major league baseball developed, the formation of teams followed the network of rail lines, a pattern that remained basically undisturbed until the late 1950s when teams began to travel by air transportation.

Many other recreational pursuits were nurtured by railroads after 1865. The widespread interest in thoroughbred and trotting racing was in large part sustained by the expansion of the railway system. Interregional races became possible, and horses and spectators were carried from all over the country to track races. Realizing the financial advantage of encouraging horse racing, many railroads transported horses at reduced prices. The rail lines capitalized on public interest in prizefighting too, despite its illegality, and scheduled excursion trains for a bout. The popularity of America's first heavyweight champion, John L. Sullivan, was acquired by his tours by train to various parts of the country.[26]

By the turn of the century, almost every realm of sport shared in the powerful impact of the railroad, and in the years up to World War II this influence continued unabated. Perhaps one of the most significant contributions of the railroad to sport in the 20th century was the opening of new areas for recreational participation. For example, the initial stimulus for the popularization of skiing was the "snow train." Cozens and Stumpf described how rail transportation nurtured skiing: "The first 'snow train' left Boston's North Station in 1931, and four years later such trains were pulling out of New York's Grand Central Station with thousands of apartment dwellers on board, intent on spending two days in the snows of New England."[27] Railroads were responsible for the development and promotion of a number of America's most popular winter sports resorts.

As important as the steam engine was to improving transportation and stimulating industrialization, its impact on the social life and transportation habits of Americans was miniscule in comparison to the development of the internal combustion engine. This invention made possible the automobile and the airplane, two modes of transportation that completely revolutionized travel and numerous other aspects of life. In addition to their contributions to transportation, the automobile and airplane created totally new industries involving billions of dollars in capital and employing millions of workers. They stimulated the construction of millions of miles of highways, and they spawned the growth of many industries and occupations related to auto and aircraft production and use. For example, the prosperity of the oil, rubber, steel, and electronic industries depend to a large extent on these two forms of transportation. The growth of metropolitan areas, especially suburban and satellite towns outside large cities, was stimulated by the automobile.

Inventors in Europe and the United States had successfully developed an internal combustion engine powered by gasoline by the last decade of the 19th century. But at first, there was little general interest in the converted bicycles that were the first automobiles because they were either used for racing or as a toy for the rich. Then a young man by the name of Henry Ford saw the potential of the automobile as a means of popular transportation. He realized that he would have to gain the financial backing for the auto through racing, so he built a huge-engined racing car, the "999," and hired a professional bicycle rider by the name of Barney Oldfield to race it. After the "999" easily won the race against its challengers, Ford wrote: "The '999' did what it was intended to do: It advertised the fact that I could build a fast motor car. A week after the race I formed the Ford Motor Company."[28] In 1895, there were four registered autos in the U.S.; by 1915 the number had grown to 2 1/2 million, and by 1975 to 70 million.

Racing was the first and foremost attraction of the automobile in the days when its usefulness for any other purpose was questioned. In 1895, H. H. Kohlsaat, publisher of the *Chicago Times-Herald,* sponsored the first automobile race in America; automobile races had already become the fad in Europe. Early automobile manufacturers recognized the commercial value of races and used them as a major marketing technique to win public interest.[29] This particular aspect of automobile racing continues to the present day. Throughout the 20th century, automobile racing has grown in popularity and now includes a bewildering array of racing forms—midget autos, stock cars, hot rods, etc.

But the automobile contributed to the rise of sport in many ways beyond auto racing. For countless millions the auto progressively opened up broader horizons in the fields of spectator and participant sport. It provided an easy means of transportation from city to city and from the country to the sports of town or city. Thus, the large stadiums and other sports facilities could be conveniently reached by large groups of people. Also for the first time, golf courses, ski resorts, tennis courts, bathing beaches, and field sports, such as fishing, camping, hunting, were within practical reach of large masses of the population. All this would have been impossible without the transportation provided by the automobile.

In 1903, Oliver and Wilbur Wright successfully flew an airplane, but it was not until World War I that airplanes were used in any large scale, first for scouting enemy movements and later in actual combat. During the 1920-40 era, aircraft design was improved, airports constructed, and regular passenger, mail, and express lines established. World War II provided for further development, and the postwar period saw the airplane become the prominent mode of long-distance public transportation. Airplanes have in effect shrunk the nation by reducing traveling time.

Airplane races have never held the spectator appeal of auto racing, but air transportation has had a significant impact on sports in other ways. Until about the mid-1950s, most professional and collegiate athletic teams traveled by rail. With improvements in all phases of air transportation, the airplane became the common carrier of teams. The expansion of professional sports franchises from the East and Midwest into the West and the South and the increased number of pro sports teams could only have been possible with air travel. Interregional collegiate football and basketball games were rare until air travel made it possible to take long trips in a short period of time. Now, interregional contests are a part of the weekly menu of collegiate sports.

Communication

As important as transportation was to the transformation of American sport, the new methods of communications over the past century and a half have been equally significant. The invention and development of the telegraph was the most important advance in communication during the first half of the 19th century. Samuel F. B. Morse perfected an electrical instrument by which combinations of dots and dashes could be transmitted along a wire, and the first telegraph line was built between Baltimore and Washington, D.C., in 1844. Soon, telegraph lines stretched between all of the principal cities, and by 1860, some 50,000 miles of line existed east of the Rockies. Meanwhile, Western Union was extending its lines to the Pacific coast, putting the Pony Express out of business a little more than a year after it was founded.

From its invention in 1844, the telegraph rapidly assumed a significant role in the dissemination of sporting news because newspapers and periodicals installed telegraphic apparatus in their offices. Only two years after its invention, the *New York Herald* and the *New York Tribune* had telegraphic equipment. By 1850, "prize fights, horse races, trotting contests, and yachting events were occasionally reported over the wires."[30]

Simultaneous with the development of the telegraph, a revolution in the dissemination of news occurred with the improvements in the presses used to print copy and other processes of newspaper and journal production. The telegraph and the improved press opened the gates to a rising tide of sports journalism, but the journalistic exploitation of sports actually did not occur until the decade following the Civil War.[31]

The Atlantic cable, successfully laid in 1866 by Cyrus Field, did for international news what the telegraph had done for national communication. The cable reduced the time it took to send a message from Europe to the U.S. from 10 days (by steamship) to a moment or so. This advance in communication was a boom to sports enthusiasts for it overcame the handicap of having to wait two or three weeks to get sports results from England and Europe. In 1869, when the Harvard crew traveled to England to row against Oxford on the Thames River, enormous national interest centered on the match. According to Mathews, in New York, "Along the sidewalks there was but one topic of conversation."[32] The results of the race were "flashed through the Atlantic cable as to reach New York about a quarter past one, while the news reached the Pacific Coast about nine o'clock, enabling many of the San Franciscans to discuss the subject at their breakfast tables, and swallow the defeat with their coffee."[33] All this was a culmination of a campaign in transatlantic news coverage that began months earlier and served as the first real test of the Atlantic cable.[34] The combination of telegraph and Atlantic cable aroused a greater interest in international sport.

The communications breakthrough in the latter 19th century was the telephone, which was first exhibited at the Centennial Exposition in Philadelphia in 1876. There, Alexander Graham Bell demonstrated that an electrical instrument could transmit the human voice. Although at first most people thought of the telephone as a plaything, business and industrial leaders saw its possibilities for maintaining communication with their far-flung interests. In 1900, there were slightly more than one million telephones in use; today, there are more than 100 million. With less than 7 percent of the world's population, the United States possesses more than one-half of the world's telephones.

Newspapers were one of the first businesses to make extensive use of telephone service, and the sports departments founded by many of the newspapers in the last two decades of the 19th century depended on the telephone to obtain the results of sports events. By the end of the century, the telephone was an indispensible part of sports journalism.

In 1896, an Italian scientist, Guglielmo Marconi, patented the wireless and showed the possibility of telegraphy without the use of wires. Within a few years, wireless telegraphy was carrying messages to all parts of the world. One of the first stories that was covered by wireless was a sports event. Marconi was hired by Associated Press in 1899 to report on the international yacht race involving Sir Thomas Lipton's *Shamrock* and the American *Columbia*. Thus, the wireless took its place along with the telegraph and the telephone in intensifying public interest in sport and stimulating the rise of sport.[35]

The next important step in electrical communication was the radio, which until 1920 was mainly a toy for amateur scientists. But in 1920, a radio station in Pittsburgh began broadcasting, the start of a new communication medium and industry was underway. In less than three decades, more than 90 percent of American families had acquired radios.[36] Radio's heyday was during the 1930s and '40s, and the broadcasting companies claimed that all but 2 percent of the American people were listeners. It was not until the early 1950s that television began to overshadow radio for information and home entertainment.

Radio broadcasting of sports events actually preceded the beginning of public broadcasting. On August 20, 1920, the radio station of the *Detroit News* went on the air to announce the results of the World Series baseball games. This was before the first public radio station in Pittsburgh made its initial broadcast in November of that year. Also in 1920, the first college football game was broadcast from a station in Texas.[37]

Radio came of age in the hectic 1920s, and while music and news broadcasts were the standard programs, sports events were rapidly absorbed into the entertainment schedule. One historian of radio noted: "Sports-casting had no crawling or creeping stages. It jumped down from the obstetrical table, kicked its heels in the air and started out to do a job."[38] Radio and sports were natural partners. Broadcasting for the first time brought all of the drama of the diamond, ringside, gridiron, and race track into homes from coast to coast.

The first heavyweight championship boxing bout to be broadcast was between Jack Dempsey and George Carpentier, on July 21, 1921. The broadcast was a widely acclaimed success, and in 1927, when Dempsey fought Gene Tunney for the championship, one department store sold $90,000 worth of radio equipment in two weeks, "most of which was attributed to the big fight."[39] While collegiate football games, prizefights, and racing events of all kinds were popular radio attractions, the World Series, first broadcast in 1926, was considered the top-ranking sports event, from a commercial broadcasting standpoint.

Persons currently under the age of 25 have been brought up watching the latest communications development—television. Indeed, some media experts claim that the present college generation has spent more time during their waking hours watching television than doing any other single thing. Americans of all ages watch an estimated average of 21 hours of television weekly.[40]

Although television had been experimentally developed prior to World War II, it was not until the late 1940s that technology and marketing combined to produce models for home use. The major TV boom occurred in the early 1950s as the number of sets rose from 10 to 60 million in a single decade, and broadcasting stations rose from 100 to 700. By 1957, TV was described by a radio editor of the *New York Times* as "somewhat in the same light as indoor plumbing . . . indisputably a fixture of the household but no longer a novelty."[41]

Interestingly, in its embryonic stage television covered sports events. According to Cozens and Stumpf: "A baseball game between Princeton and Columbia at Baker Field furnished the first telecast in the United States. . . . The Nova-Baer encounter in June, 1939, was the first televised boxing bout."[42]

As television sets became available to the public and broadcasting of programs expanded, it quickly became evident that televised sports events would be immensely popular, and throughout the past quarter of a century television has expanded its coverage of sports. The national networks now schedule over 1,000 hours of sports per year between them, and the ten most popular telecasts of 1975 were *all* sports events.[43]

Television not only broadcasts all of the traditional sports, but it has popularized several sports that had only local following until subjected to a national TV audience, i.e., arm wrestling, barrel jumping, demolition derbies. In addition, TV has created at least one sport of its own—the Superstar Championships. Furthermore, television has been largely responsible for the burgeoning professional sports enterprise. Professional sports, even major league baseball, was a struggling industry before the advent of television. Today, professional sport exists in its present form because of television. It is an industry almost entirely dependent on TV revenue (the economic dimensions of professional sports will be discussed in detail in chapter 7). What is true of professional sports is also true of big-time collegiate sports (which is, in fact, a professional sports industry). Collegiate athletic programs are heavily dependent on the revenue generated by televised events, mostly football and basketball.

While advances in electrical forms of communication were instrumental in the rise of sport, other communications media supplemented and extended the publicizing of sport. For example, the rise of sports journalism was closely tied to new inventions in printing processes and to the telegraph network that spanned the nation in the mid-1800s. As early as the mid-1830s several of the country's large newspapers were giving extensive coverage to prizefights, foot and horse races, as well as other sports. What was perhaps the most notable newspaper concerned with sports in the United States appeared in 1831 and survived until 1901; the paper was called the *Spirit of the Times.*[44] But in the antebellum era, sports were more directly aided by magazine and book publishers than they were by the newspaper press.

The expansion of sports journalism in the latter three decades of the 19th century related to the universal use of telegraphy by publishers, which made possible instantaneous reporting of sports events, and to the realization by editors of the popular interest in sport. Indeed, sport emerged as such a popular topic of conversation that newspapers and magazines increased their coverage in the 1880s and 1890s. At the same time, the number of U.S. newspapers increased sixfold between 1870 and 1900 (from 387 to 2,326). Their combined circulations rose from 3.5 million to 15 million. According to Kobre, "Publishers and editors [recognized the growing interest in sport] and began to cater to it to win wide circulations."[45] New York papers such as the *Herald, Sun,* and *World* devoted enough attention to sports that a new form of journalist, the sports journalist, emerged. It remained, however, for William Randolph Hearst to develop the first sports section for his paper the *New York Journal.*[46] Hearst bought the *Journal* in 1895 and immediately set out to outdo his rivals in the matter of reporting sports news. Where rival newspapers were printing from three to seven columns of sports news daily, the *Journal* doubled, trebled, and quadrupled the space and also began the special Sunday issues of twelve pages. In addition, Hearst signed up sports champions to write for his paper. What emerged was the modern newspaper sports section.[47]

Throughout the 20th century, the sports page has been an indispensible part of every newspaper. From a concentration on a few sports, such as baseball, college football, horse racing, and boxing, attention is now given to an enormously wide range of sports. Today, many newspapermen feel that the sports section is the most important factor in the circulation and subscription of a newspaper. Consequently, newspapers have been liberal with space for sports, and they spend millions of dollars annually in sports coverage for which there may appear to be little direct financial return to the newspapers. However, if sports coverage sells newspapers, as is believed, then it renders a considerable financial service to them. Indeed, it is contended by some newspapermen that the sports section is the advertisement section for the newspaper.[48]

But the benefits of newspaper sports coverage are reciprocal. Some years ago, Connie Mack, one of the principal founders and the long-time coach and owner of what is now the Oakland Athletics, stated: "The sporting world was created and is now being kept alive by the services extended by the press."[49] While this statement may be overdrawn, it is true that the sports section furnishes publicity and is largely responsible for making professional and big-time intercollegiate sports profitable businesses. It has stimulated the growth of all of the professional sports as well as fostered much of the interest in amateur sports. Cozens and Stumpf describe another way in which newspapers promote sports:

> The sports page of the modern newspaper is the "softest" spot for the press agent. For instance, the winter resort owner who needs business does not buy advertising space; he stages a golf or tennis tournament or a swimming meet. Prizes large enough to entice first-rate talent are offered, and the free publicity begins. First the build-up, then the detailed progress of the event, and finally the results.[50]

Along with the newspaper, magazine and book publishers have done much to attract attention to athletics in the past century and a half. Beginning in the antebellum era, a host of turf journals appeared along with many periodicals devoted to field sports and outdoor life. Sports journals proliferated greatly in the latter 19th century, so that almost every sport had at least one periodical devoted to it. This trend has continued to the present day, and by visiting any newsstand you will find that a substantial portion of shelf space is occupied by magazines about sports. The weekly circulation for *Sports Illustrated* is about 2,250,000, and its annual advertising revenue exceeds $72.2 million.

The publication of various kinds of books about sports began accelerating in the mid-19th century. Athletic almanacs and dime novels extolling the exploits of athletes and sportsmen grew in popularity. Handbooks of various kinds were published. Outing Publishing Company issued more than a hundred titles on yachting, hunting, cycling, and athletics. Two books by Thomas Hughes, *Tom Brown at Rugby* and *Tom Brown at Oxford,* were responsible for a rising desire for sports fiction. In 1896, Gilbert Patten began pouring out a story every week of the heroic sports achievements of a fictional athlete by the name of Frank Merriwell to meet the demand for boys' athletic stories. Before he was through, Patten had authored 208 titles, which sold an estimated 25 million copies.[51]

Juvenile literature has contributed significantly to arousing sports interests among young boys and girls. For many youth, the successes of fictional athletic heroes is the first step in nurturing an interest in sport. Many a teacher has found that a problem reader became an avid reader when a book about sports was substituted for one about some mid-Victorian family living in London.

Other Technological Developments and Sport

Other technological advances have had a marked influence on the transformation of sport, although they may not have been as obvious as the ones described thus far. Improvements in photography developed rapidly in the years following the Civil War, as the cumbersome equipment was replaced by the more mobile Eastman Kodak, which also produced clearer reproductions, and finally with cameras that produced the illusions of movement. Sports played an important role in the early development and popularization of the camera. In 1872, Eadweard Muybridge, with the prodding of Leland Stanford, made the first successful attempt to record the illusion of motion by photography. He was interested in discovering whether a trotting horse left the ground entirely at some point in its gait. By setting up a battery of cameras that went off sequentially, the movements of the horse were successfully photographed. The clarity of these pictures led Muybridge to realize that his photographic technique could be extended to analyze the movements of all kinds of species. He subsequently photographed a host of walking and running animals, and in his monumental 11-volume study entitled *Animal Locomotion* (1887) he included thousands of pictures of horses, birds, and even human athletes.[52] Other experimenters gradually perfected the techniques that gave birth to the true motion picture.

In its early years, the motion picture industry concentrated primarily on boxing. The first commercial motion picture was a six-round bout between Young Griffo and Battling Barnett in 1895. Motion pictures of boxing championships were one of the most popular forms of sports spectating in the first three decades of the 20th century, and served to stimulate the public appetite for organized sports. In recent years, the motion picture has become an indispensible instrument in coaching for scouting opponents and reviewing the performances of one's own athletes. Collegiate and professional coaches of some sports spend as much time viewing films as almost any other coaching task. Undoubtedly, the motion picture has contributed to the remarkable advances in the technical aspects of sports.

The impact of the still camera cannot be overlooked, however. Beginning in the early years of this century, newspapers and magazines made extensive use of pictures to show the performance of athletes in the heat of competition or to illustrate the correct (or incorrect) method of performing a skill. This has had the effect of keeping sports before the eyes of the large mass of Americans, further nurturing sports.

We have already described how advances in the use of electricity led to important developments in communication, but the use of electricity to produce light had an equally significant impact on sport. When Thomas A. Edison invented the incandescent bulb in 1879, he inaugurated a new era in the social life of Americans. With the invention of the light bulb, sports events for the first time could be held at night. Within a few years, electric lighting and more comfortable accommodations helped lure athletes and spectators into school and college gymnasiums and into public sports arenas and stadiums. Prizefights, walking contests, horse shows, wrestling matches, basketball games, and other sports were now held indoors in lighted facilities. Madison Square Garden in New York City had electric lights by the mid-1880s, and they were used for a variety of sports events (the current Madison Square Garden is the third of its kind). Betts claimed that "much of the urban appeal of indoor sport was directly attributed to the revolution which electric lighting made in the night life of the metropolis."[53]

While indoor sports were greatly stimulated by electric lighting, America's "national pastime"—baseball—did not discover the value of this invention until the 1930s. According to *The Outlook,* "social historians may record 1930 as the year of the emergence of night baseball."[54] The first ventures into nighttime baseball took place in Des Moines and Wichita in the summer of 1930. Several minor leagues quickly adopted night baseball, but it was not until 1935 that the night game was introduced for the first time in the major leagues in Cincinnati, and only in the 1940s did night baseball gain general acceptance in the major leagues.[55] (The past owner of the Chicago Cubs, Phillip K. Wrigley, never accepted night baseball; thus there are no lights at Wrigley Field, and all of the Cub games are held during the daylight hours.)

We might take one final example of how an invention changed the nature of sport. The vulcanization of rubber by Charles Goodyear in the 1830s eventually influenced sports equipment and apparel in every sport. Elastic and resilient rubber balls changed the nature of every sport in which they were used. Equipment made with rubber altered the tactics and techniques of many sports. The pneumatic tire developed in the 1880s "revolutionized cycling and harness racing in the next decade," and it played a vital role in the rise and spectacular appeal of auto racing.[56]

Industrialization, Urbanization, and Sport

The Growth of Industry and Urbanization

As noted earlier in this chapter, a series of inventions in the late 18th century and the technological advances that accompanied these inventions completely changed the means by which goods were produced. This development made possible the use of machines, large-scale production, and gradually business consolidation. It became known as the Industrial Revolution. The major characteristic and social consequence of the Industrial Revolution was the factory system. Artisans and craftsmen were transformed into an industrial proletariat. Its initial impact was on the textile industry. Spinning of thread and the weaving of cloth had traditionally been done at home on spinning wheels and hand looms, but new methods for performing these tasks enabled them to be done in factories by power-driven machinery. By 1820, the Lowell loom had been developed, making possible the spinning and weaving of cotton in the same factory. The sewing machine of Elias Howe revolutionized the making of clothes, shoes, and various leather goods.

Other industries emerged. The successful smelting of iron with the aid of anthracite coal was perfected about 1830, and by 1850 improved methods of making steel were developed. Steel production was the backbone of industrial development because the machinery for factories was primarily made from steel. Moreover, the rapidly growing railroad system depended on steel for track and rail cars.

Before 1860, industry was largely centered in New England and the mid-Atlantic states, but by 1900, industrialization and manufacturing had spread out to all parts of the country. Especially noteworthy was the movement of industry westward. In the West, new industries were created; the meat-packing industry developed in Chicago and Kansas City, while in the plains states, the production of wood products became prominent.

Developments in one field stimulated changes and growth in others. As noted above, the steel industry was enhanced by the expanding railroad network, which used steel rails for the lines being built in the West. Railroads, in turn, were stimulated by the need of the steel industry for iron ore, coal, and other materials that needed to be transported over the rails to the factories. Moreover, railroad development encouraged the westward movement, and new and fertile areas of the West produced crops and products that needed to be transported to markets, further stimulating railroad building. Simultaneously, industry produced the farm machinery that made it possible to raise larger crops. Finally, the new methods of communication promoted the growth of all kinds of business, and, in turn, were themselves stimulated by that growth.

Before the Civil War, factories were small and the most common forms of business organization were the partnership, where ownership was by two or more individuals, and the proprietorship, in which a single person owned the entire business. But as the factory system took root, a capitalistic class began to emerge and a new form of business ownership, the corporation, became a dominant form of organization. By the 1890s, corporations produced nearly three-fourths of the total value of manufactured products in the United States. The large corporations were able to develop mass production methods and mass sales, the bases of big business, because of the huge amounts of money that they controlled. They were also able to drive out small businesses and acquire control over the production and price of goods and services in a given field of business. For example, by 1880, the Standard Oil Company controlled 90 percent of the country's petroleum business. When the U.S. Steel Corporation was founded near the turn of the century, it controlled some 60 percent of the iron and steel production of the nation—from the mining of the ore to the distribution of the finished steel products.[57] Throughout the 20th century, the corporate form of business has expanded and extended into virtually every form of goods and service operation. In 1968, "the 200 largest industrial corporations controlled over 60 percent of the total assets held by all manufacturing corporations."[58] Some economists call the 20th century the "century of the corporation."

As technology increased the means of industrial production, more and more people gave up farming and came to the cities to work in the factories and offices. They were joined by a seemingly endless stream of immigrants who sought a better life in America. Factories multiplied and towns and cities grew rapidly. The first U.S. census completed in 1790 recorded a population of nearly 4 million, about six percent of whom were classified as urban; by 1890, the population had risen to 62 million, with some 35 percent now living in urban areas. The United States has witnessed a veritable population explosion in the 20th century, with a population now in excess of 225 million and an urban population of around 75 percent of the total.[59]

The Influence of Industrialization and Urbanization on the Rise of Sport

The concentration of large groups of people in towns that soon would become thriving cities made it possible for sport to be transformed from informal and spontaneous events to organized, highly competitive activities, and industrialization and urbanization were the basic causes for the rise of sport. Of course, these movements were greatly enhanced by the revolutionary transformation in communication, transportation, and other technological advances.[60]

Urban influences on the world of sport made their appearances in the pre-Civil War era, and by 1860 the increasing concentration of city populations and the monotonous and wearisome repetition of mechanical work created a demand for more recreational outlets. According to Betts: "Urbanization brought forth the need for commercialized spectator sports, while industrialization gradually provided the standard of living and leisure time so vital to the support of all forms of recreation."[61]

Towns and cities were natural centers for organizing sports. The popular sport of horse racing centered in New York, Charleston, Louisville, and New Orleans, while the first organized baseball clubs were founded in such communities as New York, Boston, Chicago, and St. Louis. Yachting and rowing regattas, footraces, billiard matches, and even the main agricultural fairs were held in or near the larger cities.[62] Betts has noted: "Millionaires who ventured into yachting, office girls and young ladies of leisure who turned to cycling, and prize fight enthusiasts who backed their favorite challengers were largely from the town or city." He goes on to summarize the influence of the city: "Urban areas encouraged sport through better transportation facilities, a growing leisure class, a higher standard of living, more available funds for purchase of sporting goods, and the greater ease with which leagues and teams could be organized."[63] Increased leisure and income are undoubtedly the main causes for the extraordinary development of participant sport in the current generation. The machine, which at first so greatly reduced free time, has finally allowed the masses to acquire a measure of leisure that they can use to play and watch sports.

Mass production of goods and corporate organization developed in sport just as it did in other industries. Although manufacturing and merchandising of sports goods were still in the pioneer stage of development in the latter 19th century, much of the growing popularity of sports and outdoor recreation was due to standardized manufacturing of bicycles, billiard tables, baseball equipment, sporting rifles, fishing rods, and numerous other items used in sports.

The first major sporting goods corporation was formed by Albert G. Spalding, a former pitcher for the Boston and Chicago baseball clubs, in 1876. Beginning with baseball equipment, he branched out into various sports, and by the end of the century, the A.G. Spalding and Brothers Company had a virtual monopoly over athletic goods. He was "the monarch of the business in the late years of the century."[64] Department stores began carrying sports goods on a large scale around the early 1880s, led by Macy's of New York City; Sears, Roebuck devoted 80 pages of their 1895 catalog to sporting equipment.[65]

With the rising popularity of numerous sports throughout the 20th century, and with the advances in technology, making possible the introduction of newer and better sports equipment, and finally with improved manufacturing and distribution methods, the sporting goods industry has become a multimillion dollar-a-year industry. Several large corporations control a large portion of the sporting goods business, but with the proliferation of sports in the past two decades, many small companies now produce a variety of sports equipment.

American business and labor organizations have contributed to the rise of sport through organized industrial recreation programs for millions of U.S. workers. During the 19th century, most industrial leaders showed little interest in the health and welfare of their employees, but by the beginning of this century, voices inside and outside industry were pleading for consideration of the worker as a human being, with special focus on the worker's physical and mental health. Business and labor leaders began to realize that perhaps opportunities for diversion, whether in intellectual directions or in such amusements as games and sport, might enhance employee health and morale, and hence increase productivity. The idea of providing company-sponsored recreation as a phase of business management caught on and programs of all sorts came into existence. In 1913, a U.S. Bureau of Labor Statistics survey found that half of the companies surveyed had some form of recreation program for their employees.[66] A similar survey conducted on 319 companies in 1927 found that 157 maintained baseball diamonds or athletic fields, 50 had tennis courts, 13 maintained golf courses, while 223 of them sponsored baseball teams, and 41 had soccer teams.[67] By the 1950s, some 20,000 organizations were sponsoring some form of industrial recreation, with more than 20 million employees participating.[68] During the 1930-50 era, the best amateur teams in basketball, baseball, and softball were company-sponsored teams. The

National Industrial Basketball League included teams such as the Phillips 66ers, Goodyear Wingfoots, and the Peoria Caterpillers. Championships of the National Baseball Congress and Amateur Softball Association were dominated by company-backed teams.

Industrial recreation programs have grown enormously over the past 50 years and today more than $1.5 billion a year is spent on employee recreation; indeed, industry spends more on sports equipment than all U.S. schools and colleges combined. More than 125 golf courses are owned by corporations, and industry is probably the biggest user of bowling lanes, Ping-Pong tables, volleyball, basketball, and softball equipment in the country. Three-fourths of all firms employing more than 1,000 people have some form of athletic program, and more than 8,000 companies now have full- or part-time recreation managers. There is a National Industrial Recreation Association, made up of industrial recreation managers and supervisors, which publishes a journal called *Recreation Management.*[69]

Labor unions, originally formed to acquire better pay and working conditions for industrial employees, gradually broadened their interests to include the health and mental welfare of their members. The United Automobile Workers established a recreation department in 1937, based on a strong policy of organized recreation for all ages. Other unions have organized recreation programs that include almost everything in the way of leisure-time activities. Among these are team and individual sports, social recreation, dancing instruction, handicrafts, orchestras, and hobby clubs. Some unions have acquired large tracts of land on which they have built elaborate recreational facilities for the use of their members.

Professional Sports as an Industry

Professional sports teams are a form of corporate organization that function very similarly in many respects to corporations of any other kind, albeit with certain tax and monopolistic advantages given to other businesses.[70] (This will be more fully discussed in chapter 7.)

The first professional baseball team was player owned and controlled, but major league teams were organized into business corporations in the latter 19th century and continue to the present as business enterprises made up of separate corporations under a cartel form of organization. Professional football began in the 1920s, and industry had a hand in its development. The Acme Packing Company in Green Bay, Wisconsin, sponsored a local team, which was fittingly called the Packers, and in Decatur, Illinois, the A. E. Staley Manufacturing Company started the team that became known as the Chicago Bears. From these humble beginnings professional football is now a $90 million-a-year business, and each franchise in the National Football League is worth in excess of $20 million.[71]

Bureaucracy and Sport

The rise of industrialization and the use of mass production methods brought about a tremendous bureaucratization in both private and public organizations. The fundamental feature of every society is embodied in a characteristic organizational form, and for our time this is bureaucracy. It dominates our age, not just in large-scale business but also in government, education, religion, the armed forces, and almost every other contemporary institution.

Bureaucracy is the immense administrative machine of all large-scale organizations. It has been the harbinger of standardization, mass production, objectivity, and impersonality in complex organizations. Bureaucracy stands in direct opposition to every emotional, unspecialized, personal, and deeply human aspect of personality. Authority in a bureaucratic organization is authoritarian and hierarchical; it is also rational, that is, it is based entirely on understood and accepted rules efficiently designed to serve the organization's goals. The interests of the organization are paramount in the development of these rules, and the formal aspects of a bureaucracy manifest these interests and rules.

According to Max Weber, the German sociologist whose ideas have greatly influenced this field, bureaucratic organization is characterized by a primary orientation toward the attainment of specific goals, e.g., the central goal of General Motors is to make profits for its shareholders, thus a central feature of bureaucratic organization is an acceptance of the priority of the organization and a belief that individuals must subordinate their wills to it. An established hierarchy with a strict authoritarian chain of command and codified policies is seen as necessary and valuable. There is a central ideology in support of technology and the domination of humans and environment by technique; therefore, science, technology, organization, and planning are prime values. Basic also to bureaucratic organization is rational authority. Under a system of rationality, the goals of the organization are to be achieved as completely as possible and at the lowest cost. This is most readily accomplished by selecting competent personnel and devising an elaborate division of labor.[72]

The first formal scheme for the rationalization of industrial work was proposed by Frederick W. Taylor in the early years of the 20th century, a time of population growth and industrial expansion. His system was called "scientific management," and its most fundamental precept was cost efficiency. He suggested that an organization could achieve its production goals only when it could achieve an optimal cost-efficiency ratio. Taylor's primary propositions were: (1) use time and motion study to find the one best way of performing a job—the way that permits the largest average rate of production over the day; (2) provide the employee with an incentive to perform the job in the best way at a fast pace—in general, do this by giving him a specified bonus over regular rates if he meets the standards of production; and (3) use specialized experts to establish the various conditions surrounding the worker's task. Taylor, a tennis champion and golf devotee, was said to have learned through sport "the value of the minute analysis of motions, the importance of methodical selection and training, the worth of time study and of standards based on rigorous exact observation."[73]

The underlying notion implicit in the "scientific management" approach with regard to human nature is that humans are bad, lazy, and incentive oriented. Scientific management treated employees as a means by assuming that they would cooperate and work only when forced to do so. This arrangement reduced employees to instruments of the organization who functioned under a hierarchical authority relationship. The climate of interpersonal relationship under this management approach was at a low level; relations between leaders, or managers, and workers were closed and inflexible; there was little opportunity for change initiated by the workers. American industry enthusiastically adopted Taylor's approach to management leadership, and this management style has frequently been used by various nonindustrial organizations such as schools, the military, and sports organizations.[74]

The influence of bureaucracy goes beyond the organizations that employ this form of administrative process; it is a source of norms regulating a large number of activities both within and beyond large-scale organization boundaries. So powerful and so pervasive are the organizations that employ bureaucratic methods that the value orientations engendered by this form of organization have attained the status of core values for American society. They permeate the fabric of every social institution and the American socialization process is largely devoted to conditioning the youth of the nation to this orientation.

As organized sport has grown prominent and powerful in the past 60 years, it has clearly adopted the assumptions and values of bureaucratic organizations. Charles Page has persuasively argued that sport has not escaped the powerful thrust of bureaucracy:

> The social revolution of sport, viewed in historical perspective, has been in large part the transition from both folk-rooted informal contests and the agonistic recreation of elites to its bureaucratization—or, in simple terms, from player-controlled "games" to the management-controlled "big time."
>
> This transition has been two-sided. On the one hand, there has been the ever- growing rationalization and formalization of sport, with the aim of maximizing athletic "output," abetted by consistently improved techniques and equipment and measured by victory, record breaking, and, of fundamental importance, sheer economic profit—on this count, sport has become big business with all of its familiar features. On the other hand, there has been the decreasing degree of autonomy of the athlete himself, whose onetime position as a more or less independent participant has been largely replaced by the status of skilled athletic worker under the strict discipline of coaches, managers,

> and, in the case of the pro, the "front office." This large-scale bureaucratization of sport, it should be stressed, is by no means confined to its professional version: rules and routine, the ascendancy of work over play, and the rise of the coach's authority within and beyond the athletic realm have penetrated deeply into collegiate and high school sports and even into the adult-controlled, highly organized "little leagues" in baseball and football.[75]

Bureaucracy has been transplanted from public and private organizations to which it was largely confined at first, to the affairs of sport, and the emergence of bureaucracy in sport has been dependent on many of the same factors that were responsible for the growth of bureaucracy in other areas of organizational life, e.g., the expansion of a money economy, the increased size of administrative units, the growth of occupational specialization, and prominence of the profit motive.[76]

The growth in organized sport has witnessed an acceptance of the priority of sports organizations and a belief that the individual must subordinate his will to them. An established hierarchy and efficiency procedures are seen as necessary and inviolate, and the domination of man and environment by technology is a central ideology. The basic concern is with athletes subjecting themselves to the will of the coach, whose primary concern is with winning athletic contests. The rise of increasingly institutionalized and codified sports teams has caused many coaches to view team members as objects in a machinelike environment who need to be conditioned to perform prescribed, fragmented tasks as instrumental to team performance. Thus, the players become another person's (the coach's) instrument, and are used to reach the objectives and goals of the organization; they are reduced to cogs in the organization's machinery. Individual players are expected to do their best to fit themselves into functions needed by the organization. This is vividly exemplified to the popular locker slogan: "There is no I in team." A system of incentives and rewards, i.e., letter awards, helmet decals, etc., are instituted to "motivate" athletes to perform. It may be seen that in this approach decisions are made by management (the coaches), after a thorough cost-efficiency analysis, and the players are expected to carry out the will of the coach for accomplishment of organizational goals.[77] As Morford has argued:

> The modern coach, instead of being the man who encourages and guides others to struggle to do their thing, has instead become the person who manipulates and controls others and their environment so as to do his thing. Thus, the individual loses his chance to struggle himself, to seek his own experience.[78]

The most important foundation of both American sport and bureaucratic organization is authority. In both activities, rigid and bureaucratized hierarchy controls more and more aspects of the workers' and athletes' lives both on and off the job or, in the case of sports, the field of play. As Hoch has said:

> In football, like business . . . every pattern of movement on the field is increasingly being brought under the control of a group of non-playing managerial technocrats who sit up in the stands . . . with their headphones and dictate offenses, defenses, special plays, substitutions and so forth to the players below.[79]

Coaches typically structure coach-athlete relationships along authoritarian lines; they analyze and structure sports team positions for precise specialization of the athletes, and they endeavor to control player behavior not only throughout practice and contest periods but also on a round-the-clock basis, e.g., grooming rules, training rules, dating behavior, etc. Under this form of management, the athletes are the instruments of organizational goals. In most cases, they are not consulted about the organizational goals (it is assumed that they want to be champions and that they are willing to "pay the price" to be winners). They are not consulted about team membership, practice methods, team strategy, or any of the other dynamic functions of a team. The assumption has been made that they have nothing to contribute towards identifying group goals and the means for achieving them. Habermas has argued that "sport . . . has long since become a sector for the rationalization of work." The training process is analyzed, dissected, calculated, and synthesized just like the production process. "Sport is a copy . . . of the world of work. And individuals become substrata of units of measurement in it."[80] What do coaches say when they want to praise an athlete? They say he is a hard worker! According to Plessner, "two worlds of work" stand opposite to each other: sport being "a copy of the world of industry" with the same formal functional rules and standards of valuation.[81]

While one may not like the notion that bureaucratic values and methods are salient throughout organized sports, it is basically true. Moreover, it serves to illustrate one way in which sport is a microcosm of American society.

Cultural Forces for the Rise of Sport

As significant as the technological and industrial revolutions were to the rise of sport, they were accompanied by an equally significant force—changing cultural attitudes, values, and beliefs about sport. Without cultural support for sport, it could not have become the prominent social institution that it now is.

Social Aristocrats, Rabble, and Immigrants

Organized sports grew in the first half of the 19th century through the support and encouragement of three social groups—the American social aristocracy, the metropolitan "rabble," and the immigrants.[82] Wealthy southern farmers and plantation owners and northern businessmen were highly influential in stimulating public interest in such sports as cricket, yachting, fox hunting, horse racing, and trotting. In the South, the seasonal nature of the crops permitted recreation in the lull periods each year, and the slack seasons were spent enjoying a wide variety of sports activities. Northern gentlemen, grown affluent from commercial or manufacturing interests, also turned to sports of various sorts. Thus, "members of the social aristocracy deserve much credit for early sporting enthusiasm."[83]

As cities grew, an element of the population that journalists referred to as "rabble" and "rowdies" stimulated organized sports interest. Wherever sports events were held, this group could be found gambling on the outcome and generally raising the emotional atmosphere of the event by wildly cheering their favorites and booing or attempting to disconcert those whom they had bet against. While sportsmen publicly condemned the actions of the "rabble," they secretly encouraged them because this group often helped to insure the financial success of sports events.

Immigrants also contributed to the rise of sports in a variety of ways. First, immigrants settled in the cities in great numbers and became a part of that urban population who sought excitement through sport and recreation as an antidote to the typically dull and monotonous jobs they held. Second, since a great many of these mid-19th-century immigrants did not possess the strict religious attitudes toward play and sport of the fundamental Protestant sects, they were free to enjoy and participate in sports of all kinds. Third, the immigrants brought their games and sports with them to America. Cricket, horse racing, and rowing were widely popular with the British immigrants. The Germans brought their love for lawn bowling and gymnastics, German turnverein (gymnastic clubs) were opened wherever Germans settled, and by the time of the Civil War, there were approximately 150 local turnverein with some 10,000 members.[84] The Scotch pioneered in introducing track and field to the United States with their annual Caledonian games. The Irish seemed to have a particular affinity for the prize ring, and some of the most famous 19th-century boxers were immigrants of Ireland.

Muscular Christianity and Intellectuals

The grasp of Puritanism on the mid-19th-century mind was so strong and conservative that sport could only penetrate into the periphery of social life. However, reaction to the Puritan belief that pleasure was the companion of sin emerged when liberal and humanitarian reform became a major concern, and one aspect of the social reform movement was the effort to improve the physical health of the population. The crusaders noted that a great deal of human misery was the result of poor health, and they believed that people would be happier and more productive if they engaged in sports to promote physical fitness and enjoy leisure.

Leaders in what became known as the "Muscular Christianity Movement" were highly respected persons, who were willing to risk their positions and reputation on behalf of exercise and sports. The Beecher family, famous for its Christian reform positions, was among the active crusaders for exercise and sport. Catharine Beecher wrote a book in 1832 entitled *Course of Calisthenics for Young Ladies,* but her most influential book was *A Manual of Physiology and Calisthenics for Schools and Families* published in 1856. This book not only advocated physical exercise for girls, but it promoted the introduction of physical education into American schools.

Support for physical activity came from other respected persons. The noted writer, Oliver Wendell Holmes, was "convinced that greater participation in sport would improve everything in American life from sermons of the clergy to the physical well-being of individuals."[85] Equally vigorous in his advocacy of sport was the renowned Ralph Waldo Emerson, and his status in the intellectual community served to increase the impact of his support. According to Lewis, the combined support of the clergy, social reformers, and intellectuals "to the problems of physical fitness and wholesome leisure had a profound effect upon attitudes because sport suddenly became important to heretofore apathetic youths."[86]

Colleges

Cultural support for the rise of sport shifted to American colleges in the latter 19th century. Gymnasiums had been established in a number of colleges prior to 1860, but no prolonged, systematic program of physical education existed before 1860, when Amherst College hired Edward Hitchcock as the first college physical educator. Other colleges followed, and by the turn of the 20th century most colleges had established an organized physical education program. Programs of this type trickled down to the high schools. These school and college programs served to introduce the youth of the country to various forms of sport and exercise, and this socialized them to be both sports participants and spectators.

Interschool athletic programs were even more important than the physical education programs to the rise of sport. After students organized teams, collegiate sports revolutionized campus life and served as a major source of physical activity for many students and a significant source of entertainment for other students, alumni, and the general public.

Intercollegiate athletics gradually became more than merely a demonstration of physical skills between rival institutions. The students, alumni, and public began to regard victory as the measure of a college's prestige. Campus and commercial editors increased their coverage, and sports events became featured items in newspapers and magazines. As a result, this increased coverage focused attention on winning and made contest results appear to be an index of an institution's merit.[87] Thus, a belief emerged throughout American colleges that winning teams favorably advertised the school, attracted prospective students, enhanced alumni contributions, and, in the case of state-supported colleges, increased appropriations from the state legislature. The notion that successful teams brought renown to the college and to the president himself must surely have been in the mind of University of Chicago president, William Rainey Harper, when he hired Yale All-American, Amos Alonzo Stagg, in 1890. He asked Stagg to "develop teams which we can send around the country and knock out all the other colleges. We will give them," wrote Harper, "a palace car and a vacation too."[88]

So the practice of using sports as a right arm of the public relations department of a college began in the latter 19th century and continues to the present day. This system of interschool sports is unique to the United States, and it has been one of the most significant forces in the development of organized sports. Not only is it the model for high school sports, but many nonschool youth sports programs have been organized to serve as "feeder" systems to the school and college programs. Finally, the intercollegiate program serves as a "farm system" for many of the professional sports.

Social Philosophy

The technological and industrial revolutions created profound changes in interpersonal relations that required moral and social justifications for the role of capitalism in human affairs. The captains of industry found their chief justifications in two related ideas—the gospel of wealth and Social Darwinism. According to the gospel of wealth, success and the acquisition of wealth were the just rewards of industry, thrift, and sobriety, while the mass of humanity remained poor because of their own laziness and natural inferiority. Government, according to this notion, should merely preserve order and protect property; it should leave control over the economy to the natural aristocracy, who won and held their leadership in competitive struggle.

Social Darwinism, however, was probably the most important social philosophy in the latter third of the 19th century, and it supplied a biological explanation for the gospel of wealth. As an integrated philosophy it was largely the product of the fertile mind of British sociologist, Herbert Spencer. Spencer was profoundly impressed by Darwin's findings in the field of biology, and he constructed his system on the principles of the survival of the fittest. Darwin had reported that in the animal world there was an ongoing fierce struggle for survival that destroyed the weak, rewarded the strong, and produced evolutionary change. Struggle, destruction, and the survival of the fit, Spencer argued, were essential to progress in human societies as well. The weak threatened the road to progress and deserved to perish. The strong survived because they were superior. Although Social Darwinism repudiated the humane and Christian principles on which American democratic tradition rested, Spencer's theories had great popularity in the United States and penetrated American thought quite markedly. This was the case for several reasons, but perhaps most importantly Social Darwinism was made to order to suit the needs of the ruling business oligarchy. It justified the "success ethic"; in the name of progress, it justified economic warfare, poverty, exploitation, and suffering in terms of the survival of the fittest.

The chief American expositor of Social Darwinism was William Graham Sumner, who, in 1875, taught one of the first sociology courses in America at Yale. Sumner based his sociology on the notion that human life encounters formidable obstacles and threats to survival. There is a fundamental struggle to "win" (a favorite word of Sumner) under the conditions imposed by nature. In this process, humans always compete with others. Sumner argued:

> Every man who stands on the earth's surface excludes every one else from so much of it as he covers; every one who eats a loaf of bread appropriates to himself for the time-being the exclusive use and enjoyment of so many square feet of the earth's surface as were required to raise the wheat.[90]

Sumner linked competition to the emergence of virtues—such as perseverance and hard work—presumed to be answers to the struggle against nature, and winning was seen as the just reward to the superior individual, while losing was viewed as the overt manifestation of an inferior being.[91]

The actual extent to which Social Darwinism became a part of American sports is a moot question, but a number of observers have noted that the rise of highly organized sport coincided with the emergent popularity of Social Darwinism in America, and that a high degree of interest in winning games is demonstrated in American sports, an orientation that is congruent with this social philosophy. Eldridge Cleaver has said:

> Our mass spectator sports are geared to disguise, while affording expression to, the acting out in elaborate pageantry of the myth of the fittest in the process of surviving.[92]

A similar notion was expressed by George Sauer, a former professional football player:

> I think football as it is now played reflects a segment of thought, a particular kind of thought, that is prevalent in our society. The way to get ahead is to compete against somebody, work your way up the ladder, and in so doing you have to judge yourself and be judged in relation to somebody else.[93]

George Atkinson, defensive back for the Oakland Raiders, has put it more succinctly: "It's [football] the law of the jungle. You know it's exactly like nature, the survival of the fittest."[94]

Anyone who doubts these indictments of football may easily confirm them by reading *Lombardi: Winning is the Only Thing,* or *Confessions of a Dirty Ballplayer,* or *Out of Their League,* or *They Call It a Game,* or *Meat on the Hoof,* where callous and brutal acts are celebrated as evidence of virtue, and notions that only the fittest survive abound.[95]

The popular dictum, "winning isn't everything, it's the only thing," popularized by the late Vince Lombardi (but the idea is hardly unique to him), exemplifies a core value of organized sports (although it is disavowed by many coaches and athletes); it may be seen by the actions of coaches and parents in youth and school programs. Its salience may be easily observed in colleges and professional teams, where coaches are fired if they do not win and athletes are dropped from scholarships or, in the case of the pros, traded or "released" if they do not perform up to expectations.

Summary

This chapter has reviewed the rise of sport in America. Current social circumstances are related to events of the past; in the case of sport, the changing social-cultural conditions of America provide excellent clues to understanding sport in its present form.

Highly organized spectator and participant sports are products of the past century and a half, and the technological and industrial revolutions played major roles in the transformation of sport. Urbanization was also a significant factor, for current sports forms could have only become possible with a large, urban population. Finally, influential persons from the clergy and intelligentsia, as well as social reformers have contributed ideas which form the bases of attitudes, values, and beliefs about sports in America. American values and their relationship to contemporary sports will be the subject of the next chapter.

Notes

1. Robert H. Boyle, *Sport—Mirror of American Life* (Boston: Little, Brown, 1963).
2. See John M. Roberts, Malcolm J. Arth, and Robert R. Bush, "Games in Culture," *American Anthropologist* 61 (August, 1959), pp. 597-605; Louis A. Zurcher, Jr. and Arnold Meadow, "On Bullfights and Baseball: An Example of Interaction of Social Institutions," *International Journal of Comparative Sociology* 8 (1967), pp. 99-117; and Janet Lever, "Soccer: Opium of the Brazilian People," *Trans-Action* 7 (December, 1969), pp. 36-43.
3. The subject of religion and sport will be examined more fully in chapter 5.
4. Foster Rhea Dulles, *A History of Recreation: America Learns to Play,* 2nd ed. (New York: Appleton-Century-Crofts, 1965), p. 7.
5. William C. Ewing, *Sports of Colonial Williamsburg* (Richmond, Va.: The Dietz Press, 1937), p. 1.
6. Dulles, *A History of Recreation,* pp. 67-83. Also see Bruce Bennett, "Sport in the South Up to 1865," *Quest* 27 (Winter, 1977), pp. 4-18.
7. Ibid., p. 84.
8. John R. Betts, "The Technological Revolution and the Rise of Sport," *Mississippi Valley Historical Review* 40 (September, 1953), pp. 232-233.
9. Dulles, *A History of Recreation,* p. 136. Professional runners, pedestrians (or peds) as they were called, were the most popular athletes of the early 19th century. For an interesting discussion of these runners see

George Moss, "The Long Distance Runners of Ante-Bellum America," *Journal of Popular Culture* 8 (Fall, 1974), pp. 370-382.

10. Antebellum refers to that period of the 19th century before the Civil War.
11. Dulles, *A History of Recreation,* p. 183.
12. Harold Seymour, *Baseball* (New York: Oxford University Press, 1960), p. 15.
13. John R. Betts, *America's Sporting Heritage: 1850-1950* (Reading, Mass.: Addison-Wesley, 1974), p. 111.
14. Jame Bryce, "America Revisited: The Changes of a Quarter-Century," *Outlook* (March 25, 1905), pp. 738-739.
15. Betts, *America's Sporting Heritage,* p. 218.
16. Ibid., p. 308.
17. *Statistical Abstracts of the United States* (Washington, D.C.: U.S. Government Printing Office, 1973), p. 208.
18. "National Adult Physical Fitness Survey," *Physical Fitness Research Digest* 4 (April) (Washington, D.C.: President's Council on Physical Fitness and Sports, 1974).
19. T. Kando, *Leisure and Popular Culture in Transition* (St. Louis: C.V. Mosby, 1975), p. 219.
20. Betts, "The Technological Revolution and the Rise of Sport," p. 256.
21. Betts, *America's Sporting Heritage,* p. 27.
22. Guy M. Lewis, "America's First Intercollegiate Sport: The Regattas from 1852 to 1875," *Research Quarterly* 38 (December, 1967), pp. 638-639.
23. Parke H. Davis, *Football, The American Intercollegiate Game* (New York: C. Scribner's, 1911), p. 45.
24. Betts, "The Technological Revolution and the Rise of Sport," p. 237.
25. Ibid., p. 235.
26. Ibid., p. 237.
27. Frederick Cozens and Florence Stumpf, *Sports in American Life* (Chicago: University of Chicago Press, 1953), p. 159.
28. Henry Ford and Samuel Crowther, *My Life and Work* (Garden City: Doubleday, 1922), p. 51.
29. Betts, *America's Sporting Heritage,* pp. 81-82.
30. Ibid., p. 33.
31. Ibid., p. 57.
32. Joseph J. Mathews, "The First Harvard-Oxford Boat Race," *New England Quarterly* (March, 1960), p. 77
33. *Frank Leslie's Illustrated Newspaper* (New York), 29 (September 28, 1869), p. 2. Quoted in Betts, *America's Sporting Heritage,* pp. 73-74.
34. Mathews, "The First Harvard-Oxford Boat Race," p. 77.
35. Betts, *America's Sporting Heritage,* p. 74.
36. Kenneth G. Bartlett, "Social Impact of the Radio," *Annals of the American Academy of Political and Social Science* 250 (March, 1947), pp. 89-97.
37. Alfred M. Lee, *The Daily Newspaper in America* (New York: Macmillan, 1937), p. 559. See also Gleason L. Archer, *History of Radio to 1926* (New York: American Historical Society, 1938), pp. 212-215.
38. Francis Chase, Jr., *Sound and Fury* (New York: Harper and Bros., 1942), p. 303.
39. *New York Times* (September 24, 1927), p. 14.
40. Roper Poll for Television Information Office, cited in *New Times* (June 27, 1975), p. 13.
41. Quoted from "Radio and Television," *Encyclopedia Americana Annual,* 1957.
42. Cozens and Stumpf, *Sports in American Life,* p. 151.
43. "The Affluent Activists," *Forbes* 118 (August 1, 1976), p. 22. See also William Leggett, "He Was Right on the Button," *Sports Illustrated* 44 (February 23, 1976), p. 48.
44. Cozens and Stumpf, *Sports in American Life,* p. 113.
45. Sidney Kobre, *The Development of American Journalism* (Dubuque, Ia.: Wm. C. Brown Co. Publishers, 1969), p. 357.
46. Betts, "The Technological Revolutions and the Rise of Sport," p. 240.
47. William H. Nugent, "The Sport Section," *American Mercury* 16 (March, 1929), pp. 328-338.
48. Stanley Woodward, *Sports Page* (New York: Simon and Schuster, 1949).

49. Connie Mack, *My Sixty-Six Years in the Big Leagues* (Philadelphia: John C. Winston, 1950).
50. Cozens and Stumpf, *Sports in American Life,* p. 121.
51. Betts, *America's Sporting Heritage,* p. 237.
52. Betts, "The Technological Revolution and the Rise of Sport," pp. 249-250.
53. Ibid., p. 247.
54. *Outlook and Independent,* CLV (August 20, 1930), p. 614.
55. Betts, *America's Sporting Heritage,* p. 227; the first World Series night game was played in 1975.
56. Betts, "The Technological Revolution and the Rise of Sport," p. 248.
57. Ross Robertson, *History of the American Economy,* 3rd ed. (New York: Harcourt, Brace, Jovanovich, 1973), pp. 321-353.
58. Economic Report on Corporate Mergers, Hearings Before the Subcommittee on Antitrust and Monopoly (Washington, D.C.: U.S. Government Printing Office, 1969), p. 3.
59. Noel P. Gist and Silvia F. Fava, *Urban Society* (New York: Thomas Y. Crowell, 1964), p. 50.
60. Betts, *America's Sporting Heritage,* p. 173-203, 308-325.
61. Betts, "The Technological Revolution and the Rise of Sport," p. 232.
62. Betts, *America's Sporting Heritage,* p. 30.
63. Ibid., p. 172.
64. Ibid., p. 205.
65. Betts, "The Technological Revolution and the Rise of Sport," p. 245.
66. Leonard J. Diehl and Floyd R. Eastwood, *Industrial Recreation: Its Development and Present Status* (Lafayette, Ind.: Purdue University, 1940), p. 75.
67. *Monthly Labor Review* (U.S. Bureau of Labor Statistics), May, 1927, pp. 2-3.
68. "Industry's Fact-Finding Board Conducts Nationwide Employee-Recreation Survey," *Industrial Sports Journal* 10 (March, 1950), pp. 18, 36.
69. "Playing on the Job," *Newsweek* (March 17, 1969), p. 100.
70. In 1922, the U.S. Supreme Court exempted baseball from antitrust legislation. Since that time, owners of baseball and other professional sports have used that decision, and more recent ones, to define their special legal and economic position. For an excellent discussion of this issue, see Steven R. Rivkin, "Sports Leagues and Federal Antitrust Laws," in *Government and the Sports Business,* ed. Roger G. Noll (Washington, D.C.: Brookings Institution, 1974), pp. 387-410, and D.Q. Voigt, *American Baseball: From Gentleman's Sport to the Commissioner System* (Norman, Oklahoma: University of Oklahoma Press, 1966.
71. Joseph Durso, *The All-American Dollar* (Boston: Houghton Mifflin, 1971), pp. 25-66.
72. Max Weber, *Theory of Social and Economic Organization,* trans. A. M. Henderson and Talcott Parsons (New York: Oxford University Press, 1947), pp. 333-336. Robert Merton, *Social Theory and Social Structure* (New York: Free Press, 1957) suggests that bureaucracies are frequently not the rational organizations they are created to be because socialization to bureaucratic roles tends to produce uncreative, rigid, overly conservative persons.
73. Charles De Freminville, "How Taylor Introduced the Scientific Method into Management of the Shop," *Critical Essays on Scientific Management"* Taylor Society *Bulletin* 10 (February, 1925), part II, p. 32.
74. In R. E. Callahan, *Education and the Cult of Efficiency* (Chicago: University of Chicago Press, 1962), the author has argued that scientific management was one of the most important historic forces to shape the administration of public schools in America. D. Riesman and R. Denny, "Football in America: A Study of Cultural Diffusion," *American Quarterly* 3 (1951) pp. 309-319, in their classic paper on cultural diffusion and American football, discuss the relation between Taylor's writings and the development of American football.
75. Charles H. Page, "The World of Sport and its Study," in *Sport and Society,* ed. John T. Talamini and Charles H. Page (Boston: Little, Brown 1973), pp. 32-33.
76. Alan G. Ingham, "Occupational Subcultures in the Work World of Sport," in *Sport and the Social Order,* eds. Donald W. Ball and

John W. Loy (Reading, Mass.: Addison-Wesley, 1975), p. 353.

77. George H. Sage, "The Coach as Management: Organizational Leadership in American Sport," *Quest* 19 (January, 1973), pp. 35-40.

78. W. R. Morford, "Is Sport the Struggle or the Triumph?" *Quest* (January, 1973), p. 86.

79. Paul Hoch, *Rip Off the Big Game* (Garden City: Doubleday, 1972), p. 9.

80. J. Habermas, quoted in *The Scientific View of Sport* ed. O. Grupe, D. Kurz, and J. M. Teipel (Berlin: Springer-Verlog, 1972), p. 44.

81. H. Plessner, quoted in ibid., p. 45.

82. Betts, *America's Sporting Heritage,* p. 15.

83. Ibid., pp. 15-16.

84. Emmett A. Rice, John L. Hutchinson, and Mabel Lee, *A Brief History of Physical Education,* 5th ed. (New York: Ronald Press, 1969), p. 169.

85. Guy Lewis, "The Beginning of Organized Collegiate Sport," *American Quarterly* (Summer, 1970), p. 225.

86. Guy Lewis, "The Muscular Christianity Movement," *Journal of Health, Physical Education, and Recreation* 37 (May, 1966), p. 42.

87. Lewis, "The Beginning of Organized Collegiate Sport," p. 228.

88. Stagg quoted Harper in a letter to his family, January 20, 1891, as quoted in Richard J. Storr, *Harper's University: The Beginnings* (Chicago: University of Chicago, 1966), p. 179.

89. Richard Hofstadter, *Social Darwinism in American Thought* (Boston: Beacon Press, 1955).

90. Albert Galloway Keller, ed., *Essays of William Graham Sumner I* (New Haven: Yale University Press, 1934), p. 386.

91. A number of social theorists rejected social Darwinism completely. The most articulate of them was Lester F. Ward. See Hofstadter, *Social Darwinism,* pp. 70-75, for a discussion of Ward's attack of this social theory. Also see Lester F. Ward, *Dynamic Sociology* (New York: D. Appleton, 1883).

92. Eldridge Cleaver, *Soul on Ice* (New York: McGraw-Hill, 1968), p. 85.

93. "The Souring of George Sauer," *Intellectual Digest* 2 (December, 1971), p. 53.

94. Robert Ward, "The Oakland Raiders' Charming Assassin," *Sport* 64 (April, 1977), p. 54.

95. Jerry Kramer, ed., *Lombardi: Winning Is the Only Thing* (New York: World, 1970); Johnny Sample, Fred Hamilton, and Sonny Schwartz, *Confessions of a Dirty Ballplayer* (New York: Dial, 1970); Dave Meggyesy, *Out of Their League* (New York: Paperback Library, 1971); Bernie Parrish, *They Call It a Game* (New York: New American Library, 1971); Gary Shaw, *Meat on the Hoof* (New York: St. Martin's Press, 1972.)

Sport and American Values 3

A recurrent theme of this book is that sport is a microcosm of American society. The types of sports, the way in which sport is organized, who participates and who does not, all provide clues about the nature of the society. Thus, the study of sport, like the study of any institution, provides important indicators about: (1) a society's values, (2) a society's social structure (social stratification and social organization), and (3) societal problems.

The objective of this chapter is to examine the reciprocal relationship between sport and American values. The relationship is interdependent because, on the one hand, societal values affect the kinds of sports that are played, the way they are organized, and the motivations for participation in them. But the converse is also true—sport affects American values. Sport, like all institutions, is conservative, primarily because it reinforces certain American values. Before discussing this interdependent relationship between sport and values, we will define what is meant by societal values and describe the American system of values.

The American Value System

Man is a valuing creature. That is, human beings live in an affectively charged world where some things are preferred over others. Some objects, people, or ideas are considered wrong, bad, or immoral, while others are believed correct, good, or moral. Some goals are deemed worthy, while others are not. Values are the bases for making decisions. *Values are the culturally prescribed criteria by which individuals evaluate persons, behavior, objects, and ideas as to their relative morality, desirability, merit, or correctness.* The phrase "culturally prescribed" is an important qualifier in this definition because it implies that human beings are taught (socialized) the criteria by which to make such judgments. Children learn from their parents, peers, and the media what is right or wrong, moral or immoral, correct or incorrect.

Although individuals may have their own idiosyncratic criteria for evaluation, we will examine those values widely held in American society. Several caveats should be mentioned, however, before we discuss the dominant American values. First, diversity in the United States precludes any universal holding of values. Persons in the counterculture (aptly named because they reject the dominant values) and members of certain ethnic and religious groups have very different values. Moreover, there are differences in emphasis for the dominant values by region, social class, age, and size of community.

Second, the system of American values is not always consistent with behavior. For example, Americans have always valued "hard work" as the means to success. Yet, rich persons who may have inherited their wealth are highly esteemed in American society. The value of equality or opportunity that all Americans verbally embrace is inconsistent with the injustices suffered by members of minority groups.

Third, the values themselves are not always consistent. How does one reconcile the coexistence of individualism with conformity? or competition and cooperation? Robin Williams, an eminent analyst of American society, has concluded that:

> We do not find a neatly unified "ethos" or an irresistible "strain toward consistency." Rather, the total society is characterized by diversity and change in values. Complex division of labor, regional variations, ethnic heterogeneity, and the proliferation of specialized institutions and organizations all tend to insulate differing values from one another.[1]

To minimize the problem with inconsistencies, we will present only the most dominant of American values in this section.[2] Let's examine these in turn.

Success (Individual Achievement)

The highly valued individual in American society is the self-made person—i.e., one who has achieved money and status through his or her own efforts in a highly competitive system. Our culture heroes are persons like Abe Lincoln, John D. Rockefeller, and Joe Namath, each of whom rose from humble origins to the top of his profession.

Success can be achieved, obviously by outdoing all others, but it is difficult often to know exactly the extent of one's success. Hence, economic success (one's income, personal wealth, and type of possessions) is the most commonly used measurement. Economic success, moreover, is often used to measure personal worth. As Robin Williams has put it, "The comparatively striking feature of American culture is its tendency to identify standards of personal excellence with competitive occupational achievement."[3]

The primary goal of sports competition is to succeed (to win). Thus, coaches do all they can to instill in their athletes the character traits they believe will bring team success (e.g., loyalty, enthusiasm, initiative, self-control, confidence, poise, and ambition). Figure 3-1 presents the ingredients of success according to John Wooden, the most successful basketball coach in history. Wooden is representative of the prevailing view in sport that participation in athletics leads to success in other facets of life.

As Jesse Hill, the former athletic director at the University of Southern California, has put it, "Athletics develop dedication and a desire to excel in competition, a realization that success requires hard work and that life must be lived according to rules."[4]

Competition

Competition is highly valued in American society. Most Americans believe it to be the one quality that has made America great because it motivates individuals and groups to

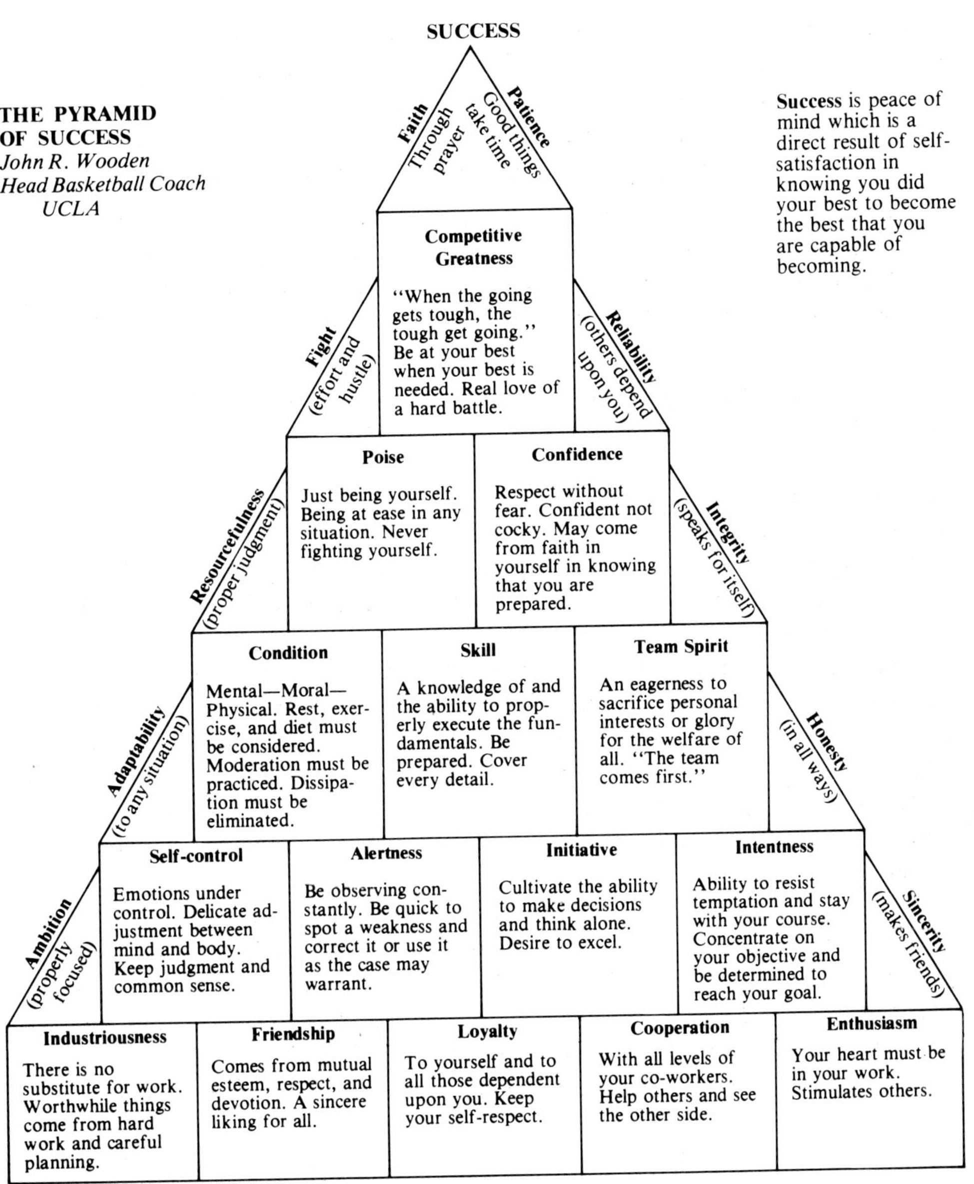

Figure 3-1. The Pyramid of Success. Success is peace of mind that is a direct result of self-satisfaction in knowing you did your best to become the best that you are capable of becoming.

Source: John Wooden and Bill Sharman, The *Wooden-Sharman Method:* A GUIDE TO WINNING BASKETBALL. Copyright 1975 by Macmillan Company Publishers. Reprinted by permission of the publisher.

be discontented with the status quo and with being second best. Motivated by the hope of being victorious in competition, or put another way, by fear of failure, Americans must not lose a war or the Olympics or be the second nation to land men on the moon.

Competition pervades almost all aspects of American society. The work world, sports, courtship, organizations like the Cub Scouts, and schools all thrive on competition. The pervasiveness of competition in schools is seen in how athletic teams, cheerleading squads, debate teams, choruses, bands, and casts are composed. In each case, competition among classmates is used as the criterion for selection. Of course, the grading system is also often based on the comparison of individuals with each other.

The Cub Scouts, because of its reliance on competition, is an all-American organization. In the first place, individual status in the den or pack is determined by the level one has achieved through the attainment of merit badges. Although all boys can theoretically attain all merit badges, there is competition as the boys are pitted against each other to see who can obtain the most. Another example of how the Cub Scouts use competition is their annual event—the Pinewood Derby. Each boy in a Cub pack is given a small block of wood and four wheels that he is then to shape into a racing car. The race is held at a pack meeting with one boy eventually being the winner. The event is rarely questioned even though nearly all of the boys go home disappointed losers. Why is such a practice accepted—indeed publicized? The answer, simply, is that it is symbolic of the ways things are done in virtually all aspects of American life.

An important consequence of this emphasis on the "survival of the fittest" is that some persons take advantage of their fellows to compete "successfully." Perhaps the best recent example is the abuses by high administration officials during the 1972 election campaign (the Watergate break-in, bugging, "laundering of money," taking of illegal contributions from individuals and corporations, use of the Internal Revenue Service to punish enemies, and the "dirty tricks" against political opponents) were done in the cause of a "higher good"—i.e., insuring the election of Richard Nixon. Sociologist Amitai Etzioni has captured the essence of this relationship between "success" and illegal means in the following statement:

> Truth to be told, the Watergate gang is but an extreme manifestation of a much deeper and more encompassing American malaise, the emphasis on success and frequent disregard for the nature of the means it takes to achieve it. Not only high level administration officials, but many Americans as well, seem to have accepted the late football coach Vince Lombardi's motto, "Winning is not the most important thing, it's the only thing." Thus, the executives of ITT who sought to overthrow the government of Chile to protect their goodies, the Mafia chieftans who push heroin, the recording company executives who bribe their records onto the top-40 list, and the citizens who shrug off corruption in the local town hall as "that's the way the cookie crumbles," all share the same unwholesome attitude. True, the Watergate boys have broken all known

American precedents in their violation of fair play, but they are unique chiefly in the magnitude of their crime—not in the basic orientation that underlies it. John Mitchell captured the perverted spirit of Watergate best when he stated that "in view of what the opposition had to offer" (i.e., McGovern), he felt justified in doing anything necessary to secure Nixon's reelection.[5]

In the business world we find theft, fraud, interlocking directorates, and price-fixing are techniques used by some individuals to "get ahead" dishonestly. A related problem, abuse of nature for profit, while not a form of cheating, nevertheless takes advantage of others, while one pursues economic success. The current ecology crisis is caused by individuals, corporations, and communities, which find pollution solutions too expensive. Thus, in looking out for themselves, they ignore the short- and long-range effects on social and biological life. In other words, competition, while a constant spur for individuals and groups to succeed, is also the source of some illegal activities and hence social problems in American society.

Similar scandals are also found in the sports world as we will note throughout this book. The most visible type of illegal activity in sports is illegal recruiting of athletes by colleges and universities. In the quest to succeed (i.e., win), some coaches have felt it necessary to violate NCAA regulations by altering transcripts to insure an athlete's eligibility, allowing substitutes to take admissions tests for athletes of marginal educational ability, paying athletes for nonexistent jobs, illegally using government work studies monies for athletes, and offering money, cars, and clothing to entice athletes to their school.[6]

The Valued Means to Achieve

There are three related highly valued ways to succeed in American society. The first is through hard work. Americans, from the early Puritans to the present day, have elevated persons who were industrious and denigrated those who were not. Most Americans, therefore, assume that poor people deserve to be poor because they are allegedly unwilling to work as hard as persons in the middle and upper classes. This type of explanation places the blame on the victim rather than on the social system that systematically thwarts efforts by the poor. Their hopelessness, brought on by their lack of education, or by their being black, or by their lack of experience, is interpreted as their fault and not as a function of the economic system.[7] This typical interpretation, however, is buttressed by the success of some members of the poor in the sports world. Athletic stars such as O. J. Simpson, Wilt Chamberlain, Hank Aaron, Althea Gibson, and others are presented as dramatic evidence that a meteoric rise in fame and fortune is possible through the blending of hard work and talent. It could be argued that these persons succeed in sports because sport is relatively immune from the racism present in the larger society.[8] However, it could also be argued that these persons succeed, not because of the openness of the system, but because they managed somehow to overcome its roadblocks.

The two remaining valued means to success are continual striving and deferred gratification. Continual striving has meaning for both the successful and the not-so-successful. For the former, one should never be content with what he or she has; there is always more land to own, more money to make, or more books to write. For the poor, continual striving means a never-give-up attitude, a belief that economic success is always possible through hard work, if not for yourself, at least for your children.

Deferred gratification refers to the willingness to deny immediate pleasure for later rewards. The hallmark of the successful person in American society is just such a willingness—to stay in school, to moonlight, or to go to night school. One observer has asserted that the difference between the poor and the nonpoor in this society is whether they are future or present-time oriented.[9] Superficially, this assessment appears accurate, but we would argue that this lack of a future-time orientation among the poor is not a subcultural trait but basically a consequence of their hopeless situation.

Progress

Societies differ in their emphasis on the past, the present, and the future. American society, while giving some attention to each time dimension, stresses the future. Americans neither make the past sacred nor are they content with the present. They place a central value on progress—on a brighter tomorrow, a better job, a bigger home, a move to the suburbs, college education for their children, and on self-improvement.

Americans are not satisfied with the status quo; they want growth (bigger buildings, faster planes, bigger airports, more business moving into the community, bigger profits, and new world's records). They want to change and conquer nature (dam rivers, clear forests, rechannel rivers, seed clouds, spray insecticides, and replace grass with artificial turf).

Although the implicit belief in progress is that change is good, some things are not to be changed, for they have a sacred quality (the political system, the economic system, American values, and the nation-state). Thus, Americans while valuing technological change, do not favor changing the system (revolution).

Material Progress

An American belief holds that "hard work pays off." The payoff is not only success in one's profession but also in economic terms—income and the acquisition and consumption of goods and services that go beyond adequate nutrition, medical care, shelter, and transportation. The superfluous things that we accumulate or strive to accumulate, such as country club memberships, jewelry, lavish homes, boats, second homes, pool tables, electric toothbrushes, and season tickets to the games of our favorite teams are symbols of success in the competitive struggle. But these have more than symbolic value because they are elements of what Americans consider the "good life" and, therefore, a right.

This emphasis on *having* things has long been a facet of American life. This country, the energy crisis notwithstanding, has always been a land of opportunity and abundance. Although many persons are blocked from full participation in this abundance, the goal for most is to accumulate those things that bring status and that provide for a better way of life by saving labor or enhancing pleasure in our leisure.

External Conformity

Societies cannot tolerate total freedom by individuals. Without a minimum of cooperation and conformity to laws and customs, there is anarchy. To this end, individuals are socialized into socially acceptable beliefs and practices. In addition, individuals universally seek the approval of *some* of their fellows and, therefore, try to be "successful" by some shared standards of achievement or conformity.[10] Conformity, then, is really a characteristic of all societies. The degree of conformity required, however, varies greatly from society to society. Analytically, we can separate conformity in American society into two levels. At one level are the official expectations of behavior by the community, state, and nation. This involves the customs and laws individuals are expected to obey. Deviants from these expectations are punished by fines, imprisonment, gossip, or other negative sanctions. The threat of these sanctions is usually enough to ensure conformity. But more than this, we are socialized to desire conformity.

At another—a more personal—level, individuals tend to conform to the groups with which they closely identify. We tend to conform to expectations of family, peers, ethnic groups, religious groups, and work groups. Thus, within the context of the societal-wide expectations for behavior, there is great diversity. Suburbanites conform, as do ghetto residents, hippies, teeny-boppers, the jet-set, union members, and businessmen. David Riesman has characterized Americans as being other-directed.[11] By this he meant, oversensitive to the opinions of others. In a sense, Americans continually have their "antennas" out picking up signals from those about them. Another observer, William H. Whyte, has pointed to this same phenomenon in the organizational context of social life.[12] Whyte has argued that the bureaucratic trend in American society forces many persons to conform. Rules must be followed, boats must not be rocked, and one will get ahead in the bureaucracy.

Societal Values and Sport

We have pointed out repeatedly that sports mirror a society's basic structure and values. The relationship between American values and the form of sports that prevail will be the theme of this section.

Many reasons exist for the tremendous popularity of sport in America. The conditions of mass society constitute an important set of factors. Individuals living in an urban and bureaucratized society tend to feel alienated; in effect, they have feelings of isolation, powerlessness, self-estrangement, and meaninglessness. These persons need to identify with others in a cause that will give meaning to their existence and an escape from an otherwise humdrum world. Sports teams representing factories, schools, neighborhoods, cities, or nations, each pursuing victory, provide an important source of identification for individuals in American society. They provide entertainment, diversion, and something to look forward to.

Another reason is that the masses have been influenced by sports publicists and the media. Television, newspapers, and magazines have generated interest in sports by creating heroes and by continually bombarding the citizenry with statistics, human interest stories, and coverage of the sporting events themselves.

A third factor that partially explains the sports mania in the United States is the increased leisure time available to most Americans. This, coupled with the relatively high standard of living that most Americans enjoy, provides much of the basis for the rise in attendance figures at sports events and the rise in sporting activity by Americans.

An important underlying factor, and the one we want to emphasize in this section, is the close relationship between American sports and American values. In learning the culture (through the socialization process), most Americans have internalized values that predispose them to be interested in the outcome of competitive situations—and competition is the sine qua non of sports.

The Values of Competition and Success in Sport

As in the larger society, there is a tremendous emphasis in American sport on competitive success. Winning is glorified by all who participate. Below are several quotes from several highly successful football coaches, which exemplify this emphasis on winning:

> "Winning is not everything. It is the only thing."
>
> Vince Lombardi (legendary coach of the Green Bay Packers)

> "I will demand a commitment to excellence and to victory, and that is what life is all about."
>
> Vince Lombardi

"Winning is living."
George Allen (coach of the Washington Redskins)

"Everytime you win, you're reborn; when you lose, you die a little."
George Allen

"No one ever learns anything by losing."
Don Shula (coach of the Miami Dolphins)

Americans want winners, whether it be in school, or business, or politics, or sports. In sports, we *demand* winners. Coaches are fired if they are not successful. Teams are booed if they play for ties. Inevitably, coaches faced with the option of taking a tie or gambling on winning (with a high probability of losing) will go for the win with the comment, "We didn't come down here to tie." The 27 teams in the National Football League that do not win the Superbowl in a given year are losers. Not even the members of the runner-up team consider themselves successful because they did not win the only game that really counts.

Coaches do all they can to socialize their athletes with the value of winning. They reinforce winners with praise, honor, and status. Negatively, they ridicule losers or quitters. As an example of a technique used to instill in athletes the desire to excel, one coach of a pony league football team (fourth, fifth, and sixth graders) in Lawrence, Kansas, had his young boys yell "I'm a girl" before they could let their legs touch the ground during a leg lift exercise. This fear of humiliation kept many boys doing the exercise beyond their normal endurance and, the coach probably assumed, increased their potential for winning.

Another technique of coaches to instill in their athletes the goal of winning has been to place slogans on the dressing room walls to exhort players to value certain behaviors. Some common slogans that espouse the competitive spirit are:

A quitter never wins, a winner never quits.
When the going gets tough, the tough get going.
It's not the size of the dog in the fight, but the size of the fight in the dog.
Never be willing to be second best.
The greatest aim in life is to succeed.
Win by as many points as possible.[13]

The demand for winners is found at all levels of sport. Even among youngsters "winning is everything," as evidenced by the pressures in little league baseball, football, and the junior Olympics. A relatively new sport for youngsters, motorcycle racing, is an excellent example of sports competition among youth. In 1973, it was reported that some 10,000 children from age 2 1/2 to 16 race undersized motorcycles competitively at some 1,500 tracks around the country. Since riders can be no better than their equipment, the competition is between the youngsters on the track and between the dads for providing the hottest bike.[14]

Another example of the emphasis on winning even among youngsters are the contests sponsored by some business corporations. Ford Motor Company sponsors a "Punt, Pass, and Kick" contest for youngsters 8 through 13, while Phillips Petroleum sponsors a similar contest for baseball skills—"Pitch, Hit, and Throw." In each contest, winners are selected at the local level and proceed through the various state and regional tournaments until a winner is found for each age category. In 1974, there were 1,112,702 entrants in the Punt, Pass, and Kick contest and only six winners. An interesting question is why an organization would sponsor an event with six winners and 1,112,696 losers. Perhaps, the answer lies in that this, too, is a microcosm of the larger society.[15]

The Soap Box Derby, sponsored by several major corporations, is another sporting activity for youngsters. The ultimate winner, like those contests sponsored by Ford and Phillips Petroleum is the one person who survives the tests from among the tens of thousands who initially entered the competition—clearly a situation of survival of the fittest. Unfortunately, the "fittest" is not always so, as attested by the scandal associated with the 1973 Soap Box Derby. In this case, winning was so important to the "winning" boy and his uncle that they used an illegal magnet that gave the vehicle an unfair advantage at the start of each race. Moreover, a later investigation revealed that one-third of the final cars (and six of the top ten) had been altered to achieve an unfair advantage.

Sports, as played in America, are expressions of Social Darwinism. It is a "survival of the fittest" approach where everyone competes to be at the top. Three quotes from ex-football players—Bob Long, Charley Taylor, and Johnny Sample—will suffice to show this highly competitive atmosphere in contemporary sports:

> I wasn't one of Vince's [Lombardi] favorites at Green Bay. When I hurt my knee in a scrimmage before the 1966 season he yelled, "Drag him off the field and let's get on with the scrimmage."[16]

> In spring training my sophomore year, I broke my neck—four vertebrae. "Hey coach," I said, "my neck don't feel good." "There's nothing wrong with your neck, you jackass," he said. So the numb went away a little, and I made a tackle. When I went to get up, my body got up but my head just stayed there, right on the ground. The coach

> says, "Hey, get this jackass off the field." So the trainer put some ice on my neck and after practice they took me up to the infirmary for an X-ray. The doctor said, "Son, your neck is broken. You got here ten minutes later, you'd be dead." Dead! Man that scared me. I mean those coaches let you lie right out there on the field and die.[17]

> I hated to see Jesse go . . . But that, I began realizing, was what the game's all about—survival of the fittest. Jesse was over the hill and any sad thoughts I had about him were far outweighed by the tremendous feeling of happiness I had over making the team.[18]

Such a heavy emphasis on winning is not a "natural" phenomenon but rather a cultural one. Games of many societies have no competitive element but reflect a different emphasis because of their cultural values. For contrast, let's examine a game from another society that would never capture the enthusiasm of Americans.

> The Tangu people of New Guinea play a popular game known as *taketak,* which involves throwing a spinning top into massed lots of stakes driven into the ground. There are two teams. Players of each team try to touch as many stakes with their tops as possible. In the end, however, the participants play not to win but to draw. The game must go on until an exact draw is reached. This requires great skill, since players sometimes must throw their tops into the massed stakes without touching a single one. *Taketak* expresses a prime value in Tangu culture, that is, the concept of moral equivalence, which is reflected in the precise sharing of foodstuffs among the people.[19]

Or, take the example of how the Zuñi Indians treat an outstanding runner, as reported by anthropologist Ruth Benedict.

> The ideal man in Zuñi is a person of dignity and affability who has never tried to lead, and who has never called forth comment from his neighbors. Any conflict, even though all right is on his side, is held against him. Even in contests of skill like their foot races, if a man wins habitually he is debarred from running. They are interested in a game that a number can play with even chances, and an outstanding runner spoils the game: they will have none of him.[20]

These examples underscore our contention that a society's sports mirror its basic values. Cooperative societies have sports that minimize competition, while aggressive societies have highly competitive games. This raises an interesting question about the nature of the most popular American sports—why are Americans so interested in aggressive and violent sports? The sports with the greatest spectator appeal in America are football and auto racing. These sports, along with the popular pseudosports of professional wrestling and roller derby, are well known for their violence.

Why are violent sports so popular with Americans? Violence is a derivative of competition. It is the ultimate way to insure the "survival of the fittest." Competition implies aggression, as noted in the following statement by former professional football player, George Sauer. He suggests that aggression enables one to get ahead in society, as well as on the football field.

> How does football justify teaching a man to be aggressive against another man? And how does it justify using that aggression for the ends that it has? I think the values of football as it is now played reflect a segment of thought, a particular kind of thought, that is pretty prevalent in our society. The way to do anything in the world, the way to get ahead, is to aggress against somebody, compete against somebody, try to dominate, try to overcome, work your way up the ladder and in doing so you have to judge yourself and be judged as what you want to be in relation to somebody else all the time. Given the influence football has on young children, the immense influence it has as a socializing force in society, its impact should be rigorously examined. People learn certain values from watching football, from watching aggression, from watching it performed violently and knowing that these guys are going to get a big chunk of money if they do it well often enough.[21]

Another explanation frequently advanced for Americans' preoccupation with violent sports is that watching or playing such sports acts as a catharsis, ridding us of the pent-up aggression that stems from living in a competitive society. Two empirical studies suggest, however, the opposite result—that watching aggressive sports leads to aggression. Let's examine each of these briefly.

The first study compared the fans attending the Army-Navy football game with fans at the Army-Navy gymnastics meet.[22] The results showed that football fans were much more hostile, resentful, and irritable than the gym spectators both before and after watching their respective sports. The hostility level of football fans increased (comparing the subjects before and after the game), while the observers of the gymnastics meet showed no such gain in hostility. Moreover, the performance of one's team had little effect on the level of hostility of the football fans.

The theory that observing violent or aggressive actions has a cathartic effect on spectators is contradicted by another study—an examination of the links between warlike sports and the presence of war in societies.[23] The study was designed to test which of the two potential explanatory schemes, the drive discharge model or the culture pattern model, is empirically valid. The drive discharge model postulates that: (1) aggression by individuals and groups is innate; (2) war is aggressive action that occurs when aggressive tensions are too great; and (3) warlike sports serve to discharge accumulated aggressive tension and, therefore, act as alternative channels—moral equivalents—to war, making it less likely. In short, there is an inverse relationship between wars and the presence of warlike sports in societies.

The alternative model postulates that: (1) individual aggressive behavior is primarily learned (there may be some innate reason for aggression, but its intensity and configuration are predominantly cultural); (2) there is a strain toward consistency in every culture, with similar values (competition) and behavior patterns (aggressiveness) found in more than one area of the culture; and (3) behavior patterns and value systems relative to war and to warlike sports tend to overlap and support each other's presence. Thus, by this line of reasoning there is a direct relationship between the presence of war and warlike sports in societies.

The researcher examined two types of data to test these alternative hypotheses. First, he chose 20 tribal societies at random (for which he had the necessary information) and found that 90 percent of the warlike societies had warlike sports, while only 20 percent of the peaceful societies had combative sports. Second, he did a time series case study of the United States to see if the popularity of combative sports (e.g., boxing, hockey, football) rose or fell during times of war. He found that during wartime combative sports indeed rose in popularity, while noncombative sports declined. Both techniques lead to the conclusion that war and combative sports are found together in societies. Combative sports are *not* alternative channels for the discharge of aggressive tensions, but rather they serve to intensify aggression. They are not alternatives to war but supportive of it by preparing persons for battle. Or, as General Douglas MacArthur put it,

> Upon the fields of friendly strife
> Are sown the seeds
> That, upon other fields, on other days,
> Will bear the fruits of victory.[24]

The Valued Means to Achieve in Sport

In sport, as in the larger society, the goal of individual achievement must be accomplished through continuous hard work and sacrifice. The work ethic is also the sports ethic—you win if you work and sacrifice enough or, conversely, you lose if you did not work hard enough.

Examples of the slogans coaches use to inspire hard work in their athletes are:

> The will to win is the will to work.
> Practice makes perfect.
> Success is 99 percent perspiration and one percent inspiration.
> No one ever drowned in sweat.
> By failing to prepare yourself you are preparing to fail.
> There is no substitute for hard work.
> It's better to wear out than to rust out.[25]

Americans do not like quitters in sports or in the other areas of social life. This is seen in the disdain accorded typically to school dropouts, hippies, persons who declare bankruptcy, persons who do not seek employment, and athletes who either quit the team or do not give 100 percent effort even when the outcome of the game is no longer in doubt. Coaches, because they believe success in sports and life is dependent on sustained effort, do all in their power to instill in their athletes a never-give-up attitude.

Sports reinforce the success values of society for spectators as well. Montague and Morais have made this point with special reference to football:

> Football validates the success model by staging a real event in which the principles of success are shown to work as promised by society. The contest actually happens before the viewer's eyes. The reality of the event is then transferred to the ideology of the success model, which is presented as accounting for the winning team's superior performance. Of course, there is a sleight of hand going on here, because "the best team always wins." The team that wins is not necessarily best; it is best because it wins. In order to set the stage for the legitimacy of the assertion that the best team does indeed win, the teams must rigidly and publicly adhere to behaviors symbolic of the success model during their training [i.e., self-denial and hard work]. It can then be argued that a team's superior performance is consonant with the expectations of the success model. The burden of proof switches to the losers: If the team that abided by the rules wins, then the team that loses must have failed to dedicate itself seriously enough.[26]

The Value of Progress in Sport

Coaches, athletes, and fans place a central value on progress. Continued improvement (in mastering new techniques, winning more games, or setting new records) is the aim of all athletes and teams. As an example, great milers such as Jim Ryun undergo great pressures to set new records each time they run competitively. The demands come from the fans, the press, promoters, and often from the athletes themselves.

Materialism in Sports

Although the value that Americans place on success in competitive situations has the most important impact on the way sport is organized in America, materialism has an important effect on the way sports are organized. Professional teams especially are formed to make a profit. Owners make lucrative arrangements with television networks, which have had a dramatic effect on sports (e.g., scheduling, timing, and number of time-outs). Teams that do not show a high enough profit may be moved to another city in the search of more money. Professional leagues have also secured exemptions from antitrust legislation from Congress to protect their investments. High-powered university teams are just as involved in profits as the pros, but they are less obvious about their material interests.

Athletes, too, are obviously motivated by material concerns. This fact is lamented by Tom Meschery, former professional basketball player and coach.

> There was a time, and it was not so long ago, when things such as honor and loyalty were virtues in sport, and not objects of ridicule. It was a time when athletes drew pleasure and satisfaction from the essence of competition, not just from their paychecks. But somehow, with the introduction of big business, the concept of sports in this country has changed. The business psyche has invaded basketball and has made the players nothing but businessmen spurred by the profit motive. In some cases players make more money with their outside financial activities than they do on the court. Their sport becomes a mere showcase to keep them before the public, like an actor's guest appearance on a television talk show. The game no longer has its roots into idealistic bedrock. It's just business: nine to five.[27]

Examples of what Meschery has said are found in all sports. Wilt Chamberlain, for example, moved from the Los Angeles Lakers to the San Diego Conquistadores for $600,000 a year because he thought of himself as a businessman who had to make the best business deal possible. The exploits of Mark Spitz as an amateur in the Olympics were parlayed into as much as $5 million over a number of years for endorsements, personal appearances, and the like. The same merchandising of a sports star occurred after Henry Aaron broke Babe Ruth's home-run record.

Athletes hire lawyers to negotiate for the highest possible bonuses and salary arrangements, and hold out individually and even strike collectively on occasion for better material comforts. Furthermore, athletes often engage in activities that may increase attendance at contests. Boxers such as Muhammad Ali are well known for this, but the best example may be the ballyhoo that preceded the Bobby Riggs-Billie Jean King tennis match. Star athletes also devote much of their energy to making money through endorsements of projects, personal appearances, and giving inspirational talks.

Sports fans, too, are influenced by material considerations. They like plush stadiums with expensive scoreboards and other amenities. They are excited by athletes playing for large stakes (e.g., the difference between the first and second place in a golf tournament may be as much as $30,000). Sonny Werblin shook up pro football by being first to offer a very big bonus—$400,000—to Joe Namath for signing with the Jets. This had the dual effect of legitimizing the Jets and making Joe Namath an instant celebrity whom the fans would turn out in great numbers to see.

The Value of External Conformity in Sport

Conformity is highly valued in American sports. Coaches, generally, demand that their athletes conform to the behavior norms of the community in hair styles, manner of dress, and speech patterns.[28] This is probably the result of two factors (both of which we will elaborate on later in this book). The first reason is that the coaches feel their precarious jobs might be in further jeopardy if they permitted their athletes to act outside community standards. The second reason is that coaches tend to be conservative.

Coaches of team sports place a high value on team unity. They place a great emphasis on subordination of self to team success as the following coaching cliches indicate:

> There is no "I" in team.
> There is no "U" in team.
> A player doesn't make the team, the team makes the player.
> United we stand, divided we fall.
> Cooperate—remember the banana, everytime it leaves the bunch, it gets skinned.[29]

Another aspect of external conformity found in both sport and the larger society is "acceptance of authority." The system (the rules, the structure of power) is not challenged. Coaches have absolute control over their team and players; if they wish to participate, they must conform to his system. This belief is illustrated by the statement of Ray Mears, successful basketball coach at the University of Tennessee:

> I'm a disciplinarian. There isn't a boy on my team that has a beard or mustache. A lot of people say it's the style. Black athletes come in and say it's part of their culture. I show them pictures of some nice looking, All-American black athletes who don't wear a mustache and beard and say, "What about their culture?" I want our boys to look like the All-American boy. To my way of thinking, and that's who's coaching the team at Tennessee, the All-American boy is clean cut, clean shaven and his hair is in order. This is how I expect them to look.
>
> Coaches must hang on to the discipline which is a part of their profession. If we can do it on the collegiate level, where we get All-Americans, so can you [Mears is writing for high school coaches]. We get players who are considered trouble-makers or who come from a deprived background. But they can learn discipline and improve their appearance. They can cut their hair short, dress sharp and look like All-Americans. I expect them to be clean shaven every day. When I say a meeting is at 2:30 I don't mean 2:32. If they want to play for Tennessee, they will fit into the program. Just because a player is having problems adjusting doesn't mean that I have to give up my principles too. You have to make some exceptions and shade a bit and I will, but I'm not going to let anybody else run the ball club. A boy's got to understand right from wrong.[30]

Summary

American values can be analyzed according to their goal and the means for attaining them. This is shown in the following quote, which also relates the values to those espoused by the very successful (and, therefore, "canonized") football coach, Vince Lombardi.

> The goal of middle-class values is success; that is, increasing accumulation of goods leading to higher social status. The means of success is hard work and continual striving on the part of the individual—a means that necessarily fosters elitism and class consciousness. The manner is basically puritanical: disciplined repression of present needs for the sake of future gratification, commitment to law and order accompanied by reliance on authority and tradition, and an optimistic pragmatism whose methods are always open to change.
>
> Now, these are exactly the values that, as his admirers see it, were fundamental in the world of Vince Lombardi. He was a good coach because he was successful; he accumulated a lot of goods for the players who were fortunate enough to be part of his [Green Bay] Packers family. He relied on individual hard work and discipline, and instilled in his men the consciousness that they were better and must achieve according to their elite status. His manner was hard and puritanical: he drove his men to their limits, promising them "success" in return. He was strictly authoritarian, yet he was an optimistic pragmatist in his ability to adjust to individuals and situations.[31]

The above quote shows that values affect sport. Just as important is the insight that sport in America, through its organization and the demands and emphases of those in power, reinforces societal values. This mutual reinforcement places sport squarely in the middle of "the American way of life." It is precisely because sport is so intertwined with fundamental American values that any attack on sport is usually interpreted as unpatriotic—the work of communists, hippies, or some other "un-American" group. Hence, criticism of sport is rarely taken seriously. We should keep this in mind as we examine the positive and negative consequences of sport in American society. Any proposed changes in sport must be related to American values. That is why the Athletic Revolution, which we will examine in this book's final chapter, is truly revolutionary—it espouses a system of sport based on a very different set of values.

Notes

1. Robin M. Williams, Jr., *American Society: A Sociological Interpretation,* 3rd ed. (New York: Alfred A. Knopf, 1970), p. 451.

2. We have relied on four sources that were especially helpful for the delineation of American values: Williams, *American Society,* pp. 438-504; Cora Dubois, "The Dominant Value Profile of American Culture," *American Anthropologist* 57 (December, 1955), pp. 1232-1239; Charles A. Reich, *The Greening of America* (New York: Random House, 1970); and Phillip Slater, *The Pursuit of Loneliness: American Culture at the Breaking Point* (Boston: Beacon Press, 1970).

3. Williams, *American Society,* pp. 454-455.

4. Quoted in Harry Edwards, *Sociology of Sport* (Homewood, Ill.: Dorsey Press, 1973), p. 71.

5. Amitai Etzioni, "After Watergate—What?: A Social Science Perspective," *Human Behavior* 2 (November, 1973), p. 7.

6. See Kenneth Denlinger and Leonard Shapiro, *Athletes for Sale: An Investigation into America's Greatest Sports Scandal—Athletic Recruiting* (New York: Thomas Y. Crowell, 1975).

7. See William Ryan, *Blaming the Victim* (New York: Pantheon Books, 1971).

8. Racism is very present also in sports, however, as we will document in chapter 9.

9. Edward C. Banfield, *The Unheavenly City: The Nature and Future of Our Urban Crisis* (Boston: Little, Brown, 1970). For a critique of Banfield's position, see William Ryan, "Is Banfield Serious?" *Social Policy* 1 (November/December, 1970), pp. 74-76.

10. Williams, *American Society,* p. 485.

11. David Riesman et al., *The Lonely Crowd* (New Haven, Conn.: Yale University Press, 1950).

12. William H. Whyte, Jr., *The Organization Man* (New York: Simon and Schuster, 1956).

13. Eldon E. Snyder, "Athletic Dressing Room Slogans as Folklore: A Means of Socialization," *International Review of Sport Sociology* 7 (1972), pp. 89-102.

14. Ernest Havemann, "Down Will Come Baby, Cycle and All," *Sports Illustrated* 39 (August 13, 1973), pp. 42-49.

15. See George B. Leonard, "Overemphasis on Winning Makes Us a Nation of Losers," *The National Observer* (April 12, 1975), p. 16; Paul Hoch, *Rip Off the Big Game: The Exploitation of Sports by the Power Elite* (Garden City, N.Y.: Doubleday Anchor Books, 1972).

16. Jerry Kramer, ed., *Lombardi: Winning Is the Only Thing* (New York: Pocket Books, 1970), p. 157.

17. Quoted in Gary Shaw, *Meat on the Hoof* (New York: St. Martin's Press, 1972), p. 121.

18. Johnny Sample, *Confessions of a Dirty Ballplayer* (New York: Dell, 1971), p. 61.

19. George B. Leonard, "Winning Isn't Everything: It's Nothing," *Intellectual Digest* 4 (October, 1973), p. 45.

20. Ruth Benedict, *Patterns of Culture* (New York: Mentor Books, 1934), p. 95.

21. Jack Scott, "The Souring of George Sauer," *Intellectual Digest* 2 (December, 1971), pp. 52-55.

22. Jeffrey H. Goldstein and Robert L. Arms, "Effects of Observing Athletic Contests on Hostility," *Sociometry* 34 (March, 1971), pp. 83-90.

23. Richard Sipes, "War, Sports and Aggression: An Empirical Test of Two Rival Theories," *American Anthropologist* 75 (February, 1973), pp. 64-86. Indirect negative evidence for the violence as catharsis hypothesis is found in Dane Archer and Rosemary Gartner, "Violent Acts and Violent Times, *American Sociological Review* 41 (December, 1976), pp. 937-963.

24. Quoted in Hoch, *Rip Off the Big Game,* p. 70.

25. Snyder, "Athletic Dressing Room Slogans as Folklore," pp. 89-102.

26. Susan P. Montague and Robert Morais, "Football Games and Rock Concerts: The Ritual Enactment of American Success Models," *The American Dimension: Cultural Myths and Realities,* eds. W. Arens and Susan P. Montague (Port Washington, N.Y.: Alfred Publishing, 1976), p. 42.

27. Tom Meschery, "There is a Disease in Sports Now," *Sports Illustrated* 37 (October 2, 1972), p. 56.

28. See George H. Sage, "Occupational Socialization and Value Orientation of Athletic Coaches," *Research Quarterly* 44 (1973), pp. 269-277; George H. Sage, "Value Orientations of American College Coaches Compared to those of Male College Students and Businessmen," *Sport and American Society,* 2nd ed., ed. George H. Sage (Reading, Mass.: Addison-Wesley, 1974), pp. 207-228.

29. Snyder, "Athletic Dressing Room Slogans as Folklore," pp. 89-102.

30. Ray Mears, "Staff Organization," *The Basketball Bulletin* (Fall, 1976), p. 38.

31. Robert J. Beuter, "Sports, Values and Society," *The Christian Century* 89 (April 5, 1972), p. 389.

Sport and American Education 4

Sport and education are inexorably intertwined in American society, especially at the high school and college levels. Statistics in 1973 showed that 89 percent of the 22,000 high schools fielded a basketball team, 76 percent had track teams, and 72 percent had football teams.[1] If all interschool sports are included (there are at least 27), then virtually every secondary school is probably engaged in some interschool sports competition. The same is true at the college level, where schools without interschool sports are so rare that as exceptions they prove the rule.

But while sport is found in almost all education establishments, it is difficult to ascertain the degree to which it contributes to the educational process. The conventional view is that participation in sport has educational benefits. This is exemplified by the platform statement of the Division of Men's Athletics, American Alliance for Health, Physical Education, and Recreation:

> Athletics, when utilized properly, serve as potential educational media through which the optimum growth—physical, mental, emotional, social, and moral—of the participants may be fostered. During the many arduous practice sessions and in the variety of situations that arise during the heat of the contests, the players must repeatedly react to their own capabilities and limitations and to the behavior of others. These repeated reactions, and the psychological conditioning that accompanies them, inevitably result in changes—mental, as well as physical—in the players. Because each contest is usually surrounded by an emotionally charged atmosphere and the players are vitally interested in the outcome of the game, the players are more pliable and, hence, more subject to change than in most educational endeavors. To ensure that these changes are educationally desirable, all phases of athletics should be expertly organized and conducted.[2]

A contrary view, less widely held, is critical of sport as now constituted in American schools. From this perspective, sport is believed to detract from the educational goals of schools. Moreover, critics assert that while athletic participation may lead some individuals to be good sports, others are bad sports; while some play by the rules, others circumvent them; and while there is integrity in some sport programs, there is hypocrisy in others. In short, these critics feel that sport and education are incompatible. As Thorstein Veblen in 1899 characterized the situation: "the relation of football to physical culture is much the same as that of the bullfight to agriculture."[3]

The remainder of this chapter is directly or indirectly related to this controversy. We will describe first the role of sport in American education. Second, we will explore the positive and negative consequences of sport for the school, community, individuals, and society. Finally, we will assess the relationship between sport and education by examining inherent problems and dilemmas.

The Role of Sport in Secondary Schools

Although the thrust of this book is on corporate sport in America, much of the material in this chapter is devoted to organized sport—sport at the high school and college levels. We shall see, however, that sport in American education varies from "organized" to "corporate." Even at the high school level rudimentary traces of corporate sport may be found.

Interschool sports are an extremely important part of contemporary American education. This activity began in the colleges in the 19th century primarily as a diversion from the boredom of classroom work. The first intercollegiate sports contest was a rowing race between Harvard and Yale in 1852. At first, such activities were organized by students. This has changed to the extent that now students have virtually no voice in athletic policies (a point to which we will later return), control being vested in coaches, school administrations, athletic corporations, leagues, and national organizations.

Interschool sports competition at the college level grew rapidly in the early 20th century. This provided an important stimulus for similar activities at the high school level. High school sports were also consciously encouraged by school officials for two reasons. First, sport was needed to upgrade the physical fitness of Americans since a high proportion of poorly conditioned youth were discovered when given physicals during World War I. A second reason was that educators stressed the potential of sports for developing desirable citizenship and character traits.[4]

From modest beginnings, interschool sports have become vitally important in American schools.[5] So integral have they become that contemporary schools would appear to an outsider as more concerned with athletics than scholarly endeavors.

> A visitor entering a school would likely be confronted, first of all, with a trophy case. His examination of the trophies would reveal a curious fact: the gold and silver cups, with rare exception, symbolize victory in athletic contests, not scholastic ones. The figures adorning these trophies represent men passing footballs, shooting basketballs, holding out batons; they are not replicas of the "The Thinker." The concrete symbols of victory are old footballs, basketballs, and baseballs, not works of art or first editions of books won as literary prizes. Altogether, the trophy case would suggest to the innocent visitor that he was entering an athletic club, not an educational institution.
>
> Walking further, this visitor would encounter teenagers bursting from classrooms. Listening to their conversations, he would hear both casual and serious discussions of the Friday football game, confirming his initial impression. Attending a school assembly that morning, he would probably find a large segment of the program devoted to a practice of school cheers for the athletic game and the announcement of a pep rally before the game. At lunch hour, he would be likely to find more boys shooting baskets in the gymnasium than reading in the library. Browsing through a school yearbook, he would be impressed, in his innocence, with the number of pages devoted to athletics.

> Altogether, this visitor would find, wherever he turned, a great deal of attention devoted to athletics. As an impressionable stranger, he might well suppose that more attention is paid to athletics by teenagers, both as athletes and as spectators, than to scholastic matters. He might even conclude, with good reason, that the school was essentially organized around athletic contests and that scholastic matters were of lesser importance to all involved.[6]

A consequence of the extraordinary popularity of sport in American secondary schools is its generation of status for males. Of special interest is that it ranks above scholarship, the presumed goal of education, as a means of determining prestige in the social system of the American high school. Tannenbaum examined student attitudes in a large New York City high school toward these categories of male students: brilliant versus average, studious versus nonstudious, and athletes versus nonathletes. Six hundred fifteen high school juniors were given written descriptions of the traits of stereotyped fictitious students. On the basis of the traits ascribed to each imaginary student, a mean acceptibility rating was calculated. The eight fictitious characters were thus ranked from most to least acceptable:[7]

1. Brilliant nonstudious athlete.
2. Average nonstudious athlete.
3. Average studious athlete.
4. Brilliant studious athlete.
5. Brilliant nonstudious nonathlete.
6. Average nonstudious nonathlete.
7. Average studious nonathlete.
8. Brilliant studious nonathlete.

These ratings reveal several interesting patterns in the criteria for status among adolescents. Foremost, the male athlete, regardless of his other attributes, is favored over the nonathlete. A second pattern shown in these ranks is that brilliance is valued if one is not studious. Being studious is a trait almost as denigrating as being a nonathlete. The irony of these values is that a person who is compulsive in his quest to achieve in his studies is the object of scorn, while the athlete who compulsively shoots 500 baskets a day or runs 100 miles a week is admired. The one is a "curve-raiser" or a "grind," the object of ridicule, but there are no analogues in athletics, where the "grind" is respected for his dedication. Coleman has argued that the reasons for this contradiction is that the hard worker in school achieves at the expense of the classmates, while the athlete's success brings glory to the entire school.

> Thus the boy who goes all-out scholastically is scorned and rebuked for working too hard; the athlete who *fails* to go all-out is scorned and rebuked for not giving his all. Why this difference? The answer . . . lies in the structure of activities. The scholar's efforts can bring glory to no one but himself, and serve only to make work more difficult

> for the others. But the athlete's achievements occur as part of a collective effort. He is working for his school, not merely for himself, and his extra efforts bring acclaim from his classmates, while loafing brings rebukes—all a consequence of the structure of activities in a school, which allocates interscholastic games to athletics, and allocates interpersonal competition (in the form of grades) to academic work.[8]

In his elaborate study of ten Illinois high schools in 1957 and 1958, Coleman documented the vital significance of athletics in American secondary education.[9] He found that regardless of school size, location, or socioeconomic compositions, athletics dominated school life.

1. Membership in a school's elite group ("leading crowd") varied by sex. Girls were included because of ascribed characteristics (parents' achievement, good looks, possessions). However, membership for boys was based on achievements, especially in athletics.

2. The most important attribute for male popularity was "being an athletic star." This trait was consistently considered more important than (in order of importance): being in the leading crowd, being a leader in activities, high grades and honor roll, having a nice car, and coming from the right family.

3. When asked how they would most like to be remembered, 44 percent of the boys said as an athletic star, 31 percent said as a brilliant student, and 25 percent replied, most popular. This was in contrast to the parents' response as to how they wanted their sons to be remembered; three-fourths of the boys' parents wanted brilliant students.

One implication of these findings is that athletics introduces an important democratizing factor in the status system for high school boys that is not present for girls. Although success in athletics is partially ascribed—height, weight, coordination—these traits are presumably found randomly throughout the social class structure. Thus, individuals with requisite physical characteristics can, if motivated, learn and practice the skills necessary for athletic success. In short, achievement in athletics, not social background, is for the most part the basis for status among male peers.

The system of peer group rewards acts as a deterrent to academic achievement—a more important implication for the goals of schools. It does so because persons with greatest academic talent are encouraged to divert their energies away from scholarship to athletics and social activities. Thus, groups and individuals in the school (with the aid of the administration and community) actually work against the academic objectives of the school.

Coleman's thesis is that adolescents form a subculture. They comprise a group with values and interests antithetical to the larger society and the school. His use of the concept subculture is similar to what Yinger has called a contraculture. This is a culturally homogeneous group with values and norms that differ from the larger society because the group opposed the larger society. This type of group is in conflict with the dominant culture and thus can be understood only by reference to the dominant group.[10]

But is there an adolescent subculture? Bennett Berger has argued that adolescents do not form a relatively autonomous social system in opposition to the larger society.[11] Rather, according to Berger, the sources of the antiintellectual character of adolescent life are in the *adult* world. School athletics are initiated and supported by adults—school administrators, coaches, parents, local booster organizations, and businessmen. Adults reward athletic achievements of youth more than scholarly achievements. Consider the difference, for example, in community response to state basketball champions and state debate champions.

This criticism of Coleman is only of his interpretation that youth, because they want to be popular and are much more interested in sports than scholarship, comprise a subculture. This criticism should not cloud the important contributions of his book—the empirical verification of the importance of athletics in American high schools and in adolescent status systems.

The empirical evidence since Coleman's study does not support his contention that high school athletes are uninterested in academic achievement.[12] Schafer and Armer, for example, found from a sample of 585 high school boys that athletes had a grade point average (GPA) of 2.35 compared to 1.83 for nonathletes.[13] Other studies have noted an association between athletic participation and higher educational aspirations.[14]

Some problems of interpretation exist, however, whenever athletes are compared with nonathletes.[15] The two categories are different not only in physical characteristics but on other significant dimensions as well. For instance, when grades are compared, athletes will have a higher GPA than nonathletes because athletes must meet a minimum level to be eligible. This may keep students poor in academic performance from ever attempting to participate in athletics or such persons may be removed from athletic teams. A second caveat is that the relationship between athletic involvement and academic achievement should not be viewed as a causal one. Indeed, Lueptow and Kayser found, when comparing athletes with nonathletes, that the former did not show an improvement in grades during their high school years.[16]

Although the relationship between athletics and educational attainment and expectations must be qualified, the data negate the conclusion of Coleman that athletic participation is counterproductive in the educational enterprise. Similarly, the data should lay to rest the "dumb jock" stereotype.

Coleman's assertion that athletics detracts from scholastics has been contradicted by recent studies, but the question remains whether athletics continues to be foremost in the status system of American high schools. Significant changes have occurred in

American society in the intervening years, such as the rise of the counterculture, increased drug usage by youth, heightened racial unrest in schools, and an increasing tendency to question persons in authority roles (teachers, principals, coaches, ministers, parents, police, and government leaders). Quite possibly, these and other factors have led to the athlete being replaced as the "big man on campus" by student activists, rock musicians, scholars, or some other social category.

The evidence is unclear; occasional articles appear in the popular press suggesting that boys still want desperately to be athletes because athletics remains the most highly rewarded activity in their school and community. This has been recently documented, for example, for: Benton, Illinois; Yates Center, Kansas; Stockbridge, Michigan; and Tracy, California.[17] At the same time, however, there is evidence that increasing numbers of high school youngsters are becoming disenchanted with sports. In a survey for the Athletic Institute, an organization supported by the sporting goods industry, Frank Jones felt that this disenchantment was especially strong among minority groups in the inner city who resent racism, the lack of opportunity except for a favored few, and the lack of athletic facilities. But the affluent youngster in the suburbs is also losing interest in sports, according to Jones. Apathy or antagonism toward athletic programs by the affluent is the result of the regimentation demanded in sports and the denial of creativity of self-expression. Jones stated that while this increased questioning of sports appears to be an urban and suburban phenomenon, high school sports continue to flourish and go unquestioned in rural America, where they are the "only show in town."[18]

Eitzen replicated Coleman's study 16 years later to determine whether athletic prowess continued as the single most important criterion for high status.[19] Eitzen's study included 14 schools, which ranged in student population from 92 to 2,937 and in community size from 400 to 622,236. The data, taken from two questions—How would you like to be remembered? and What does it take to be popular?—showed that athletics remain just as important in the status system of teenage males as Coleman found in the 1950s. Regarding the first question, Coleman found that 31 percent of the boys wished to be remembered as a brilliant student, 44 percent as an athletic star, and 25 percent as most popular. The percentage from Eitzen's replication 16 years later were 25, 45, and 30, respectively. As for the popularity ranking, the data again showed that athletic participation remained important (see table 4-1). However, these findings may obscure the possibility that some categories of adolescents have become disenchanted and apathetic about athletics and have shifted their interests elsewhere. Thus, the second question of this research was, How do adolescent boys vary in the importance they attach to athletics by individual, school, and community characteristics? The findings summarized are as follows:

Table 4.1. The Ranking of the Criteria Boys and Girls Use to Rate the Popularity of Boys.

Boys' Ranking of Criteria to be Popular with Boys

	Average Ranking	
Criteria for Status	**Eitzen**	**Coleman***
Be an athlete	2.2	2.2
Be in leading crowd	2.15	2.6
Leader in activities	2.77	2.9
High grades, honor roll	3.66	3.5
Come from right family	3.93	4.5

Girls' Ranking of Criteria for Boys to be Popular with Girls

Criteria for Status	**Eitzen**
Be in leading crowd	2.17
Be an athlete	2.38
Have a nice car	3.03
Come from right family	3.32
High grades, honor roll	3.80

*These ranks are approximations extrapolated from a bar graph supplied by James S. Coleman, *The Adolescent Society* (New York: Free Press, 1961), p. 44. Coleman did not present the data for how girls ranked the criteria for boys being popular with girls.

Individual factors:

1. Nonwhite boys were more interested in sport than whites.
2. The younger the adolescent, the more interested in athletics.
3. The lower the educational attainment of fathers, the more athletic-minded the sons.
4. The more involved in school activities, the more boys wanted to be remembered as athletes.

School-related factors:

1. The smaller the school, the more importance attached to athletics.
2. The more rigid the authority structure of the school, the more the boys wanted to be athletes.

Community-related factors:

1. The smaller the community, the more interested were the boys in athletics.
2. The more rural the community, the greater the importance given to athletics.

3. The greater the number of families living in poverty (incomes of less than $3,000), the more athletics were valued by boys.

These findings suggest that while boys generally continue to want to be athletes, some groups tend to be less enthused about sports (i.e., sons of college-educated fathers from large urban or suburban schools in relatively affluent communities). Thus, if this tendency becomes more widespread (because now boys even in these categories choose sports over the other possibilities but are less inclined to do so), several societal trends suggest that the enthusiasm for sports may wane in the future. School unification makes schools larger, a larger proportion of youngsters attend suburban schools each year, each generation is better educated, and schools are generally more permissive than in the past. If these conditions lead to somewhat less enthusiasm for sports, then sport participation as the dominant criterion for social status will diminish in the future.

The Consequences of Sport for Schools, Communities, and Individuals

Clearly high school and college athletes receive substantial rewards for their activities. They receive fame and acclaim from peers, neighbors, teachers, and even from strangers. A high school star can become a legend in his own time, a deity canonized in newspapers and immortalized through countlessly retold exploits.[20] But even nonstars have celebrity status. They are the recipients of praise and honor, of special favors by businessmen, and of popularity with the opposite sex. Moreover, schools and communities are usually much more willing to spend great sums of money for athletic equipment and arenas than they are for academic equipment and buildings. They are willing to allow a disproportionate amount of time to be spent on athletics and related activities.

But why are athletes and athletics given such extraordinary importance? The answer is that sports have positive consequences for the participants, schools, and communities.

Positive Consequences of Sports for the School

All organizations must have a minimal amount of unity; members must give an organization some allegiance for it to survive. Allegiance can stem from pay, ideology, chance for promotion, or cooperative need to accomplish a collective goal. Schools, however, do not have the usual means to motivate their members. Grades, the equivalent of pay, do not always work because part of the school population is indifferent to them and because they are so often dependent on defeating one's peers. Moreover, students are forced by custom and by law to attend school, a fact that ensures their physical presence, but not their involvement in the school's academic objectives. Aside from athletic contests, schools do not have collective goals, only individual ones. So, any activity that promotes loyalty to the school serves a useful and necessary purpose. James Coleman in the following quotation shows how athletics provides an unifying function for the school.

> Athletic contests with other schools provide, for these otherwise lifeless institutions, the collective goals that they lack. The common goals shared by all make the institution part of its members and them part of it, rather than an organization outside them and superimposed upon them. The results are evident to any observer: The adolescent social system is centered at the school, not at the drugstore; the name by which the teen-agers identify themselves is that of the school ("Those are East High Kids; I'm from Tech."); the teen-agers think of the school, the team, and the student body as one and use the pronoun "we" in referring to this entity ("We're playing Parkville Friday.") . . .
>
> Thus, the importance of athletic contests in both high schools and colleges lies at least in part, in the way the contests solve a difficult problem for the institution—the problem of generating enthusiasm for and identification with the school and of drawing the energies of adolescents into the school.[21]

Interschool sports competition, then, is a means of unifying the entire school. Different races, social classes, fraternities, teachers, and students unite in a common cause—the defeat of a common enemy outside the group. Potentially hostile segments of the school are often kept from fragmenting the school by athletics.[22] School morale can also be lifted through the collective following of an athletic team, thereby serving to unify the school. Kent State University was in a shambles after the campus disorders of 1970. The killing of several students by the National Guard left many groups bitter and divided. In 1972, however, the Kent State football team won the Mid-American Conference championship for the first time in its history and wound up in the Tangerine Bowl. Mike Lude, the athletic director, has been quoted as saying that the athletic program at that school helped to keep the school functioning normally and serving as a rallying point for the university's battered morale.[23] But although athletics in this instance may have helped unify the school, it also may have served negatively as an "opiate of the masses," keeping them from working to change conditions that caused the Kent State tragedy in the first place.

There is also the larger question as to why schools need to achieve unity through athletics. Reacting to a statement by the student editor of the Notre Dame newspaper that football, more than any other single activity, helps to unite all the people connected with Notre Dame, Sage replied:

> Unite them for what? Is there an enemy out there preparing to attack Notre Dame? It makes one wonder about the academic climate of a university which must depend upon

> a game for its unity. It is curious that an institution of higher education cannot find support, nourishment, intellectual stimulation, and even unity, if that is necessary from its scholars—its students and faculty.[24]

Athletics serves to unify not only school student bodies but to minimize the conflicts of students and teachers.

> There is a tendency for the school population to split up into hostile segments of teachers and students and to be fragmented by cliques among both groups. The division of students into groups prevents a collective morale from arising and thereby complicates administration; the split between students and teachers is even more serious, for these two groups tend to become definite conflict groups, and conflict group tensions are the very antithesis of discipline. This condition athletics alleviates. Athletic games furnish a dramatic spectacle of the struggle of picked men against a common enemy, and this is a powerful factor in building up a group spirit which includes students of all kinds and degrees and unifies the teachers and the taught.[25]

In addition to the unifying function of athletics, there is also the social control function. Waller, writing in 1932, gave the following advice to school administrators:

> The organization of the student body for the support of athletics, though it is certainly not without its ultimate disadvantages, may bring with it certain benefits for those who are interested in the immediate problems of the administration. It is a powerful machine which is organized to whip all students into line for the support of athletic teams, and adroit school administrators learn to use it for the dissemination of other attitudes favorable to the faculty and the faculty polity.[26]

Assuming that school administrators could manipulate students through sport, what social control functions would be performed? First, athletic activity may make students more tractable because it drains off their surplus energies. For athletes and nonathletes alike, sports furnishes a diversion of attention from undesirable to desirable channels. It gives them something to think about and something to do with their time, thereby keeping them from mischief and from questioning the system. Second, athletes, because they must obey school rules and training rules if they want to compete, serve as examples of good behavior. Athletes have high status in the school system. Thus, by virtue of their favored position, they tend to have the conservatism of the privileged classes. If this assumption is correct and nonathletes tend to admire them, then athletes serve to preserve the system as it is.

The school encourages sports participation for self-serving reasons (school and community cohesion, financial support, social control). Administrators and school boards encourage participation not only because they want to encourage physical fitness but, more importantly, because they believe that sports participation inculcates the values of society into individuals. As David Matza has put it, "The substance of athletics contains within itself—in its rules, procedures, training, and sentiments—a paradigm of adult expectations regarding youth."[27] Schools want individuals to follow rules, to be disciplined, to work hard, to fit in—sports accomplishes these. Thus, sports are believed by those in authority to be justified.

A final social control function of athletics is its dampening of violent rivalries between towns, neighborhoods, and schools. Athletic contests are often symbolic contests between rivals. Because they are routinized and institutionalized (the rules of the game, the sanctions that can be applied for violations), the official goal of civil order (by minimizing real violence) is believed to be accomplished. A problem with this, however, is that ritualized violence may erupt into actual violence between players and/or spectators at any time. It has been generally assumed by school authorities that the benefits outweigh the potential for actual conflict.[28] At the present time, however, especially in urban areas, sporting events between schools have actually enhanced the probability of violence. As a consequence, some contests have either been cancelled or held without spectators.[29]

Sports can also be used by the school to encourage intellectual activities by the students. A contingency for participation in sports is the maintenance of a certain grade point average, so participants must at least meet this minimum. The existence of sports may also keep some youngsters from dropping out of school because of their desire to participate. Some schools have even used the interest that many youngsters have in sports to stimulate their interest in reading and other academic skills. At DeWitt Clinton High School in New York City, for example, an innovative summer school course has been designed. Students with below-average reading scores spend their mornings in the classroom reading stories about basketball and their afternoons playing the game. Daily attendance in this program averaged better than 90 percent of those enrolled, as compared with 62 percent average attendance among students during the regular school year. This program is a two-pronged attempt to use sports to motivate students to learn academic skills. They read enjoyable sports stories and are rewarded by a chance to play. The goal is to interest students enough to foster reading on their own. As one instructor said, "we want to register the idea about reading that, as with sports, if you want to be good at it, you've got to work at it."[30]

One other positive consequence of school sports is related to the unifying function. Teams representing a school provide a rallying point for persons who might otherwise be only loosely identified with the school. This often increases monetary support for the school, especially at the college level as James Reston has noted:

> Nobody in America has really analyzed the positive effects of sport on the remarkable growth and development of state university education in America. No doubt state university sport has been professionalized and corrupted, but it has produced football teams which have become symbols of state pride. It has kept the alumni in touch with

> the university. More important it has held the interest and the allegiance of legislators in the state capitols, and has in the process helped produce educational appropriations for all these land-grant institutions on a scale that would never have been possible without the attraction and the pride engendered by these sporting events at the universities on autumn Saturday afternoons.[31]

Positive Consequences for the Community

We have already noted that school athletics appear to be effective means for channeling interest and loyalty of the community for the school. Clearly, this enthusiasm generated by sports is a unifying agent for the community. Persons, regardless of occupation, education, race, or religion, can and do unite in backing the school's teams against the common enemy.

Sports are even a cohesive force between generations, as Edgar Friedenberg has noted:

> High school athletics require real skill and competence; at their best they are beautiful to watch. Football and basketball provide almost the only occasion in American life when adults can empathize with and take pride in the qualities of youth with a minimum of guilt or envy. If this opportunity is frequently exploited to serve viciously competitive ends, it is also frequently the occasion for a real appreciation and affection for the young, in response to what they are actually like. Athletic events, therefore, could serve as a real force for integration.[32]

Sports provide action in an otherwise humdrum world. They not only provide excitement but also fantasy and escape. Murray Kempton has even suggested that "the prime social function of sport is to unite us in the feeling that we are all still in high school."[33]

The Consequences of Sport for the Participant

Individuals participate in sports for a variety of reasons. Perhaps most important is the desire for high status and the approval of fans, press, peers, parents, teachers, and others. They may also participate because they enjoy the activity and being physically fit. They may also derive great pleasure from being part of a cohesive unit, striving for a common goal. Sometimes forgotten, however, is that many persons participate because all the normative influences pull them in that direction. There are many constraints to participate, whether one wants to or not. Of course, youngsters are socialized to desire participation so they may not feel the constraints.

We noted in our earlier discussion of sports as a character builder that a negative side exists as well, a position that Banham summarizes:

> It [the conventional argument that sport builds character] is not sound because it assumes that everyone will benefit from sport in the complacently prescribed manner. A

> minority do so benefit. A few have the temperament that responds healthily to all the demands. These are the ones able to develop an attractively active character. Sport can put fresh air in the mind, if it's the right mind; it can give muscle to the personality, if it's the right personality. But for the rest, it encourages selfishness, envy, conceit, hostility and bad temper. Far from ventilating the mind, it stifles it. Good sportsmanship may be a product of sport, but so is bad sportsmanship.[34]

The research on whether sport builds character is contradictory.[35] The problem is that sports produce positive outcomes for some individuals and negative ones for others. Orlick sums up this dualism nicely:

> For every positive psychological or social outcome in sports, there are possible negative outcomes. For example, sports can offer a child group membership or group exclusion, acceptance or rejection, positive feedback or negative feedback, a sense of accomplishment or a sense of failure, evidence of self-worth or a lack of evidence of self-worth. Likewise, sports can develop cooperation and a concern for others, but they can also develop intense rivalry and a complete lack of concern for others.[36]

Two problems for individual high school athletes are often overlooked. First, for many erstwhile athletes, sport leads to a series of failures. Either they fail to make the team or their team loses many more times than it wins. In a success-oriented society, what happens to all of the failures that sport generates? At the individual level, failure can be devastating for some. As Jeansonne has put it:

> Keep score and somebody has to lose. It doesn't matter that people grow bigger, stronger and faster each day; each game, each event still has its loser, frightfully narrowing one's odds of going through life undefeated, untied and unscored upon. The majority won't even make the playoffs. Yet there is no sympathy for the loser, often even from the loser himself. The word—loser—leaves vile smells and tastes among players, coaches and watchers of games. . . . "The word loser," says former basketball star Bob Cousey in his recent book, *The Killer Instinct,* "is a dirty word in our society. Call a man a son of a bitch and he may grin; you've made him sound tough and manly. Call him a loser and he may fight you because you've made him sound unmanly."[37]

Another problem is one of adjustment after one's career in sport is finished. In 1972, about one million boys played football in high school, 31,000 played college football, and only about 1,000 were professional football players.[38] Clearly, most boys, even if stars, will not make it at the next level. After the glory years, what happens to them when they are considered has-beens? Does participation in sport have carryover value to other endeavors where there is no hero-worship, no excitement, and notoriety? What happens to the jock who finds himself suddenly outside the world that has until now been the center of importance in his life? Does he become embittered and turn away from sport, or does he fill his time with reliving the past, attending games, Monday morning quarterbacking, and watching sports on television? How does he, when compared to nonathletes, adjust to his job, marriage, upward or downward mobility? Little research has been done on this very important series of questions. Although novelists have dealt with the matter,[39] much sociological research remains to be done.

Manifest and Latent Consequences of Interschool Sports for Society

The previous section has enumerated the consequences of sports in American education at three levels: community, school, and individual. Although these are important and some have implications for the larger society, we will concentrate here on a very important intended consequence for society—enculturation—and an important but often overlooked latent (unintended) consequence—reinforcement of the sex roles.

The Enculturation Function of Interschool Sports

Educational philosophers have suggested that schools tend to emphasize either of two goals—enculturation or maturation.[40] The enculturation model holds that schools exist to equip youngsters with the skills, values, and knowledge (culture) that guarantee the continuation of the political, economic, and religious heritage of the society. Thus, schools stress such objectives as developing economically useful vocational skills, loyalty to the nation, acceptance of the prevailing values, and accommodation to authority. Implicit in this goal of enculturation is the school's role in the selection of persons to fit into the various occupational and status systems of society.

At odds with the enculturation goal of education is the goal of enhancing the maturity of individual students. In this model, schools exist to encourage students to be genuinely autonomous. Instead of relying only on authority, tradition, or one's peers, decisions are based on rationality. Advocates of this position agree that the accumulated knowledge and skills of the culture must be transmitted and learned, but it is even more vital that each student develop a questioning, critical attitude. Just as important is the role of the school in the development of a sense of unconditional self-worth in each student, one that is not dependent on performance, achievement, conformity, or external approval.

Public schools in the United States, in both their overt curricular content and in the covert curricula inherent in the teaching-learning process, more closely approach the enculturation model than the maturity model. We agree with Schafer's argument that:

> . . . most schools demonstrate a much greater concern for inculcating so-called "correct" attitudes than for fostering inquisitiveness; for teaching the blind following of authority than a desire for actively searching for the truth; for fostering uncritical loyalty to the nation-state and its current leadership than for developing a critical and

> questioning citizenry; for turning out followers than for developing innovators; for teaching supposedly marketable skills than for stimulating a life-long enjoyment of learning; and for turning out people who base their acceptance of self and others on performance and "right" attitudes than on intrinsic worth and dignity. In short, greatest stress is given to learning how to "fit in."[41]

As our discussion in the previous chapter on sport and values showed, participation in sport is a very important mechanism of enculturation.

The Reinforcement of Sex Roles

Sport in American schools has historically been almost exclusively a male preserve. This is clearly evident as one compares by sex the number of participants and facilities.*

What is the impact on a society that encourages its boys and young men to participate in sports, while expecting its girls and young women to be spectators and cheerleaders? The answer is that sport thereby serves to reinforce societal expectations for males and females. Males are to be dominant, aggressive—the doers—while females are expected to be passive supporters of men, attaining status through the efforts of their menfolk. Kathryn Clarenback of the University of Wisconsin has made this point well in the following passage:

> The overemphasis on protecting girls from strain or injury; the underemphasis on developing skills and experiencing teamwork, fits neatly into the pattern of the second sex. Girls are the spectators and the cheerleaders. They organize the pep clubs, sell pompons, make cute, abbreviated costumes, strut a bit between halves and idolize the current football hero. This is perfect preparation for the adult role of women—to stand decoratively on the sidelines of history and cheer on the men who make the decisions.[42]

Problems, Dilemmas, and Controversies

While, as we have noted, sport in schools has positive consequences for the school, participants, and spectators, more and more critics are wondering about the educational benefits of such activities. In this section, we will discuss some of these criticisms and suggest some alternatives for sport in higher education and secondary education.

Sport-Related Problems in Higher Education

School sports, especially at the intercollegiate level, have become increasingly dominated by high pressure, commercialism, and a philosophy of winning at any cost.

*Since we will examine sexism in sport in greater detail in chapter 10, our discussion here will be limited to the unintended ways in which school sport works to maintain the conventional expectations for masculine and feminine roles.

These are manifested in a strong tendency for schools in the "big time," or those striving for that level, to use illegal recruiting practices and to abuse athletes, physically and psychologically, for the good of the program. In short, intercollegiate athletics has in very fundamental ways corrupted the goals and ideals of higher education.

Cheating

Cheating involves a violation of the rules to gain an unfair advantage on an opponent. It occurs at all levels of sport and may be done by individual players, teams, or coaches.[43] The types of cheating depend on the sport and the ingenuity of the participants. The following are some examples:

Some players are coached to use illegal but difficult to detect techniques, such as holding or tripping by offensive linemen in football. In basketball, it is often advantageous to touch the lower half of the shooter's body because the referee usually watches the action around the ball. A form of cheating often taught players is to fake being fouled in basketball. The intent is to fool an official who is out of position.[44]

Coaches sometimes break the spirit of a rule if not the rule itself. A former school teacher wrote the following in a letter to sport columnist Jim Murray (this occurred at the high school level, but it indicated what also happens in colleges and universities):

> I was disgusted by the deceit practiced in the athletic department—men to whom our boys look for leadership. For example, our league had a rule against having more than a certain number of practices during the summer months preparatory to the beginning of football season. But—by pure coincidence—the whole football team would show up in full uniform on unscheduled days. Also, the coaching staff would miraculously appear. I will say that, in some cases, the coaches and team did not come in direct contact, that is, they were separated by, probably, 20 yards, but this infuriated me as an educator. As far as I was concerned, the only thing we were teaching those kids was how to cheat. And what seemed even more ridiculous was that these coaches were breaking their own rules—rules they themselves had made.[45]

When the pressure to win becomes too great, the result can be a policy of cheating—offering athletes more than the legal limit to lure them to your school. In a 1929 report, the Carnegie Foundation decried the widespread illegal recruiting practices of American colleges and universities. Not only has the problem continued, but it has intensified because the economic rewards for winning are now so much greater. A losing season can mean a considerable loss of alumni contributions (as well as gate receipts). When the Ohio State football team went from a 7-2 record in 1966 to 4-5 the next year, alumni contributions dropped by almost $500,000. Conversely, a winning team can dramatically aid a program financially, as evidenced by the contributions in excess of $1 million to North Carolina State's athletic scholarship fund after that school won the 1974 NCAA basketball championship.[46]

The extent of recruiting irregularities is unknown. A reasonable speculation is that recent scandals involving such schools as Long Beach State, Southwest Louisiana, Minnesota, Oklahoma, and Michigan State are only the visible portion of the iceberg.[47]

> A 1974 survey by the National Association of Basketball Coaches said that one of every eight major colleges made illegal offers to prospects, that all the cheaters were offering money, 80 percent were offering cars, and more than half were offering clothing. The survey was conducted among 25 recently graduated college players, 25 current high school standouts, 25 sets of parents, and 25 athletic directors of major-college basketball programs. Of the 50 players interviewed, 40 percent said they had received illegal offers.[48]

In addition to the illegal offering of material things, coaches have also altered transcripts to insure an athlete's eligibility, had substitutes take admissions tests for athletes of marginal educational ability, provided jobs for parents, paid athletes for nonexistent jobs, illegally used government work studies monies for athletes, and the like. Clearly, such behaviors not only corrupt coaches and athletes alike, but they demean the ideals of higher education.

A different form of cheating involves the use of drugs so that one might compete at a higher-than-normal level of ability. This may be done on the insistence of trainers and coaches or by an athlete on his or her own. Two groups of drugs are used by athletes. The first type—restorative—aids in healing a traumatized part of the body. The second type—additive—is alleged to improve an individual's performance. Two additive drugs—amphetamines and anabolic steroids—are used with some regularity by many athletes. Amphetamines stimulate the athlete. They literally help him in getting "psyched up." Anabolic steroids are male hormones that aid in adding weight and muscle.[49]

Hypocrisy

Sport is frequently proclaimed to be a citadel of law and order. At the same time, some of the most outspoken of these claimants are guilty of cheating. As already noted, many coaches, in their quest for success, have condoned giving illegal payments and other gratuities to players.[50]

Many athletes in universities are bound to become cynical about their education. Coaches proclaim that their athletes are students first and athletes only secondarily. This is the typical recruiting speech to prospects and their parents. But in practice, the reverse is often true. The athlete has signed a contract and is paid for his athletic services. He is an employee and the relationship between a coach and his athlete is essentially employer-employee. Athletes are often counseled to take easy courses, whether or not those courses fit their educational needs. Because of the enormous demands on their time during the season, athletes frequently must take a somewhat reduced course load, and, thus, they will not usually graduate in the normal amount of time. Study halls and tutors are frequently available, even required, for college athletes, but the primary function of these adjuncts is to insure athletic eligibility, not necessarily the education of the athlete. If the athlete achieves an education in the process, it is incidental to the overriding objective of big-time sport. As the University of Virginia football coach honestly put it: "We've stopped recruiting young men who want to come here to be students first and athletes second."[51] This philosophy is echoed by Alabama's legendary coach Bear Bryant:

> I used to go along with the idea that football players on scholarship were "student-athletes," which is what the NCAA calls them. Meaning a student first, an athlete second. We were kidding ourselves, trying to make it more palatable to the academicians. We don't have to say that and we shouldn't. At the level we play, the boy is really an athlete first and a student second.[52]

Dehumanizing Aspects of Collegiate Sport

Some coaches, in their zeal to be successful, are also guilty of behaviors that brutalize and demean their athletes—actions that in other contexts would not be tolerated. The common charge of critics of these practices is that the athletes have become tools of the schools, dehumanized as they work endless hours to develop machinelike precision. The athletes are dehumanized as coaches demean and belittle them in an effort to increase their performances. The athlete is dehumanized further when forced to participate in incredibly rigorous conditioning drills or drills designed to force marginal players to quit in humiliation and pain.

Let's examine one extensive example of these dehumanizing occurrences from Gary Shaw's experiences while a football player at the University of Texas. All freshmen football players and those others whom the coaching staff wanted to discourage reported to daily sessions conducted by the trainer. These sessions took place in a room heated to 120°F. The athletes wore sweat suits, wrist weights, ankle weights, a 30-pound vest, and held a 30-pound dumbbell in each hand. They did calisthenics with each exercise continuing until someone faltered. Whoever faltered became the target of derision from the trainer and the other players (who suffered because they had to do the exercise over). One day, Shaw recalled, they did 500 sit-ups (several players vomited) and the concrete rubbed them raw.[53]

Another dehumanizing practice at Texas was the "shit drill." These drills were for all players below the fourth team. They were designed, according to Shaw, to get the marginal players to quit. Coaches wanted to get rid of these players because they held scholarships and if their scholarships were vacated, someone else could replace them. Since scholarships were nearly impossible to take away, the job was to get players to "voluntarily" give them up. Three techniques were used: trainer sessions (see above), running the stadium steps every morning from 4:30 to 5:00 with a 30-pound vest on, and "shit drills." The "shit drills" were a series of violent drills where players would run headlong into each other helmet to helmet, and where individual tackling and even gang tackling (all against one) were practiced. This 2 1/2-hour physical punishment continued daily during the season. Concomitant with the physical abuse was psychological abuse (questioning a player's masculinity, running down his ability, and so on). Many, of course, ultimately quit the Texas football team, "voluntarily" giving up their scholarships. Shaw noted that these persons invariably also quit school. They were physically and psychologically beaten. In the latter case, they had been socialized by the system not to be quitters, yet they finally broke under the strain and were quitters.[54]

Sports Illustrated has noted dehumanizing activities conducted at Kansas State, Florida State, Tennessee, Kentucky, and other universities for athletes required to enroll in conditioning classes in the off-season. At Florida State, for example, the athletes were required to wrestle in rooms with a false ceiling of chicken wire suspended four feet above the wrestling mats; the loser had to wrestle the next match. At Kansas State, one grueling activity was to harness the players back to back; one had to drag the other 20 feet across the floor.[55]

Another example of dehumanization is when an injured player is forced to play before an injury is properly healed.

> "Someone needs to brainwash coaches so they'll understand their job is to coach and teach . . . They're too damned concerned with winning and not with the boys." That appears to be the ultimate problem—those coaches who are more concerned with winning football games than they are with the health of their young charges. It is a fact that coaches who do not win rather consistently lose their jobs. But pressuring players, trainers and doctors to cut short the time needed to heal injuries fully is not the way to retain a job. Most coaches can find other jobs. No injured player has ever been able to find another body.[56]

These examples occur at prominent universities. Even when publicized, nothing happens to the coach unless he loses too many games. However, the player in such a situation, if he is relatively aware, must realize that he is just a piece of machinery to be used, abused, and discarded, to be replaced by another replaceable part. Clearly, corporate sport, in its quest for winning and making money, has lost sight of the original purpose of sport—participation for enjoyment.

Authoritarian Leadership

Most teams are dictatorships. Rules are made and enforced from the top. Game strategy is the province of the established leadership. Lineups are determined by the authorities. As the former football coach at the University of Pittsburgh once said,

"Football is not a democracy. There's nothing to debate. The players can debate in political science class."[57] The rationale is simple: winning teams are in shape, well disciplined, efficient, and composed of persons who think and act as one. But this may be a myth; the key variable may be that winning teams are composed of better players than everybody else from the start. But the point is that coaches *believe* that they must have strict external discipline to win. Thus, players' lives are controlled by coaches. Their freedom is restricted because coaches feel they have the right to control even those things unrelated to actual performance (e.g., clothing and hairstyles). As Melvin Cratsley, former coach at Carnegie Tech, reasoned:

> I wanted my players to wear blazers, get haircuts, wear a tie, take a bath once in a while, be on time. They didn't want to do these things. I object to players telling me they want beards, long hair and all the rest, because the next thing they want to do is run the team. More important than the beard is what it represents—rebellion. If you can't tell them what to do, they don't need a coach.[58]

But what is the effect on the athletes who, whether they are teenagers or adults, are told how to dress, when and how to cut their hair, and when they should be in bed? Does such autocratic behavior by coaches build autonomous, self-reliant, self-disciplined individuals, prepared to live in a democracy? Many critics of sport argue that such behavior does not and is, therefore, incompatible with the goals of education.[59]

The sociological explanation for cheating, hypocrisy, brutality, and authoritarianism by some coaches lies not in their individual psyches but in the intensely competitive system within which they operate. In American society, the success or failure of a team is believed by most persons to rest with the coach. This pressure to win brings some coaches to use illegal inducements to attract athletes to their school, or teach their linemen to hold without getting caught, or to look the other way when athletes (who face the same pressures to succeed) use drugs to enhance their performance. The absolute necessity to win also explains why some coaches drive their players too hard. Thus, what some persons might label brutality has been explained by some coaches as a necessity to get the maximum effort from players. Finally, authoritarianism can be explained by the constraints on the coaching role. Democracy is unthinkable to most in the coaching profession because coaches are liable for the outcome in an extremely uncertain situation. Since they cannot control injuries, officiating, mental lapses by athletes, and the bounce of the ball, most coaches are convinced that they must seek to control as much else as possible.[60]

College Sport Is Big Business

Perhaps the source of all the problems noted above is that the colleges in question are involved in a commercial entertainment enterprise.[61] Because winning teams bring greater economic rewards to the universities, the pressure to win is so great that participants cheat, players are dehumanized, drugs are used to enhance performance beyond normal limits, and the like.

The businesslike character of big-time college sport is more directly responsible for one additional problem. Young men (and more recently young women) are paid slave wages (room, board, and tuition) to bring honor and dollars to their university. Whereas, the average professional football player, for example, earns more than $50,000 per year and basketball players more than $110,000, the average college player in these sports earns about $5,000 (in services rather than money). Thus, there are two questions of morality: (1) the use of student-athletes to hustle money for the university; and (2) the exploitation of the athletes by paying them indecent wages.

There are two possible solutions to the problems related to "corporate sport" at the university level. One solution is to take the fantasy and hypocrisy out of college sports. Norman Cousins has proposed this with respect to football. Cousins believes that football is terribly important to most schools. It provides schools with an image, increases financial support, unites alumni, students, faculty, and townspeople behind the school, and finances minor sports. Thus, football is so completely metabolized into higher education that it would be impossible to abolish it. Furthermore, it is unrealistic to try to maintain a strictly amateur program because recruitment, scholarships, and bonuses occur no matter what is done to disguise them. The answer is to stop pretending that it is an amateur sport. The evidence is clear that major college football is *not* amateur sport. Thus, Cousins asserts that we should:

> Recognize and run it as an out-and-out professional enterprize. Allow colleges to sponsor professional teams. Regard football as a legitimate money-making and prestige activity. Players should not be required to enroll as students or attend classes. Colleges now own and operate, or have substantial interests in, various businesses, large and small. They invest in real estate and maintain large portfolios of stocks in corporations. Why should they not be permitted to invest in a football team, equip it with the finest players they can find, paying them salaries appropriate to their skills, and attracting crowds large enough to help raise revenue for paying decent salaries to the faculty, maintaining a good library, and carrying on a strong program of research?
>
> The question is not whether football should be regarded as a proper activity of American colleges. That question has already been affirmatively decided. The question is whether it ought to be continued in its present disguise, cutting into the self-respect of college presidents, making liars and cheats out of faculty members who have to pretend that empty seats are occupied and that phantoms are scholars, and teaching young men how to take money under the table and then swear they know nothing about it. Far better to hire the performers in the open, the way a college hires janitors or night watchmen or other persons essential to the operation of the school, than to maintain an elaborate disguise which no one believes. . . .

> There is no point in arguing that it would be awkward or inappropriate for the American college to associate itself with professional sports. It is doing so already. What now needs to be done is to call things by their right names—one of the basic purposes of education in the first place.[62]

The other alternative solution would be to shift the level of college sport from the "corporate" to the "organized" level. The assumption behind such a change is that there is no place for professional sport in an educational institution. The demand for winning and making money has become so important that educators have condoned practices antithetical to sportsmanship, honesty, and fair play. Just as important, the athletes's enjoyment in the activity has been lost in the process. Jack Scott, principal spokesman for the "radical" critique of contemporary "corporate sport," has argued that sport has become corrupt, dehumanized, commercialized, political, authoritarian, and racist.[63] Scott has argued that athletics should be returned to the athlete who can participate for the sheer inherent enjoyment of the activity. He seeks greater participation in sport by men and women of all ages. He wants coaches to teach, not police, to serve instead of being served. A few schools do maintain this type of program, including Massachusetts Institute of Technology, Brooklyn College, and Hampshire College.[64]

In summary, there are massive problems in American intercollegiate sport. What began as "organized sport" has in many schools and conferences become "corporate sport." Over the years, the original intent of such competition—pleasure for the participants—has been lost to the big-business, highly competitive, and often corrupt aspects of contemporary college athletic programs. If schools sponsor athletic teams as part of the educational process, then there must be a reassessment of their programs. We would offer as a guide to such a reevaluation, a statement by Robert Pritchard, director of athletics at Worcester Polytechnic Institute:

> The place of the athletic program reveals priorities. It also can reveal the acquiescence to pressures. The test lies in "What does the program do for the person?" If the participant is not the reason for the existence of the program, then it becomes nearly a professional program. If the purpose is to make money, to publicize the school, to satisfy the alumni ego or assuage a state legislature, then much of the educational value of an intercollegiate program is lost.[65]

Sports-Related Problems in Secondary Education

Many of the problems found in intercollegiate sports are also found at the interscholastic level. One problem at both levels—excessive pressure to win—is manifested in the existence of high-pressure coaches, authoritarian coaching regimes, cheating, and the separation of sport from the athlete. Commercialism, hypocrisy, and the brutalization of athletes have also filtered down to interscholastic sport.

In this section, we will focus on one fundamental problem of interscholastic sport as it is presently organized—that it is not designed to maximize its educational potential. Implicit in this criticism is the assumption that sports participation is a worthwhile school-related activity if it is congruent with educational goals.

Educators agree that all school programs should be designed to realize their educational potential. Illustrative of this is the statement by the American Alliance for Health, Physical Education, and Recreation regarding the goal of athletics in schools:

> Athletics when properly utilized, serve as potential educational media through which optimum growth—physical, mental, emotional, social, and moral—of the participants may be fostered.[66]

Unfortunately, research has shown that the athletic program in most high schools is not designed for the optimum growth of most students. Talamini examined athletic programs in 60 schools, ranging in pupil size from 456 to 2,850.[67] He compared the athletic practices in each school with the norms established by the Educational Policies Commission for Schools.[68] This famous report has been widely quoted by authorities as the guide for athletics programs if they are to be consonant with educational goals. Among the recommendations of the commission were that schools: (1) should abolish postseason tournaments because, when measured in terms of educational values, such tournaments do more harm than good; (2) should emphasize intramural sports that can be played in adulthood (carry-over sports); (3) should carefully choose coaches for their values and skills (not just their winning record) since they serve as significant role models for youth; and (4) should finance athletics entirely by taxes rather than gate receipts or other methods that contribute to the commercialization of athletics.

The results from Talamini's study showed that schools did not measure up to these norms. In the first instance, 93 percent of the schools would participate in postseason championships if they had the chance. With regard to carry-over intramurals, 30 percent of the schools had *no* intramural sports at all for boys and 27 percent had no offerings for girls' intramurals. Of the remaining schools, only 17 percent equally sponsored carry-over and non-carry-over sports. The third norm, that coaches should be selected primarily for their moral character and teaching ability, was not adhered to since the paramount concern of schools in the selection of coaches was "Is he a winner?" Finally, with regard to how schools athletics are financed, Talamini found that 50 percent of the schools met the criterion by exclusively using tax funds to run the athletic program.

Talamini's conclusion was that the vast majority of schools do not follow the standards set forth by the Educational Policies Commission—that there is a real discrepancy between ideal norms and situational realities. High school sports programs are, for the most part, overly competitive and commercialized and, therefore, not serving the educational goals of schools.[69]

Several criticisms of present interscholastic sports programs are implied in the lack of congruence between athletic programs and the standards of the Educational Policies Commission. First, excessive stress on winning, rather than on participation, makes sport work rather than play. Moreover, there is the possibility of physical and psychological damage to youngsters who must participate in twice-a-day practices, summertime practices, Saturday practices, and Sunday evening movies of the previous Friday's game. As Willard Waller said back in 1932:

> A more serious indictment of the social system which allows the livelihood of a man and his family to depend upon the athletic achievements of boys is that the coach is so pressed that he uses his human material recklessly. He trains his "men" (aged sixteen) a bit too hard, or he uses his star athletes in too many events, or he schedules too many hard games; all this he does from a blameless desire to gain a better position or a rise in salary for himself, but he often fails to consider the possible effects upon the physical well-being of the rising generation.[70]

Evidence of such an overemphasis on winning is prevalent in American high schools, clearly implying that sporting activity has lost its fun element. The solution is difficult, however, because there must be an across-the-board deemphasis on high school athletics. This can be accomplished partially by severely limiting practice time (in and out of season) and monitoring of practices to ensure players' rights. There needs to be a corresponding emphasis on sports participation for its own sake. The stress should be on enjoyment of the process, not the outcome. As Tom Meschery, former pro basketball player and coach, has put it:

> Young players today spend all their time learning skills when they should be enjoying competition. We stress the learning process at the expense of absorbing simple, genuine enthusiasm. Pre-high school sports [and we would add high school sports] should be directed toward spontaneity, not organization. They should be directed toward lessening tension, not creating it. There is no need for high school state basketball tournaments. This may seem drastic, but at that age it seems counterproductive to arrive at an ultimate winner when we could have half a dozen winners. It is good for the young to argue the never-to-be settled championship.[71]

A second criticism implied by the Educational Policies Commission report is that interscholastic sport programs are elitist. They are for the few, not the many. If sports participation is believed to have educational benefits, then how can schools justify limiting basketball squads to twelve and football squads to fifty? Why should participation be limited almost exclusively to the fast and/or strong (football) or the tall (basketball)? Further, how can schools justify letting these few have almost exclusive rights to the athletic facilities. The solution to this problem lies in: (1) increasing the emphasis on intramural programs; (2) having no limit as to the size of squads; and (3) dividing players by age, height, and weight with interschool competition at each level (this is done presently for boxing and wrestling and could be used for football, basketball, and track).

A final criticism of high school sports (and collegiate sports as well), but one omitted by the Educational Policies Commission, is the almost total control that coaches exercise over their players' lives. Many coaches, for example, exert control over hairstyles, clothing, dating, whom one associates with, church attendance, and the like. Walter Schafer has criticized these practices:

> Coaches have no business, in my judgment, requiring conformity to a particular set of moral standards—their own or those of the dominant adult community—that are unrelated to athletic training or performance. . . . The reaction by many to what I am saying will surely be—but the coach needs ultimate and unquestioning authority in order to maximize performance and success by the athlete and his team. My response is that while the coach indeed needs authority, it must be exercised in a humane, dignified, and supportive fashion if the desired personal outcomes we have discussed are to be achieved. Moreover, it is vital to distinguish between *scope* and *strength* of authority. While a coach no doubt needs *strong* authority over his athletes, that authority ought to be narrow rather than broad in scope in that it is exercised over behavior, clearly and directly related to training or performance.[72]

There is certainly a legal question whether coaches have the right to infringe upon the civil liberties of their charges. Beyond that, there is the question of the educational value of controlling these youngsters on and off the field. It would appear that a system that denies personal autonomy fosters dependence and immaturity, rather than the presumed virtues of participation—leadership, independence, and self-motivation. Moreover, does existence in an autocracy prepare one for life in a democracy?

There is a radical experiment with democracy in football that goes one step further than that advocated by Walter Schafer. It is the system used by George Davis, a football coach in several California high schools and a junior college.[73] While at St. Helena High School, his teams won 45 straight games. But the Davis system of coaching was unique. His players voted on who should be in the starting lineup; they decided what positions they wanted to play; and they established the guidelines for discipline. In other words, his revolutionary system was democratic.[74] Davis believed that such a system on an athletic team would:

1. Increase confidence between players and coaches.
2. Promote team cohesion.
3. Teach responsibility, leadership, and decision making, thereby fostering maturity rather than immaturity, independence instead of dependence.
4. Increase player motivation—instead of having to be driven by fear, harassment, and physical abuse, by the coach, the players would have to impress their peers.

5. Free the coach to *teach* skills, techniques, and strategies.
6. Allow the players to experience the benefits of democracy.

But will such a system work? Won't players choose their friends? Davis is convinced that they rather than the coach know who is best, and because they do not want to lose or be embarrassed, they will choose the best personnel for each position. Given a choice between good and mediocre blockers, backs are going to choose the best. They will not let cliques or prejudice influence their vote.

Davis summed up his system this way:

> What does the vote achieve? It takes the problems of discipline and responsibility and puts them where they belong, with the players. The coach becomes a teacher, what he is being paid to do, a resource unit. My job is to teach, to help athletes reach a level of independence. At any level this is how democracy works and why it succeeds.[75]

Summary

It is difficult to imagine an American high school or college without an interschool sports program for students. Sport and education are intimately interrelated because sport provides important consequences for schools, communities, and individuals.

The theme of this chapter has been on the relationship between school sport and educational goals. Our conclusion is that for sport to be compatible with educational goals in American schools, it should be structured to be "organized sport" not "corporate sport." The data presented in this chapter, however, suggest that school sport is moving in the direction of corporate sport (big-time athletic universities are already there, by definition).

Sport at the elementary school level tends to accomplish educational goals (e.g., the fostering of good health practices, learning of skills, the value of teamwork, and the striving for a goal) in a playful, enjoyable atmosphere. At each successive educational level, however, the nature of sport changes, becoming more serious, bureaucratized, and elitist, and its outcome more crucial. Figure 4-2, provided by Snyder and Spreitzer, shows the progression in school sports from "informal sport" to "corporate sport."

The serious question for educators is whether there is a place for "corporate sport" in education. But the problem, of course, is not limited to education. As Harry Edwards has said:

> What's "wrong" with sport and sport in education in America reflects America itself—particulary the relationships between contemporary social, political, and economic realities and this nation's value priorities, its attitudes, and its perspectives.[76]

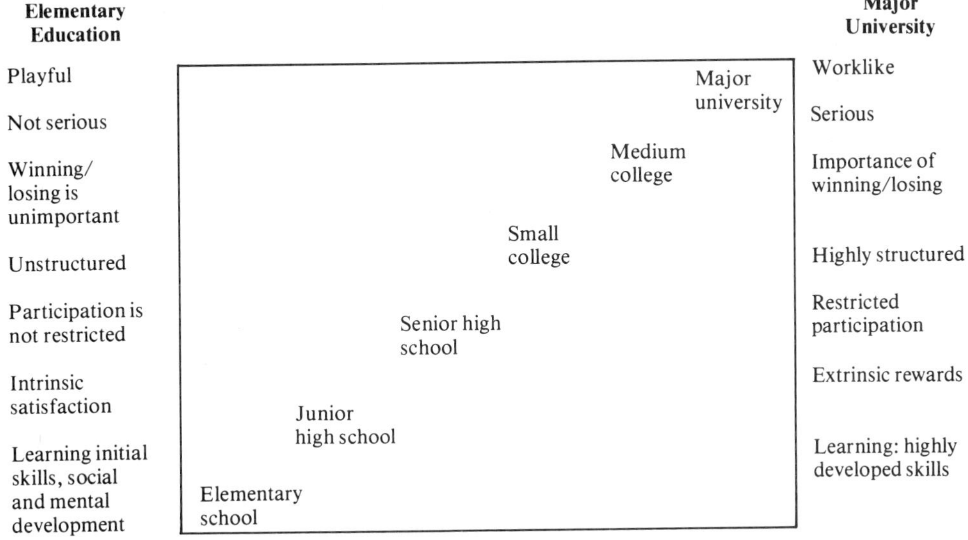

Figure 4-2. Attributes of Sports at Different Educational Levels.

Source: Eldon E. Snyder and Elmer A. Spreitzer, "Sport and Education," *Encyclopedia of Physical Education,* vol. 5, eds. George H. Sage and Gunther Luschen (Reading, Mass.: Addison-Wesley, in press).

Notes

1. "1973 Sports Participation Survey," mimeographed (Elgin, Ill.: The National Federation of State High School Associations, 1973).
2. "Athletics in Education," A Platform Statement by the Division of Men's Athletics, American Alliance for Health, Physical Education and Recreation (Washington, D.C.: 1963).
3. Thorstein Veblen, *The Theory of the Leisure Class* (New York: Mentor Books, 1953), pp. 173-174. This book was first published in 1899.
4. Frederick Cozens and Florence Stumpf, *Sports in American Life* (Chicago: University of Chicago Press, 1953), chapter 6.
5. The degree of importance of sport in education varies, of course, from society to society. Even among advanced industrial societies, there is a wide variance. French schools, for example, attach relatively low priority to school sports, while English schools attach more importance, and East German schools still more. Although it is an empirical question, most research suggests that American schools are among those that attach the greatest importance to sport in schools. See UNESCO, *The Place of Sport in Education: A Comparative Study,* Educational Studies and Documents, no. 21 (Paris: UNESCO, 1956).
6. James S. Coleman, *Adolescents and the Schools* (New York: Basic Books, 1965), pp. 35-36.
7. Abraham J. Tannenbaum, "Adolescents'

Attitudes Toward Academic Brilliance," (Ph.D. diss. New York University, 1960). Quoted in James S. Coleman, *The Adolescent Society* (New York: The Free Press, 1961), pp. 309-310.

8. Coleman, *The Adolescent Society,* p. 309.
9. Ibid. A summary of the role of athletics by Coleman is also found in "Athletics in High School," *Annals of the American Academy of Political and Social Science* 338 (November, 1961), pp. 33-43; and *Adolescents and the Schools* (New York: Basic Books, 1965), chapter 3, "Athletics in High School."
10. J. Milton Yinger, "Contraculture and Subculture," *American Sociological Review* 25 (October, 1962), pp. 625-635.
11. The points that follow are generally the insights of Bennett M. Berger, *Looking for America* (Englewood Cliffs, N.J.: Prentice-Hall, 1971), pp. 44-53.
12. For a more elaborate analysis of the relationship between athletic involvement and academic achievement, see Eldon E. Snyder and Elmer Spreitzer, "Sport and Education," *Encyclopedia of Physical Education,* vol. 5, eds. Gunther Luschen and George H. Sage (Reading, Mass.: Addison-Wesley, forthcoming).
13. W. E. Schafer and J. M. Armer, "Athletes Are Not Inferior Students," *Trans-action* 5 (November, 1968), pp. 21-26, 61-62. See also Richard A. Rehberg and Michael Cohen, "Athletes and Scholars: An Analysis of the Compositional Characteristics and Damage of These Two Youth Culture Categories," *International Review of Sport Sociology* 10 (1975), pp. 91-107.
14. See R. A. Rehberg and W. E. Schafer, "Participation in Interscholastic Athletics and College Expectations," *American Journal of Sociology* 73 (May, 1968), pp. 732-740; W. G. Spady, "Lament for the Letterman: Effect of Peer Status and Extracurricular Activities on Goals and Achievement," *American Journal of Sociology* 75 (January, 1970), pp. 680-702; E. A. Spreitzer and M. D. Pugh, "Interscholastic Athletics and Educational Expectations," *Sociology of Education* 46 (Spring, 1973), pp. 171-182; and Luther B. Otto and Duane F. Alvin, "Athletics, Aspirations, and Attainments," *Sociology of Education* 42 (April, 1977), pp. 102-113.
15. See the excellent summary of the methodological problems found in such studies in Christopher L. Stevenson, "Socialization Effects of Participation in Sport: A Critical Review of the Research," *Research Quarterly* 46 (October, 1975), pp. 287-301.
16. L. B. Lueptow and B. D. Kayser, "Athletic Involvement: Academic Achievement and Aspirations," *Sociological Focus* 7 (Winter, 1973-74), pp. 24-36.
17. See Frederick C. Klein, "Hoopster Hoopla: High School Basketball is a Serious Matter in a Small Illinois Town," *Wall Street Journal* (March 1, 1970); William Johnson, "The Greatest Athlete in Yates Center, Kansas," *Sports Illustrated* 35 (August 9, 1971), pp. 27-31; Tom Ricke, "A Town Where Boys are Kings and the Court Business is Basketball," *Detroit Free Press* (March 14, 1971); Diane Divoky and Peter Schrag, "Football and Cheers," *Saturday Review* (November 11, 1972), pp. 59-65.
18. Frank B. Jones, "Intercollegiate and Interscholastic Athletic Programs in the 1970's," *Sportscope* (June, 1970), pp. 1-20.
19. D. Stanley Eitzen, "Sport and Social Status in American Public Secondary Education," *Review of Sport & Leisure* 1 (Fall, 1976), pp. 139-155. See also D. Stanley Eitzen, "Athletics in the Status System of Male Adolescents: A Replication of Coleman's 'The Adolescent Society,' " *Adolescence* 10 (Summer, 1975), pp. 267-276. For a replication of the Coleman study at the elementary school level, see Hugh Troy Buchanan, Joe Blankenbaker, and Doyice Cotten, "Academic and Athletic Ability as Popularity Factors in Elementary School Children," *Research Quarterly* 47 (October, 1976), pp. 320-325.
20. An excellent example of this is the story of Mike Peterson found in Johnson, "The Greatest Athlete in Yates Center, Kansas," *Sports Illustrated* 35 (August 9, 1971), pp. 27-31. For a discussion of the same process in the ghetto playgrounds of New York City, see Pete Axthelm, *The City Game* (New York: Harper's Magazine Press Book, 1970).
21. Coleman, *Adolescents and the Schools,* p. 49.
22. Unity occurs when teams win. Losing teams may actually increase the possibility of division in a school.
23. Quoted in Robert Markus, "Athletics Have

Helped Kent State Overcome Tragedy," *NCAA News* 10 (February 1, 1973), p. 2.

24. George H. Sage, "The Collegiate Dilemma of Sport and Leisure: A Sociological Perspective," *Proceedings of the National College Physical Education Association for Men,* (1976), pp. 203-208.

25. Willard Waller, *The Sociology of Teaching* (New York: John Wiley and Sons, 1965), pp. 115-116. This was first published in 1932.

26. Waller, *The Sociology of Teaching,* p. 116. Many of the insights about the social control functions of sport in schools that follow derive from this source.

27. David Matza, "Position and Behavior Patterns of Youth," *Handbook of Modern Sociology,* ed. Robert E. L. Faris (Chicago: Rand McNally, 1964), p. 207.

28. Ibid., p. 205-206.

29. See Clifford B. Fagan, "Player Brawls Must Be Eliminated," *NCAA News* 9 (March 15, 1972), p. 7; Karol Stonger, "Racial Strife Dooms Sports in Big Cities," Associated Press release (March 25, 1971); and "Brawls, Blood on Basketball Court Seen as Sign of Times," Associated Press release (February 15, 1972). These instances of violence run counter to the belief that sports contests relieve tensions. They support the findings by social scientists mentioned in the chapter on sport and values: see Richard Sipes, "War, Sports and Aggression: An Empirical Test of Two Rival Theories," *American Anthropologist* 75 (February, 1973), pp. 64-86; Jeffrey H. Goldstein and Robert L. Arms, "Effects of Observing Athletic Contests on Hostility," *Sociometry* 34 (1971), pp. 83-90.

30. Iver Peterson, "Summer School Course Uses Sports to Inspire Youths to Read," *New York Times* (August 15, 1972).

31. James Reston, "Sports: Therapy with Our Fun," *New York Times* (October 6, 1966).

32. Edgar Z. Friedenberg, *Coming of Age, in America: Growth and Acquiescence* (New York: Vintage Books, 1967), p. 158.

33. Murray Kempton, "Jock-Sniffing," *New York Review of Books* 16 (February 11, 1971).

34. Charles Banham, "Man at Play," *Contemporary Review* 207 (August, 1965), p. 62.

35. For summaries of the research supporting both sides of this issue, see Lowell Cooper, "Athletics, Activity, and Personality: A Review of the Literature," *Research Quarterly* 40 (March, 1969), pp. 17-22; Robert N. Singer, *Coaching, Athletics and Psychology* (New York: McGraw-Hill, 1972); Charles R. Kniker, "The Values of Athletics in Schools: A Continuing Debate," *Phi Delta Kappan* 61 (October, 1974), pp. 116-120.

36. T. D. Orlick, "The Sports Environment: A Capacity to Enhance—A Capacity to Destroy," paper presented at the Canadian Symposium of Psycho-Motor Learning and Sports Psychology (1974), p. 2.

37. John Jeansonne, "Loser, A Word to Lose," *The Basketball Bulletin* (Fall, 1976), p. 88.

38. From a speech by Wayne Duke, Big 10 Commissioner, reported in *NCAA News 9* (August 15, 1972), p. 1.

39. See, e.g., John Updike, *Rabbit Run* (New York: Knopf, 1960).

40. Much of the discussion in this section comes from Walter E. Schafer, "Sport, Socialization and the School: Toward Maturity or Enculturation?" a paper presented at the Third International Symposium on the Sociology of Sport, Waterloo, Ont. August 22-28, 1971.

41. *Ibid.,* p. 5. This point has been made by a variety of educational observers, see especially Charles E. Silberman, *Crisis in the Classroom* (New York: Random House, 1970).

42. Cited in Bil Gilbert and Nancy Williamson, "Programmed to be Losers," *Sports Illustrated* 38 (June 11, 1973), p. 73. See also Paul Hoch, *Rip Off the Big Game* (Garden City, N.Y.: Doubleday Anchor Books, 1972), p. 149; Diana Divoky and Peter Schrag, "Football and Cheers," *Saturday Review* (November 11, 1972), pp. 59-65.

43. For a survey of the literature and numerous insights about the phenomenon of cheating in sports, see Gunther Luschen, "Cheating in Sports," *Social Problems in Athletics,* ed. Daniel M. Landers (Urbana: University of Illinois Press, 1976), pp. 67-77; D. Stanley Eitzen, "Sport and Deviance." *Encyclopedia of Physical Education,* vol. 5, eds. Gunther Luschen and George H. Sage (Reading, Mass.: Addison-Wesley, forthcoming).

44. Frank Ramsey, while a Boston Celtic, wrote an article in *Sports Illustrated* describing nine

moves by which a skillful basketball player could take unfair advantage of his opponents by deceiving the referees—Frank Ramsey, "Smart Moves by a Master of Deception," *Sports Illustrated* 19 (December 9, 1963), pp. 57-63. One observer has argued that basketball itself is a game of deceit and that this explains why it is so uniquely American; see Leonard Koppett, *The Essence of the Game is Deception* (New York: Associated Features, 1973).

45. Jim Murray, syndicated columnist (March 10, 1972).

46. Kenneth Denlinger and Leonard Shapiro, *Athletes for Sale: An Investigation into America's Greatest Sports Scandal—Athletic Recruiting* (New York: Thomas Y. Crowell, 1975). See also Joseph Durso, *The Sports Factory: An Investigation into College Sports* (New York: Quadrangle, 1975); Jim Benagh, *Making It to #1: How College Football and Basketball Teams Get There* (New York: Dodd, Mead, 1976).

47. For the details of the Long Beach State case, see Ray Kennedy, "427: A Case in Point," *Sports Illustrated* 40 (June 10, 1974), pp. 87-100 and (June 17, 1974), pp. 24-30. For a statement of the problem and some suggested changes to deal with the problem of cheating, see the statement by William L. Wall, past president of the National Association of Basketball Coaches—William L. Wall, "Time to Clean Up Basketball," *Sports Illustrated* 36 (February 14, 1972), pp. 20-21. For the efforts of the NCAA to control recruiting violations, see Larry Van Dyne, "College Sports' Enforcement Squad," *The Chronicle of Higher Education* 14 (March 7, 1977), pp. 1, 14, and (March 14, 1977), pp. 5-6.

48. Kenneth Denlinger and Leonard Shapiro, *Athletes for Sale* (New York: Thomas Y. Crowell, 1975), p. 42.

49. The extensiveness of drug usage in sports is debatable. For some indications, see Bil Gilbert, "Drugs in Sport," *Sports Illustrated* 30 (June 23, 1969), pp. 64-72 (June 30, 1969), pp. 30-42, and (July 7, 1969), pp. 30-35; Jack Scott, "It's Not How You Play the Game, But What Pill You Take," *New York Times Magazine* (October 17, 1971), pp. 40ff. For a statement about the ethical implications of drug usage in sports, see Robert J. Bueter, "The Use of Drugs in Sports: An Ethical Perspective," *The Christian Century* 89 (April 5, 1972), pp. 394-398.

50. For an excellent review of the problems big money has brought to sport, see the critique by former basketball player and coach Tom Meschery, "There is a Disease in Sports Now . . ." *Sports Illustrated* 37 (October 2, 1972), pp. 56-63.

51. Sonny Randle, quoted in "Scorecard," *Sports Illustrated* 43 (September 1, 1975), p. 12.

52. Quoted in James A. Michener, *Sports in America* (New York: Random House, 1976), p. 203.

53. Gary Shaw, *Meat on the Hoof: The Hidden World of Texas Football* (New York: St. Martin's Press, 1972), pp. 78-91.

54. Ibid., pp. 122-134.

55. Pat Putnam, "A Case of Volunteer-or Else," *Sports Illustrated* 39 (July 23, 1973), pp. 22-25.

56. George Simpson, "College Football's B.M.O.C. Crisis: Battered and Maimed on Campus," *Sport* 63 (November, 1976), p. 26.

57. Quoted in Shaw, *Meat on the Hoof,* p. 39.

58. Quoted in John Underwood, "The Desperate Coach," *Sports Illustrated* 31 (August 25, 1969), pp. 70-71.

59. Glenn Dickey, *The Jock Empire* (Rednor, Penn.: Chilton Books, 1974), chapter 16, "Athletes and the Self-Discipline Myth."

60. Harry Edwards, *Sociology of Sport* (Homewood, Ill.: Dorsey Press, 1973), pp. 135-141.

61. The following critique is taken primarily from George H. Sage, "The Collegiate Dilemma of Sport and Leisure: A Sociological Perspective," *Proceedings of the National College Physical Education Association for Men,* (1976), pp. 203-208.

62. Norman Cousins, "Football and the College," *Saturday Review* (September 28, 1963), p. 36.

63. For statements of Jack Scott's philosophy, see Jack Scott, *Athletics for Athletes* (Oakland, Cal.: Other Ways Books, 1969); Jack Scott, *The Athletic Revolution* (New York: Free Press, 1971).

64. See John Underwood, "Beating Their Brains Out," *Sports Illustrated* 42 (May 26, 1975),

pp. 84-96; John Papanek, "Of Subways and Salami," *Sports Illustrated* 45 (November 22, 1976); Jay Evans, "At Hampshire the Players are in Charge," *New York Times* (October 17, 1976), p. 2S.

65. Robert W. Pritchard, "Worcester Polytechnic Institute Has Something for Everyone," *NCAA News* 10 (August 15, 1972), p. 3.
66. American Alliance for Health, Physical Education, and Recreation, "Athletics in Education," *Journal of Health, Physical Education and Recreation* (September, 1962), p. 24.
67. John T. Talamini, "School Athletics: Public Policy Versus Practice," *Sport and Society: An Anthology,* eds. John T. Talamini and Charles H. Page (Boston: Little, Brown, 1973), pp. 163-182.
68. Educational Policies Commission, *School Athletics* (Washington, D.C.: National Educational Association, 1954).
69. Ibid.
70. Willard Waller, *The Sociology of Teaching* (New York: John Wiley and Sons, 1965), pp. 114-115.
71. Meschery, "There is a Disease in Sports Now," p. 58.
72. Schafer, "Sport, Socialization and the School," pp. 13-14.
73. For a complete description of the George Davis experiment, see Neil Amdur, *The Fifth Down: Democracy and the Football Revolution* (New York: Delta Books, 1972). In 1977 at least two college basketball teams—Eastern Washington and Northern Colorado—were using this radical approach.
74. Some critics in Willits, a community where Davis wanted to establish this system, were upset with it. They accused Davis of shirking responsibility, promoting disunity, and aiding communist agitators. The irony is that these evils were the presumed consequences of a democratic system.
75. Amdur, *The Fifth Down: Democracy and the Football Revolution*, p. 218.
76. Edwards, *Sociology of Sport,* p. 361.

52

Sport and Religion 5

On the one hand, there may seem to be little in common between sport and religion; going to church on Sunday, singing hymns, studying the Bible, worshipping God all seem quite alien to the activities that we associate with sport. On the other hand, it has been contended that contemporary sport has all the trappings of formal religion. It has its gods: superstar athletes; its saints: those who have passed to the great beyond, such as Vince Lombardi, Knute Rockne, Jim Thorpe, George Gipp, etc.; its scribes: the sports journalists and sportscasters, who disseminate the "word" of sports deeds and glories; its houses of worship: the Astrodome, Yankee Stadium; and masses of highly vocal "true believers." Indeed, Harry Edwards has argued that "if there is a universal popular religion in America it is to be found within the institution of sport."[1]

While it may be too superficial to suggest that sport has many of the characteristics of religion, it is nevertheless true that the two have become increasingly intertwined, and that each is making inroads into the traditional activities and prerogatives of the other. In previous generations, Sunday was the day reserved for church and worship, but with the increase in opportunity for recreational pursuits, both as participant and spectator, and the virtual explosion in televised sports, worship on weekends has been replaced by worship of weekends.[2] As a result, sport has captured Sunday, and churches have had to revise their schedules to oblige sport. At most Roman Catholic churches, convenient Saturday late afternoon and evening services are now featured in addition to traditional Sunday masses, and other denominations frequently schedule services to accommodate the viewing of professional sports events. In a three-part series on "Religion in Sport" for *Sports Illustrated,* Frank Deford noted that "the churches have ceded Sunday to sports. . . . Sport owns Sunday now, and religion is content to lease a few minutes before the big games."[3]

At the same time that sports seem to be usurping religion's traditional time for worship and services, many churches and religious leaders are attempting to weld a link between the two activities by sponsoring sports events under religious auspices and/or proselytizing athletes to religion and then using them as missionaries to spread the "word" and recruit new members. Thus, contemporary religion uses sport for the promotion of its causes.

Sport uses religion as well, and in more ways than just seizing the traditional day of worship. For those involved in sports—as participants or as spectators—numerous activities with religious connotations are employed in connection with the contests. Ceremonies, rituals, taboos, fetishes, and so forth, all of which are part of religious practices, are standard observances in the world of sport.

In this chapter, we shall examine the multidimensional relationship between two universal social institutions—religion and sport.

Religion and Society

The Province of Religion

Religion is the belief that supernatural forces influence human lives. According to J. Milton Yinger, a leading scholar in the sociology of religion, religion is "a system of beliefs and practices by means of which a group of people struggle with those ultimate problems of human life. It is the refusal to capitulate to death, to give up in the face of frustration, to allow hostility to tear apart one's human association."[4] As a social institution, religion is a system that functions to maintain and transmit beliefs about forces considered to be supernatural and sacred. It provides codified guides for moral conduct and prescribes symbolic practices deemed to be in harmony with beliefs about the supernatural.[5] For all practical purposes, the universality of religious behavior among human beings may be assumed, since ethnologists and anthropologists have not yet discovered a human group without traces of behavior we call "religious."[6]

Societies have a wide range of forms and activities associated with religion, including special officials (priests), ceremonies, rituals, sacred objects, places of worship, pilgrimages, and so forth. In modern societies, religious leaders have developed elaborate theories or theologies to explain the place of humans in the universe. Moreover, the world religions—Christianity, Hinduism, Buddhism, Confucianism, Judaism, and Muhammadanism—are cores of elaborate cultural systems that have dominated world societies for centuries.

Social Functions of Religion

The term "social functions" as used here refers to the contribution that religion makes to the maintenance of human societies; the focus is on what religion does, with what it contributes to the survival and maintenance of societies and groups.[7]

Religions exist because they perform important functions for society and the individual. At the individual level, psychic needs are met by religious experience. The unpredictable and sometimes dangerous world produces personal fears and general anxiety that reverence for the powers of nature, or seeking cooperation through religious faith and ritual, may alleviate. Fears of death are also made bearable by beliefs in a supernatural realm into which a believer passes.

Religion also assigns moral meaning and makes comprehensive human experiences, which might seem otherwise a "tale told by an idiot, full of sound and fury, signifying nothing." If one can believe in a God-given scheme of things, the universal quest for ultimate meaning is validated, and human strivings and sufferings seem to make some sense. Finally, the need to celebrate human abilities and achievements and the sense of transcendence are met and indeed fostered by many religions through ceremonies and rituals that celebrate humans and their activities.[8]

For the society, one function of religion is so crucial that it almost includes all the others—social integration. Religion promotes a binding together, both of the members of a society and of social obligations that help to unite them. August Comte, considered by many as the founder of sociology, believed that a common belief system held people together. Comte summarized the function of religion as an integrative tool in this way:

> Our being is thus knit together, within and without, by a complete convergence both of the feelings and of the thoughts towards that Supreme Power which controls our acts. At this point there arises Religion in its true sense, that is, a complete unity, whereby all the motives of conduct within us are reduced to a common object, whilst our conduct as a whole submits with freedom to the necessity imposed by a power without.[9]

Religion is an important integrative force in society because it organizes the individual's experience in terms of ultimate meanings that include but also transcend the individual. When many people share this ordering principle, they can deal with each other in meaningful ways and can even transcend themselves and their individual egotisms, sometimes even to the point of self-sacrifice.[10]

Since all human social relationships are dependent on symbols of one kind or another, religion supplies the ultimate symbols, the comprehensive ones, the ones on which all other ones make sense. As Smelser has said: "Religion is a symbolic canopy stretched out over the network of social institutions, giving them an appearance of stability and 'rightness' that they would otherwise lack. In this manner, religion functions to maintain and perpetuate social institutions."[11]

Religious ceremonies and rituals also promote integration, since they serve to reaffirm some of the basic customs and values of society. Here, the societal customs, folkways, and observances are symbolically elevated to the realm of the sacred. In Johnstone's words: "In expressing common beliefs about the nature of reality and the supernatural, in engaging in joint ritual and worship activities, in retelling the sagas and myths of the past, the group (society) is brought closer together and linked with the ancestral past."[12]

Another important integrative function religion performs is to bring persons with diverse backgrounds into meaningful relationships with each other. To the extent that religious groups can reach people who feel isolated and abandoned and are not being relieved of their problems elsewhere, to that extent religion is serving society.

Religion also serves as a vehicle for social control; that is, religious tenets constrain the behavior of the community of believers to keep them in line with the norms, values, and beliefs of society. In all the major religions, there is an intertwining of religion and morals, and schemes of other worldly reward or punishment for behavior, such as that found in Christianity, become a powerful force for morality; the fear of hell fire and damnation has been a powerful deterrent in the control of Christian societies. The virtues of honesty, conformity to sexual codes, and all the details of acceptable moral behavior in a society become merged with the religious beliefs and practices.

A third social function of religion is what Smelser calls "social structuration," which means that religion tends to legitimize the secular social structures within a society. There is a strong tendency for religious ideology to become united with the norms and values of secular structures, producing, as a consequence, religious support for the values and institutions of society.[13]

From its earliest existence, religion has provided rationales that served the needs and actions of leaders. It has legitimized as "God-given" such disparate ideologies as absolute monarchies and democratic forms of government. Moreover, when obedience to the social agents of control is interpreted as a religious duty and disobedience is interpreted as sinful, this social function of religion is well served.

The Changing Relationship of Sport and Religion

Primitive Societies

According to Rudolph Brasch, athletic activities began as religious rites: "Its roots were in man's desire to gain victory over foes seen and unseen, to influence the forces of nature, and to promote fertility among his crops and cattle."[14] The Zũni Indians of New Mexico played games which they believed would bring rain and thus enable their crops to grow. In southern Nigeria, wrestling matches were held to encourage the growth of crops, and various games were played in the winter to hasten the return of spring and to ensure a bountiful season. One Eskimo tribe, at the end of the harvest season, played a cup-and-ball game to "catch the sun" and thus delay its departure. Playing games was a way for these primitive peoples to assure revival of nature and the victory of vegetation.[15]

The Ancient Greeks

The ancient Greeks worshipped beauty and entwined religious observance with their athletic demonstrations in such a way that it is difficult to define where one left off and the other began. Greek gods were anthropomorphic and sculptors portrayed the gods as perfect physical specimens, to be both admired and emulated by their worshippers. The strong anthropomorphic conceptions of gods held by the Greeks led to their belief that gods took pleasure in the same things as mortals—music, drama, and displays of physical excellence. The gymnasia located in every city-state for all male adults provided facilities and a place for sports training as well as for discussions of intellectual topics. Furthermore, there were facilities for religious worship; an altar and a chapel were located in the center of each gymnasium.

The most important athletic meetings of the Greeks were part of religious festivals: the Olympic games were held in honor of Zeus, king of the Greek gods; the Pythian games took place as a festival in honor of Apollo; the Isthmian games were dedicated to the god Poseidon; and the Nemean games were held in honor of Zeus. Victorious athletes presented their gifts of thanks upon the altar of the god or gods whom they thought to be responsible for their victory. The end of the ancient Olympic games was a result of the religious convictions of Theodosius, the Roman emperor between 392 and 395 A.D. He was a Christian and decreed the end of the games as part of his suppression of paganism in favor of Christianity.[16]

The Early Christian Church

Religious support for sport found no counterpart to the Greeks in Western societies until the beginning of the 20th century. The Roman Catholic church came to dominate society in Western Europe from 400 A.D. until the Reformation in the 16th century, and since then Roman Catholicism has shared religious power with Protestant groups.

At first opposing Roman sport spectacles, such as chariot racing and gladiatorial shows, because of the paganism and brutality, the Christians eventually came to regard the human body as an instrument of sin. The early Christians did not view sports as evil *per se* for the Apostle Paul wrote approvingly of the benefits of physical activity;[17] but the paganism prominent in the Roman sports events was abhorrent to the Christians. Moreover, early Christianity gradually built a foundation based on asceticism, which is a belief that evil exists in the body, and, therefore, the body should be subordinate to the pure spirit. As a result, church dogma and education sought to subordinate all desires and demands of the body to exalt the spiritual life. St. Bernard argued: "Always in a robust and active body the mind lies soft and more lukewarm; and, on the other hand, the spirit flourishes more strongly and more actively in an infirm and weakly body."[18] Nothing could have been more damning for the promotion of active recreation and sport.

Until the Reformation, spiritual salvation was the dominating feature in the Christian faith. According to this view, the cultivation of the body must be subordinated to salvation of the spirit, especially since the body can obstruct the realization of this aim. An otherwise enlightened Renaissance scholar, Desiderius Eramus, while a monk at a monastery (before he became a critic of Roman Catholicism), wrote an essay "On the Contempt of the World," in which is articulately characterized the Christian attitude toward body and soul:

> The monks do not choose to become like cattle; they know that there is something sublime and divine within man which they prefer to develop rather than cater for the body. . . . Our body, except for a few details, differs not from an animal's body but our soul reaches out after things divine and eternal. The body is earthly, wild, slow, mortal, diseased, ignoble; the soul on the other hand is heavenly, subtle, divine, im-

> mortal, noble. Who is so blind that he cannot tell the difference between body and soul? And so the happiness of the soul surpasses that of the body.[19]

The Reformation and the Rise of Protestantism

The Reformation of the early 16th century signaled the end of the vicelike grip that Roman Catholicism had on the minds and habits of the people of Europe and England. With this religious conversion, one might think that the pejorative view of sports might have perished where the teachings of Martin Luther and John Calvin prevailed. But Protestantism had within it the seeds of a new asceticism, and the Calvinism imported to England, in its Puritan form, became a greater enemy to sport than Roman Catholicism had been.

Puritan influence grew throughout the 16th century, and by early 17th century had come to have considerable influence on English life. Moreover, since Puritans were some of the earliest English immigrants to America, they had considerable influence on the social life in the colonies. Perhaps no Christian group had greater opposition to sports than the Puritans. Dennis Brailsford asserted that "the Puritans saw their mission to erase all sport and play from men's lives."[20] They gave England the "English Sunday" and the equivalent in the United States, the blue laws, which, until a few decades ago, managed to debar sports on the Sabbath and severely limit the kinds of sports that were considered appropriate for a Christian. As a means of realizing amusement and unrestrained impulses, sport was suspect for the Puritan, and as it approached mere pleasure or involved physical harm to participants or animals (boxing, cockfighting), or involved gambling, sport was, of course, altogether evil. The English historian, Macaulay, claimed that the Puritans opposed bearbaiting not so much because it was painful for the bear but because it gave pleasure to the spectators.[21]

Religion and Sport from the Colonial Period to the 20th Century

The principal relationship of the church and sports in the American colonies was restriction and probation, especially with regard to sports on the Sabbath. Legislation prohibiting sports participation on Sunday began soon after the first English settlement in the colonies and was enacted by a group of Virginia ministers. But such repressive acts are more commonly associated with the Puritans in New England because they, too, enacted legislation of this type. Actually, most of the colonies passed laws against play and sport on the Sabbath, and it was not until mid-20th century that industrial and economic conditions brought about the repeal of most of these laws, although most had been annulled by custom.[22]

There were a number of reasons for Protestant prejudice toward play and sport in the colonies. One prominent objection was that participation would detract attention away from spiritual matters. There was also the belief that play and its resultant pleasure might become addictive because of the inherent weakness of human nature. There was, of course, the practical matter that survival in the colonies and on the frontier required hard work from everyone, and, thus, time spent in play and games was typically considered time wasted. Finally, the associations formed and the environment in which play and sport occurred conspired to cast these activities in a bad light. The tavern was the center for gambling and table sports, dancing had obvious sexual overtones, and field sports often involved gambling and cruelty to animals.

Churchly opposition to leisure pursuits was firmly maintained in the first few decades of the new republic, and each effort to liberalize attitudes of habits toward leisure pursuits was met with new attacks on sport as "sinful." Sports were still widely regarded by the powerful Protestant religious groups as snares of the Devil himself. But social problems became a prominent concern of social reformers beginning in the 1830s, many of whom were clergy and intellectual leaders. Crusades against slavery, intemperance, industrial working conditions, and support for the emancipation of women, public education, and industrial reform was widespread; indeed, every facet of American life came under scrutiny, and one aspect of this comprehensive social reform movement was the concern for human health and physical fitness.

Social conditions had begun to change rapidly under the aegis of industrialization—the population shifted from rural residence to urban, labor changed from daylong agricultural toil to toil for wages under squalid working and living conditions. The physical health of the population became a major problem, leading a number of reformers to propose that people would be happier, more productive, and have better health if they engaged in vigorous sports activities. Surprisingly, some of the leading advocates of play and sport were clerics, and from their pulpits they presented forceful arguments that physical prowess and sanctity were not incompatible. Intellectual leaders joined the movement. Ralph Waldo Emerson said: "Out upon the scholars . . . with their pale, sickly, etiolated indoor thought! Give me the out-of-door thoughts of sound men, thoughts all fresh and blooming."[23] Esteemed poet and novelist, Oliver Wendell Holmes joined the attack on the physical condition of the youth. He wrote:

> I am satisfied that such a set of black-coated, stiff jointed, soft-muscled, paste complexioned youth as we can boast in our Atlantic cities never before sprang from the loins of Anglo-Saxon lineage.[24]

Holmes argued that widespread participation in sports would make for a more physically fit citizenry, as well as create a more exciting environment.

The proposals of support for physical fitness and wholesome leisure had a profound effect on the church. Responding to the temporal needs of the people, the clergy began to shed much of the other-worldly emphasis and seek to alleviate immediate human problems. Recognizing the need for play and the health benefits of leisure amusements, the church began to soften its attitude toward play and sports. In summarizing the change that occurred, sports historian Guy Lewis said:

> Sport, within a few decades of the 1856 to 1860 period, became an integral part of the life in the nation. Its emergence began with the concern of a few intellectuals for the health and well-being of their fellow countrymen. Although the "Muscular Christianity" phase of social reform directly affected only a small segment of the population, its total impact must be measured in terms of the end result—the establishment of a new American institution.[25]

Although the development of a more liberal attitude toward sport by church leaders began to appear in the antebellum period, not all church authorities subscribed to the trend. The staid Congregationalist magazine, the *New Englander,* vigorously attacked sport:

> Let our readers, one and all, remember that we were sent into this world, not for sport and amusement, but for labor; not to enjoy and please ourselves, but to serve and glorify God, and be useful to our fellow men. That is the great object and end in life. In pursuing this end, God has indeed permitted us all needful diversion and recreation. . . . But the great end of life after all is work. . . . It is a true saying . . . *"We come into this world, not for sports."* We were sent here for a higher and nobler object.[26]

In official publications and public speeches, some church leaders fought the encroaching sport and leisure mania throughout the latter 19th century. Militant organizations, such as the American Sabbath Union, the Sunday League of America, and the Lord's Day Alliance, were visible proof of the vitality of the strong forces still mobilized in support of this phase of Protestant doctrine.[27] But there was a growing awareness that churches were fighting a losing war. Churchmen gradually began to reconcile play and religion, as medical, educational, and political leaders emphasized that physical, mental, and, indeed, moral health was developed through games and sports. City churches began to minister to the social, physical, and economic needs of their members and residents in the neighborhood, extending their role beyond just preaching salvation of the soul. To meet the social needs of rural and city members, churches adopted sports and sponsored recreations to draw people together, and church leadership played an important role in the promotion of community recreation and school physical education in the latter 19th century. Many clergy used their church halls and grounds as recreation centers for the neighborhood. Rainwater proposed that the beginning of the playground movement in America began in 1885, when the sand gardens were opened in the yards of West End Nursery and Parmenter Street Chapel in Boston.[28] The New York City Society for Parks and Playgrounds was begun in 1890 with the support of clergymen, who delivered sermons to their congregations on children's need for playgrounds.[29]

Support for physical education found its way into denominational journals and meetings, and religious support for physical education played an important role in its acceptance into colleges and eventual adoption by public school boards across the country. The Young Men's Christian College at Springfield, Massachusetts (now Springfield College), made sport and physical fitness one of the cornerstones of a proper Christian education and life-style.

Increasingly, churches broadened their commitment to play and sport endeavors as a means of drawing people together. Bowling leagues, softball leagues, and youth groups, such as the Catholic Youth Organization (CYO), were sponsored by churches for their young members. The church's prejudice against pleasure through play had broken down almost completely by the beginning of the 20th century.

Religion and Sport in 20th-Century America

Churches have been confronted with ever-increasing changes in the 20th century; economic pressures, political tendencies, and social conditions have been the chief forces responsible for the drastically changed relationship between religion and sport. Increased industrialization turned the population into a nation of urban dwellers, while higher wages were responsible for an unprecedented affluence. The gospel of work (Protestant work ethic) has become no longer acceptable to everyone, and increased leisure has enhanced the popularity of sports. The story of changes in the attitudes of religionists in the 20th century "is largely one of accelerating accommodation." Much of Protestant America has come "to view sport as a positive force for good and even as an effective tool to promote the Lord's work."[30] Sports and leisure activities have become an increasingly conspicuous part of the recreation program of thousands of churches and many church colleges. Swanson summarized the new role of the church:

> Throughout the twentieth century, the church has moved steadily further into recreation. Camping programs, athletic leagues, organized game periods at various group meetings, and even full-time recreation directors are all evidences of a positive relationship between religion and play.[31]

Perhaps the best example of the change in the symbolic relationship between religion and sport within the last century occurred at the dedication of a Sports Bay in the Cathedral of St. John the Divine in New York in 1929. At the ceremony, Bishop William T. Manning said:

> Clean, wholesome well-regulated sport is a most powerful agency for true and upright living. . . . True sport and true religion should be in the closest touch and sym-

> pathy. . . . A well played game of polo or of football is in its own way as pleasing to God as a beautiful service of worship in the Cathedral.[32]

The Roman Catholic and Protestant clergymen who over the centuries had preached that sport was a handmaiden of the devil must have shifted uneasily in their graves at such an oration. Times had certainly changed, the church included, and reconciliation between sports and organized religion had approached finality. Perhaps the change in church attitude toward sports is best described by Cozens and Stumpf: "If you can't lick 'em, join 'em!"[33]

Sport as Religion

In the past two decades, the power and influence of sport has increased enormously, while at the same time formalized religion and the institutional church has suffered a decline of interest and commitment. Sport has taken on so many of the characteristics of religion that some have argued that sport has emerged as a new religion, supplementing, and in some cases even supplanting, the traditional religious expressions.[34] Rogers contends that "sports are rapidly becoming the dominant ritualistic expression of the reification of established religion in America."[35]

A few examples will illustrate how organized sports has taken on the trappings of religion. Every religion has its idols (saints and high priests) who are venerated by its members. Likewise, sports fans have persons whom they worship: the saints who are now dead, such as Knute Rockne, Babe Ruth, and, of course, Vince Lombardi, who earned a place among the saints for his fierce discipline and the articulation of the basic commandment of contemporary sport—"Winning is the only thing." The high priests of contemporary sports, such as George Allen, "Bear" Bryant (whom some have claimed can "walk on water"), and "Woody" Hayes direct the destinies of large masses of followers.

In addition to the fundamental commandment of sport, according to St. Vince, numerous proverbs fill the world of sport: "Nice guys finish last"; "When the going gets tough, the tough get going"; "Lose is a four-letter word"; etc. These proverbs are frequently written on posters and hung in locker rooms for athletes to memorize.[36]

The achievements of athletes and teams are manifested in numerous shrines built throughout the country to commemorate and glorify sporting figures. These "halls of fame" have been built for virtually every sport played in America, and some sports have several halls of fame devoted to them. According to Redmond:

> Athletes become "immortal heroes" as they are "enshrined" in a sports hall of fame, when "devoted admirers" gaze at their "revered figures" or read plaques "graven in marble" before departing "often very moved" (or even "teary-eyed") from the many "hushed rooms, filled with nostalgia." This is the jargon of the churches of sport in the twentieth century.[37]

Symbols of fidelity abound in sports. The athletes are expected to give total commitment to the cause, including abstinence from smoking, alcohol, and, in some cases, even sex. The devout followers who witness and invoke traditional and hallowed chants show their devotion to the team and add "spirit" to its cause. It is not unusual for these pilgrims to travel hundreds of miles, sometimes braving terrible weather conditions, to witness a game, as a display of their fidelity.

Like religious institutions, sport has become a function of communal involvement. One cheers for the Green Bay Packers, the New York Yankees, or the Denver Nuggets. The emotional attachment of some fans for their teams verges on the religious fanaticism previously seen in holy wars against heretics and pagans. Opposing teams and their fans, as well as officials, are occasionally attacked and brutally beaten.

Religion Uses Sport

Churches Sponsor Sports for Social Service and Integration

From a position of strong opposition to recreation and sport activities, the church has made a complete reversal within the past century, and now heartily supports these activities as effective tools to promote "the Lord's work." Social service is a major purpose behind religious leaders providing play and recreation under the auspices of the church. Church-sponsored recreation and sport programs provide a service to its members, and sometimes the entire community, that is often unavailable in an accepted form anywhere else. Church playgrounds and recreation centers in urban areas have facilities, equipment, and instruction that municipal governments often cannot provide. YMCA, YWCA, CYO, and other church-related organizations have performed a variety of social services for old and young alike, one of which is the sponsorship of sports leagues.

The church also promotes sport to strengthen and increase fellowship among the congregation, which has been beneficial to the church as well as to its members. At a time when churches were just beginning their extensive support for recreational and sports programs, one clergyman said: ". . . there is a selfish reason why the church should offer recreation of some sort—because it aids the church and enlivens the people."[38] In a time of increasing secularization, such as the United States has witnessed in the past 50 years, it is understandable why churches would accommodate activities that solidify and integrate membership.

Religious Leaders Use Sport

Not content to merely provide recreational and sports opportunities under the sponsorship of the church, some religious leaders outwardly avow the association between religion and sport in their preaching. Bob Richards, an Olympic pole-vault champion and a minister, said: "I motivate people with sports stories and witness to my Christian faith. . . . Pastors should get out of their pulpits and into sports."[39] One example of this approach is evangelist Mike Crain, director of the Judo and Karate for Christ Camp in Kentucky, who practices "karate for Christ" by splitting 10 inches of concrete with his hand in a demonstration of God's power.[40]

One of the most popular contemporary evangelists, Billy Graham, enthusiastically supports the virtues of sports competition and the sanctity of Christian coaches and athletes. He has made sports a basic metaphor in his ministry. According to Graham, the basic source of Christianity, the Bible, legitimates sport involvement. He has said: "The Bible says leisure and lying around are morally dangerous for us. . . . Sports keep us busy."[41]

Church Colleges Use Sport

Intercollegiate sports programs were originally organized and administered by the students merely for their own recreation and amusement. But the programs gradually changed form and character by the early years of the 20th century, and one of the new features that emerged was the use of the collegiate sports teams to publicize the school and bind alumni to their alma mater. Church-supported colleges and universities—both Roman Catholic and Protestant—began to use their athletic teams to attract students, funds, and public attention to impoverished and often academically inferior institutions. The classic, but by no means only, example is Notre Dame.[42] Recently, the chaplain of the Notre Dame athletic department acknowledged that the athletic program had been used to promote the university. He said: "Of course Catholic schools used athletics for prestige. Notre Dame would not be the great school it is today, the great academic institution, were it not for football."[43]

The most recent example of a religious university deliberately using intercollegiate athletics for its promotion is Oral Roberts University in Tulsa, Oklahoma. When evangelist Oral Roberts founded this university in 1965, one of his first actions was the establishment of an athletic program to bring recognition and prestige to the university. With respect to the program, Roberts has said:

> Athletics is part of our Christian witness. . . . Nearly every man in America reads the sports pages, and a Christian school cannot ignore these people. . . . Sports are becoming the No. 1 interest of people in America. For us to be relevant, we had to gain the attention of millions of people in a way that they could understand.[44]

Religious Organizations for Athletes

One of the most notable outgrowths of religion's use of sport has been the nondenominational religious organizations composed of coaches and athletes that provide a variety of programs designed to recruit new members to religion. The first of these groups was the Fellowship of Christian Athletes (FCA), which was founded in 1954. The avowed purpose of the FCA is "to confront athletes and coaches and through them the youth of the nation, with the challenge and adventure of following Christ and serving him through the fellowship of the church. . . ."[45] It attempts "to combat juvenile delinquency, to elevate the moral and spiritual standards of sports in an unprincipled secular culture; to challenge Americans to stand up and be counted for or against God and to appeal to sports enthusiasts and American youth through hero worship harnessed."[46]

The FCA uses older athletes and coaches to recruit younger ones to Christ; it has a mailing list of more than 55,000 persons and a staff of more than 35. Its most important single activity is the annual week-long summer conferences attended by more than 10,000 participants, where coaches and athletes mix religious and inspirational sessions with sports instruction and competition. With regard to the activity at these conferences, the executive director of the FCA said: "It's 50 percent inspirational and 50 percent perspirational."[47] Another important facet of the FCA is the high school and college group session programs known as the "huddle-fellowship program" in which high school and college athletes in a community or campus get together to talk about their faith, engage in Bible study, and pray. They also engage in projects such as serving as "big brothers" for delinquent or needy children, visiting nursing homes, and serving as playground instructors. There are now some 1,600 high school huddles in the United States and more than 200 college fellowships, the bulk of which are found in the South, Southwest, and Midwest. Most of the members are white, middle-class boys; however, in recent years, female athletes have been admitted to the FCA, and their membership in the organization is growing rapidly. In addition to these activities, FCA sponsors state and regional retreats, provides various informational materials such as films, records, tapes, and it publishes a monthly periodical *The Christian Athlete.*

Another religious group formed mostly by former athletes is a division of the Campus Crusade for Christ and is called Athletes in Action (AIA). With a special dispensation from the NCAA, the AIA fields several athletic teams made up of former college athletes. These teams compete against amateur teams throughout the country each year, and as part of each appearance the AIA athletes make brief evangelical speeches and testimonials to the crowds and distribute free religious materials.[48]

Other organizations also enlist the assistance of athletes in spreading the gospel. The Pro Athletes Outreach (PAO) was founded largely as an intramural peacekeeping force because the AIA and the FCA were squabbling over enlisting the best missionary athletes for their programs. The PAO sends phalanxes of professional athletes on what it calls "speaking blitzes" of the country. The athletes deliver religious and testimonial speeches to groups of largely young people. An officer previously with the AIA has recently set up the Institute for Athletic Perfection in Prescott, Arizona.

Religion Uses Athletes and Coaches to Attract Converts

Of all of the purposes and/or consequences of religion's association with sport, certainly one of the most important is the use of athletes, coaches, and the play environment to recruit new members to the church. The use of play as a "drawing card" has been a major consideration of many religious leaders. An often used slogan nicely sums up this principle: "There are many a one who comes to play and remains to pray." Getting persons into church recreation and sports programs is often viewed as a first step into the church and into Christian life. Playgrounds and recreation centers in or near churches, and the supervision of these facilities by clergy or lay persons with a strong religious commitment, provide a convenient setting for converting the non-church-going participant. A great deal of "informal" missionary work is done in these settings, often resulting in conversions to religion. However, due to the prominence and prestige of famous athletes and coaches, religious leaders have realized that they could be used as effective missionaries, and virtually every religious group has used coaches and athletes to recruit new members.

In a three-part series for *Sports Illustrated,* Frank Deford reported that "the use of athletes as amateur evangelists is so widespread that it might be fairly described as a growth industry." He goes on to observe that it "is almost as if a new denomination has been created: Sportianity."[49] *The Wittenburg Door,* a contemporary religious journal, has derisively labeled this movement, "Jocks for Jesus."[50]

The practice of using "jock evangelists" is explained by one of the directors of FCA in this way: "Athletes and coaches . . . have a platform in this country. Athletes have power, a voice."[51] Billy Zeioli, one of the "Sportianity's" leading evangelists, said: ". . . the fact is the people view athletes . . . as stars, and we can't change that. So we say: let's . . . teach them to be right and moral, and then take them to the people."[52] Another advantage of using athletes to reach other athletes is access. As one former AAU wrestling champion and AIA assistant athletic director noted: ". . . I can get into a fraternity, a locker room, where nobody else would be permitted."[53]

Athletes and coaches are used to sell religion. The technique is fairly straight-forward and simple: Those who are already committed to religion convert the athletes. Since athletes are among the most visible and prestigious persons in our society, they may be used for "missionary work" in spreading the gospel to their teammates and others with whom they interact.[54] As Deford observed: "Jesus has been transformed, emerging anew as a holler guy, hustler, a give-it-100-percenter."[55] Combining the popular appeal they have as celebrities with the metaphors of the sports world, athletes are able to catch and hold the attention of large groups of people. Roger Staubach, Dallas Cowboy quarterback, in a pep talk on "the game of life" at the International Student Congress on Evangelism, said: "the goal we must get across is our salvation . . . [and] God has given us a good field position."[56]

Sportianity and Social Issues

There is little inclination on the part of religious leaders and the various organizations that make up Sportianity to confront the pressing social issues of sport or the larger society. Virtually all of the leaders in the Sportianity movement are fundamentalists who preach a conservative theology. They are generally reluctant to take a stand on moral issues within sports or the wider society. According to Frank Deford: "In the process of dozens of interviews with people in Sportianity, not one even remotely suggested any direct effort was being considered to improve the morality of athletics."[57]

In an interview with the directors of the communications department of the FCA, the editor for *The Wittenburg Door* asked: "Your magazine is the mouthpiece of FCA. Do you see your role as trying to change athletics?" The response was: "The FCA board and officers would not see that. . . . Stick with the positive, don't deal with the evils in athletics . . . the board would rather have us not stir the waters. Just print the good story about the good ole' boy who does good things."[58]

The various Sportianity organizations and their members have not spoken out against racism, sexism, cheating in sport, the evils of recruiting, or any of the other well-known unethical practices, excesses, and abuses in the sports world. Deford articulately described this indifference to sports problems:

> Sportianity does not question the casual brutality—spearing, clotheslining, gouging—that sends players . . . to the hospital every year. It does not censure the intemperate behavior of coaches like Woody Hayes and Bobby Knight.[59]

In the final analysis, sports morality does not appear to have been improved by the Sportianity movement. Instead, Sportianity seems willing to accept sports as is, more devoted to maintaining the status quo than resolving the many problems in sport today.

Value Orientations of Religion and Sport

The value orientations underlying competitive sports in America may seem remotely connected with religion, but most of those that are central to sports are more or less secularized versions of the core values of Protestantism, which has been the dominant religious belief system throughout American history.

The classic treatise on the Protestant ethic and its relationship to other spheres of social life is Max Weber's *The Protestant Ethic and the Spirit of Capitalism,* originally published near the turn of the century.[60] The essence of Weber's thesis is that there is a relationship—a parallel—between the Calvinist doctrine of Protestantism as a theological belief system and the growth of capitalism as a mode of economic organization. Weber understood the relationship between Protestantism and capitalism as one of mutual influence; he used the term "elective affinity."[61] The relationship existed in this way: For John Calvin, God could foresee and, therefore, know the future; thus, the future was predestined. In a world whose future was foreordained, the fate of every person was preestablished. Each person was, then, saved or doomed from birth by a kind of divine decree; nothing the individual did could change what God had done. Although each person's fate was sealed, the individual craved for some visible sign of his fate, and since Calvin taught that those elected by God acted in a godly manner, the elected could exhibit their salvation by glorifying God, especially by their work in this world. According to Weber, "the only way of living acceptably to God . . . was through the fulfillment of obligations imposed upon the individual by . . . his calling."[62] Thus, the best available sign of being among the chosen was to do one's job, to follow one's profession, to succeed in one's chosen career. According to Weber, "In practice this means that God helps those who help themselves."[63] Work per se was exhalted; indeed, it was sacred. The clearest manifestation of being chosen by God was success in one's work. Whoever enjoyed grace could not fail, since success at work was visible evidence of election. Thus, successful persons could think of themselves, and be thought of by others, as the righteous persons. The upshot was that this produced an extreme drive toward individual achievement resulting in what Weber called "ascetic Protestantism"—a life of strict discipline and hard work as the best means of glorifying God.

Although the Protestant ethic gave divine sanction to the drive to excel and encouraged success in business, industry, and science, it condemned the material enjoyment of success. The chosen person merely used success to document salvation. Persons who used success for personal gratification and luxury merely showed that they were doomed by God. To avoid the accumulation of vast personal wealth, Calvinism promoted the reinvestment of profits to produce more goods, which created more profits and, in turn, represented more capital for investment, ad infinitum—the essence of entrepreneurial capitalism. In addition, the avoidance of waste, distractions, and pleasure, the reliance on technical knowledge, and functional rationality were advocated as a means of demonstrating salvation.

Weber's study of the relationship between religious beliefs and capitalism investigated the religious principles that provided a rationale for the ideology of capitalism and for the authority of the capitalist. The spirit of capitalism, according to Weber, consisted of several principles, each of which was compatible to Protestant principles. Collectively, they constituted a clear elective affinity between Calvinist Protestantism and the spirit of capitalism.[64]

What does this have to do with sports? No one who is familiar with contemporary sports and the Protestant ethic can overlook the unmistakable link between them (there is, of course, also a correspondence between capitalistic ideology and modern sports, but that will not be examined here). The emergence of sport as a pervasive feature of

American life undoubtedly owes its development to various social forces, one of which may be Protestant Christianity, the value orientations of which form the basis of the fundamental doctrine of the American sports creed. The notion of a sports creed in American sports was proposed by sociologist Harry Edwards, who suggested that persons involved with sports, especially coaches and athletes, adhere to a particular kind of institutional ideology, the overriding orientation of which is individual achievement through competition.[65] The phrase "ideology of sport" is used as a generic designation for all ideas espoused by or for those who participate in and exercise authority in sports, as they seek to explain and justify their beliefs.

If we place the values inherent in the Protestant ethic and the sports creed side by side, it immediately becomes apparent that the two are congruent. That is, they share a significant equivalence. Without attempting to claim a causal link between the two belief systems, it does seem possible to suggest an elective affinity between them.

The Protestant stress on successful individual achievement is in keeping with the values of sport. The notion that one's achievement stamps the "chosen" from the "doomed" is seen in the "winning is everything" ideology in sports. Winners are the good people; personal worth, both in this and the other world, is equated with winning. The loser is obviously not one of God's chosen people, just as failure in one's occupation stamps the Protestant as doomed to hell.

In the final analysis, the sports creed mirrors the core values of the Protestant ethic and vice versa. Success, self-discipline, and hard work—the original tenets of the ethic—are the most valued qualities of an athlete. The characteristics of the good Christian are also those needed by the successful athlete, and the temper of organized sports is competitive, with an overriding sense of wins and losses. In describing the intercollegiate athletic program at Oral Roberts University, its founder Oral Roberts, said: "Just playing the game is not enough. It's all right to lose some but I'm not much for losing. We're geared up for winning here."[66] The founder of AIA aspires that the teams representing that organization become the best amateur teams in America because he believes that they cannot be effective missionaries if they are losers.[67] The notion that nothing converts like success is confirmed by Dallas Cowboy quarterback, Roger Staubach, who said: "When the Cowboys played Miami in the Super Bowl, I had promised that it would be for God's honor and glory, whether we won or lost. Of course, the glory was better for God and me since we won, because victory gave me a greater platform from which to speak."[68]

The notion that dedication, self-discipline, and sports participation may be an "occupational" calling, is central to the theology of Sportianity. God is glorified best when athletes give totally of themselves in striving for success and victory. As one spokesman for Sportianity put it, no athlete "can afford to discredit Jesus by giving anything less than total involvement with those talents that he has been given in this training and competition.''[69] Just as the businessman is responsible to God to develop his talents to the fullest, so is the athlete equally responsible. If God has granted one athletic abilities, then one is obligated to use these abilities to glorify and honor God; anything less than total dedication to the task is insufficient.[70] Discipline, sacrifice, training, and unremitting work by athletes not only leads to success (''workers are winners''), but they are seen as ways of using God-given ability as a way of glorifying God, an important Protestant requirement. Success can be considered as the justly deserved reward of a person's purposeful, self-denying, God-guided activity.

Any belief system that can help provide athletes and coaches with a rationale for their deep commitment to athletics provides a means for expressing the essence for their striving and is most welcome. Protestant theology does help give expression to the ''essence and striving'' of athletes and coaches. In short, it is a belief system to which the athlete and coach can hold an elective affinity. Whether they actually hold such an elective affinity remains a matter of speculation. Moreover, we hasten to add that although Protestantism certainly is not responsible for the creation of the sports creed, it does provide religious reinforcement for it. According to Edwards, ''There are strong indications that the predominant emphasis upon this orientation in sport does not stem solely from Protestant religious traditions . . . though the latter undoubtedly heightens and legitimizes the achievement value.''[71]

Perhaps it is not coincidental that the belief systems of Protestantism and modern sports are so congruent. The two institutions use similar means to respond to their members' needs. They try to enforce and maintain through a strict code of behavior and ritual a strict belief system that is typically adopted and internalized by all involved in that particular institution. They serve cohesive, integrative, and social control functions for their members, giving them meaningful ways to organize their world. Because of the sacredness nurtured by these systems, both religion and sport resist social change, and, in this way, support the status quo.

Sport Uses Religion

Uses of Religion by Athletes and Coaches

Religious observance and competitive sports constantly impinge on each other, and magico-religious practices of various kinds are found wherever one finds athletics. Religion can be viewed from one point of view as an important means of coping with situations of stress. There are two main categories of stress situations, both of which involve situations in which persons have a great deal of emotional investment in a successful outcome. The first category includes situations in which individuals or groups suffer the death of other persons who are important to them. In the second category are those situations in which largely uncontrolled and unpredictable natural forces may imperil the vital personal and social concerns of an individual or group. Athletic competition falls into the latter category of stress, since competition involves a great deal of uncertainty about the typically important outcome.

Coaches and athletes are well aware of and have great respect for the technical knowledge required for successful performance, but they are also aware of its limitations. As a supplement for the practical techniques, sports participants often employ magico-religious practices in conjunction with sports competition. The coaches and athletes do not believe that these practices make up for their failure to acquire necessary skills or employ appropriate strategy. However, these practices help them to adjust to stress by providing opportunities to dramatize their psychological anxieties, thus reinforcing self-confidence. Religion invokes a sense of "doing something about it" in undertakings of uncertainty in which practical techniques alone cannot guarantee success. The noted anthropologist Bronislaw Malinowski concluded from his research that when the outcome of vital social activities is greatly uncertain, magico-religious or other comparable techniques are inevitably used as a means of allaying tension and promoting adjustment.[72]

Prayer is perhaps the most frequently employed use of religion by athletes—prayer for protection in competition, prayer for good performance, and prayer for victory are three examples. Sometimes the act of prayer is observed by a Roman Catholic crossing himself before shooting a free throw in basketball or a team at prayer in the huddle before a football game. The first historical example of prayer and the direct intervention of gods in sports competition is described by Homer in the *Iliad.* During the funeral games held in honor of Patroclus, who was killed in battle, one of the events was a footrace in which three men compete. Ajax takes the lead from the start, followed closely by Odysseus:

> Thus Odysseus ran close behind him and trod in his footsteps before the dust could settle in them, and on the head of Ajax fell the breath of the godlike hero running lightly and relentlessly on.

As they neared the finish line, Odysseus prays for divine assistance and his prayer is answered by Athene, who not only inspires Odysseus to make a last minute dash but causes Ajax to slip and fall in a mass of cow dung, and Odysseus wins the race. Ajax received an ox as second prize:

> He stood holding the horns of the ox and spitting out dung, and exclaimed: "Curse it, that goddess tripped me up. She always stands by Odysseus like a mother and helps him."[73]

Very little is known about the actual extent to which individual athletes use prayer in conjunction with their participation, but it seems probable that if some athletes are seen praying, others may be doing so without outward, observable signs. In some cases, coaches arrange to have religious services on the Sabbath or on game days. At present, almost every major league baseball and football team—more than 50 of them—hold Sunday chapel services, at home and away, and Sunday services are also held in sports as varied as stock-car racing and golf.[74] One of the claims for this type of service is that the sharing of rituals and beliefs strengthens a group's sense of its own identity and accentuates its "we feeling." The chaplain for Notre Dame athletics says about the game-day mass, ". . . it provides unity."[75] There are probably other reasons why coaches sanction locker room prayers. Sportswriter Larry Merchant suggests that prayer may be used simply because it cannot do any harm: "It might not help, but how much can it hurt? The other coach does it and you can't let him get the edge."[76]

Many sports contests are started with two ceremonies: the playing of the national anthem and a religious invocation. Some invocations are brief and to the point, while in others, clergy use the invocation to conduct a religious service or attempt to dramatize metaphorically the relationship between athletics and religion. An example of the latter was the following invocation delivered at the dinner before the 1976 World Hockey Association All-Star game:

> Heavenly Father, Divine Goalie, we come before You this evening to seek Your blessing. . . . Keep us free from actions that would put us in the Sin Bin of Hell. . . . Help us to stay within the blue line of Your commandments and the red line of Your grace. Protect us from being injured by the puck of pride. May we be ever delivered from the high stick of dishonesty. May the wings of Your angels play at the right and left of our teammates. May You always be the divine Center of our team, and when our summons comes for eternal retirement to the heavenly grandstand, may we find You ready to give us the everlasting bonus of a permanent seat in Your coliseum. Finally, grant us the courage to skate without tripping, to run without icing, and to score the goal that really counts—the one that makes each of us a winner, a champion, and All-Star in the hectic Hockey Game of Life. Amen."[77]

Although there is little empirical work on the use of prayer by athletes and coaches, Marbeto collected data on male baseball, basketball, football, and tennis athletes and coaches from 23 colleges and universities in California. Fifty-five percent of the coaches and athletes indicated that they pray at least sometimes in connection with athletic contests.[78] They pray for a variety of specific reasons, but personal excellence and a winning performance are the most frequently expressed reasons. Most who prayed did so before the contest, fewer did so during the contest, and even fewer did so after the contest.

Marbeto reported that those who pray in athletics are likely to be regular churchgoers with a strong religious upbringing. His data on church attendance and the use of prayer suggested that the prayers for assistance in the game are said primarily out of habit. According to Marbeto:

> Quite often the person who goes to church regularly prays in numerous phases of his daily living. Thus, the athlete who prays at game time probably does it because of his past conditioning, not because the contest elicits such prayers any more that other stressful episodes in his life.[79]

Marbeto further divided his respondents into those at church-affiliated colleges and those at public institutions and found that athletes and coaches at church-affiliated schools indicated that they feel more dependent on a spiritual power or ultimate being than their counterparts at public colleges. There was also considerable difference in the two types of institutions with respect to team prayers. Eighty-two percent of the coaches at church colleges have team prayers in connection with the contest, while only 10 percent of the coaches from the public schools encouraged or set aside time for team prayer.[80]

Marbeto reported that 51 percent of the respondents who prayed believe that the use of prayer may indirectly affect the outcome of the game. One athlete responded: "I never play my best if I haven't recited the Lord's Prayer first." Another said: "My experience tells me that sincere prayer can be the winning factor."[81]

Uses of Magic in Sport

Religion supplies an important means by which humans meet situations of stress. In practice, religion and magic are closely entwined, but there are important distinctions in the two. Both magic and religion are alike in assuming the existence of supernatural powers, but there is a significant difference in the ends they seek. Religion's goals are oriented to the other-worldly, toward a supreme supernatural god, and religion typically centers on overarching issues, such as salvation and the meaning of life and death. While the physical and social welfare of humans is often a concern of religion, it always has a transcendental point of reference, which is not true of magic. The practitioner of magic seeks ends that are in the everyday world of events. Religion is concerned with ultimate issues; magic is oriented toward immediate, practical goals. Moreover, religious worshippers possess an attitude of awe and reverence toward the sacred ends they pursue, but the users of magic are "in business" for practical and arbitrarily chosen ends. The latter are manipulators of the supernatural for their own private ends rather than worshippers of it; the attitude of magic users is likely to be utilitarian. In this respect, Malinowski noted that magic has an end, in pursuit of which the magical ritual is performed. The religious ritual has no purpose—that is, the ritual is not a means to an end but an end in itself. Malinowski said: "While in the magical act the underlying idea and aim is always clear, straightforward and definite, in religious ceremony there is no purpose directed toward a subsequent event." Furthermore, the content of magic and religion differ. The content of magic has no unified inclusive theory but instead tends to be atomistic, somewhat like a book of recipes. On the other hand, religion tends to encompass the whole of life; it often provides the comprehensive theory of both the supernatural and human society.[82]

Magic flourishes in situations of uncertainty and threat; it is most commonly invoked in situations of high anxiety about accomplishing desired ends. The origin of most magical rites can be traced to fears experienced individually or collectively. They are associated with human helplessness in the face of dangers and unpredictability, which give rise to superstitious[83] beliefs and overt practices to ward off impending danger or failure and bring good luck. According to Malinowski:

> We find magic wherever the elements of chance and accident, and the emotional play between hope and fear have a wide and extensive range. We do not find magic wherever the pursuit is certain, reliable, and well under control of rational methods. . . .[84]

In support of this contention, Malinowski compared two forms of fishing among natives of the Trobriand Island of Melanesia: lagoon and open-sea fishing:

> It is most significant that in the lagoon fishing, where man can rely completely upon his knowledge and skill, magic does not exist, while in the open-sea fishing, full of danger and uncertainty, there is extensive magical ritual to secure safety and good results.[85]

Malinowski's thesis about the conditions under which magic appears is applicable to the world of sport. Athletes and coaches are engaged in an activity of uncertain outcome and in which they have a great deal of emotional investment. Even dedicated conditioning and practice, and the acquisition of high-level skill do not guarantee victory because opponents are often evenly matched, and player injury and other dangers are often present. Thus, "getting the breaks" or "lucking out" may be the determining factor in the outcome of a contest. Having a weakly hit baseball fall in for a base hit or a deflected football pass caught by an unintended receiver are examples of luck or "getting the breaks" in sports. Although the cliche "the best team always wins" is part of the folk wisdon of sports, athletes and coaches commonly believe that this is not always so, and indeed believe that factors leading to a win or a loss are somewhat out of their control.

Drawing on Malinowski's theory, it appears that athletes and coaches would use magic to bring them luck and to assure that they "get the breaks," thus supplying them with beliefs that serve to bridge over the uncertainty and threat in their pursuit of victory. It would also enable them to carry out their actions with a sense of assurance and confidence, and to maintain poise and mental integrity in the face of opponents. In Malinowski's words:

> The function of magic is to ritualize man's optimism, to enhance his faith in the victory of hope over fear. Magic expresses the greater value for man of confidence over doubt, of steadfastness over vacillation, of optimism over pessimism.[86]

It is difficult to assess just how extensive the uses of magic are in sport. Stories about athletes and coaches in newspapers and magazines leave little doubt, though, that magical beliefs and practices play a prominent role in the life of athletes and coaches. They tend to employ almost anything imaginable that might ensure "getting the breaks," and this often involves some form of ritualistic superstitious behavior. Indeed, stories about the magical rites that pervade sports make a witch doctor look like a super sophisticate.

Empirical study of magic in sport is virtually nonexistent, but Gregory and Petrie investigated magical practices among members of six intercollegiate athletic teams at a Canadian university and found that the ranking for sport superstitions were similar between team and individual sport athletes. They also reported that team athletes indicated greater support for superstitions related to equipment and its use, order of entering the sports arena, dressing room rituals, repetitive rituals, and sports personalities. Individual sport athletes showed greater support for superstitions related to wearing charms, lucky lane numbers, team cheers, and crossing oneself before participation (table 5-1). They concluded that magical practices were prevalent among athletes of their sample, and "that 137 respondents endorsed 904 superstitions (with repetition) which could be grouped into 40 categories clearly indicating the strength of superstition in sport."[87]

Various forms of magic are practiced in sports—ritual, taboo, fetishes, witchcraft—that coaches and athletes employ to enhance their chances of victory or to protect them from injury.

Rituals

Rituals are standardized actions directed toward entreating or controlling the supernatural powers in regard to some particular situation. There is an almost infinite variety of rituals practiced in sport, since all athletes are free to ritualize any activity they consider important for successful performance. Typically, rituals arise from successful performances. When an athlete plays well, the successful outcome frequently leads to the idea that something must have been done in addition to the actual skill or strategy to have produced the successful outcome; thus successful performance becomes associated with a certain type of behavior. Former professional baseball player and anthropologist George Gmelch related how he attempted to prolong a batting streak through ritual:

> I . . . ate fried chicken every day at 4 P.M., kept my eyes closed during the national anthem and changed sweat shirts at the end of the fourth inning each night for seven consecutive nights until the streak ended.[88]

He also told of one baseball pitcher who had the complex ritual of touching a crucifix in his back pocket, straightening his cap, and then clutching his genitals before each pitch.[89]

Table 5-1. Frequency of Endorsements of Sport Superstitions Among Athletes by Sex.

Sport Superstition Category	Athletes (N = 137) Male (N=66)	Female (N=71)	Overall *f*
Uniform	77	117	194
Equipment	81	25	106
Clothes	52	32	84
Routines	46	27	73
Charms	14	23	37
Food	19	14	33
Numbers	8	17	25
Order or Playing Position	20	12	32
Balls	12	11	23
Coaches' Beliefs	11	8	19
Religion	14	5	19
Repetitive Actions	14	5	19
Spectators' Beliefs	14	3	17
Sports Persons	9	3	12
Speaking	2	10	12
Hair	1	19	20
Dressing Room	15	4	19
Team Cheers	2	11	13
Crossing Self	7	3	10
Personal Beliefs	6	4	10
Jewelery	9	4	13
Coins	10	3	13
Colors	3	3	6
Facilities	4	4	8
Travel	7	0	7
Hands	2	4	6
Date Toss of Coin	5	3	8
Pregame Night	1	6	7
Scoring	0	5	5
Whites	6	1	7
Time	5	1	6
Good Samaritan	5	0	5
Rabbits' Feet	2	0	2
Shaving	2	3	5
Rules	1	2	3
Sex	1	0	1
Weather	2	1	3
Injury	2	0	2
Concentration	0	1	1
Horseshoes	0	1	1
Touching Wood	0	1	1

Adapted from: C. Jane Gregory and Brian M. Petrie, "Superstitions of Canadian Intercollegiate Athletes: An Inter-sport Comparison," *International Review of Sport Sociology* 10 (No. 2, 1975), p. 63.

Coaches, as well as athletes, have their favorite rituals. According to Larry Keith, basketball coaches practice more superstitious rites than a witch doctor:

> When driving to a home game, Michigan's Johnny Orr is careful to avoid being stopped by a particular Ann Arbor traffic light. While waiting in his motel room for a road game, Southern Illinois' Paul Lambert undresses, turns off the heat and watches television for hours under a mound of blankets. Cincinnati's Gale Catlett would rather find a penny before a game than his opponent's playbook. Marshall's Bob Daniels would put his student manager in uniform rather than dress 13 players for a game. Before daring to walk out of his dressing room, Arkansas' Eddie Sutton must shake the hand of each assistant in a prescribed order and then drink a Coca-Cola.[90]

In addition to individual rituals, there are a number of team rituals. In basketball, the ritual of stacking hands is frequently employed just before the team takes the floor to begin the game and after time-outs. The most universal hockey ritual occurs just before the start of a game when players skate in front of their goal and tap the goalie on the pads for "good luck." Green Bay Packer coach Vince Lombardi had his players pat a small Buddha statue for luck.[91] Gmelch reported that one major league baseball team wore the same uniforms in every game during a 16-game winning streak and refused to let them be washed because they feared that their good luck might be washed away with the dirt.[92]

Taboos

A taboo is a strong social norm prohibiting certain actions that are punishable by the group or by magical consequences. There are numerous institutional taboos in each sport and, of course, many personal taboos. Two of the strongest taboos in baseball are crossing the handles of bats and mentioning a no-hitter that the pitcher has in progress. Crossing bats is believed to bring bad luck and mentioning a no-hitter to the pitcher is believed to "break the spell" the pitcher has on the hitters, ending his chances to complete a no-hit game.

Some athletes develop taboos about touching portions of the playing surface, such as not stepping on the chalk foul lines (just like children avoid stepping on sidewalk cracks) or not wearing certain parts of the uniform.

Fetishes

Fetishes are revered objects believed to have magical power to attain the desired ends for the person who possesses or uses them. Fetishes are standard equipment for coaches and athletes. They include a bewildering assortment of objects: rabbits' feet, pictures of heroes or loved ones, pins, coins, remnants of old equipment, certain numbered uniforms, etc. Typically, these objects obtain their power through association with successful performance. For example, if the athlete or coach happens to be wearing or using the object during a victory, the individual attributes the good fortune to the object; it then becomes a fetish embodied with supernatural power. The seriousness with which some athletes take fetishes was described by Gmelch:

> I once saw a fight caused by the desecration of a fetish. Before the game, one player stole the fetish, a horsehide baseball cover, out of a teammate's back pocket. The prankster did not return the fetish until after the game, in which the owner of the fetish went hitless, breaking a batting streak. The owner, blaming his inability to hit on the loss of the fetish, lashed out at the thief when the latter tried to return it.[93]

Judy Becker recently described the numerous rituals, taboos, and fetishes employed by athletes at that bastion of intellect and rationality, Yale University. For example, in hockey, the use of the word "shut-out," as in "let's protect the shut-out," was taboo. Once, in a game in which Yale went into the locker room with a 4-0 lead and someone violated this rule; it disturbed the entire team. Within 10 minutes after the teams returned to the ice, the opponents had tied the score. One of the most common magical practices involved clothes fetishes, such as wearing a particular article of clothing. One track athlete believed that "new shoes go fast," so he got new spikes before each meet. Becker reported that uniform numbers had magical connotations for many athletes, and they would go to great lengths to obtain their lucky number.[94]

Magic and the Malinowski Thesis Applying the Malinowski thesis to baseball players, Gmelch hypothesized that magical practices should be associated more with hitting and pitching than with fielding, since the first two involve a high degree of chance and unpredictability whereas average fielding percentages or success rate is about 97 percent, reflecting almost complete control over the outcome. From his observations as a participant in professional baseball, Gmelch reported that there was indeed a greater incidence and variety of rituals, taboos, and use of fetishes related to hitting and pitching than to fielding. He concluded:

> . . . nearly all of the magical practices that I participated in, observed or elicited, support Malinowski's hypothesis that magic appears in situations of chance and uncertainty. The large amount of uncertainty in pitching and hitting best explains the elaborate magical practices used for these activities. Conversely, the high success rate of fielding, . . . involving much less uncertainty, offers the best explanation for the absence of magic in this realm.[95]

Witchcraft

Magical practices harmful in intent or whose intent is to bring misfortune on others are called black magic or witchcraft. In sport, those who employ this form of magic believe that the supernatural powers are being employed to harm or bring misfortune on opponents. In Africa, witchcraft dominates some sports. Medicine men who claim they can make the ball disappear or cast a spell on opposing players are especially active in soccer. It is estimated that about 95 percent of Kenyan soccer teams hire witch doctors to help them win matches, and matches have been marred by witchcraft-inspired riots.[96]

We may laugh when reading about African soccer teams traveling with a witch doctor but not give a second thought to the clergyman traveling with one of our teams. In discussing this issue, one observer noted:

> In Nairobi, Kenya, one team spent $3,000 on witch doctors last year. Sports leaders there have tried to discourage witchcraft as well as the practice of players painting their bodies with pig fat to ward off evil spirits. Athletic teams in our country, of course, are much too sophisticated to travel with witch doctors and wear pig fat. Our teams travel with clergymen and wear medals.[97]

Actually, witchcraft is not confined to African sports. During the 1975 ABA championship playoff between the Indiana Pacers and the Denver Nuggets, the Pacers employed a witch doctor by the name of Dancing Harry to cast hexes on the Denver players. Denver counteracted with The Wicked Witch of the West, equipped with a cauldron, to mix up evil spirits designed to reduce the Pacers' effectiveness.

Summary

In this chapter, we have examined the reciprocal relationships between sport and religion. Although sports and religion may seem to have little in common, we have attempted to demonstrate that contemporary sport and religion are related in a variety of ways. For many centuries, Christian church dogma was antithetical to play and sport activities, but over the past century, with the enormous growth of organized sport, churches and religious leaders have welded a link between these two activities by sponsoring sports events under religious auspices and/or proselytizing athletes to religion and then using them as missionaries to convert new members.

While contemporary religion uses sport for the promotion of its causes, sport uses religion, as well. Numerous activities with a religious connotation—ceremonies, rituals, and so forth—are employed in connection with sports contests.

Notes

1. Harry Edwards, "Desegregating Sexist Sport," *Intellectual Digest* 3 (November, 1972), p. 82.
2. Editorial, "Sport: Are We Overdoing It?" *Christianity Today* 20 (February 20, 1976), p. 22.

3. Frank Deford, "Religion in Sport," *Sports Illustrated* 44 (April 19, 1976), pp. 92, 102.
4. J. Milton Yinger, *Religion, Society and the Individual* (New York: Macmillan, 1957), p. 9.
5. David Dressler, *Sociology: The Study of Human Interaction* (New York: Alfred Knopf, 1969), p. 658.
6. Elizabeth K. Nottingham, *Religion: A Sociological View* (New York: Random House, 1971), pp. 7-9.
7. Functionalism as used in the social sciences involves applying to social systems the biological notion that every organism has a structure made up of relatively stable interrelationships of parts. Each of these parts performs a specialized task, or function, which permits the organism to survive and to act. With respect to societies, this notion assumes that they consist of elements that perform specific functions that contribute to the overall survival and actions of the society.
8. Leonard Broom and Philip Selznick, *Sociology,* 5th ed. (New York: Harper and Row, 1973), pp. 393-395.
9. August Comte, *System of Positive Polity,* trans. by Frederick Harrison (New York: Burt Franklin, 1875), pp. 16-17.
10. Emile Durkheim, *Suicide,* trans. John Spaulding and George Simpson (Glencoe, Ill.: The Free Press, 1951), p. 159. See also Emile Durkheim, *The Elementary Forms of the Religious Life* (New York: Collier Books, 1961); this book is one of the classics in the sociology of religion.
11. Neil J. Smelser, ed., *Sociology: An Introduction* (New York: John Wiley and Sons, 1967), p. 340.
12. Ronald L. Johnstone, *Religion and Society in Interaction* (Englewood Cliffs, N.J.: Prentice-Hall, 1975), p. 143.
13. Smelser, *Sociology,* pp. 343-344.
14. Rudolph Brasch, *How Did Sports Begin?* (New York: David McKay, 1970), p. 1.
15. Ibid., pp. 2-4. See also Hans Damm, "The So-Called Sports Activities of Primitive Peoples: A Contribution Toward the Genesis of Sport," in *The Cross-Cultural Analysis of Sport and Games,* ed. Gunther Luschen (Champaign, Ill.: Stipes, 1970), pp. 52-69.
16. P.C. McIntosh, *Sport in Society* (London: C.A. Watts, 1963) pp. 3-4.
17. See for example, I Corin. 6:12-20, 9:24-26; I Timothy 4:8
18. Cited in G.G. Coulton, *Five Centuries of Religion,* vol. 5 (Cambridge, Eng.: Cambridge University Press, 1923), p. 532.
19. Albert Hyma, *The Youth of Erasmus* (Ann Arbor: University of Michigan Press, 1930), p. 178.
20. Dennis Brailsford, *Sport and Society* (London: Routledge and Kegan Paul, 1969), p. 141. For a more sympathetic but not altogether convincing argument about the Puritan attitude toward sport, see J. Thomas Jable, "The English Puritans—Suppressors of Sport and Amusement?" *Canadian Journal of the History of Sport and Physical Education* 7 (May, 1976), pp. 33-40.
21. Thomas B. Macaulay, *The History of England,* vol. 1 (London: Longman, Green, Longman, and Roberts, 1861), p. 162.
22. John Scollard, "Birth of the Blue Laws," *Mentor* 18 (May, 1930), pp. 46-49, 58-60; William C. White, "Bye, Bye Blue Laws," *Scribners* 94 (August, 1933), pp. 107-109; J. Thomas Jable, "Sunday Sport Comes to Pennsylvania: Professional Baseball and Football Triumph Over the Commonwealth's Archaic Blue Laws, 1919-1933," *Research Quarterly* 47 (October, 1976), pp. 357-365.
23. Van Wyck Brooks, *The Flowering of New England, 1815-65* (New York: Random House, The Modern Library, 1936), p. 253.
24. "The Autocrat of the Breakfast Table," *Atlantic Monthly* 1 (May, 1858), p. 881.
25. Guy Lewis, "The Muscular Christianity Movement," *Journal of Health, Physical Education, and Recreation* 37 (May, 1966), p. 42.
26. "Amusements," *New Englander* 9 (1851), p. 358. Cited in Ralph Slovenko and James A. Knight, eds., *Motivation in Play, Games, and Sports* (Springfield, Ill.: Charles C. Thomas, 1967), pp. 124-125.
27. Arthur M. Schlesinger, *The Rise of the City, 1878-1898* (New York: Macmillan, 1933), p. 335.
28. Clarence E. Rainwater, *The Play Movement in the United States* (Chicago: University of Chicago Press, 1922), pp. 22-23.

29. Ibid., p. 5.
30. William R. Hogan, "Sin and Sports," in *Motivations in Play, Games, and Sports,* ed. Ralph Slovenko and James A. Knight (Springfield, Ill.: Charles C. Thomas, 1967), pp. 133-134.
31. Richard A. Swanson, "The Acceptance and Influence of Play in American Protestantism," *Quest* 11 (December, 1968), p. 58.
32. "Modern Sport Symbolized," *Sportsmanship* 1 (January, 1929), p. 9; cited in Frederick W. Cozens and Florence S. Stumpf, *Sports in American Life* (Chicago: University of Chicago Press, 1953), p. 104.
33. Cozens and Stumpf, *Sports in America,* p. 93.
34. A. James Rudin, "America's New Religion," *Christian Century* 89 (April 5, 1972), p. 384; Cornish Rogers, "Sports, Religion and Politics: The Renewal of an Alliance," *Christian Century* 89 (April 5, 1972), pp. 392-394; and Michael Novak, *The Joy of Sports* (New York: Basic Books, 1976).
35. Rogers, "Sports, Religion, and Politics," pp. 392-394.
36. Eldon E. Snyder, "Athletic Dressing Room Slogans as Folklore: A Means of Socialization," *International Review of Sport Sociology* 7 (1972), pp. 89-102.
37. Gerald Redmond, "A Plethora of Shrines: Sport in the Museum and Hall of Fame," *Quest* 19 (January, 1973), pp. 41-48.
38. Fred Eastman, "Rural Recreation Through the Church," *The Playground* 6 (October, 1912), p. 234.
39. Bob Richards.
40. Lee Gutkind, "Striking a Blow for Christ," *Sports Illustrated* 38 (July 30, 1973), pp. 32-34.
41. "Are Sports Good for the Soul?" *Newsweek* (January 11, 1976), p. 51.
42. Many Roman Catholic colleges and universities have used football and basketball to publicize the institution. Protestant institutions have followed the same pattern, with Brigham Young University and Southern Methodist University among the most visible.
43. Quoted in Deford, "Religion in Sport," p. 96.
44. Robert H. Boyle, "Oral Roberts: Small BUT OH, MY," *Sports Illustrated* 35 (November, 1970), p. 64.
45. This statement appears on most of the Fellowship of Christian Athletes official publications. It appears on the title page of each issue of *The Christian Athlete.*
46. Fellowship of Christian Athletes Summer Conference Guide, Kansas City, Missouri, 1975, p. 2.
47. Quoted in Joe McGuff, "Sporting Comment," *The Kansas City Star* (May 24, 1970).
48. Joe Jares, "Hallelujah, What a Team!" *Sports Illustrated* 46 (February, 1977), pp. 41-42.
49. Deford, "Religion in Sport," p. 92.
50. *The Wittenburg Door* 24 (April-May, June, July, 1975).
51. Quoted by Frank Deford, "The Word According to Tom," *Sports Illustrated* 44 (April 26, 1976), p. 69.
52. Ibid.
53. Quoted in Deford, "Religion in Sport," p. 92.
54. Deford, "The Word According to Tom," pp. 65-66.
55. Deford, "Religion in Sport," p. 98.
56. "The Christian Woodstock," *Newsweek* (June 26, 1972), p. 52.
57. Deford, "Religion in Sport," p. 100.
58. *The Wittenburg Door* 24 (April-May, June, July, 1975), pp. 19-20.
59. Deford, "The Word According to Tom," p. 67.
60. Max Weber, *The Protestant Ethic and the Spirit of Capitalism,* trans. Talcott Parsons (New York: Charles Scribner's, 1958). This essay is probably the most famous work in the sociology of religion. It has aroused a great deal of controversy among sociologists and historians. The whole notion of a relationship between Protestantism and capitalism is called into serious question by Kurt Samuelsson, *Religion and Economic Action: The Protestant Ethic, The Rise of Capitalism, and the Abuses of Scholarship* (New York: Basic Books, 1961). For an excellent collection of the views of Weber's critics, see Robert W. Green, ed., *Protestantism and Capitalism:*

The Weber Thesis and Its Critics (Boston: D.C. Health, 1959).

61. Reinhard Bendix, *Work and Authority in Industry* (New York: John Wiley and Sons, 1956), observed that "Weber stated . . . that he was investigating whether and at what points certain 'elective affinities' are discernible between particular types of religious beliefs and the ethics of work-a-day life" (p. 63). Werner Stark, "The Theory of Elective Affinity," in *The Sociology of Knowledge* (Glencoe, Ill.: The Free Press, 1958), notes that the term elective affinities implies that "human groupings of whatever kind, will, for their part, always be on the look-out for appropriate ideas to give expression to their essence and their striving" (p. 257). In the Talcott Parsons translation of Weber's study, the word "correlation" is substituted for elective affinity.

62. Weber, *The Protestant Ethic,* p. 80.

63. Ibid., p. 115.

64. Weber made it quite clear that he was not suggesting that one social process was a *causal* agent for the other. In his final paragraph, he said: "It is . . . not my aim to substitute for a one-sided materialistic an equally one-sided spiritualistic causal interpretation of culture and history" (Weber, *The Protestant Ethic,* p. 183).

65. Harry Edwards, *Sociology of Sport,* (Homewood, Ill.: Dorsey Press, 1973), pp. 64, 334.

66. Boyle, "Oral Roberts" p. 65.

67. Deford, "Religion in Sport," p. 90.

68 Noted in Michael Roberts, *Fans!* (Washington, D.C.: New Republic, 1976), pp. 117-118.

69. Jay Dirkson, "The Place of Athletics in the Life of the Christian," *Sport Sociology Bulletin* 4 (Spring, 1975), p. 54.

70. Ibid.

71. Edwards, *Sociology of Sport,* p. 335.

72. Bronislaw Malinowski, *Magic, Science, and Religion and Other Essays* (Glencoe, Ill.: The Free Press, 1948).

73. Louise R. Loomis, ed., *The Iliad of Homer,* trans. Samuel Butler (Roslyn, N.Y.: Walter J. Block, 1942), pp. 368-369.

74. Deford, "Religion in Sport," p. 92.

75. Quoted in Frank Deford, "Reaching for the Stars," *Sports Illustrated* 44 (May 3, 1976), p. 60.

76. Larry Merchant, *And Every Day You Take Another Bite* (New York: Doubleday, 1971), p. 36.

77. Quoted in Deford, "The Word According to Tom," p. 65.

78. Joseph A. Marbeto, Jr., "The Incidence of Prayer in Athletics as Indicated by Selected California Collegiate Athletes and Coaches" (master's thesis, University of California, Santa Barbara, 1967).

79. Ibid., p. 68.

80. Ibid., p. 72.

81. Ibid., p. 87-88.

82. Malinowski, *Magic, Science, and Religion,* pp. 12-30.

83. The word superstition is "a belief that one's fate is in the hands of unknown external powers governed by forces over which one has no control." G. Johoda, *The Psychology of Superstition* (London: Penguin Press, 1969), p. 139. Superstition is a form of magical belief.

84. Malinowski, *Magic, Science, and Religion,* p. 116.

85. Ibid., p. 14. See also A.R. Radcliffe-Brown, *Structure and Function in Primitive Societies* (New York: The Free Press, 1965) and G. Homans, *The Human Group* (New York: Harcourt, Brace, World, 1950) for alternative explanations of magic.

86. Malinowski, *Magic, Science, and Religion,* p. 70.

87. C. Jane Gregory and Brian M. Petrie, "Superstitions of Canadian Intercollegiate Athletes: An Inter-Sport Comparison," *International Review of Sport Sociology* 10 (No. 2, 1975), p. 59.

88. George Gmelch, "Baseball Magic," *Trans-Action* 8 (June, 1971), p. 40. A number of rituals, taboos, and fetishes employed in baseball are described in the chapter "The Folklore of Baseball" by Tristram P. Coffin, *The Old Ball Game* (New York: Herder and Herder, 1971).

89. Gmelch, "Baseball Magic," p. 40. For a discussion of some bizarre rituals of hockey goalies, see Jerry Kirshenbaum, "Reincarna-

tion and 13 Pairs of Socks," *Sports Illustrated* 46 (March 28, 1977), pp. 30-33.

90. Larry Keith, "Nuts About the Game," *Sports Illustrated* 45 (November 29, 1976).

91. Jerry Kramer, *Instant Replay* (New York: Signet Books, 1969), p. 193.

92. Gmelch, "Baseball Magic," p. 40.

93. Ibid., p. 54.

94. Judy Becker, "Superstition in Sport," *International Journal of Sports Psychology* 6 (No. 3, 1975), pp. 148-152.

95. Gmelch, "Baseball Magic," p. 54.

96. "Soccer Witchcraft Anything But Charming," *Rocky Mountain News* (July 2, 1975), p. 38. Also see Douglas Hill, *et al., Witchcraft, Magic and the Supernatural* (London: Octopas, 1974), pp. 20, 150 for a discussion of the Italian sorcerer who puts the "evil eye" on the opponents of his favorite soccer team.

97. Cited in Merchant, *And Every Day You Take Another Bite,* p. 37.

Sport and the Polity 6

In an interview for the student newspaper at the University of Kansas, the school's director of athletics said: "I don't think athletics has a thing to do with politics. They shouldn't even be mentioned together. There's no relationship between the two. They're entirely different subjects."[1] This type of statement is often made by sports officials of universities, professional leagues, and the United States Olympic Committee. The argument of this chapter, however, is just the converse—that sport and politics are very closely intertwined. Several characteristics inherent to sport serve to guarantee this strong relationship.

First, sports participants typically represent and have an allegiance to some social organization (e.g., school, factory, neighborhood, community, region, or nation). Much of the ritual accompanying sporting events is aimed at symbolically reaffirming fidelity to the sponsoring organization (slogans, chants, music, wearing of special clothing, etc.). Goodhart and Chataway have argued that there are four kinds of sport: sport as exercise, sport as gambling, sport as spectacle, and representative sport. This latter type

> . . . is a limited conflict with clearly defined rules, in which representatives of towns, regions, or nations are pitted against each other. It is primarily an affair for the spectators: they are drawn to it not so much by the mere spectacle, by the ritual, or by an appreciation of the skills involved, but because they identify themselves with their representatives. . . .
>
> Most people will watch [the Olympic Games] for one reason only: there will be a competitor who, they feel, is representing them. That figure in the striped singlet will be their man—running, jumping, or boxing for their country. For a matter of minutes at least, their own estimation of themselves will be bound up with his performance. He will be the embodiment of their nation's strength or weakness. Victory for him will be victory for them; defeat for him, defeat for them.[2]

This last point is worthy of emphasis. Evidence from any recent Olympics or other international competition shows that for many nations and their citizens, victory is an index of that nation's superiority (in its military might, its politico-economic system, and its culture). Clearly, the outcomes of international contests are very often interpreted politically.

A second basis for a close relationship between sports and politics is inherent in the process of organization itself. As sport has become increasingly organized, a plethora of teams, leagues, player's associations, and ruling bodies has been created. These groups acquire certain power that by their very creation is distributed unequally.[3] Thus, there may be a power struggle between players and owners (e.g., the NFL player strike in 1974), or between competing leagues (e.g., NBA vs. ABA in professional basketball), or between various sanctioning bodies (AAU vs. NCAA in amateur athletics).

The linkage between sport and politics is quite obvious when the impact of the federal government on sports is considered. Several illustrations make that point: (1) legislation has been passed exempting professional sports from antitrust laws; (2) tax laws give special concessions to owners of professional teams; (3) the blackout of televised home games has been lifted for professional football despite the protests of the league commissioner and the owners; and (4) the Congress decides which sport organization will have the exclusive right to select and train athletes for the Olympic Games.

Another indication of the close relationship between sports and politics is that sports events and political situations have reciprocal effects on each other. A famous example of a sports event affecting politics is the tour of China in 1971 by the American table tennis contingent. This tour proved to be the prelude to political exchanges between the two nations. Another example was a war that erupted between El Salvador and Honduras after a soccer match between the two countries. There are also many examples of political situations that have affected sports. The apartheid policies of South Africa have resulted in that nation being barred from Olympic competition.[4] After the Soviet Union's suppression of the Hungarian revolt of 1956, participants from the two countries engaged in a very bloody water polo match at the Olympic Games in Melbourne, Australia.

In the early 1970s, a U.S.-Russian track meet was cancelled because of increased tensions between the two countries. And, as a final example, Canada under pressure from the People's Republic of China announced, just weeks before the 1976 Olympic Games were to open, that it would bar Taiwanese athletes from competing as representatives of the Republic of China.

The institutional character of sport is a final source of the strong relationship between sport and politics. Sport, as with the institutions of the polity and religion, is conservative; it serves as a preserver and legitimator of the existing order. The patriotic pageants that accompany sporting events reinforce the political system. Moreover, sport perpetuates many myths, such as, anyone with talent regardless of race or social station has an equal chance to succeed. Sport also legitimizes ideas such as "winning is not everything, it is the only thing."[5] Sport is a model of law and order. As former Texas football coach Darrell Royal has said, ". . . football is the last bastion of traditional American values. It's the last institution where you have rules to obey—in bed at ten, lights out at eleven, breakfast at seven."[6]

We have seen that the very nature of sport makes politics endemic to it. The remainder of this chapter will cement this relationship further by examining in greater detail the various political uses of sport. The final section will focus on the political attitudes of persons in sport (especially coaches and athletes).

The Political Uses of Sport

Sport as a Propaganda Vehicle

Success in international competition frequently serves as a mechanism by which a society's ruling elite unites its citizens and attempts to impress the citizens of other countries. A classic example of this was Adolf Hitler's use of the 1936 Olympic Games to strengthen his control over the German people and to introduce Nazi culture to the entire world. According to Mandell in his book *The Nazi Olympics,* the festival planned for these Games was a shrewdly propagandistic and brilliantly conceived charade that reinforced and mobilized the hysterical patriotism of the German masses.[7]

More recently, the communist nations have used sport for promoting their common cause. During the 1972 Olympics, 600 medals were awarded. Since about ten percent of the athletes at that Olympics were representatives of communist countries, on a proportional basis one would expect that they should win about 60 medals. They won an astounding 285 medals, however, or 47 1/2 percent of the total. This, the Communists argued, was evidence of the superiority of the communist politico-economic system. Similarly, when Cuba won 20 times more gold medals than did the United States, on a per capita basis, at the 1971 Pan American Games, Cuban Premier Castro proclaimed to Latin America that this was proof of the superiority of the Cuban people and the Cuban system.

The most striking example of success in the 1976 Olympics was from East Germany. Although a nation smaller in population than California (17 million), East Germany placed third in the overall number of medals awarded with a total of 90, whereas the United States had 94 and the Soviet Union, 125. East Germany spends an estimated $300 million annually on its massive sports program. From the age of 7, children are tested and the most promising athletes are enrolled in sixteen special schools, where they receive special training and expert coaching in addition to their normal schooling. After their formal education is completed, the star athletes are given special jobs, permanent military deferments, and new apartments.[8] But why would a nation devote so much money, time, and talent to sport? One reason is the competition between East and West Germany. Another is the goal of international acceptance of East Germany as a sovereign state. Third is the desire to demonstrate the superiority of the communist way of life. East Germany is not unlike the other communist countries in using sport for the accomplishment of political goals. The emphasis on sport by the Eastern bloc countries—the Soviet Union, East Germany, Poland, Yugoslavia, Rumania, Hungary, Czechoslovakia, and Bulgaria—is seen by their winning 53 percent of all the medals awarded at the 1976 Olympics.

But the use of sport as a propaganda vehicle internationally is not limited to communist countries. International sports victories are just as important to the United States. After the 1972 Olympics, when the Americans fared worse than expected (especially in track and basketball) many editorial writers and politicians advocated plans whereby American athletes would be subsidized and receive the best coaching and facilities to regain athletic supremacy. This did not happen and the cry arose again after the 1976 Olympics. The clear assumption behind these plans was that if Americans were allowed to devote as much time and money to athletics as the Communists, Americans would prevail—proving the superiority of the free enterprise system.

The United States government uses athletes to promote international goodwill and enhance the American image abroad. The State Department, for example, sponsors tours of athletes to foreign countries for those purposes. Arthur Ashe, the black American tennis star, toured Africa for eighteen days in 1971 under the sponsorship of the U.S. Information Agency. He gave exhibitions, clinics, and interviews. The tour cost $12,000 plus $60,000 for film. The film was then offered to schools, clubs, and public theaters around the world (except in the United States), especially in Africa.[9]

Sport as an instrument of national policy is not limited to the industrialized nations of the world. The developing countries use sport even more for this purpose. A study of the 133 members of the United Nations in 1973 showed that while 26 percent of the nations had a cabinet level post related to sport, 87 percent of the nations classified as developing had such a position.[10] The probable reason for this keen interest in sport by developing nations is that sport provides a relatively cheap political tool to accomplish national objectives (prestige abroad and unity at home).

Sport and Nationalism

Success in international sports competition tends to trigger pride among that nation's citizens. As mentioned previously, the Olympics and other international games tend to promote an "us vs. them" feeling among athletes, coaches, politicians, the press, and fans. It can be argued, then, that the Olympic Games represent a political contest, a symbolic world war in which nations win or lose. Because this interpretation is commonly held, citizens of the nations involved unite behind their flag and their athletes.[11]

The integral interrelationship of sport and nationalism is easily seen in the blatantly militaristic pageantry that surrounds sports contests. The playing of the national anthem, the presentation of the colors, the jet-aircraft flyovers, the band forming a flag or a liberty bell, are all political acts supportive of the existing political system. The following is a description of the nationalistic flavor of an opening night ceremony:

> The inaugural festivities . . . include appearances by the bands of the 371st Army from Ft. Leavenworth, Kan., and the 1st Infantry (Big Red One) from Ft. Riley, Kan. Fifty

> regular Army men from Ft. Riley will feature one portion of the program—with each carrying the flag of a different state. Things will be wrapped up militarily with a color guard from the United States Naval Reserve here and the first pitch thrown out by Lt. Cmdr. Joseph Charles Plumb, Jr., of Overland Park, recently released after five and one-half years as a prisoner of war in North Vietnam.[12]

The irony of this, however, is that such a nationalistic display is not generally interpreted politically. Recognition of the explicit acceptance of the political content of these festival rituals was manifested in 1970 by the refusal of the American Broadcasting Company (ABC) to televise a halftime program in which the University of Buffalo band presentation featured three themes: antiwar, antiracism, and antipollution. The network refused because the halftime show was a "political demonstration." But later that same season ABC televised the halftime of the Army-Navy game where several Green Berets who had staged a raid on a prisoner of war camp in North Vietnam were honored. That one of these halftimes was labeled political while the other was not is revealing. Clearly, both were political, but only those demonstrations or ceremonies that were controversial and antiestablishment were so labeled and frowned on.[13]

In this vein, sports columnist Jerry Isenberg has speculated:

> I wonder, for example, if just once during that long string of half-time shows someone had called for a minute of silence for all the cancer victims who did not benefit from research because the funds were spent on the space program, whether or not the management might not have judged that to be political, with no place in the sports arena. I wonder how many airplanes in what kind of formation the government would have agreed to send over for that one.[14]

An important question is why are patriotic displays commonplace at sports contests, but not at most other public events (e.g., plays, lectures, concerts, and movies)? The support for these patriotic rituals is so strong, that when an administrator decided to *not* play the national anthem at a track meet, as was the case at Madison Square Garden in early 1973, he was forced by public opinion and politicians to reverse himself. Typically, a bill was introduced before the New York City Council that would make it unlawful "to commence any sporting event, open to the public and for which admission is charged, without first playing the national anthem, either by live musicians or by mechanical reproductions."[15]

Athletes who do not show proper respect for the flag or for the national anthem are subject to stiff penalties. When Tommie Smith and John Carlos raised gloved, clenched fists and bowed their heads during the national anthem at the 1968 Olympics, the Olympic Committee stripped them of their medals and banned them from further Olympic competition. The Olympic Committee made such a decision even though they claim the Olympics are a nonpolitical event.[16] Vince Matthews and Wayne Collett received a similar penalty for their alleged disrespect for the U.S. national anthem at the 1972 Olympics.

Why are athletic events so overladen with patriotic themes? Tom Wicker, of the *New York Times,* made the following speculation:

> What is the correlation, if any, between patriotism and people battering one another in the boxing ring or in football games—or for that matter between patriotism and track meets, baseball games and other athletic events that are not so violent?
>
> The explanation probably is that symbols like the flag and the anthem, appropriate as they are to the warlike spirit, are equally appropriate to sports events, with their displays of the instinct to combat and the will to win. Even the so-called "noncontact" sports exalt competition and the pursuit of victory, including the kind of individual heroism and team spirit that are evoked in wartime.[17]

For whatever reason, sport competition and nationalism are closely intertwined. When American athletes compete against those of another country, national unity is the result (for both sides, unless one's athletes do poorly). Citizens take pride in their representatives' accomplishments, viewing them as collective achievements. This identification with athletes and their cause of winning for the nation's glory tends to unite the citizenry regardless of social class, race, and regional differences. Thus, sport can be used by political leaders whose nations have problems with divisiveness.

Sport as an "Opiate" of the Masses

We have shown that sport success can unite a nation through pride. After Brazil won the World Cup in soccer *(futebol)* for the third time in succession, one observer noted:

> The current *futebol* success has promoted a pride in being Brazilian and a unifying symbol without precedent. Even the lower classes of the cities, thanks to television, felt a sense of participation in something representing national life. They know that Brazil is now internationally significant, not necessarily for reasons of interest to the scholar or public figure, but of importance to the common man. It is estimated that over 700 million soccer fans throughout the world watched Brazil defeat England and Italy. The Englishman in his pub, the French worker, the German with a Volkswagen all know that Brazil is not just another large "tropical country," but the homeland of the world's best *futebol* and a legend named Pele.[18]

This pride in a nation's success, because it transcends the social classes, serves as an opiate of the masses. Sanders has asserted that *futebol* in Brazil enables the poor to forget partially the harshness of their life. It serves also as a safety valve for releasing tensions that might otherwise be directed toward disrupting the existing social order.[19]

The same situation appears to be true of the United States. Virtually all homes have television sets, making it possible for almost everyone to participate vicariously in and identify with local and national sports teams. Because of this, the minds and energies of many persons are deflected away from the hunger and misery that is disproportionately the lot of the lower classes in American society. Bill Bradley, former Rhodes scholar and professional basketball player, has pointed out that it deflects us away from seeking solutions to the problems of war and racism.

> Life is full of ironies. . . . It's really ironic the way the fans come out to cheer the Big Game when there's a war on; people being bombed to death; racism, and all the rest of it. . . . It's also ironic that when 100,000 people will be at tomorrow's rally [a New York peace rally], the Knicks and me will be going over tonight's game films. . . . And Bill Bradley wonders hard about the morality of providing what he calls a "fix," a temporary escape from the problems of the world to a sports dreamworld; an escape that is really no escape because it permits those problems to go on just as before.[20]

Sport also acts as an opiate by perpetuating the belief that persons from the lowest classes can be upwardly mobile through success in sports. Chapter 9 will deal with this topic more fully, but, meanwhile, it's enough to say that for every major leaguer who came up from poverty, tens of thousands did not. The point, however, is that most Americans *believe* that sport is a mobility escalator and that it is merely a reflection of the opportunity structure of the society in general. Again, poor youth who might otherwise invest their energies to changing the system, work instead on a jump shot. The potential for revolution is thus impeded by sport.

At the other end of the social spectrum, sport may also divert the energies and interests of those who are the decision makers. An editorial made this point about Richard Nixon during his presidency.

> Nixon has that ability to turn off the rest of the world when a sports event is on. He watched college football on TV one afternoon when peace marchers descended on Washington, and probably his only complaint was that there wasn't enough beer in the White House refrigerator. And who can forget that performance by the Washington Monument, when he walked out in the early morning to talk to the peace marchers about the football teams at their schools.[21]

The Exploitation of Sport by Politicians

Politicians may use athletics and athletes in at least five ways. First, an athlete can use his fame and free publicity as an aid to getting elected or appointed to office. Of course, these persons may have had the political skills to win anyway, but athletic fame undoubtedly helps. In 1974, for example, at least four prominent Congressmen were former star athletes: "Vinegar Bend" Mizell, Bob Mathias, Jack Kemp, and Ralph Metcalfe; there was also a Supreme Court Justice in "Whizzer" White; and a U.S. President, Gerald Ford.

When appropriate, political candidates inform the voters of their athletic prowess.

Among the presidential candidates in 1976, for example, the prospective voters were informed that Morris Udall was a former professional basketball player, Birch Bayh was a shortstop at Purdue and a former state Golden Gloves boxing champion. Another Golden Gloves champion was George Wallace. And, of course, the voters were reminded that Gerald Ford played center on a national championship football team at the University of Michigan. Representative Jack Kemp, a 13-year National Football League veteran, argued that people admire the qualities presumed to be a by-product of athletic participation:

> There are many lessons of athletic competition that do apply to our free enterprise way of life . . . tenacity, never giving up, knowing what adversity is, not shrinking in the face of challenge. There is a basic honesty about sports competition, a willingness to stand up to problems. I think this is what people admire about Gerald Ford.[22]

Politicians also find it beneficial to get the approval and active campaign support of athletes. Wilt Chamberlain and Jim Brown, for example, campaigned actively for Richard Nixon in 1972. His opponent George McGovern also sought athletes. His newsletter a year before the election noted that

> Ray Schoenke, first-string offensive guard for the Washington Redskins, is in the process of putting together a large group of athletes who will work for the candidacy of Senator McGovern. The list now includes: John Wilbur, Bill Brundidge and Charlie Harraway of the Redskins; Paul Warfield, Miami Dolphins; Steve Carleton, St. Louis Cardinals; Lou Pinella, Kansas City Royals; Dan Conners, Oakland Raiders; Dave Bing, Detroit Pistons; and Kermit Alexander, Los Angeles Rams. After the fall season ends, several players will be traveling full time for the McGovern campaign.[23]

In the 1976 presidential campaign, Gerald Ford used prominent sports figures such as coaches Paul "Bear" Bryant, Woody Hayes, Tom Landry, and Billy Martin; sportscaster Joe Garagiola; and athletes Chris Evert, Peggy Fleming, Willie Shoemaker. Jimmy Carter, too, used athletes such as Tommy Nobis and Henry Aaron in his campaign.[24]

The preceding examples show that athletes, because they are well known and admired, can get votes for either themselves or candidates whom they support. But sport itself is so popular in American society that politicians may use examples of sport or sport metaphors to communicate with the public. Moreover, they find it useful to identify with teams, to attend sports events, and to talk with coaches and athletic heroes. Richard Nixon, more than any recent president, identified with sports. But governors, congressmen, mayors, and other officials tend more and more to identify with sports. James Reston has argued that, because of the increased popularity of sport, politicians have shifted recently from proving fidelity to religion to proving their affinity for sport to win votes.

> It is an interesting switch. Politicians used to feel that they had to identify themselves with the church in order to pick up votes, and they quoted the Bible to prove their fidelity to the old faith. Now they telephone football coaches instead of bishops and issue pronouncements on the cunning confusion of the modern Texas wishbone offensive strategy, which is now the new holy trinity of football.
>
> Who can blame them? Politicians go where the votes are. The stadium is now more popular in America, or at least more exciting and more decisive, than the church. The game of football, unlike the "great game of politics," is mathematical and understandable. Its rules are plain; four tries to make ten yards, measurable by the sticks. The field is clearly marked with its sidelines and goal lines. It has a kick-off, a half-time and an end marked to the second by the clock and referees and a head-linesman to call the close ones and spot the dirty tricks and instant replay cameras to let the people judge the decisions.
>
> In short, football is not a metaphysical exercise. It has pageantry and a short practical clash between the weak and the strong, and at the end you know who has won. It is not like a theological philosophy or a foreign policy, where you have to wait for a generation and sometimes even a lifetime to discover how it all comes out.[25]

Politicians capitalize on the popularity of athletes by using them to support the system. In the United States, for example, athletes are often sent overseas to maintain the morale of servicemen. Athletes are also used in advertisements that urge the viewer or reader to join the army or ROTC, to vote, and to avoid drugs. They are also asked to give patriotic speeches on holidays and other occasions.

Use of athletes for the maintenance of the status quo is used in other countries as well. In communist countries, the avowed goal of sports is to aid in the socialist revolution. Subsidized by the state, athletes visit factories and villages to hold demonstrations and make political speeches. These activities spread the philosophy of the rulers and bolster the morale of the factory and farm workers to increase production.[26]

A final way that sport can be exploited by politicians is related to the manipulation of sports audiences. As noted before, militaristic displays and patriotic pageants can be used to promote nationalism among the spectators. Moreover, this captive audience can be manipulated by politicians to win votes. The sporting crowd is viewed by many politicians as a type of ethnic or regional group worthy of courting for votes.[27]

Sport as a Socializing Agent to Transmit the Values of Society

We have frequently pointed out that sport is widely believed to be a vehicle by which the American values of success in competition, hard work, perseverance, discipline, and order are transmitted. This is the explicit reason given for the existence of little league programs for youngsters and the tremendous emphasis on sports in American schools. While vice president, Spiro Agnew voiced the prevailing view well in a speech delivered to the Touchdown Club of Birmingham, Alabama. The following are some excerpts:

> Not the least of these values is the American competitive ethic which motivates young Americans . . . to strive toward excellence in everything they undertake. For such young Americans—whether on the athletic field, in the classroom, or on the job—the importance of our competitive ethic lies in the fact that it is only by trial of their abilities—by testing and challenging—can they discover their strengths and, yes, their weaknesses. Out of this process of self-discovery, painful though it may be at times, those young Americans who compete to excel learn to cope with whatever challenges lie ahead in life. And having given their best, they also emerge from the competitive test with greater ability to determine for themselves where their individual talents lie. Life is a great competition. In my judgment it will remain so despite the efforts of the social architects to make it a bland experience, controlled by their providing what they think is best for us. Success is sweet but it entails always the risk of failure. It is very, very important to learn how to lose a contest without being destroyed by the experience. For a man who has not known failure cannot fully appreciate success. A person cannot know pleasure to any greater degree than he has known pain. And from defeat, from failure, from hardship, something builds within a person. If a person can throw off disappointment and come back and try again, he develops a personal cohesiveness that holds him together as a man throughout his life—and that gives him the durability to convert temporary defeat into ultimate victory. . . .
>
> And so, to me, that is the message of competitive sports: not simply trying to win, and to achieve, but learning how to cope with a failure—and to come back. In this regard, let me say something about my personal philosophy concerning the meaning of success and failure in sports for young Americans.
>
> First, I believe that sports—all sports—is one of the few bits of glue that holds society together, one of the few activities in which young people can proceed along avenues where objectives are clear and the desire to win is not only permissible but encouraged.
>
> Opponents of the free-enterprise system tell our young people that to try for material success and personal status is bad; that the only thing worthwhile is to find something to wring your hands about; that the ultimate accomplishment is to make everybody feel better.
>
> I, for one, would not want to live in a society that did not include winning in its philosophy; that would have us live our lives as identical lemmings, never trying to best anybody at anything, all headed in the same direction, departing not from the appointed route, striving not for individual excellence. In short, I would rather be a failure in a competitive society which is our inheritance than to live in a waveless sea of nonachievers.[28]

Agnew, of course, overlooked the noncompetitive aspects of corporate sport—e.g., professional teams are exempt from the Sherman Antitrust Act, team owners receive a special statutory tax break, professional teams play in tax subsidized stadiums. In short, he neglected to say that team owners do not compete.[29] He did voice, however, what most people believe.

Whether sport actually transmits these values or whether only the most competitive individuals survive is an empirical question. We do know that societies differ in the sports they emphasize and that these correlate with the values of society (or those values that the leaders desire to promote). As an example of a society that uses sport to promote quite different values than those enumerated by Vice President Agnew, let's look briefly at China.

Sport in China, as reported by Americans, has a very different emphasis than that found in America.[30] Sport is found throughout the country—in factories, communes, and schools—but winning in a competitive situation is not the major objective. The goals, rather, are teamwork, cooperation, working for a group goal, friendship, and physical fitness. In chapter 4, we noted that American schools and communities shower great rewards on their athletes. Winners receive ribbons, medals, and trophies—all prominently displayed. This is in sharp contrast to what is found in China. After a tour there, William Johnson noted that he had not seen a single sports trophy or pennant in all the schools and universities he had visited. He asked a school coach about this, whose response was: "It is true that sometimes we are awarded modest banners for winning, but I do not know where they are. Perhaps in a desk drawer. We consider friendship first, learning good technique second, victory banners third or perhaps even less."[31] Johnson received similar replies from other coaches, athletes, and factory workers. Clearly, a socialist system is better served if its citizens learn cooperation and teamwork, while a capitalist society is best served by encouraging everyone to strive to outdo one's fellows.

Sport as a Vehicle to Change Society

A recurring theme of this book is that sport reflects the dynamics of the larger society. So, with the social and political turmoil in American society in the last decade, one would expect that the sports world would be similarly affected.

Sport and sporting events have been used by revolutionaries and reformers to attack two major societal problems—racism and the recent American involvement in the Vietnam war. Racism has been attacked in a number of ways. Most dramatic was the proposed boycott of the 1968 Olympics by black athletes. Harry Edwards, a black sociologist and former athlete, was a leader of this boycott. His rationale for the protest was as follows:

> The roots of the revolt of the black athlete spring from the same seed that produced the sit-ins, the freedom rides, and the rebellions in Watts, Detroit, and Newark. The athletic revolt springs from a disgust and dissatisfaction with the racism prevalent in American society—including the sports world.[32]

Another boycott was directed against the New York Athletic Club's annual indoor track meet. The goal of this action was to dramatize and change the club's policy of excluding Jews, blacks, and other minorities from membership. And, black athletes at schools such as San Jose State and the University of Wyoming participated in a symbolic protest against Brigham Young University, a Mormon supported university. These athletes wore arm bands to symbolize their contempt for the racial policies of the Mormon Church.

Prior to the 1972 Olympic Games, the International Olympic Committee ruled that Rhodesia would be allowed to participate. This infuriated the African nations violently opposed to the separatist policies of the ruling elite in Rhodesia. These nations, along with blacks from the United States, threatened to boycott the 1972 Games unless Rhodesia was barred from competition. Ultimately, the International Olympic Committee bowed to this pressure and rescinded its earlier action.

The African nations also used the 1976 Olympics to embarrass apartheid countries. Some 27 countries (with more than 700 athletes) boycotted the Olympics because New Zealand's national rugby union team toured in South Africa.[33] Two months after the 1976 Olympics, perhaps as a result of this action and worldwide public opinion, South Africa officially ended racial segregation in sports.

The most blatant use of a sports event for political purposes was the Palestinian guerrilla attack on Israeli athletes at the 1972 Olympic Games. This was obviously a continuation of the terrorist tactics against the Israelis. But the choice of the Olympics with its worldwide press coverage was an ideal one for a group wishing to present a message to the world.

American athletes who opposed their country's involvement in the Vietnam war used sport to inform the establishment of their political stand. They signed petitions, participated in demonstrations, wore arm bands, and even (although rarely) refused to participate in an athletic contest unless changes were made. An example of the latter was the refusal of nine Harvard track men to compete in a meet against Army at West Point.[34]

More typical than boycotts by American athletes were their symbolic efforts. For example, some 50 University of Michigan football players signed a petition calling for an antiwar show at halftime of their homecoming game. This petition said, in effect, bring all the troops home—let's have a real homecoming this year.[35]

Nonathletes, of course, also have used athletic events to dramatize and register their protest. For example, the Stanford Students for the Defense of Angela Davis and all Political Prisoners staged a demonstration at the 1972 Rose Bowl game.

These examples show once again how sports and politics are intertwined. The worldwide popularity of sport and the importance attached to it by fans and politicians alike make sport an ideal target for political protest. However, it should be noted that the use of sport for protest, although an important means of dramatizing social problems, is generally unsuccessful in effecting a meaningful change. This is a tribute to the institutional character of sport with its built-in bias for preserving and legitimizing the status quo.

The Political Attitudes of Coaches and Athletes

Sociologists are interested in the political attitudes of various social categories, such as social classes, occupations, and religious groups. This interest is based on the assumption that individuals in similar social situations are constrained to view the world and evaluate events and ideas from the same perspective. The remainder of this chapter will focus on the political attitudes of two categories—coaches and athletes—that face somewhat similar pressures and, therefore, have congruent attitudes.

Liberalism-conservatism is a multidimensional phenomenon. Some of the many dimensions involved are attitudes about welfare, foreign aid, racial integration, the free-enterprise system, morality, and social change. Few persons, therefore, hold a consistent pattern of thought across these dimensions. This fact makes our analysis difficult and doubtless oversimplified. Nevertheless, the discussion that follows will consider political conservatives to be persons who support the existing socioeconomic-political system. This means that they have a great respect for tradition, authority, law and order, the free-enterprise system, patriotism, and the "tried and true" values of hard work, goal orientation, and Christian morality. This implies, further, that they tend to be intolerant of challenges against traditional values.

Despite an occasional political protest, athletes as a group are politically conservative. Although athletes such as Dave Meggysey, George Sauer, and Bernie Parrish have been critical of sport in American society, they are clearly exceptions to the rule. The response of the vast majority of athletes, coaches, reporters, and others in the sports world to critiques of contemporary sport is indicative of this conservative tendency. We will attempt to examine and explain this conservativism, focusing particularly on the political attitudes of coaches and athletes. Two caveats before we begin. First there is little empirical research in this area. We will supply what information is available, but much additional research is needed. Second, the available data are limited to males.

Political Attitudes of Coaches

Generalizations about any social category are always difficult because few such groups are homogeneous. The coaching profession is no exception. There are harsh coaches and lenient ones; bigoted and nonbigoted coaches; and hawks and doves on America's military policies. Despite these differences, however, coaches as a category can be characterized as politically conservative. Let's examine the available evidence from three sources: anecdotes, surveys, and scientific research.

A good deal of anecdotal evidence supports the contention that coaches tend to be politically conservative. As David Nelson, athletic director at the University of Delaware and formerly its head football coach, has summarized: "Having been a coach . . . I know that most of us are almost Harding Republicans and three degrees to the right of Genghis Khan."[36]

Item: When one of his players sat down during the playing of the national anthem, Coach Ellis of Adelbert College suspended him, saying: there are "no rules about standing for the national anthem, but no rules about dropping a player who doesn't do it, either."[37]

Item: When some University of Kansas students staged a sit-in at the chancellor's office to protest alleged discriminatory practices, the football coach, Jack Mitchell, said to his players, "you're not here to demonstrate. You're here to play football."[38]

Item: A college recruiter was questioning a high school coach about a black athlete. After asking the standard questions about height, weight, speed, test scores, and class rank, the recruiter found it necessary to ask: "Is he militant?"[39]

Item: Melvin Cratsley, basketball coach at Carnegie Tech for 17 years, said: "I object to players telling me they want beards, long hair and all the rest, because the next thing they want to do is run the team. More important than the beard is what it represents—rebellion. If you can't tell them what to do, they don't need a coach."[40]

Item: Tony Simpson, coach of a Houston junior high school, has argued: "It is time that American coaches stopped allowing themselves to be personally represented by male athletic teams and individuals who look like females. It is time that American coaches realized that a male's hair is not just an American tradition but an issue involving biblical principles; time that coaches stopped rationalizing and compromising their common sense; time to show the American athlete that his most valuable characteristic is not physical ability but respect for authority."[41]

These extreme statements may not be representative of coaches and certainly should not be taken as proof of the basic conservatism of this occupational category. They may indicate, however, the tendency of coaches to support the existing political and social orders. Let's now examine some more reliable evidence.

One source of such evidence is questionnaires distributed to coaches. The two examples given below illustrate the policy of coaches regarding changing norms:

Item: Of the 1,098 respondent coaches in Florida, 82 percent *disagreed* with this statement in a questionnaire: "A member of an athletic squad should be able to dress (hair, beard, sideburns, clothes) any way he wishes."[42]

Item: A study of 50 southern California high school basketball coaches revealed that 42 percent controlled their athletes off-court activities.[43]

Several studies indicate that physical education teachers (and most coaches are trained in this field) tend to be more conservative than teachers in other fields. One study compared prospective high school physical education teachers with prospective high school liberal arts teachers at a large midwestern university. The researcher found the physical educators to be more traditional, dogmatic, authoritarian, and more conservative in political and religious values.[44]

Physical education teachers at the college level have also been found to be more conservative than professors in other fields. The 1969 survey by the Carnegie Commission on Higher Education of the political opinions of over 60,000 full-time college faculty members found that physical education faculty ranked second out of 30 fields in percentage of respondents who characterized themselves as strongly and moderately conservative (only agriculture faculty members were found to be more conservative).[45]

Unfortunately, there has been little research on the political attitudes of coaches to support the impressionistic observations and indirect evidence given above, but existent research tends to support these notions. One study, by sport psychologists Ogilvie and Tutko, concluded that

> We know that coaches are aggressive people, self-assertive; we know that they are highly organized and ordered; . . . they are also inflexible in their profession as coaches; they dislike change and experimentation; and they are extremely conservative—politically, socially and attitudinally. . . .[46]

In a comparison of high school football coaches with government teachers in Kansas, the former were found to be more conservative on political attitudes and more willing to impose patriotic attitudes on students. This second finding is especially interesting since the coaches were more inclined to do the government teacher's job than the government teacher. Apparently, government teachers felt that it was their duty to pass on the facts and let the students decide, while the coaches felt a responsibility to impose their values on their students.[47]

Sage, in a study comparing college head coaches (football, basketball, and track) with college students and businessmen, found the coaches to be more conservative than the students but somewhat less so than the businessmen.[48] Using the Polyphasic Values Inventory, Sage found the coaches to be significantly more conservative than the college students on 14 of the 20 items. Of special interest were the items of greatest conservatism: the value of obedience to authority and the value of good conduct. Sage concluded:

> The total response profile of the college coaches showed them to possess moderate-conservative values. . . . Although conservatism is not extreme among coaches, it is more pronounced than it is among college students. . . . The findings of this study support the notion that coaches possess a greater conservatism than college students. But an item by item analysis of the response choices certainly does not support the

assertions which have been made recently that coaches are extremely conservative—even reactionary—in value orientation.[49]

The available but sketchy evidence suggests that coaches tend to be conservative. Research has shown, moreover, that coaches, regardless of their sport and of their age, tend to have similar political and social outlooks.[50] The question remains, then, why is there a tendency for coaches to be politically conservative?

The first of at least five reasons for this relationship has to do with the particular lifelong socialization of coaches.[51] There is considerable evidence that coaches, when compared to other faculty members, come from markedly lower socioeconomic backgrounds.[52] For example, while 22 percent of fathers of college professors in general held high status jobs, only six percent of college football and basketball coaches had fathers in high status occupations. Moreover, 58 percent of the basketball coaches and 54 percent of the football coaches had fathers in the low or very low occupational prestige categories. There are two related reasons why this is significant for our discussion. Considerable social science research shows that child rearing practices differ by social class. Working-class parents, for instance, are much more likely than middle-class parents to use physical punishment, to be more authoritarian, and more rigidly conventional.[53] In addition, working-class parents tend to hold particular values: law and order, obedience to authority, and political conservatism.[54] Because parental values are transmitted to their offspring and then internalized, it follows that persons growing up in working-class families will themselves tend to possess values stressing political and social conservatism.

The second reason for the propensity for conservatism among coaches is that almost invariably they are former athletes. As we will see in the next section, athletics is a ruthless selection process that encourages certain traits and discourages others. Coaches are products of the American athletic system, and the thesis of this chapter is that this system is conservative.

Third, coaching is an occupational subculture, and socialization theory suggests that members of a group tend to possess similar value orientations. There are two reasons for this: selection and assimilation. Occupational choice is often made on the basis of compatible values. That is, the individual is attracted to a particular occupation because he is in agreement with the values of that occupation. Typically, too, an individual who aspires to a particular occupation will internalize the values, attitudes, and behaviors characteristic of persons in that occupation, especially the characteristics of the most successful ones (this process is called "anticipatory socialization").[55]

In addition to selection and assimilation, the individual will also feel overt pressure to adopt the attitudes, values, and behaviors of those in the occupation. Communities, school boards, and fans demand that their coaches support the traditional values because these persons are hired to mold the character of youth. Thus, those coaches or potential coaches who harbor political and social views outside the mainstream will have a great difficulty finding or retaining a job, thereby leaving the vast majority of the jobs to those considered politically safe.

The subcultural character of the coaching profession is maintained by the open opposition from the academic community. This hostility strengthens the isolation of coaches by creating alienation and polarization. This opposition stems from the belief that coaches are antiintellectual, dehumanizing, and insensitive to the individuality of their athletes. Whether these beliefs are accurate or not, the result is an antagonistic relationship that develops solidarity among coaches and tends to reinforce their unity around specific beliefs.[56]

Finally, and perhaps most crucially, the success or failure of teams depends almost entirely on whether the coach is considered competent (in other words, whether his teams win more than they lose). Thus, there is a strong tendency for coaches to control the situation as much as possible. Since they will be held responsible for the outcome, they will make the decisions (who will play, what plays will be called, and strategy). Moreover, they will control as much of the players' lives as possible because what they eat, when they sleep, whom they date, whether they have long hair may make a difference in their (the coaches') uncertain world.

The rationale for controlling the lives of players off the field is summed up in this statement given by a coach to the players on his team: "Our school, our team, our coaches, and our community are judged by your behavior. It is very important that you be gentlemen in all your actions."[57] Apparently, this coach felt the need to control an area that is more certain than the outcome of a game, and which also has a bearing on whether he keeps his job or not. For all these reasons, coaches find it difficult to be tolerant of behavior outside of community norms. As Edwards has put it, "the apparent inflexibility of coaches then derives at least in part from the institutionalized demand that they be totally liable for outcomes in a situation wrought with uncertainties."[58]

The Political Attitudes of Athletes

Existing research that contrasts athletes with nonathletes consistently finds that the former are the more politically conservative. Walter Schafer examined this relationship, especially among high school students, and has concluded:

> Interscholastic athletics serve first and foremost as a social device for steering young people—participants and spectators alike—into the mainstream of American life through the overt and covert teaching of "appropriate" attitudes, values, norms and behavior patterns. As a result school sports tend to exert more of a conservatizing and integrating influence in the society than an innovative or progressive influence.[59]

Two studies support Schafer's contention. The first was a study of 937 male seniors from eight high schools in New York. The researchers found: (1) the greater the participation in extracurricular activities (athletics and others), the greater the acceptance of authority; (2) athletes are more likely than nonathletes to believe that the American way of life is superior to that of any other country; (3) athletes were less likely than nonathletes to endorse a statement calling for fundamental structural change in American society; and (4) athletes, more than nonathletes, believed that resistance to the draft was basically wrong.[60]

Research on college students has produced essentially the same findings. When compared with college nonathletes, college athletes were found to be more conservative, less interested and active in politics, more tolerant of violations of civil liberties, and more tolerant of repressive reactions to campus unrest.[61]

However, one qualification exists to the generalization that athletes tend to be conservative. Petrie and Reid studied the political attitudes of Canadian athletes and found them to be generally liberal.[62] This may mean that the conservatism of sport is situationally specific, i.e., specific to a particular culture. If true, this would reconfirm the thesis that sport mirrors society.

Why do American athletes tend to be politically conservative? A number of reasons have been advanced. First, athletes are the prestige leaders in their school and community. Because they benefit from the way things are, they rarely criticize the status quo. Second, since athletes devote substantial time and energy to sports activities, they have less time than nonathletes to become involved in or even consider social criticism. Third, athletes are more likely to have grown accustomed to accepting, rather than questioning, authority.[63] A fourth reason is that it is almost impossible to remain radical in the sports world. Athletes whose views and behavior are nonconventional will soon be weeded out from the regimented world most coaches insist on.[64]

No research has yet been undertaken contrasting the political attitudes of professional athletes and nonathletes with similar educational backgrounds. Presumably, two factors should operate to make professional athletes especially conservative: (1) they have been successful school athletes with all the attendant pressures by the schools and the communities on athletes to be conventional; and (2) they are successful in both monetary and prestige dimensions, making it difficult to question the system.

A most important reason why athletes at all levels are politically more conservative than nonathletes is that most persons who wield authority in the sports world are conservative. Athletes, then, hear a consistent viewpoint and feel a consistent set of constraints on their behavior from powerful others. Let's examine who these powerful persons are, first at the school level and then the professional level.

Athletes in school are affected most by their coaches and school administrators. We have already noted that coaches tend to be very conventional, politically conservative, and resistant to change. School administrators, too, tend to be politically conservative. Their significant reference group is the school board or board of regents, which represent the school's constituency. These groups do not want school representatives deviating from community expectations.

At the college level, a most significant reference group is the school's alumni, especially those who are likely to be the biggest financial contributors. We can assume that as persons become wealthier, they will tend to be more conservative. These persons pressure school administrators, at least indirectly, to keep their school's representatives in line. According to Jack Scott:

> The conservatism that engulfs the American sporting scene to this day stems in no small measure from the alumni groups that control intercollegiate athletic programs throughout the country. Not surprisingly, alumni who have the time, finances, and inclination to involve themselves in, and contribute to the financing of, a professionalized athletic program for college students are conservative men. Despite the existence at nearly all colleges of athletic advisory boards comprised of faculty, administrators, and students, it is these wealthy alumni who play the most influential role in the hiring and firing of college coaches and athletic directors. Berny Wagner, the head track and field coach at Oregon State, openly admits that coaches are not hired primarily to serve college athletes, but to please "alumni and other interested private parties" who finance the athletic programs.
>
> Just how do Mr. Wagner and other coaches please "alumni and other interested private parties"? The most obvious way is by producing winning teams that the alumni can proudly and vicariously identify with. Another less obvious but perhaps more important way is by molding young boys into clean-cut, obedient, yet competitive, acquisitive adults who will take their "proper" place in American society.[65]

Another set of persons who exert a powerful influence on amateur athletes are those running the various leagues or sanctioning bodies (e.g., State High School Activities Association, The Big Eight, The National Collegiate Athletic Association, The Amateur Athletic Union). Decision makers in these organizations have great power over athletes and athletic programs. They decide on matters of eligibility, investigate cases of alleged violations of rules, negotiate television contracts, sanction postseason play, etc. These leaders, like school administrators, are image conscious. To obtain television contracts or favorable treatment from Congress, one must not condone unconventional politics. So, Walter Byers, the executive director of the NCAA, insisted that the decision by the American Broadcasting Company not to show the peace-oriented halftime show at the previously described Buffalo-Holy Cross football game was correct. Moreover, his editorials in the *NCAA News* have praised Vice President Spiro Agnew (before Agnew's resignation from office) and condemned Harry Edwards, leader of the black boycott of the 1968 Olympics. Ironically, however, Byers has insisted that "college athletics are not political and he regularly condemns anyone who attempts to inject 'politics' into the intercollegiate athletic arena."[66]

Professional athletes, in addition to the conservative pressures exerted on them during their school days, experience constraints on their behavior from several additional sources. Foremost are owners of professional teams. By definition, these are wealthy persons who have benefitted from the existing system. Moreover, their teams can exist only with community support. Hence, there is a strong tendency among owners to promote patriotic pageantry at games and to expect their athletes to conform to community norms.

Sports announcers and sports writers also tend to be biased toward the conservative end of the political spectrum. Sports announcers are controlled totally by the team owners or by the networks. Thus, the attitudes expressed are those of powerful (and conservative) others. To a lesser extent, this is also true of sports writers. These persons, if they travel with the team, receive all kinds of consideration—from meals and travel, to permission to interview—if they are in the good graces of the team owner. Leonard Shector has described it this way:

> George Weiss, recently retired president of the New York Mets, once put it this way: "To hell with the newspapermen. You can buy them with a steak." This might be overstatement. Sports reporters who like their jobs so much have a tendency to *want* to please the management of the sporting organizations. They easily become what are called "house men." The man who covers a baseball team year after year spends a good deal more time with the management of the ball club than with his own editors; indeed, with his own wife. He becomes, if he is interested enough in his job to want to keep it, more involved with the fortunes of the team than that of his newspaper.[67]

In addition to the owners and the media, professional athletes are constrained to be conservative by their coaches and their league or sanctioning body. A classic example of the latter was the action taken by the persons who control boxing in the United States to strip Muhammad Ali of his world title because of his stand as a conscientious objector. The concern of league officials is exemplified in the efforts of Pete Rozelle, commissioner of the National Football League, to have all players show proper respect for the national anthem (the athletes are told how to stand, how to hold their helmets, etc.). The NFL is also responsible for the patriotic festivals that accompany the Super Bowl (perhaps the/ best example being the re-creation of the Battle of New Orleans from the War of 1812 during halftime of the 1971 Super Bowl).

Summary

Two themes have dominated this chapter: sport is political in character, and persons connected with sport in almost any capacity tend to be conservative. The basic conservativism of sport has two important implications for American society. First, the athletic program of American schools, to which most persons are exposed, supports and reinforces a view of the world and society that perpetuates the status quo. This is accomplished through the promotion of American values and support of the American politico-economic system.

A second implication, given the institutional character of sport, is that efforts to change sport will not come from those who control sport. Moreover, any attack on sport will be defined as an attack on society itself. Thus, change in sport will be slow and, more likely than not, the result of a real struggle.

Notes

1. *University Daily Kansan,* (December 12, 1971).
2. Phillip Goodhart and Christopher Chataway, *War Without Weapons* (London: W.H. Allen, 1968), p. 3.
3. See Ralf Dahrendorf, *Class and Class Conflict in Industrial Society* (Palo Alto: Stanford University Press, 1959); and Robert Michels, *Political Parties* (New York: Dover, 1959, first published in 1914).
4. See Richard Edward Lapchick, *The Politics of Race and International Sport: The Case of South Africa* (Westport, Conn.: Greenwood Press, 1975).
5. Jerry Isenberg, *How Many Miles to Camelot? Only Thing* (New York: Pocket Books, 1971), p. ix. The "canonization" of Lombardi in itself is an interesting commentary on sport in American society. Somehow his brutal methods are overshadowed by his success at winning football games.
6. Quoted in James Toback, "Longhorns and Longhairs," *Harpers Magazine* (November, 1970), p. 72.
7. Richard D. Mandell, *The Nazi Olympics* (New York: Macmillan, 1971).
8. See "Diplomacy Through Sports," *Newsweek* (September 4, 1972), p. 42; Jerry Kirshenbaum, "Assembly Line for Champions," *Sports Illustrated* 45 (July 12, 1976), pp. 56-65; and Michael Novak, "War Games: Facts and Coverage," *National Review* (September 3, 1976), pp. 953-954. For a similar study of the Soviet Union's emphasis on sport, see Robin Herman, "The Soviet Union Views Sports Strength as a Power Tool," *New York Times* (July 11, 1976), p. 15S. See also, Andrew Strenk, "Sport as an International Political and Diplomatic Tool," *Arena Newsletter* 1 (August, 1977), pp. 3-9.
9. Frank Deford, "The Once and Future Diplomat," *Sports Illustrated* 34 (March 1, 1971), pp. 63-75.
10. Robert M. Goodhue, "The Politics of Sport: An Institutional Focus," *Proceedings,* North American Society for Sport History (1974), pp. 34-35.
11. See Donald W. Ball, "Olympic Games Competition: Structural Correlates of National Success," *International Journal of Comparative Sociology* 13 (September-December, 1972), pp. 186-199; and Goodhart and Chataway, *War Without Weapons.*
12. "Military to Flank Royals in Opener," *Kansas City Star* (April 1, 1973).
13. Sandy Padwe, "Sports and Politics Must be Separate-At Least Some Politics, That Is," *Philadelphia Inquirer* (December 14, 1971), p. 35.
14. Jerry Isenberg, *How Many Miles to Camelot?* (New York: Holt, Rinehart and Winston, 1972), p. 197.
15. Neil Amdur, "Garden to Hear Anthem at Track Meet, After All," *New York Times* (January 14, 1973), p. 29. Similarly, when the Baltimore Orioles decided to limit the playing

of the anthem to special occasions, fans were outraged and the city council passed a resolution suggesting that the song be played before *every* Baltimore baseball game; see J.D. Reed, "Gallantly Screaming," *Sports Illustrated* 46 (January 3, 1977), pp. 52-60.

16. A claim that could not be further from the truth. The playing of the winner's national anthem, athletes representing nations, and decisions made as to where the Olympics will be held, and what nations may or may not compete are just some of the more overt examples of the political nature of the Olympic Games.

17. Tom Wicker, "Patriotism for the Wrong Ends," *New York Times* (January 19, 1973).

18. Thomas G. Sanders, "The Social Functions of Futebol," *American Universities Field Staff Reports,* East Coast South America Series, vol. XIV, no. 2, (July, 1970), p. 7.

19. Ibid., pp. 8-9; see also Janet Lever, "Soccer: Opium of the Brazilian People," *Trans-Action* 7 (December, 1969), pp. 36-43.

20. Paul Hoch, "The World of Playtime, USA," *Daily World* (April 27, 1972), p. 12.

21. Glenn Dickey, "The White House and Superfan," *San Francisco Chronicle* (November 30, 1971), p. 50.

22. Quoted in Kathleen Maxa, "Presidential Candidates as Sportsmen," *The Washington Star* (August 24, 1975), p. G-4.

23. "Athletes for McGovern," *McGovern for President Newsletter #7* (November, 1971).

24. "Famous Faces in the Races," *Time* (November 1, 1976), p. 38.

25. James Reston, "Sports and Politics," *New York Times* (November 26, 1971).

26. See John N. Washburn, "Sport as a Soviet Tool, *Foreign Affairs* 34 (April, 1956), pp. 490-499.

27. See Brian M. Petrie, "Sport and Politics," *Sport and Social Order,* ed. Donald W. Ball and John W. Loy (Reading, Mass.: Addison-Wesley, 1975), pp.199-207.

28. Excerpts from the press release of the address by the Vice President of the United States, Spiro Agnew, Birmingham, Alabama (January 18, 1972), pp. 5-6.

29. For a critique of the Agnew position, see Nicholas von Hoffman, "The Sport of Politicians," *Washington Post* (January 24, 1972), p. B1.

30. See William Johnson, "And Smile, Smile, Smile," *Sports Illustrated* 38 (June 4, 1973), pp. 76-78; William Johnson, "Courting Time in Peking," *Sports Illustrated* 39 (July 2, 1973), pp. 12-15; William Johnson, "Sport in China," *Sports Illustrated,* 39 part 1 (September 24, 1973), pp. 82-100, and part 2 (October 1, 1973), pp. 42-53; and Jonathan Kolatch, *Sport, Politics and Ideology in China* (Middle Village, N.Y.: Jonathan David, 1972.)

31. William Johnson, "Faces on a New China Scroll," *Sports Illustrated* 39 (September 24, 1973), p. 86.

32. Harry Edwards, *The Revolt of the Black Athlete* (New York: The Free Press, 1969), p. xv. See also Jack Scott and Harry Edwards, "After the Olympics: Buying Off Protest," *Ramparts* (November, 1969), pp. 16-21.

33. See "World Athletes: Victims of Political Games," *U. S. News & World Report* (July 26, 1976), p. 52; Larry Eldridge, "Like Clockwork, Politics Jars Olympics," *Christian Science Monitor* (July 6, 1976), p. 11; and Frank Deford, "More Dark Clouds over Montreal," *Sports Illustrated* 45 (July 19, 1976), pp. 32-41.

34. Bob Monahan, "Harvard Trackmen Boycott Meet Over Politics," *Boston Globe* (April 20, 1972).

35. *Des Moines Register and Tribune* (October 24, 1971).

36. David Nelson, quoted in *The Oregonian* (December 28, 1970), sports section, p. 1.

37. Quoted in John Underwood, "The Desperate Coach," *Sports Illustrated* 31 (August 24, 1969), p. 71.

38. Ibid., p. 30.

39. Rod Paige, "Racial Empathy and the White Coach," *Scholastic Coach* 41 (October, 1971), p. 62; see also "Black Athletes Stir Campuses at Risk of Careers," *New York Times* (November 16, 1969), p. 1.

40. F. Melvin Cratsley, cited in Underwood, "The Desperate Coach," pp. 70-71.

41. Tony Simpson, "Real Men, Short Hair,"

Intellectual Digest 4 (November, 1973), p. 76, excerpted from *Texas Coach* (May, 1973).

42. Don Viller, "Survey '71," *The Athletic Journal* (October, 1971), p. 58.
43. Gordon L. James, "The Changing Nature of the Coaching Challenge," *Scholastic Coach* 41 (February, 1972), p. 57.
44. Gerald S. Kenyon, "Certain Psychological and Cultural Characteristics Unique to Prospective Teachers of Physical Education," *The Research Quarterly* 36 (March, 1965), pp. 105-112.
45. S.M. Lipset, M.A. Trow, and E.C. Ladd, *Faculty Opinion Survey* (Carnegie Commission on Higher Education, no date).
46. Bruce C. Ogilvie and Thomas A. Tutko, "Self-Perception as Compared with Measured Personality of Male Physical Educators" in *Contemporary Psychology of Sport* ed. Gerald S. Kenyon (Chicago: The Athletic Institute, 1970), pp. 73-77; see also Eldon E. Snyder, "Aspects of Social and Political Values of High School Coaches," *International Review of Sport Sociology* 8 (1973), pp. 73-87.
47. Michael Boman and D. Stanley Eitzen, "The Political Attitudes of Football Coaches" (University of Kansas, 1973).
48. George H. Sage, "Value Orientations of American College Coaches Compared to Those of Male College Students and Businessmen," *Sport and American Society,* 2nd. ed., ed. George H. Sage (Reading, Mass.: Addison-Wesley, 1974), pp. 207-228.
49. Ibid., pp. 222-223.
50. George H. Sage, "Occupational Socialization and Value Orientations of Athletic Coaches," *The Research Quarterly* 44 (October, 1973), pp. 269-277.
51. Many of the insights that follow come from George H. Sage, "An Occupational Analysis of the College Coach," *Sport and Social Order,* ed. Donald W. Ball and John W. Loy (Reading, Mass.: Addison-Wesley, 1975), pp. 395-455; John D. Massengale, "Coaching as an Occupational Subculture," *Phi Delta Kappan* 61 (October, 1974), pp. 140-142; and John D. Massengale, "Occupational Role Conflict and the Teacher/Coach" (Paper presented at the Western Social Science Association meetings, Denver, May 2, 1975).
52. John W. Loy and George H. Sage, "Social Origins, Academic Achievement, Athletic Achievement, and Career Mobility Patterns of College Coaches" (Paper presented at the annual meeting of the American Sociological Association, New Orleans, August, 1972).
53. For a summary of the research findings, see D. Stanley Eitzen, *Social Structure and Social Problems* (Boston: Allyn and Bacon, 1974), pp. 255-261.
54. M.L. Kohn and C. Schooler, "Class, Occupation, and Orientation," *American Sociological Review* 34 (October, 1969), pp. 659-678.
55. See Morris Rosenberg, *Occupations and Values* (Glencoe, Ill.: The Free Press, 1967).
56. Massengale, "Coaching as an Occupational Subculture," p. 141.
57. From a statement on the policies concerning individual conduct, Shawnee Mission South High School (Shawnee Mission, Kansas, 1973).
58. Harry Edwards, *Sociology of Sport* (Homewood, Ill.: Dorsey Press, 1973), p. 140.
59. Walter W. Schafer, "Sport, Socialization and the School: Toward Maturity or Enculturation?" (Paper presented at the Third International Symposium on the Sociology of Sport, Waterloo, Ont., August, 1971), p. 6.
60. Richard A. Rehberg and Michael Cohen, "Political Attitudes and Participation in Extra-Curricular Activities with Special Emphasis on Interscholastic Activities," mimeographed. (New York: State University of New York at Binghamton, no date).
61. Derrick J. Norton, "A Comparison of Political Attitudes and Political Participation of Athletes and Non-Athletes," (master's thesis, University of Oregon, 1971).
62. Brian M. Petrie and Elizabeth L. Reid, "The Political Attitudes of Canadian Athletes," *Proceedings of the Fourth Canadian Psycho-Motor Learning and Sports Psychology Symposium* (Waterloo, Ont.: University of Waterloo, 1972), pp. 514-530.
63. These first three reasons are taken from Walter E. Schafer, "Sport and Youth Counterculture: Contrasting Socialization Themes" in *Social Problems in Athletics* ed. Daniel M. Landers (Urbana, Ill.: University of Illinois Press, 1976), pp. 183-200.

64. Bruce C. Ogilvie and Thomas A. Tutko, "Sport: If You Want to Build Character, Try Something Else," *Psychology Today* 5 (October 5, 1971), pp. 61-63; see also Terry Nau, "The Games People Play," *The Daily Collegian* (Pennsylvania State University, May 6, 1971).

65. Jack Scott, *The Athletic Revolution* (New York: The Free Press, 1971), pp. 187-188.

66. Ibid. See also "Out of Right Field," *Newsweek* (January 5, 1970), p. 35.

67. Leonard Shecter, *The Jocks* (New York: Paperback Library, 1969), p. 23.

abc
7

Sport and the Economy 7

In chapter 1, we characterized three levels of sport: "informal" sport, "organized" sport, and "corporate" sport, the latter referring to levels of sporting activity dominated by factors—economic or political—extrinsic to sport itself. "Corporate" sport, in which the relatively spontaneous, pristine nature of "informal" sport has been corrupted, characterizes sport in contemporary America. And as the tendency toward "corporate" sport has increased, sports have become more regimented, conservative, and less "playful."[1] Economic factors have contributed to the emergence of "corporate" sport in 20th-century America. As Senator William B. Spong remarked while testifying before the Senate Antitrust and Monopoly Subcommittee, "Today organized professional sports have become so overlaid with business that whatever value emanates from competitive athletics is in my judgment in great danger of being eroded."[2] In this chapter,* we will examine the intimate interrelationship of the economy and sport, its growing commercialization, and the implications of this trend for sport itself. We will also analyze the economic systems of professional and amateur athletics, focusing on their assumptions, dynamics, and functions.

The Interrelationship of Sport and the Economy

As previously noted, the 20th century has witnessed an accelerating sports boom, involving individuals as spectators, participants, and promoters. Not only has the growth of the American economy and the emergence of unprecedented affluence, especially since World War II, had an impact on sports, but, in turn, the growing interest in sport has had a substantial economic impact. Sports and leisure-time pursuits have become one of the nation's major industries. Billions of dollars—more than the cost of national defense—are spent annually on a broad array of sporting activities as diverse as snowmobiling, bicycling, snorkeling, and sky surfing.[3] Merely in terms of paid admissions to major sports events, the estimated figures for 1974 are staggering: $71.6 million in the NFL, $156.2 million for college football, $91.9 million for major league baseball, $49.3 million for college basketball, and $32.9 million for professional basketball.[4]

The Economic Climate and Sport

Sport is understandably affected by a society's economic health. A substantial expansion of the economy will be reflected in a society's sporting activities, as has been the case with the rising affluence of the American population and its effect on the 20th-century sports boom. By the same token, an economic depression or recession will have a negative effect on sports.

*Norman R. Yetman, professor of sociology and American studies, University of Kansas, coauthored this chapter.

The influence of economic factors on sport has become very evident in the impact of the "energy crisis," which first generated alarm in the autumn of 1973. Because so much fuel is consumed by travel for spectators and teams and by stadium lights (see table 7-1), energy shortages could conceivably affect nearly all sporting activities. Proposals for playing major league baseball games during the day rather than primarily at night to save energy brought immediate protests from owners, who contended that attendance would decline so drastically that baseball could not survive economically. Possible other changes that an energy shortage might bring are: declining numbers of spectators, restricted schedules, pooled scouting, and curtailment of minor league, and school sports.[5] At present, the United States has not really confronted the full impact of energy shortages on sport—either as spectators or participants. Leisure time will probably increase in the future, thereby providing more pressures for additional sporting activities. Just how Americans will deal with the changes dictated by decreased energy resources will be interesting to observe.

Table 7-1. Estimated Gallons of Fuel Consumed in Leisure-Time Pursuits, 1972*.

Activity	Gallons Consumed
Football**	564,043,166
Basketball	238,394,571
Horse Racing	97,522,973
Auto Racing	93,639,696
Rodeos	88,000,000
Bowling	40,000,000
Baseball	33,657,289
Wrestling	27,108,185
Golf	14,560,000

*Includes spectator travel, team travel (for football and auto racing), and electricity.

**The fuel usage estimated for the NFL was 47,708,700 gallons a year, college football 141,097,216 gallons, and high school football 376,237,250 gallons.

Source: Automobile Competition Committee of the U.S. Statistics, reported in William Johnson, "No Fueling, the Crisis is Here," *Sports Illustrated* 39 (December 3, 1973), p. 37.

Sport Values and Capitalistic Values

As we have previously noted, many of the values attributed to sport also provide the justifying ideology for the American business system. The emphases on success, individual competition, hard work, perseverance, discipline and order, and paradoxically, on the necessity for submerging individual efforts for the good of the team are as integral to the American business creed as to the American sports credo.[6] Given this identity in values, it is not surprising that many successful athletes are drawn into the business world. Moreover, interest or participation in sports itself is a value; sports knowledge is perceived as a positive personal attribute, and a person lacking such interests or knowledge is frequently regarded at best as strange or curious, at worst as unmasculine. Finally, the business value of sports is reflected in heavy corporate investment in sports as a form of business entertainment.

Sport and the Corporation

Even more explicit, however, are the operational ties between sports and modern corporations. Historically, the relationship of professional sports teams and business enterprise has been strong. The first professional football teams were sponsored by and bore the names of businesses, and thus were promotional entities. Bil Gilbert has shown how extensively modern American industry supports sports programs for its employees. "American industry is the world's greatest patron of fun and games. Currently about $1.5 billion is being spent on employee recreation."[7]

Moreover, sporting events have historically been sponsored by industrial companies with concern for their image and their belief that sports will provide a profitable form of advertising and investment. This is true not only in media (radio, TV, and magazine) advertising, but in promotional activities ranging from little league sponsorships to the rights to naming a municipal stadium (e.g., Schaefer Stadium in suburban Boston, Busch Stadium in St. Louis, and Rich Stadium in Buffalo).

The Super Bowl, the NFL championship, has come to epitomize the intimate relationship between sports and commercial interests. Of 90,000 seats available for the 1973 game in Los Angeles, over 10,000 were awarded to individuals or corporations with commercial or promotional ties to the league, including the presidents of the CBS and NBC television networks, who symbolically shared pro-football commissioner Pete Rozelle's private box. Seated nearby were top executive officers from Chrysler Corporation, one of the prime advertisers for the entire NFL season. Finally, Super Bowl tickets annually prove a coveted prize for winners of sales incentive contests in many American companies—including Tasters Choice, Ford, Chrysler, and Sears.[8]

The most blatant use of sport for commercial purposes occurs in automobile racing. Here drivers and owners of race cars receive a fee for using a particular brand of tire, oil, brake linings, or whatever, so that the companies can use this publicity to sell their products. In 1974, for example, driver A.J. Foyt received $225,000 from Goodyear for using their tires, and 20 other drivers in the Indianapolis 500 received payments from either Goodyear or Firestone ranging from $10,000 to $300,000. These companies budget $8 million and $3 million, respectively, for automobile racing.[9]

Commercial interests have long used successful athletes to advertise their products. Two of the most successful athletes in the merchandising game have been Mark Spitz and O.J. Simpson. Spitz, winner of seven gold medals in the 1972 Olympics, sold his services to a number of companies for a long term contract of $5 million.[10] O. J. Simpson, the legendary football player, does commercials for Kenner Products (children's toys), Hyde Spot-bilt shoes, Shick, Foster Grant, Chevrolet, R. C. Cola, Hertz, Trau and Loevner (T-shirts), and others.[11]

Table 7-2. The Super Bowl-1977

Site: Rose Bowl (rental fee: $112,000).

Attendance: 100,451 (cost per ticket $20).

Television spectators: 78 million (est.).

- Cost to NBC to purchase television rights: $3.5 million.
- Cost to NBC for breakfast for 1,000: $75,000.
- Cost per minute to television advertisers: $250,000.

Expected gross to NFL (ticket sales and broadcast revenues): $5.5 million.

- Cost of NFL cocktail party: $75,000.
- Cost of travel, lodging, and players' shares: $2.5 million.
  - Pay per winning player: $15,000.
  - Pay per losing player: $7,500.
  - Pay per official: $1,500.

Amount of money wagered: $260 million (est.).

Economic impact to the Los Angeles area (using a multiplier of 5): between $85 million and $105 million.

Sources: Bob Collins, "Just Your Basic Sports Classic," *Rocky Mountain News* (January 9, 1977), p. 57; "The Super Show," *Time* (January 10, 1977), pp. 28-34; and "It's Super Bowl Fever at its Highest Pitch," Associated Press release (January 7, 1977).

Another form of advertising is for a corporation to sponsor an event such as a tournament in bowling, golf, tennis, and skiing. This sponsorship has been especially crucial for the recent gains in women's professional sports. Corporations selling products such as Virginia Slims, Carlton, Colgate, L'eggs, Bonnie Bell, Sarah Coventry, Sears, S & H Green Stamps, and Sealy have underwritten women's golf and tennis tournaments (about $20 million in 1976) raising the prize money and the visibility of womens' sports significantly.[12]

Sports and the Media

Business interests use the popularity of sport to sell their products.

> To illustrate the effect of advertising, consider the impact on the beer market in New York of the rise of the Mets. From the standpoint of the sponsor, Rheingold, the Mets provided a means of promoting beer sales in its home territory, where its local rival Ballantine sponsored the Yankees until 1967. And, indeed, while Ballantine sales fell from 4.5 million barrels in 1965 to 2.2 million in 1969, Rheingold sales increased from 3.0 million barrels in 1965 to 3.5 million in 1969. Similarly, Schaefer Brewing of New York, which sponsored the Giants, Knicks, and Rangers, increased sales from 4.6 million barrels to 5.4 million during this same period.[13]

As Bob Carey, president of NFL properties, has characterized one role of professional football:

> We imagine pro-football as a power grid, pulsating and popularly rooted. A national promotion guy clamps his wire into the grid and gets the benefit of the power. He uses the popularity of the game to sell his product, and if it's a good product, everybody benefits.[14]

This is the rationale for business interests underwriting sports on television. Because business is willing to pay over $250,000 per minute of advertising during a Super Bowl game, $112,000 for a World Series minute, $105,000 for a Monday Night Football minute, and $25,000 for a one minute commercial during the baseball "Game of the Week," the three major networks provided 1,100 hours of sports at a cost of $315 million in 1976.[15]

The media have been crucial to the rise of the sports industry in America. The historical development of sports journalism shows the essentially symbiotic relationship between sports and the media. The telegraph, newspapers, popular sports books and magazines, the movies, radio, and television are all media forms that have influenced and been influenced by public interest in sports. Television, however, has had by far the most dramatic effect. It would be difficult to list the ways in which television has transformed sport, but so pervasive has been its impact that Johnson's claim that it "has produced more revolutionary—and irrevocable—changes in sports than in any other force since man began playing organized games" does not seem exaggerated.[16]

The most immediate apparent effect of television on sports has been the changes in patterns of viewing them. As fans turned to watching major league or major college sports on television, attendance at minor league, community, and interscholastic games declined dramatically. High school sports activities, previously community social events, were seriously affected as fans' allegiances and identifications shifted from local areas to teams from major urban areas.[17] The impact of television on minor league baseball is perhaps most striking. In 1939, major league baseball attendance was nearly 9 million; minor league attendance was more than 15 million. By 1949, at the zenith of minor league baseball, more than 42 million fans watched minor league baseball, but twenty years later, after television had become virtually universal in America, minor league attendance had declined to merely 10 million and the number of minor league clubs had dropped from 488 in 1949 to 155 in 1969.[18] Television probably contributed to the demise of semipro and amateur town and neighborhood teams as well.

What are the implications of these shifts in fan loyalties and identification from local communities to urban centers? Although empirical studies are presently lacking, it does suggest that America has become a nation of TV spectators, producing a qualitative change in sporting events and in the spectator's relation to it. An integral component of any sporting spectacle is the crowd. As individuals increasingly view sporting events alone or in small groups, much of the crowd contagion has been lost. William Johnson has alluded to this change:

> The Spectator leaned close to his flickering screen, the better to see. Well, it was good. He supposed the crowd did have to shrink and jostle about, spilling popcorn on itself and blowing choking billows of cigar smoke at the ceiling. But the Spectator was insulated from all social contact, seated on cushions miles away from all maddening environments. No expenditure of physical commitment, psychological dishevelment or cold cash had been required.[19]

If anonymity is one consequence of the urban environment, television is an ideal urban sports viewing medium.

On the other hand, if television has spelled the demise of many small town and community athletic teams as a focal point of community integration, it may well have contributed to a far broader sense of community and greater identification within a larger metropolitan area; indeed, as we have previously argued, television sports has enabled millions of Americans to identify with and participate in nationally common symbols, myths, and rites, and in this sense has contributed to a sense of national identity. Professional football in general and the Super Bowl spectacular in particular have had this effect. No other single event can regularly attract the attention of 85 million people. In cities having successful football teams, sport transcends all other phenomena as an integrating mechanism. Entire cities are united as they celebrate their heroes on the tube; crime drops precipitiously. Although every city with a Super Bowl competitor has experienced the same phenomenon, it was nowhere more apparent nor more noteworthy than in 1973 in Washington, D.C., a city whose inhabitants are usually urbane, blase, unimpressed with celebrities, and torn by partisan bickering. However, as their beloved Redskins approached their fated annihilation at the hands of the Miami Dolphins, from the President to the city's most humble citizen, little else was discussed; the city went on an emotional binge that permitted it to suppress the realities of war, inflation, and scandal in high places. Such effects, of course, occurred before the advent of television, but never on such a widespread and all-enveloping scale.

Economically, increased revenues from radio and television for organized sports have been staggering; the effect has been to make sports economically dependent on television. Revenue from radio and television broadcasting for major league baseball rose from *nothing* in 1929 to $884,000 in 1939 to $3,365,000 in 1950 to more than $50.8 million in 1976.[20] In 1975, the National Football League received $59 million—or $2.28 million per team—from broadcasting, without which the league as a whole would have had accounting losses.[21]

A substantial television contract is essential to a professional sports league's financial health—indeed, to its survival. An NBC television contract saved the fledgling American Football League from an early demise and ultimately led to its congressionally sanctioned merger with the National Football League. The lack of such a contract led to the demise of the American Basketball Association and the World Football League.

The relationship between television and professional sports has, therefore, become a mutually dependent one. To obtain television coverage, a league needs an appealing product, but to achieve that product, it needs television coverage to publicize it adequately. William C. Ford, former owner of the Detroit Lions, commented on the dependence of sports on the media. "There is no way we could survive without television. We couldn't make it without the income and the exposure. TV creates more interest and this influences box office sales."[22] Ford's claim is questionable, for it is likely that pro football could indeed survive, although not in the manner to which all—players, coaches, and owners—in the industry have become accustomed. Nevertheless, Ford's point does exemplify the essentially symbiotic relationship between the two.

The figures cited above merely indicate the magnitude of the economic impacts of television on sports and of sports on television. However, they provide no indication of the qualitative effects for sport of this huge outlay. Given this dependence on television, one of the primary considerations in moving professional sports franchises from one city to another or in establishing a new franchise in a city is potential radio and television revenues available. Testimony before the special senate subcommittee investigating professional basketball, for instance, revealed that the shifts of the Kansas City Athletics to Oakland and the Milwaukee Braves to Atlanta were dictated primarily by the fact that broadcasting revenues would be increased between half and a million dollars per year.[23] Moreover, expansion to new franchise cities is dependent on market surveys evaluating the size and tastes of the potential media audiences.[24] This dependence has enabled the media to dictate starting times of games to achieve the largest possible audiences, to dictate time-outs during games (which can radically transform games such as soccer and hockey, in which no time-outs normally occur), and even to dictate schedules.[25] Coaches recognize the promotional and recruiting value of national television exposure. Commenting on Atlantic Coast Conference schedule changes that enabled nationally ranked Maryland and North Carolina State to play a nationally televised basketball game immediately prior to the 1973 Super Bowl, the Maryland sports information director declared, "We'd play a game at 2A.M. to get it on national television."[26] William Johnson concludes that "the geography, the economics, the timing, the esthetics, the very ethos of sports as we know it have been profoundly altered and have come to be totally dependent upon television's wired-up world of arcane circuitry and undressed commercialism."[27]

Who Benefits Economically from Sports?

The sports boom has benefitted a wide range of individuals and economic enterprises. One of the best indices of the boom is the growth of the sporting goods industry, which caters to and creates the needs of the American public for adequate sporting equipment. Annual sales of sporting and recreational goods have increased dramatically, rising from $9.6 billion in 1967 to $24.7 billion in 1976.[28] The sporting goods industry is extremely diverse, providing equipment for such diverse activities as sky diving, hang gliding, boating, and handball. The money involved is enormous. For example, in 1976, $100 million was spent on waterskiing, $500 million for fishing, and $4 billion on golf. The Ski Retailers Council estimated that 4.5 million skiers have spent at least $400 each for their outfits (clothing, boots, and skis), for a total of $1.8 billion. Even cheerleading provides a lucrative market for entrepreneurs, who by producing and distributing pompons and other paraphernalia, operate a business that grosses more than $10 million annually. Additionally, more than 250 cheerleader clinics, training more than 100,000 schoolgirls, grossed $7 million in 1976 (up from $5 million in 1972).[29]

Only a small percentage of those participating in sporting activities derive direct economic benefits from them (the instrumental use of sports—businessmen using golf, tennis, etc., as a means of entertaining clients or customers—is another situation). As we will document more fully in chapter 8, the number of professional athletes competing in major league competition is extremely small. For instance, the total number of full-time players in the four major American team sports—baseball, basketball, football, and hockey—is less than 2,500 annually. Add to this only some 100 golfers who earned more than $20,000, a handful of tennis players, race-car drivers, and jockeys, and it is apparent that the business of professional sport is based on the exploits of a very small group of talented individuals. For those who have attained major league status, the financial benefits have become substantial. However, this has only been the case for a handful of recent superstars, whose well-publicized salaries have given the public a distorted and inflated idea of professional athletes' incomes. These salaries should also be balanced against the brief, often tenuous career of a professional athlete. For instance, the median length of a professional football player's career is 4.4 years, which does not even qualify the typical player for a pension under the 1973 NFL player-management agreement.

Successful professional athletes receive many additional benefits through product endorsements; banquet and speaking appearances; jobs as actors, entertainers, and sports announcers; opportunities for investments in business ventures as diverse as sports camps, real estate developments, quick-order franchises, motels, restaurants; and many others. A sports celebrity such as golfer Arnold Palmer can command as much as $10,000 for a brief personal appearance, but Uni-Managers International exemplifies the process by which the celebrity status of the athlete has become highly commercialized. Uni-Managers have developed a "rent-a-golfer" system whereby a prominent professional golfer will rent his services (for fees up to $5,000 a day) to individuals or corporations either as a gift to the man who has everything or by a company seeking to impress a client.[30] Moreover, professional athletes today have a much greater range of income-producing opportunities than ever. And because they are better educated, their post-playing career opportunities have improved, as well.

For most whose livelihood is dependent on athletic abilities, the financial rewards are not nearly so great.

Item: More than 2,500 individuals presently play minor league baseball, and only seven percent of them will make it to the major leagues. None is covered by the minimum salary scales of major league baseball. In contrast to the $48,000 average annual salary (1976) among major league players, the average salaries in classes AAA and A minor league baseball are $4,500 and $2,000, respectively.

Item: In professional golf, only 300 men follow the tour seeking part of the $9 million a year in prize money. "But it is a costly road. Of the 300 men who follow the tour, a couple of dozen make a great deal of money. Another three dozen make a very good living. Another two dozen more than clear expenses. For the rest of them, for more than 200, the tour is a losing proposition from a financial standpoint."[31]

Item: In professional basketball, a lucrative sports career awaits the successful athlete (average annual salary of $110,000 in 1976). But when both the NBA and ABA were flourishing, there were only 400 players and room only for about 50 rookies each year.

Item: The scholarship athlete in college is virtually paid slave wages for his services. Calculated on the basis of room, books, meals and tuition allowed by the NCAA, a college athlete's salary does not greatly exceed the federal government's stated poverty level and is about at the federally established minimum per hour pay scale.

Coaching is a category of professional athlete frequently overlooked in calculating the economic effects of sports in America. The number of coaches involved in nominally professional coaching roles is extremely small, but when one considers the number of coaches in colleges, junior colleges, high schools, junior high and elementary schools, this becomes a substantial number.

In addition to those directly involved in producing the sport product, many auxiliary businesses benefit from the sports boom. Sport is alleged by its promoters to have an important impact on a community's economy, because hotels, taxies, restaurants, and other business establishments can increase their volume of business. The director of the New York Business Bureau has estimated that the New York Yankees generate $50 million annually to the city's economy. A study of the economic impact of the Pittsburgh Pirates estimated that Pittsburgh benefitted by approximately $21 million ($5.7 million in direct spending by the team, $8.3 million by fans and visiting teams, and another $7.5 million in indirect spending). As a final example, the Miami Department of Publicity and Tourism estimated that the 1976 Super Bowl brought its city about $40 million in income.[32] Huge sports spectaculars—such as the Kentucky Derby, the Indianapolis 500, the Super Bowl, and the World Series—have become major tourist attractions, bringing an economic bonanza to numerous businesses ancillary to sport.

The concessions business is a lucrative one. In 1972, fans consumed 20 million hot dogs, 30 million soft drinks, 25 million cups of beer, and 5 million bags of peanuts, and the largest concessionaire, Sportservice, grossed $100 million. Sportservice and its parent corporation, Emprise, hold exclusive rights to feed fans of seven major league teams, eight professional football teams, five professional basketball teams, four hockey teams, a number of minor league teams, fifty horse and dog tracks, plus contracts with jai-alai frontons (courts), bowling establishments, golf tournaments, and ski lodges.[33] The methods used to obtain these exclusive rights have come under investigation by the government for possible links with organized crime and for antitrust violations.

Benefits from sports accrue to some illicit economic activities as well, foremost of which is gambling. Certainly billions of dollars are bet annually on the outcome of sports events in informal bets, in office pools, and in other relatively unorganized operations.[34] But it is in organized gambling, which focuses extensively—some estimates place it as high as 85 percent—on sport, that the amounts wagered are phenomenal. Government estimates have placed the amount of money involved in illegal organized gambling at some $50 billion annually. In New York City alone, $15 billion was gambled in 1973.[35] Nationally, between 12 and 15 million Americans bet on pro-football on any given weekend.[36] This activity is openly acknowledged and supported by the press wire services and such prestigious publications as the *New York Times,* which regularly carry "point spreads" indicating the point difference of the betting range. And, to reflect its rise to national prominence, football's Super Bowl has become the country's biggest single wagering event, surpassing even the Kentucky Derby.

As the sports mania has pervaded the country, public pressure to legalize sports betting has grown. Such pressure is exerted both by the financial distress of most state governments and by bet-eager constituents. The former presents a formidable argument for legalized betting. The state of Florida in 1975, for example, received $45.4 million in revenue alone from its percentage of the bets on greyhound racing.[37] However, the consequences of legalized state-supported sports betting have not yet been fully assessed. A local study of off-track betting in New York City suggests that it may have several unanticipated effects. First, illegal gambling increased substantially—62 percent—in New York City after the legalization and state control of off-track betting. Second, increasing ease of access to betting sources drew many new gamblers, unsophisticated in betting techniques and, therefore, more likely to lose, into illegal activities. These thousands of new "losers" were reported to include housewives gambling away supermarket money, students betting their allowances, and businessmen raising prices on their goods to make up their losses.[38]

Another form of illicit economic activity that has not been adequately studied is the practice of "scalping"—selling tickets to sports events at prices above those established by management. Such activities are, of course, dependent on market conditions and are possible only in high-demand situations. Thus, to be a scalper in San Diego is hardly a rewarding enterprise, whereas in New York City, in which major sporting events are almost invariably sellouts, the scalper can make a profit and rationalize his activity by declaring that he is performing a service.[39]

The Economics of "Corporate Sport"

We have argued throughout this book that big-time sport in America has transcended the "informal" and "organized" stages to the "corporate" stage—a level where sport is a bureaucratized, commercial, working situation devoid, for the most part, of the joyousness and the challenges of the game per se. Sport *is* big business. Owners of professional teams and their counterparts in big-time college sports are interested in maximizing profits. Athletes are vitally concerned with their salaries, bonuses, retirement benefits, and similar monetary concerns. In this section, we will examine closely the business side of professional and amateur sport. We will look first at professional sports, focusing on team owners and athletes.

Franchise Ownership for Profit

It should be recognized at the outset that there are psychic gratifications in owning a professional team. Many sports owners derive great personal satisfaction from knowing athletes personally—an expensive form of "jocksniffing." In addition, owners are feted by the community as service leaders and achieve a degree of prominence otherwise unattainable in their other business ventures.

Apart from the "psychic income" of team ownership, which from an economist's perspective is an irrational or noneconomic factor, there are very substantial economic motives.[40] Indeed, for most investors the primary motivation would seem to be a rationally economic one—that sports is a profitable long-range investment. But ownership of sports franchises also provides celebrity status, social prestige, and publicity that can enhance other facets of an individual's business. This reality was perhaps most explicitly articulated by Mike Burke, president of the New York Yankees, when he announced the purchase of the Yankees from CBS by a regionally diverse group of 15 prominent businessmen that included a shipping magnate, a General Motors vice president, the managing partner of a prominent New York law firm, and the son of a Texas oil multimillionaire. According to Burke, "The identity with New York and the Yankees is a visibility they (the new owners) couldn't get elsewhere."[41]

Moreover, the value of sports franchises has consistently increased. During the period 1967-73, when owners were publicly claiming player salaries were driving them to corporate bankruptcy, the value of most franchises increased dramatically. The Boston Celtics franchise increased in value from $2.8 million in 1965 to $6.2 million in 1969. The value of the then-San Diego Rockets, created in 1967 at a cost of $1.7 million, increased to $5.7 million in 1971—a profit of $4 million in four years.[42] In 1974, a New Orleans franchise was admitted to the National Basketball Association at a cost of $6.15 million, each of the existing 17 teams receiving a $380,000 share of this purchase price. Similarly, in 1971, the business journal, *Forbes,* reported that the aggregate franchise value of major league baseball franchises had increased $47.3 million for the American League and $114.9 million for the National League since their initial acquisition.[43]

Roger Noll, after a systematic examination of the financial status of professional teams, concluded that although certain teams have been in financial distress, most teams in most years make a profit. Even in basketball, the least profitable of the four major professional team sports, "probably only the weakest teams do not have a positive cash flow."[44] Two factors, in addition to ticket sales and media revenues, make a sport team profitable—tax advantages and availability of arenas at ridiculously low costs. Let's examine these in turn.

The bleak financial picture painted by some owners of professional teams is misleading because it refers only to accounting losses (expenses exceed income). However, the tax benefits available to sports promoters have been largely unpublicized. Rather than being a losing proposition, professional sports ownership has been profitable and, even in those cases where owners have not profited from their investment, it is far less of a liability than publicly stated accounting losses would indicate. In short, for many wealthy individuals, owning a sports franchise has lucrative tax advantages.

Investment in professional franchises enables a wealthy owner to offset his team's gate losses or to minimize taxable profits for his team or other investments by large depreciation allowances and by having profits on the sale of a team given preferential tax treatment as a capital gain. The purchase of a professional sports franchise includes (1) the legal right to the franchise, (2) player contracts, and (3) assets such as equipment, buildings, cars, etc. However, since the most valuable aspect of a pro sports team is its players, most of the purchase cost will be attributed to player contracts, which, in turn, can be depreciated in the same way a steel company depreciates the investment costs of a new blast furnace. Similarly, acquisition of a player from another team will enable his new owner to depreciate his value over a period of years, usually five or less. It is in this sense that the player's status as property is most apparent, for no other business in America depreciates the value of human beings as part of the cost of its operation.

An excellent example of the manner in which depreciation operates to provide the appearance of minimal profits and maximum losses from a sports investment is revealed in the 1973 sale of the New York Yankees by the CBS network to a national syndicate of wealthy businessmen for $10 million. Assuming that $1 million is attributed to franchise cost and $500,000 to equipment, this leaves $8.5 million that can be allocated to player costs. This can then be depreciated over a five-year period at $1.7 million a year. This means that the Yankees could achieve a $1 million profit a year for five years and still show a tax loss of $700,000 a year, which may, in turn, be prorated to each investor. Thus, if the syndicate were comprised of 10 men, each would receive a $70,000 tax loss against his own personal income tax return *in addition to* the $100,000 tax-free return he received as his share of the profits. It is, in this case, possible for the Yankees to have a profit of $1.7 million a year before they or their owners pay any income tax on that profit.[45] Because ownership of professional sports franchises provides this kind of tax shelter—even if the team shows accounting losses—it has become an attractive investment for many wealthy businessmen. This is particularly true for those in extremely high tax categories who can use losses and player depreciation as a means of offsetting other taxes on individual income (see example 7-1). As Roone Arledge, president of ABC Sports has noted, "Sports used to be run as a hobby by team owners. Now, it's a tax shelter for a lot of them or their corporations."[46] Lawyer Tom Evans, one of the syndicate that purchased the Yankees, remarked that "of all the traditional tax-shelter deals, this is clearly the best."[47]

These factors contribute to high turnover of sports club ownership. Since a team can depreciate the value of their players over a relatively short period (five years or less), expansion teams or newly franchised teams comprised of players purchased from other owners can depreciate, but new leagues and established teams cannot, except with players purchased from previously established clubs. Thus, buying and selling teams is more profitable than retaining them for extended periods of time. "Regardless

Example 7-1. How Pro Sports Owners Play the Tax Game.

In 1976, Mr. Sport and his three partners buy a professional sports franchise for $10 million, $1 million in cash and $9 million in long-term notes with principal payments beginning in 1980. The partnership estimates the value of the franchise at $1.5 million, player contracts at $8 million, equipment at $300,000 and the stadium lease at $200,000. The team has a net income of $450,000 before depreciation, but lists depreciation at $1.62 million for the year, thus showing a net loss of $1.2 million. So, Mr. Sport's taxable income would be $500,000 without the team, but is only $200,000 with it. Thus, because of his tax category, Mr. Sport would owe $321,000 without the team, but with the team, he owes $111,000. He saves $210,000 in taxes. In addition, he receives a $112,500 share of the income from the team, for a total cash benefit of $322,500.

Team Income

Gate receipts	$2,900,000
TV and radio	1,400,000
Concessions	345,000
Other	80,000
Total:	$4,725,000

Team Expense

Player salaries	$1,700,000
Staff	350,000
Administration and overhead	1,050,000
Training	175,000
Rent	100,000
Total:	$4,275,000

Depreciation

Player contracts	$1,600,000
Equipment	30,000
Stadium lease	20,000
Total:	$1,650,000

Total income	$4,725,000
Total expense	4,275,000
Total depreciation	1,650,000
Net loss	$1,200,000

Mr. Sport's Income

Normal taxable income	$ 500,000
Normal tax liability	321,000
Team loss share	300,000
New taxable income	200,000
New tax liability	111,000
Tax savings	210,000
Cash from team	112,000
Total gain	$ 322,000

Source: House Ways and Means Committee, reported by the Associated Press (September 17, 1975).

of the outcome of the merger proposal, the tax laws will always provide a strong financial incentive for ownership changes."[48]

The tax advantages for team owners are significant in making their investment successful. This is important to emphasize because so often we hear of the lofty ideals of the owners, that they want to provide community service without losing money. Although this may motivate some owners, we must conclude that owners tend to be primarily motivated by profit maximization, not public service.

Sports are considered primarily as financial investments and policies are dictated accordingly. Evidence for this is found in the moving of franchises from city to city in the search for greater profits. Two examples are especially noteworthy because the teams were moved despite a profitable situation in the cities they left—the Brooklyn Dodgers to Los Angeles and the Milwaukee Braves to Atlanta.[49] Clearly, in both instances the ownership saw an even brighter economic situation elsewhere. Further evidence is seen in the admission price. Data from professional basketball indicate clearly that although owners could achieve a substantial profit on their investment and keep prices low, they tend to increase the price of tickets with higher demand.[50]

The Economics of Sports Facilities

Since adequate facilities are essential to the financial success and spectator appeal of professional and big-time amateur sports, they are of great concern to sports promoters. Conventional wisdom holds that the presence of major league sports teams enhances a city's prestige, and, therefore, sports teams are avidly sought by city officials and chambers of commerce, who view them as tourist attractions and, hence, as definite business assets. The sports stadium has become a symbolic monument of modern urban America and of the integral role of corporate sport in its economic activity. They "have come to symbolize a city's willingness to undertake ambitious projects and they provide highly visible evidence of 'big-league' status."[51] As Michael Burke, New York Yankee president, commented in justifying New York City's purchase and renovation of Yankee Stadium for the use of the team, "A baseball club is part of the chemistry of the city. A game isn't just an athletic contest. It's a picnic, a kind of town meeting."[52]

One of the major inducements for shifting a franchise from one city to another or for establishing a new franchise is frequently the promise of nominal rental payment for the city's publicly owned sports facilities. The recommended rental price of newly renovated Yankee Stadium to the Yankees was $1 per year.[53] In Washington, D.C., rentals of Robert F. Kennedy Stadium were so low that not once in the stadium's 10-year history did the combined rental payments of the Redskins and the Senators cover even half the $831,611 interest on the stadium loan.

As the boom in sports in America has increased, so also has the demand for facilities to accommodate the apparently insatiable demands of fans for entertainment and of promoters for profits. Former professional football player Bernie Parrish, in congressional testimony, calculated that major colleges in the United States had more than 5 million stadium seats. At an estimated cost of $100 per seat, this would total more than a half a billion dollar investment, one built primarily with taxpayers monies and public donations. And this figure excludes expenditures for field houses, gymnasiums, tracks, and for all these facilities by minor colleges, junior colleges, and high schools.[54] Since 1965, many new sports facilities, including 15 stadiums for the use of professional football and/or baseball teams, have been constructed and three other stadiums have been renovated at taxpayer expense. The average cost of the construction of the publicly subsidized stadiums exceeded $43 million, with costs ranging from a low of $18 million for Atlanta's stadium, completed in 1965, to the mammoth New Orleans Superdome, the costs of which has risen to $163 million, and even more recently to the sports and entertainment complex in East Rutherford, New Jersey (football stadium for the New York Giants, harness racing track, etc.), which cost $340 million.[55]

About 70 percent of these stadiums are publicly financed, generally through revenue bonds—allegedly to be paid off from the revenue from the project. However, whenever revenue bonds are used to finance a public project that cannot pay for itself, the obligation becomes a general public one. This usually occurs with stadium construction bonds, since initial estimates of construction costs are understated and estimated revenues from its construction are often overstated. New York City's plan to renovate and modernize Yankee Stadium and "rehabilitate" the surrounding neighborhood to keep the baseball team in the city doubled in cost estimates in a year—from $24 million to more than $49.9 million, and eventually cost $100 million. The New Orleans Superdome provides the most extreme example of this inflationary process. After being told it would cost $35 million, Louisiana voters in 1966 approved a state constitutional amendment permitting its construction. However, actual costs for the giant facility exceeded $163 million. Commenting on the deception of the public that characterized the politics of the Superdome, a New Orleans businessman who played a prominent role in its creation disputed the notion that there was any impropriety in bypassing the public in this manner. "The man who built the Taj Mahal didn't ask the permission of the people. Ditto here."[56]

These new facilities, most of them publicly financed, are being built at the same time that the human needs of housing, schools, and medical facilities have reached crisis proportions, especially in U.S. cities. On the same day that New York's Mayor Lindsay announced that the city would spend $24 million to purchase and renovate Yankee Stadium, the city's board of education announced it was dropping more than

6,000 teachers from its school system for lack of funds. Similar financial problems have afflicted other urban areas, such as Cincinnati (which built a $45 million sports facility and cut school budgets from $77 million to $62 million), Philadelphia, Kansas City, and Buffalo.

Construction of such stadiums has not been without public criticism, although it is significant that bond elections for stadium construction have often succeeded when other proposed expenditures (e.g., for education and municipal facilities) have been defeated. Numerous critics have scorned the priorities involved in their construction and have argued that sports facilities represent a direct subsidy to the sports industry by the public, most of whom are not even sports fans and few of whom are able to use or to benefit from the facilities their money support.

In 1971, there were 90 professional sports teams using 77 different sports facilities in the United States. In a systematic examination of the effects and policy implications of sports facility financing, Okner undertook a cost-benefit analysis of the 54 publicly owned and financed facilities. Costs of stadiums include the loss of property tax monies that would ordinarily accrue to the city from this property, office and administrative expenses, maintenance, and additional policing. The primary cost of a stadium is, of course, the cost of construction and interest on the financing loans. For stadiums constructed during the 1960s, the cost was roughly $500 per seat, or an annual municipal cost of approximately $1.5 million, although Okner estimates that as land and construction costs have risen, these figures would rise to a cost of $700 a seat and $2 million a year.[57] Assuming this average cost of $1.5 million, all public stadiums receiving less than that in rent are subsidizing the team owners for the difference. Table 7-3 shows that only 19 of 20 public stadiums used for professional football received *less* than $1.5 million. Now, this $1.5 million in average cost is very conservative, since many stadiums have been built or enlarged since the 1960s at a much higher cost than $500 a seat. The Superdome in New Orleans, to take an extreme example, must pay interest on $163 million. At an annual rate of eight percent, that would amount to $1.3 million a year, *without* reducing the principal. Obviously, the taxpayers will pay the difference, a direct subsidy to the team owners.

An indirect subsidy to the owners involves property taxes. Publicly owned stadiums do not pay property taxes. Okner, after studying 44 publicly owned facilities used in professional sports in 1970-71, estimated a loss to local governments of between $8.8 and $13.4 million that would have been theirs if the facilities were privately owned.[58]

Clearly, it is in the interest of owners to have the public provide and maintain their stadiums. For this reason, the owners of Mile High Stadium in Denver transferred it to public ownership in 1968. Such a move, seemingly incongruous, meant that the owners were absolved of property taxes, and that the city would pick up the tab for future bills.

Table 7-3. Publicly Owned Stadiums in the NFL: Costs and Revenues, 1975.

Team	Stadium Costs	Total Gross Income to the Stadium Owner
Detroit Lions	Publicly owned by Wayne County. Cost of $64 million in bonds.	$1,967,977 (9 games)
Washington Redskins	Publicly owned by District of Columbia. Cost of $19.6 million in bonds.	$1,312,000 (11 games)
Philadelphia Eagles	Owned by the city of Philadelphia. Cost of $42.2 million in bonds.	$1,041,072 (9 games)
Pittsburgh Steelers	Owned by city of Pittsburgh. Cost of $37 million in bonds.	$968,000 (11 games)
Cincinnati Bengals	Owned by Hamilton County. Cost of $44 million in bonds.	$790,649 (9 games)
San Francisco '49ers	Owned by city of San Francisco. Built with city revenue bonds.	$766,157 (9 games)
Buffalo Bills	Owned by Erie County. Built with county obligation bonds.	$824,677 (10 games)
New Orleans Saints	Owned by Louisiana. Cost of $163 million in bonds.	$845,000 (11 games)
Oakland Raiders	Owned by Oakland and Alameda County.	$676,900 (9 games)
Chicago Bears	Owned by Chicago Park District. Built with bonds.	$655,320 (9 games)
Denver Broncos	Owned by city of Denver. Expansion at cost of $25 million.	$720,000 (10 games)
Green Bay Packers	Owned by Milwaukee County. Cost of $6 million in bonds.	$345,000 (5 games)
Dallas Cowboys	Owned by city of Irving. Cost of $30 million in bonds.	$681,020 (10 games)
Atlanta Falcons	Owned by Atlanta and Hamilton county. Built with city-county revenue bonds.	$675,278 (10 games)
Baltimore Colts	Owned by city of Baltimore. Built with $5 million in bonds.	$489,267 (9 games)
Kansas City Chiefs	Owned by Jackson County. Built with $43 million in bonds.	$576,800 (11 games)
Miami Dolphins	Owned by city of Miami. Expansions financed by bonds.	$543,427 (11 games)
Minnesota Vikings	Owned jointly by Minneapolis, Richfield, and Bloomington.	$484,000 (10 games)
Cleveland Browns	Owned by city of Cleveland. Built with city bonds.	$405,800 (10 games)
San Diego Chargers	Owned by city and county of San Diego. Built with city-county revenue bonds.	$382,718 (11 games)

Source: "Bronco's Stadium Rent Deal Sweet in Comparison," *Rocky Mountain News* (March 22, 1976), p. 6.

In the ensuing years, the city paid for $265,000 to install more lights so that it would qualify for Monday Night Football telecasts and $25 million to enlarge the stadium. Now the owners are only responsible for a nominal rental fee.[59]

Recalling the illustration earlier of the 12 persons investing $833,333 each to buy the New York Yankees, one can now see the tremendous bargain. Not only are profits generated, even if the team loses money, because of favorable tax laws, but for a total investment of $10 million, their team will play in a $100 million stadium refurbished at taxpayer expense.

However, several stadium benefits accrue to the supporting municipality: taxes on tickets, concessions, taxes that stadium employees pay, as well as direct income from the rental of the stadium. Other benefits to the city are indirect—money spent by fans in establishments throughout the city improves not only the general economic climate of the city but also provides additional tax revenue. As previously indicated, the president of the New York Convention and Business Bureau estimated that, if the New York Yankees left "Fun City," it would experience a minimum economic loss of $50 million a year. Equally emphasized by those who maintain that stadium money is soundly invested are the intangibles of stadium investment—the prestige and acclaim that a sports team brings a city.

Okner's analysis (which is concerned with football and baseball stadiums, not arenas) indicates that a stadium's financial benefit to a city depends on how well its teams draw at the gate. Most stadiums in the United States, however, do not pay their full cost to the city through stadium rental. Okner concluded that the prime beneficiaries of these arena subsidies are the owners of sports teams—themselves wealthy men—and those most likely to bear the costs are low income people. Some have argued that this subsidy works for the benefit of taxpayers because it keeps admissions low. But, even this works to benefit the wealthy, according to Okner:

> Even if the entire subsidy amount is passed on to spectators in the form of reduced admissions to sporting events, the benefits to the total community are not uniformly distributed. Although there is little information available on the economic status of sports fans, some inferences can be drawn from typical ticket prices. In the early 1970's admission to games averaged about $3 per seat for baseball, $7 for professional football, and $4 for basketball. Since spectator sporting events are discretionary purchases, preceded by expenditures for such things as food, clothing, and shelter, it is reasonable to assume that these events are not frequented by the poorest people in the community. Thus, there is probably a regressive impact on the distribution of income in the community from the benefit side of the stadium subsidy as well as from the cost side.[60]

The Relationship Between Owner and Athlete

Ownership of a professional team has tended to be profitable because the courts have allowed sport exemption from the antitrust laws. In 1922, Supreme Court Justice

Oliver Wendell Holmes ruled that baseball was a game that did not involve interstate commerce and was, therefore, exempt from federal antitrust laws. The special legal status conferred on professional sport by this decision persisted until the mid-1970s. In the interim, the Holmes decision allowed professional sports leagues to act as cartels, restricting competition and dividing markets among the franchises. This meant that each league controlled three activities: the competition for players, the location of league franchises, and the sale of broadcasting rights.[61] We will focus here on the most significant of these—control of the players.

The 1970s have seen a concerted attack by athletes on the employment practices of sport. Unlike in other businesses, athletes were not free to sell their services to whomever they pleased. Players' salaries were determined solely by the owner. The situation, before the landmark cases of the mid-1970s, worked this way for the athletes in baseball: once a player signed a contract with a club, that team had exclusive rights over him, and he was no longer free to negotiate with any other team. In succeeding years, the player had to sell his services solely to the club that owned his contract unless it released, sold, or traded him, or he chose to retire. Thus, once having signed a contract, the player was confronted by a single buyer who thereafter alone specified his salary. The reserve clause specified that the owner had the exclusive right to renew the player's contract annually, and, thus, the player was bound perpetually to negotiate only with one club; he became its property and could be sold to another club without his own consent.

Professional football was in one respect more restrictive of athletes than baseball and more open (at least on paper) in another. Unlike baseball, football had a draft of college players and the selected athletes had no choice of the team for which they would play. The player would play for the team that drafted him and at the salary offered or else join a team in the Canadian League (the number of Americans allowed to play in Canada is limited, however, so that option was not a real one except for the most sought after athletes). As in baseball, after signing with a team the player was bound to that team. He could, however, play out his option—i.e., play a year without signing a contract at 90 percent of his previous salary, whereupon he would be free to negotiate with another team. This apparent freedom of movement for the players was severely limited, however, by the "Rozelle Rule." This rule allowed the NFL commissioner, Pete Rozelle, to require the team signing any such free agent to compensate the club the player left with other athletes or money of equal value. Thus, it was not usually in a club's interest to sign free agents, and, in reality, the free agent did not have full economic freedom.

These provisions in baseball and football (and they were similar to the situation in basketball and hockey, too) were clearly one-sided, giving all the power to the owners. As Michael Sovern, dean of Columbia University's school of law, has described this asymmetrical relationship: "The reserve clause binds the employee without binding the employer. . . . The owner is free to decide whether to continue the relationship: the player is not."[62] Or, as another observer put it: "After the Civil War settled the slavery issue, owning a ball club was the closest one could come to owning a plantation."[63] Is such an unfair system necessary? The rationale for such a limitation on the freedoms of the players is that sports depend on competitive balance for survival. Without the binding of players to a team, talent would soon become maldistributed with the richest owners in the best markets (e.g., New York and Los Angeles) acquiring a monopoly of superior players. However, it should be noted that the ability of professional teams to sell and acquire players from other clubs invites the same possibility. Sixteen percent of all major league baseball players are traded in a single season, with the average number of trades for an individual's career being 1.7 times. More than 750 major league baseball players are traded, sold, or released in a season. Moreover, player testimony before the Senate Antitrust and Monopoly Subcommittee indicated that 68 percent of all players in the National Basketball Association had switched teams at least once during the years 1968-70.[64]

Indeed, the possibility of buying and selling contracts by owners raises the same problem of the acquisition of the best talent by wealthier teams, which is precisely what occurred several times during the extremely successful history of the New York Yankees. Thus, the absolute power of professional sports owners doesn't prevent player movement; it merely ensures that any player changes are in the owner's, not necessarily in the player's, interest.[65] The major difference in a free market system and one subject to the reserve system is that in the former the player alone would be paid for a team change; in the latter, the owner is paid what should accrue to the player. As Michael I. Sovern has argued:

> Companies with star salesmen, universities with star professors, law firms with star partners receive no special compensation if their stars leave and cause them financial loss. If they wish to protect themselves, they must offer sufficiently attractive terms to hold their stars; or they can enter into long-term contracts with both parties bound, both the employer and the employee.[66]

Moreover, it is problematic whether, in fact, the mechanisms of the draft and the reserve clause are necessary to achieve the balance sought by the owners or whether, given the existence of these constraints in the past, they have effectively operated to equalize team competition. From an economic standpoint, a single owner would be foolhardy to attempt to acquire a monopoly on a sport's best players, for attendance revenues would suffer from the absence of a real contest between teams.

> The first peculiarity of the economics of professional sport is that receipts depend upon competition among the sportors or the teams, not upon business competition among the

> firms running the contenders, for the greater the economic collusion and the more the sporting competition, the greater the profits.[67]

In other words, the closer the competition between teams, the greater the fan interest likely to be generated and, consequently, the greater the attendance revenues. Surely, in a free market system an owner would have a vested interest in *not* obtaining a monopoly, *not* acquiring all the stars, but in ensuring that some remain on other teams. Teams cannot be economically successful unless their competitors survive, too. An example of this occurred from 1968 to 1973, when each team of the NBA was paying part of the salary of the superstars signed by the league members. This led to the potentially embarrassing situation where a club owner would be paying for the services of a player who was playing to defeat his team. Rick Barry, for instance, was lured away from the ABA by San Francisco with the league members agreeing to pay all of his salary above $100,000, or $6,985.30 each.[68]

Owners know that the differences in the quality of play must not be too great. Economists have argued that such a result does not require collusion—only the free operation of market forces. Thus, a balance of competition is in the mutual interest of all concerned—players, fans, and owners. The question is whether the draft and reserve clause practice is the only way it can be achieved.

The "natural forces of competition" argument has also been made. A team overstocked with superstars will probably have morale problems or problems of combining their talents effectively. Those superstars who feel that they are not playing enough or whose talents are not being sufficiently or adequately utilized or publicized will sign contracts with other clubs. It is noteworthy that when the Los Angeles Lakers acquired Wilt Chamberlain to accompany superstars Elgin Baylor and Jerry West, they still failed to win the NBA championship. Similarly, when Philadelphia acquired Julius Erving in 1976 to complement superstars George McGinnis and Doug Collins, the NBA championship eluded them.

Finally, the most telling argument against the draft and the reserve clause is that neither has worked in distributing talent equitably. If these mechanisms had worked in the anticipated manner, one would anticipate that league champions would, over an extended period of time, be distributed randomly. In other words, over the years one would expect that team A would be a champion as frequently as teams B, C, D, and E. Obviously, this has not been the case in American professional team sports. Each major sport has had certain long-standing champion teams and others that have been almost perpetual losers. The dynasties of the New York Yankees from 1921 to 1964, the Boston Celtics during the 1950s and '60s, the Green Bay Packers during the 1960s, and the league domination of the St. Louis Cardinals, N.Y. Giants, and Brooklyn Dodgers from 1940 to 1960 are examples. Clearly, the existing rules have resulted in unequal distribution of talent.

Moreover, it is problematic whether the draft alone can alter a club's situation radically (except, perhaps, in basketball, where, because of the smaller number of team members, the acquisition of a single superstar, such as Kareem Abdul-Jabbar or Bill Walton, can have such an effect). The only difference between the teams selecting first and last in a player draft is a single player per year, and in most sports the addition of a single outstanding player per year will make little difference in a team's ultimate success. Indeed, the emphasis placed on the draft system attributes an undue rationality to it. Of the quarterbacks of teams reaching the 1971 NFL playoffs, three were signed as free agents, two were 10th round draft choices, one was picked as an expendable player in the expansion draft, and only two were first round draft choices.

Not only do sports promoters argue that the common draft and reserve clause are necessary to ensure equal distribution of playing talent and to prevent rich clubs from acquiring a monopoly of outstanding players, but they contend that these mechanisms are the only means of avoiding financial ruin for professional sports, because competitive bidding for players would otherwise become prohibitive. This latter argument led professional football to obtain congressional exemption from the antitrust laws in 1966 and professional basketball leagues to seek a similar exemption in 1971. Although the football merger bill passed through congress virtually unopposed, by the time professional basketball promoters sought a similar exemption, players in all major sports had become much more effectively organized and aware of the effect of a merger agreement in reducing player salaries.

The existence of rival leagues provides a much greater opportunity for athletes to realize their full economic value. Both players and owners agree that salaries increase substantially when two leagues are in competition for player talent and that a merger agreement would, because it controls or limits player bargaining power, depress player salaries. There is little doubt that the financial position of players greatly improves under competitive conditions. In professional football, average salaries rose from $4,000 per year in 1946 to $8,000 per year in 1949 when the National Football League and the All-America Conference competition had ceased. After the demise of the All-America Conference, the average salary of NFL players was only $1,200 higher than it had been in 1949.[69]

After the formation of the American Football League in 1960, competitive bidding for professional football players was resumed until it was ended by the merger agreement in 1966. Bob Kellerman has described the effects of the merger: "The owners of both leagues realized their competition was only benefitting the consumers (the fans) and the producers (the players)."[70]

The merger enabled owners to raise costs to consumers in the form of higher ticket prices, which rose 35 percent from an average cost per ticket of $5.36 in 1966 to $8.59 in 1973. In addition, the cost of preseason tickets nearly doubled during the same time period.[71] Further still, broadcasting revenues increased substantially during the same time period, thereby dramatically improving the owner's financial position. Moreover, because rookie players were being paid much less, average NFL player salaries after 1969 stayed the same and in 1970 declined. Since that time collective bargaining has brought about an increase in average salaries, which rose from $25,604 in 1970 to $27,500 in 1973. The average salaries in professional football increased $500-600 a year since the 1966 merger, less than the increase in the cost of living during that same period.[72]

The advent of the World Football League again brought competition into the determination of salaries, and the average salary rose sharply from $27,500 in 1973 to $42,000 in 1975. The impact of competition on player salaries was again seen with the demise of the WFL and the concomitant drop in NFL player salaries.[73]

Thus, the real benefits of the merger accrued not to the players, and especially not to the fans, who paid much higher spectator costs, but to the owners, whose net income more than doubled from 1966 to 1970.[74] The effect is thus, to quote Kellerman again, that the owners "*avoid* competition with each other at all costs while, at the same time, they sell a product whose main ideological function is to perpetuate the belief in competition."[75]

Interleague competition for players had equally dramatic effects on salaries within the National Basketball Association, which since 1967 has been confronted with competition from the rival ABA. The average rookie salary in the NBA in 1960-61 was $8,000; in 1966, it had risen to $12,500, but in 1970-71, under the pressures of the threat of the ABA, average rookie salaries had nearly quadrupled, to $46,000. In 1966, before the new league was founded, the median salary in the NBA was less than $20,000, fringe benefits were minimal, and there was no player medical or life insurance. In 1971, a minimum salary of $16,500 had been established, fringe benefits had become substantial, and the median salary had risen to $43,000.[76] In 1976, the last year of the two leagues, the average salary was a phenomenal $110,000. If that is what basketball players were worth with two leagues, one would think that is what they are worth, period. The effect of the merger on basketball salaries should be instructive.

The late 1960s was a period in American history where various downtrodden groups became militant in the attempt to change existing power arrangements. Within this society-wide framework, athletes, too, began to recognize their common plight and organized to change it. Most fundamentally, they felt that the owners had all the power and that this resulted in athletes not receiving their true value in the marketplace. The result was that athletes, singly and as player associations, began to assert themselves against what they considered an unfair system.

Several instances were especially instrumental in the modification of the reserve clause in baseball. First, there was the case of Curt Flood who was traded by the baseball Cardinals to Philadelphia but refused to play for them. He did not play the next year (1970) in protest and brought suit against organized baseball, alleging that the reserve system constituted a system of peonage. The U.S. Supreme Court ruled 5-3 against Flood but recognized that the system should be changed by congressional action.

In 1974, Catfish Hunter of the Oakland Athletics was allowed by an arbitrator to be released from his contract because the owner had failed to make payments on an insurance policy that was part of the contract. The bidding for Hunter's services resulted in his signing a multiyear contract with the New York Yankees for $3.5 million. This showed the other athletes very clearly that they were not being paid their true worth and had much to do with the increased militancy of the athletes.

Finally, the reserve system in baseball died in December, 1975, with the decision by an arbitration panel that two players, Andy Messersmith and Dave McNally, were free agents because they had played out their existing contracts plus an additional year. McNally did not pursue his career further because of an injury but Messersmith signed a three-year, no-cut contract with Atlanta for about $1 million.

These landmark cases led to an agreement between the owners of professional baseball teams and the Players' Association in July, 1976. The provisions allowed: (1) players without 1976 or 1977 contracts to become free agents; and players with six or more years in the major leagues to become free agents without waiting for a one-year option period. Most importantly, there would be no compensation for the free agent's former team.

The first test of baseball's free agent system occurred in November, 1976, when the eligible players entered the reentry draft (called by some the "auction of freed slaves"). What happened had several important implications for the future of baseball.[77] First, contrary to many predictions, not many athletes took the free agent route—only 24 out of the pool of some 600. This was probably the consequence of the second implication, salaries were raised to mollify the athletes under contract. Third, again contrary to expectations, the competitive balance of baseball was generally enhanced. Of the 12 teams with winning seasons in 1976, three signed a total of four new players. Of the 12 with losing records, seven teams purchased 14 free agents (by the end of 1976, six players remained unsigned). Fourth, the owners' profits were now being shared more equitably with the athletes, especially the star athletes. The first 14 free agents signed long-term agreements ranging from three to 10 years that totaled $20.5 million in bonuses, salary, and deferred payments. To put this in perspective, Gene Autry purchased the Angels in 1960 for $2.1 million. In 1976, he paid more than $5 million for three athletes: Joe Rudi, Bobby Grich, and Don Baylor. Baseball was still profitable for owners, just less so. The attendance for major league baseball in 1976 was 33 million. When this is multiplied by the average cost of tickets ($3.45), the total is $117,300,000, not counting parking and concessions. Moreover, according to Marvin Miller, executive director of the Players' Association, radio and television revenues produce 150 percent of baseball's payroll.[78] So, while baseball owners continue to make profits, the momentous decisions in baseball clearly restructured the power relationship between owner and athlete. When the other sports are considered, the year 1976 can truly be considered the year of "jock liberation."

Professional football did not have as far to go as baseball to remove the reserve clause. Players were already allowed to play out their option. The obstacle, as we noted earlier, was the Rozelle Rule. The Rozelle Rule was voided after two court cases. The first, brought by quarterback Joe Kapp, occurred when Kapp signed a nonstandard contract with the New England Patriots, and it was voided by Commissioner Rozelle. Kapp gave up his career and sued the league. A district court judge ruled in Kapp's favor in 1974, saying that the standard player contract violated federal antitrust laws and that the Rozelle Rule was illegal.

Since the Kapp case involved an individual player rather than the entire NFL system and was subject to a prolonged appeal process, the NFL Players' Association brought suit to change the system for all. In December, 1975, a U.S. court judge decided that the Rozelle Rule was illegal. He directed the NFL and its 26 teams to cease enforcing the rule. The result was that in May, 1976, 24 new free agents began searching for the best offers, and Larry Csonka signed for more than $1 million covering four seasons. John Riggins, who as a New York Jet played his option year for $67,500, put his price at $1.5 million for five years, payable at $100,000 a year until 1990.[79]

In response to the court cases, the fear of additional litigation, and owner-player strife, the owners and the National Football League Players' Association reached a five-year, $107 million agreement early in 1977. The essentials of this contract were:[80]

1. The Players' Association was recognized as a union with all players required to pay annual dues even if they refused membership.
2. No arbitrary hair or dress codes would be exercised for the players.
3. The Rozelle Rule was modified so that compensation for free-agent veterans changing teams would be a set number of draft choices awarded to his former team, depending on the salary of the player.
4. The player draft was changed, giving draftees several alternatives: (a) if selected in the draft, they must be offered a contract with a salary of at least $20,000 a year or be declared a free agent; (b) if the player refuses terms, he will be subject to the next year's draft, and if unchosen then he becomes a free agent. The draft itself was reduced from 17 rounds to 12, thereby freeing 140 collegians unselected to free-agent status.
5. Minimum salaries would start at $15,000 for undrafted rookies (going up to $17,000 in 1980) and rise to $30,000 for a five-year veteran (up to $32,000 in 1980). Also, a player released because of injury the previous season must be paid half his salary up to $37,500.
6. After four years, no option clause is allowed without the player's permission,

and he is to be paid 110 percent of his salary while he plays out the option year. If waived, a veteran of four years may declare himself a free agent and sign on with any team.

Basketball, unlike football and baseball, reached a settlement with considerable cooperation between owners and athletes. It should be noted, however, that this spirit of cooperation by the owners was prompted by the court decisions in the other sports—decisions with a clear message—owners could no longer treat their players as highly paid slaves. The provisions of this settlement were:[81]

1. The option clause was to be eliminated from nonrookie player contracts, beginning with those that expired with the 1976 season. In other words, veterans were no longer bound to a team for one year after their contracts ran out.
2. In 1980, the owner of a player whose contract had expired has the right of first refusal if that player is offered a contract by another team. By equalling the best offer, the owner can keep his player. If not, the player is free to join the new team.
3. The compensation rule (similar to the Rozelle Rule) will be void beginning in 1980.
4. The owners agreed to pay $4.5 million in equal shares to approximately 500 players for the harm done by the old system, plus $1 million for the players' legal fees.

Although the reserve clause appears to be dead in professional sports, some issues considered "freedom issues" by the athletes remain unresolved (e.g., the player draft in football). A favorable judgment by the courts in these issues will indicate the degree to which the balance of power has shifted in professional sports between the owners and the athletes.

The recent death of the reserve clause provides an opportunity to see whether or not the rich owners will accumulate all the best players, as defenders of the clause predict. We have already seen one result—a large increase in salaries, especially for the superstars. An interesting question is what will be the effect of these huge salaries on the fans. Their once-noble athletic heroes are now businessmen. Athletes demand huge salaries—to play a game. They threaten to not play. They no longer seem to have loyalty for their team or city. Robert Angell observed that fans do not seem to object as much to the large salaries by the superstars, but resent the across-the-board affluence of athletes.

> But large payments to athletes are not enjoyed or approved of by us, the fans, if the payment is made broadly, to all the athletes engaged in a particular trade at the big-league level—all basketball players, all hockey players, and so on. "The players have gotten too greedy," "They're all paid too much"—these are current grandstand convictions, which I also hear from other people, in and out of the sports world. As I pick up this complaint, however, it seems to apply more to a well-paid journeyman than to the

superstar—more to Rusty Staub or Roy White, say, than to Johnny Bench or Jim Palmer. It would be extremely interesting to measure this, if we could. What it means, I think, is that high pay for athletes is resented if they are seen as *employees*. And when these employees behave like contemporary workmen, trying to extract the most money and the most favorable working conditions and retirement benefits from a typically reluctant and unsympathetic employer, and forming a union to press their demands—which is what the baseball and football and basketball players have all done in recent years—then they are resented even more deeply, almost to the point of hatred. This is an extraordinary turn of events in a labor-conscious, success-oriented society like ours.[82]

Interestingly, the fans have tended to take the side of the team owners in many salary disputes, strikes, and other disruptions. Ironically, the owners over the years have had the monopoly, they have taken economic advantage of their athletes, and they have had the temerity to move franchises to more lucrative communities. Again, the next few years will provide the data as to whether this resentment toward the businessmen/athletes is a short-lived phenomenon or not.

The final irony, as noted by columnist Red Smith is that fans resent the high salaries of athletes but take in stride the huge salaries of other entertainers.

The fact that a few young men can make a million or two playing a game seems to offend some people, especially people outside baseball. They say they read about nothing but money on the sports pages these days and it makes them sick because where does a .267 hitter like Reggie Jackson come off with his gaudy demands? They say the fun has gone out of sports and there is nobody around today like Babe Ruth, who would have played for nothing and thanked you for the chance.

Some of these same people go out to Las Vegas and tear their pants getting up $25 or $35 to hear Frank Sinatra sing a few songs for $100,000 a night. They see nothing out of line when Robert Redford gets $2 million or more for making faces in one movie.

They forget that ballplayers are in the entertainment business, same as Sinatra and Redford, and that the measure of an entertainer's value is how he draws at the gate.[83]

The Economics of "Amateur" Sports

The trend toward greater bureaucratization, commercialization, and institutionalism—toward "corporate sport"—is not restricted to professional athletics alone; it is also true of much of organized amateur athletics in the United States. Analysis of the "sports industry" must, therefore, deal with both categories of sports participation, although, in reality, they are often virtually indistinct.

The amateur concept was a product of the late 18th-century leisure class, whose ideal of the patrician sportsman was part of their pursuit of conspicuous leisure. Consequently, to be a pure amateur required independent wealth, since the true amateur derived no income from his sports participation. Explicit in the amateur ideal is the idea that an individual's athletic endeavors must be unrelated to his work or livelihood, and that sport itself is somehow sullied, tarnished, or demeaned if one is paid for performing.

Jack Scott has pointed out that "the cardinal virtue of amateur athletics is that since athletes are not paid for competing, the activity is more likely to maintain a *participant orientation* rather than a *spectator orientation*."[84] Elaborating on this point, Scott quotes from H.A. Harris: "So long as sport is true to itself, the only purpose of the organization of it is the enjoyment of the players, as soon as the interests of the spectators are allowed to become predominant, corruption has set in and the essence of the game has been lost."[85]

Given this distinction, much of what presently passes for amateur sport in the United States apparently does not conform to this definition. Not only is its conduct highly organized and rationalized (not by players but by professional managers and officials), but the monetary stakes are high. Amateur athletics is a big-business proposition. For instance, before the AAU would sanction a 1973 United States tour by the Russian gymnastics team, the AAU insisted on a contract ensuring that Olga Korbut, the Olympic sensation and the primary reason that each performance on the tour was a sellout, would perform.[86] The U.S. Olympic Committee, which has rigidly and ritualistically invoked an anachronistic, outmoded amateur concept, is comprised of 714 committee members responsible for policy in 37 sports, including a 16-member executive committee and a 59-member Board of Directors.[87] Moreover, the USOC has an investment portfolio valued at nearly $6 million, yielding between $400,000 and $500,000 annually.[88] In 1972, over $8.5 million in contributions was raised, including minimum contributions of $30,000 each from companies, such as Coca-Cola, Gillette, and Sears, Roebuck, for rights to use the USOC trademark for promotional activities.[89]

In most cases today, the distinction between professional and amateur is artificial. Considerable popular criticism in the United States has been directed toward the "amateur" status of athletes in many communist countries who are state-supported, either as members of the military, nationally owned factories, or students. In the United States, however, so-called amateur athletes are supported in a variety of ways. Track stars, for example, are given lucrative "expense money," which has frequently been sufficient to support an individual for several years. It has only been recently that tennis, one of the most formal and staid of American sports, has laid aside the idea that amateurs and pros cannot compete against each other, in essence making the distinction defunct.

Finally, the most frequent means of subsidizing "amateur" athletes is through scholarships to colleges and universities. Ignoring for the moment the long-range value of a college degree, the typical athletic scholarship (a "legal" maximum of room, books, board, tuition, and fees is specified by the NCAA) would have an annual value of $3,000 at a state-supported school with low tuition, and $7,000 at a private school with high tuition. This does not include the widespread illicit payments frequently discovered through NCAA investigations. Although college scholarships do not provide income comparable to a "professional" contract, it should be recognized, nevertheless, that the college athlete is being compensated financially for his athletic exploits. Most athletes in highly competitive sports are subsidized in some way, and thus the distinction between "amateur" and "professional" is primarily one of degree. Chris Chataway, a former Olympic middle-distance runner, noted the impossibility of remaining an amateur:

> The winners of the track and field events in Rome [the 1960 Olympic Games] this year will, almost every one of them, have trained at least two hours a day for at least two years. None of these, unless he has private means, can have done that, and travelled over the world to get the necessary competition, and at the same time have remained in any meaningful sense of the word an amateur.[90]

Finally, definitions of what comprises "amateur" status has changed over time. Recognition of this is explicit in the charter of the U.S. Olympic Committee, which stipulates that all Olympic athletes must conform to the "*current* interpretation of the amateur rule" (our underscoring) of the International Olympic Committee. In 1928, for instance, the IOC sanctioned the practice of "broken time," which meant that an athlete competing in the Olympic Games should be reimbursed by the Games to an amount equal to the salary he would have lost while he was competing, a practice not accepted today. Similarly, in 1973, the NCAA changed its amateur definition to permit individuals who are professionals in one sport to compete in intercollegiate athletics in another.

The Economics of Collegiate Sport

The business dimension of "amateur" sports is most fully developed in the athletic programs of U.S. colleges and universities. The intercollegiate sports system, initially student-organized and student-run, came under the control of school administrators early in the 20th century. It has since become a major business proposition. For example, the total sports revenue for the University of Michigan for fiscal 1976 was $4,803,192.[92] As Jim Kehoe, University of Maryland athletic director, described his university's athletic program, the annual budget of which exceeds $2 million, "This is business, a multi-million dollar a year business. I've got to run it like one."[91] In 1969, NCAA member institutions spent more than $300 million on intercollegiate athletics and realized receipts of more than $200 million, with university subsidies making up the difference. The average expenditure by each school was $548,000. However, although 50 largest athletic schools averaged expenditures in excess of $1.3 million, the modal pattern among all NCAA schools was an athletic expenditure of less than $100,000 a year.[93]

Operating an athletic program as a business proposition means that financial losses are unacceptable. However, in 1974, nine of ten college athletic budgets were operating in the red.[94] There have been different responses to this financial crisis in intercollegiate sports. The NCAA itself has responded by permitting freshmen to compete in varsity athletics, reducing the maximum number of scholarships that each school may annually award, and eliminating the $15 "laundry" money previously allowed athletes each month. Some schools have reduced their commitment to intercollegiate athletics, either deemphasizing the level of competition of their athletic programs or dropping support of specific sports; typically these are "minor sports," such as golf, tennis, swimming, soccer, rugby, and lacrosse.[95] But the financial losses have most frequently prompted individual athletic programs to redouble their efforts "to remain competitive" and thus approach fiscal solvency. One response is to fire the incumbent coach and replace him with another who promises to reverse the institution's athletic fortunes (his agreement to coach frequently having been obtained by the university's commitment of greater financial outlays to support his new and invigorated program). But the most far-reaching consequence of these escalating costs is that they further intensify the pressures to recruit athletes legally and illegally.

The extensive financial involvement of American colleges and universities in athletics makes it difficult to distinguish their operation from noncollegiate "professional" enterprises. In fact, there are many universities whose average game attendance in football and, especially, in basketball exceeds that of professional teams. Yet, the costs, especially player salaries, are not nearly so great for colleges as for professional sports.

As mentioned above, the salaries paid college athletes raises the question of how college athletes are to be distinguished (except qualitatively) from "professionals." In other words, the money an admitted professional receives is merely greater than the typical college player and, furthermore, the professional player is not confronted with the necessity of diverting his energies to his studies, to the hassle of remaining "academically eligible"; he is free to devote himself solely to developing his athletic skills.

Because the professional-amateur distinction is difficult to make realistically, it is not surprising that college athletics has instituted collusive practices similar to those employed by professional promoters. As with professional athletes, a free market does not exist for college athletes either, since they are subject to severe restrictions by the NCAA, the major governing body of college athletics, which functions as a cartel.[96] NCAA regulations regarding recruiting, scholarships, and eligibility are collusive, and like the reserve clause in professional sports, their effect is to prevent one team from "raiding" players on another. Although colleges have not yet fully rationalized procedures to the point of instituting a "draft" of eligible high school and junior college players, there *is* fierce competition; the national and conference letters of intent, require a player to declare his intention of enrolling and competing for a specific school, which "has the effect of insulating a given university-firm from competition for inputs by other university-firms in its conference."[97] In other words, once high school hero Tommy Touchdown signs a letter of intent with Silo Tech, conference arch-rival Snob Hill U. stops bidding for his services.

The effects of such practices are, of course, advantageous for competing schools; it enables them to restrict their feverish recruiting activity for schoolboy talent to several months of the year. NCAA rules also preclude "tampering" with players who have already committed their services to a school. Silo Tech cannot recruit a player already at Snob Hill unless the *player* is willing to be penalized by being declared ineligible for a year. This rule against transfers has an effect similar to the option clause in professional sports. If the player is willing to forego competing for a year, he can transfer his services to another team. This practice, however, does not apply to the coaches of intercollegiate teams, only to the players. Koch has noted that this rule against transfers, as other aspects of the NCAA economic system, is "stacked in favor of the university-firm at the expense of the student athlete."[98]

Other NCAA regulations also seriously limit the freedom of college athletes to compete. First, players may not compete for more than four years in a single sport, nor may they compete in intercollegiate athletics after they have received a baccalaureate degree. This rule has led to the somewhat common situation of a player having the requisite number of hours or courses to fulfill his institution's graduation requirements but refusing to accept his degree until he has completed his intercollegiate athletic eligibility. By contrast, graduate students in English universities compete in British collegiate sports, whereas graduate students in the United States are precluded from doing so. Moreover, the NCAA stipulates that an athlete cannot compete more than five years after he initially enters college (except in the cases of interruption of college career for military or missionary service—revealing exemptions). The student who drops out of school, for whatever reason, midway through his career and returns several years later is, therefore, precluded from participating in intercollegiate athletics.

Thus, as Koch has concluded, the effect of these NCAA regulations is to permit American colleges to operate their athletic programs in a monopolistic manner by regulating and limiting the freedom of potential athletes. They establish a ceiling on athlete's salaries, and regulate the length and criteria for participation and limit player mobility.[99]

Yet, despite the pervasive commercialization of college sport, it still retains (or attempts to retain) an aura of wholesomeness. Walter Byers, executive director of the NCAA, explicitly contrasted the purported value of "amateur" with professional sport in America today:

> I submit that this country could well survive—it would be painful—the loss of professional sports, but I hold the personal view, having spent some twenty-five years in intercollegiate athletics, and being intimately familiar with interscholastic athletics, that this country might not survive the deterioration and eventual elimination of interscholastic and intercollegiate athletics.[100]

But we must recognize the professional aspect of the "big-time" college athletic sport system. Especially true in football and basketball, and to a lesser but increasing extent in baseball and hockey, intercollegiate sports serve as the minor league farm systems for major league professional team sports.[101] They also serve as a source of free publicity for future pro stars. Collegiate sports participation has historically been the primary prelude to professional competition in basketball and football, whereas this has infrequently (although increasingly) been the case for baseball and hockey. Although the minor league system of major league baseball has, as we noted above, diminished considerably from its heyday immediately after World War II, it is still much more extensive than in any of the other major professional team sports. The primary difference between the baseball and hockey minor leagues and those of other pro sports is that there is little mobility among the latter, whereas it is highly atypical for a baseball or hockey professional not to have served even a minimal apprenticeship in the minor leagues. And, conversely, it is highly atypical for a professional basketball or football player to have begun his career in a minor league before reaching the big time.

Recognition of the professional nature of collegiate sports and their function as "minor leagues" or training grounds for future major leaguers has led to the suggestion that the professional nature of collegiate athletics be explicitly recognized. This would be accomplished by having a college athlete's "letter of intent" be considered a legal contract with that school in the same way that a professional athlete's contract is "owned" by his team. Major league owners desiring the services of such an athlete would have to purchase the contract from his school, thereby reimbursing Jock State for the costs of player developmental or "minor league" training and, simultaneously, improving the financial positions of schools supplying the pros with their raw material.

Recognizing this natural source of player development, professional basketball and football has, until very recently, entered into informal agreements with U.S. colleges and universities. The pro teams promised that they would not tamper or try to negotiate with undergraduate players until their entering class had completed its four years of athletic eligibility. Thus, a player like Wilt Chamberlain, who competed for only three of a possible four years at Kansas, was unable to play during that fourth year in the NBA because he was not yet deemed eligible for a draft. The effect of these arrangements within the professional leagues is clearly collusive and was legally ruled so soon after the fledgling American Basketball Association challenged the rule by signing undergraduate players to contracts in their sophomore and junior years. The more established NBA refused to permit this practice unless the player is deemed a "hardship" case in which, because of his family's alleged dire economic condition, he must receive more substantial wages than his university can provide for his services. This practice was a sham, however, as virtually anyone of talent was labeled a "hardship" case.

But the professional football leagues have refused to sign such "ineligible" players under any conditions. They, thus, protect their relationships with their "minor leagues" and simultaneously preclude the possibility of professional play for many college sophomores and juniors by decreeing, in effect, that any football player who enters college must wait four years until he may play professional football. (In exceptional cases individuals have been drafted from junior college teams. Also, it is probable that very few players have developed sufficiently by their sophomore or junior years to play professional football, but that is really irrelevant to the point being made here—that the professional drafting arrangements preclude such a possibility for the individual player.) The parallel between the monopoly powers of professional owners and those of college coaches was nowhere made more explicit than in the testimony of William L. Wall, past president of the National Association of Basketball Coaches before the U.S. Senate. Wall argued that the proposed professional basketball merger bill be amended to include a "four-year protection rule." This rule would explicitly forbid professional teams from signing an undergraduate athlete until late in the fourth year after his initial matriculation, and after the close of the collegiate basketball season.[102] It would also prohibit pros tampering with undergraduate stars. Such a rule would have a stabilizing effect for college coaches, but it would deprive the undergraduate star of maximum freedom. In other words, the moment a player enrolls in a four-year college, he would immediately waive for four years his right (despite his or her family's economic situation) to earn a living by playing professional basketball.

Summary

We have shown the economic side of sport in this chapter. The message is clear—in professional and in big-time collegiate sport the "dollar is king." Sport is used by big business in a multimillion dollar effort to sell products. Owners squeeze as much money as they can from fans and taxpayers. Players seem incapable of being satiated with enough money. The result is the ultimate corruption of sport—corporate sport rather than sport as a meaningful, joyous activity in itself. Let's review briefly the various components that demonstrate the businesslike atmosphere of sport.[103]

1. Sport has sold out to the demands of television. In return for large contracts, the leagues and the NCAA allow the television networks to dictate schedules, time-outs, and the like.

2. The principle of supply and demand operates in the amount of admission charged for athletic events. If sport were truly a game rather than a business, the most successful teams (New York Knicks, Ohio State) would charge the lowest ticket prices, but this is not the case.

3. The owners of professional teams are in constant search of better markets. The possibility that a franchise will move increases the probability that municipalities will provide facilities or other inducements at taxpayer expense (to entice teams to their city or to encourage them to remain there).

4. Athletes seemingly put self-interest ahead of team play and loyalty to their fans. Players demand very high salaries and other monetary inducements (bonuses, retirement benefits, insurance policies, interest-free loans, etc.). The frequent result is pugnacious negotiation between owners and athletes.

5. A struggle exists between athletes (through unionlike organizations) and entrepreneurs for power to regulate sports and apportion profits. This is manifested in court battles, player strikes, owner lockouts, and press agentry by both sides to sway public opinion.

In sum, instead of being a release from the daily world of money, strikes, strife, and legal complexities, sport has become similar to the world of work. As such, it reveals, in microcosm, the values of the larger society. As Angell has said of baseball (but true of all corporate sport):

> Professional sports now form a noisy and substantial, if irrelevant and distracting, part of the world, and it seems as if baseball games taken entirely—off the field as well as on it, in the courts and in the front offices as well as down on the diamonds—may now tell us more about ourselves than they ever did before.[104]

Notes

1. For an insightful discussion of these processes, see Bil Gilbert, "Gleanings from a Troubled Time," *Sports Illustrated* 37 (December 25, 1972), pp. 34-46.

2. *Hearings before the Subcommittee on Antitrust and Monopoly of the Committee on the Judiciary,* U.S. Senate, 92nd Congress, 1st session (1971), p. 337. Hereafter cited as *Hearings.*

3. *New York Times* (December 31, 1972), p. 14.

4. These figures are conservative estimates multiplying admissions times $5 for college football, $7 for NFL football, $3 for major league baseball, $2 for college basketball, and $4 for professional basketball. The totals exclude income from parking, concessions, and other adjunct commercial enterprises.

5. See Leonard Koppett, "Impact of Energy

Crisis on Sports? No Answer, Yet," *New York Times News Service* (November 21, 1973).

6. For a discussion of the American business creed, see Francis X. Sutton et al., *The American Business Creed* (Cambridge, Mass.: Harvard University Press, 1956). For an extensive discussion of the American sports creed, see Harry Edwards, *Sociology of Sport* (Homewood, Ill.: Dorsey Press, 1973), pp. 317-330.
7. Bil Gilbert, "Sis-Boom-Bah for Amalgamated Sponge," *Sports Illustrated* 22 (January 25, 1965), p. 54.
8. Tom Buckley, "Business in a Front Seat for Today's Super Bowl," *New York Times* (January 14, 1973), p. 1.
9. Douglas S. Looney, "The Salesmen Run a Costly Race at Indy," *The National Observer* (May 25, 1974), p. 18.
10. See Jerry Kirshenbaum, "On Your Mark, Get Set, Sell," *Sports Illustrated* 38 (May 14, 1973), pp. 36-46.
11. See Edwin Shrake, "The Juice on a Juicy Road," *Sports Illustrated* 41 (August 19, 1974), pp. 36-40. For a similar account of the commercialization of Bruce Jenner, see Barry McDermott, "Back to Bruce in a Moment. First, this Commercial," *Sports Illustrated* 47 (September 26, 1977), pp. 42-48.
12. Marty Bell, "Is She Paying Off?" *Women-Sports* 3 (December, 1976), pp. 61-64.
13. Ira Howoritz, "Sports Broadcasting," *Government and the Sports Business,* ed. Roger G. Noll (Washington, D.C.: The Brookings Institution, 1974), p. 315.
14. Quoted in Gilbert, "Gleanings from a Troubled Time," p. 38.
15. Will Grimsley, "TV Sports—$315 Million a Year," Associated Press release (November 24, 1975); "Broadcasters to Pay $81.5 Million," Associated Press release (August 9, 1976).
16. William O. Johnson, Jr., *Super Spectator and the Electric Lilliputians,* (Boston: Little, Brown, 1971), p. 26; see also Barry D. McPherson, "Sport Consumption and the Economics of Consumerism," in *Sport and Social Order,* ed. Donald W. Ball and John W. Loy (Reading, Mass.: Addison-Wesley, 1975), pp. 243-275.
17. *Hearings,* pp. 1087-1098.
18. Ibid.
19. Johnson, *Super Spectator,* pp. 10-11.
20. *Hearings,* p. 38; *Sports Illustrated* 38 (March, 1973), p. 16; and Associated Press release (March 7, 1976).
21. Associated Press release (July 1, 1975).
22. Quoted in William O. Johnson, Jr., "After TV Accepted the Call, Sunday was Never the Same," *Sports Illustrated* 32 (January 5, 1970).
23. *Hearings,* p. 382.
24. Johnson, *Super Spectator,* pp. 56ff.
25. See Ross Atkin, "NBA Series Tailor-Made to Form-Fit TV Schedule," *The Christian Science Monitor* (May 26, 1976), p. 7.
26. *Washington Post* (January 14, 1973), p. C8.
27. Johnson, *Super Spectator,* p. 27.
28. "People are Shelling Out More Than Ever for a Good Time," *U.S. News & World Report* (February 21, 1977), pp. 40-42; "The Affluent Activists," *Forbes* (August 1, 1976), pp. 22-25.
29. Greg Thompson, "Cheerleading Turns into Big Business," Associated Press release (November 25, 1976); *New York Times* (October 28, 1972), p. 39.
30. James F. Lynch, "For the Golfer Who Has Everything, . . ." *New York Times* (December 12, 1971), section 5, p. 11.
31. "Making It on Pro Golf Tour Reserved for Few," Associated Press release (March 23, 1976).
32. "Super Bowl $40 Million Attraction for City of Miami," Associated Press release (January 11, 1976; "Money Players," *Sports Illustrated* 46 (March 27, 1977), p. 14.
33. John Underwood and Morton Sharnik, "Look What Louis Wrought," *Sports Illustrated* 36 (May 29, 1972), pp. 40-54.
34. See "Everybody Wants a Piece of the Action," *Newsweek* (April 10, 1972), pp. 46-52.
35. *New York Times* (January 10, 1974), p. 52.
36. See Larry Merchant, *The National Football Lottery* (New York: Holt, Rinehart and Winston, 1973).
37. David Anable, "The Greyhound Racing

Boom—and the Pitfalls," *The Christian Science Monitor* (May 13, 1976), pp. 18-19.

38. Gerald Eskenazi, "Rise in Illegal Gambling Blamed on OTB Climate," *New York Times* (January 10, 1974), p. 1.

39. Gerald Eskenazi, "Scalpers: Shadowy Profiteers in Sports," *New York Times* (December 28, 1970), p. 1.

40. Jonathan Brower, "Professional Sports Team Ownership: Fun, Profit and Ideology of the Power Elite," *Journal of Sport and Social Issues* 1 (1976), pp. 16-51.

41. Quoted in *New York Times* (January 11, 1973), p. 46.

42. *Hearings,* p. 19.

43. "Who Says Baseball is Like Ballet?" *Forbes* (April 1, 1971), p. 30.

44. Roger Noll, "The U.S. Team Sports Industry," *Government and the Sports Business,* p. 13.

45. See William Johnson, "Yankee Rx is Group Therapy," *Sports Illustrated* 38 (February 12, 1973), pp. 46-49; Red Smith, "Some Buy on Yanks," *New York Times* News Service (January 5, 1973); Ron Scherer, "How Costly Baseball Players Save Owners Taxes," *The Christian Science Monitor* (August 11, 1976), p. 11; and especially Benjamin A. Okner, "Taxation and Sports Enterprises," *Government and the Sports Business,* pp. 159-183.

46. Quoted in Johnson, *Super Spectator,* p. 83.

47. Quoted in Johnson, "Yankee Rx is Group Therapy," p. 49.

48. *Hearings,* p. 675.

49. For a complete analysis of the economics and legality of the move by the Braves from Milwaukee to Atlanta, see S. Prakesh Sethi, *Up Against the Corporate Wall: Modern Corporations and Social Issues of the Seventies* (Englewood Cliffs, N.J.: Prentice-Hall, 1971), pp. 267-280.

50. Roger G. Noll, "Attendance and Price Setting," *Government and the Sports Business,* pp. 136-138.

51. Charles G. Burck, "It's Promoters vs. Taxpayers in the Superstadium Game," *Fortune* 87 (March, 1973), p. 105.

52. Joseph Durso, "The $24 Million Picnic," *New York Times* (April 5, 1971), p. 39.

53. *New York Times* (November 15, 1973), p. 13.

54. *Hearings,* p. 961.

55. Claire Walter, "Football Giants Move to a Brand New Home," *The Christian Science Monitor* (September 13, 1976), p. 16.

56. Quoted in Burck, "It's Promoters vs. Taxpayers," p. 182. See also J.D.Reed, "The Louisiana Purchase," *Sports Illustrated* 41 (July 22, 1974), pp. 67-80.

57. Benjamin A. Okner, "Subsidies of Stadiums and Arenas," *Government and the Sports Business,* pp. 339-342.

58. Ibid., pp. 342-343.

59. "Robbing Peter to Pay Paul—with the Taxpayers as Peter," *Rocky Mountain News* (March 25, 1976), p. 54.

60. Okner, "Subsidies of Stadiums and Arenas, pp. 000.

61. See Noll, "The U.S. Team Sports Industry," pp. 1-10.

62. *Hearings,* p. 326; and Leonard Koppett, "Don't Blame It All on the Free Agents," *The Sporting News* (July 2, 1977), pp. 4 and 16.

63. Alex Ben Block, "So, You Want to Own a Ball Club," *Forbes* (April 1, 1977), p. 37.

64. *Hearings,* p. 870.

65. Thomas N. Daymont, "The Effects of Monopsonistic Procedures on Equality of Competition in Professional Sport Leagues," *International Review of Sport Sociology* 10 (No. 2, 1975), pp. 83-99.

66. *Hearings,* p. 323.

67. Walter C. Neale, "The Peculiar Economics of Professional Sports," *The Quarterly Journal of Economics* 78 (February, 1964), p. 2.

68. Paul L. Montgomery, "Top NBA Stars Were Subsidized," *New York Times* (March 21, 1976), pp. S1 and 6.

69. Ibid.

70. Quoted in Paul Hoch, *Rip Off the Big Game: The Exploitation of Sports by The Power Elite* (Garden City, N.Y.: Doubleday Anchor Books, 1972), p. 121.

71. *Hearings,* pp. 780, 792.

72. Gerald Scully, as reported in *New York Times* (January 27, 1974), p. 48.

73. Bob Collins, "NFL Player Salaries Drop with WFL's Credibility," *Rocky Mountain News* (March 23, 1975), p. 72.

74. *Hearings,* p. 795.

75. Quoted in Hoch, *Rip Off the Big Game,* p. 121; italics in original.

76. *Hearings,* p. 196.

77. Larry Keith, "After the Free-for-all was Over," *Sports Illustrated* 45 (December 13, 1976), pp. 29-34; "Baseball Labor Unions Finally Gain Dignity," Associated Press release (December 26, 1976); Ross Atkin, "Baseball Settles Its Differences," *The Christian Science Monitor* (August 14, 1976), p. 8; Ron Fimrite, "He's Free at Last," *Sports Illustrated* 45 (August 30, 1976), pp. 14-17; Joseph Durso, "The Year in Sports," *New York Times* (December 19, 1976), p. 38; Red Smith, "Sports in 1976: Jock Lib," *New York Times* (December 19, 1976), p. 35.

78. Quoted in Red Smith, "When Prices Go Up, Up, Up," *New York Times* (November 28, 1976), p. 35.

79. Ron Reid, "He's Free, But Not Cheap," *Sports Illustrated* 44 (June 7, 1976), pp. 69-72.

80. "Behind Pro Football's Labor Peace," *New York Times* (March 6, 1977), p. S9.

81. Douglas S. Looney, "The Start of a Chain Reaction?" *Sports Illustrated* 44 (February 16, 1976), pp. 18-20.

82. Robert Angell, "The Sporting Scene: In the Counting House," *The New Yorker* (May 10, 1976), pp. 109-110; see also Randall Poe, "The Angry Fan," *Harper's* (November, 1975), pp. 86-95.

83. Quoted in Red Smith, "When Prices Go Up, Up, Up," *New York Times* (November 28, 1976), p. 3S.

84. Jack Scott, *The Athletic Revolution* (New York: The Free Press, 1971), p. 96.

85. Quoted in Scott, *The Athletic Revolution,* p. 97.

86. Martha Duffy, "Hello to a Russian Pixie," *Sports Illustrated* 38 (March 19, 1973), p. 26.

87. Neil Amdur, "U.S. Olympic Group Top-Heavy," *New York Times* (November 5, 1972), section 5, p. 1.

88. Ibid., p. 4.

89. This activity, incidentally, is explicitly contrary to the Congressional charter of the U.S. Olympic Committee: "It shall be unlawful for any person, corporation, or association other than the United States Olympic Association or its subordinate organizations and its duly authorized employees and agents. . . to induce the sale of any article whatsoever by using. . . the emblem of the United States Olympic Association. . . ." *Articles of Incorporation of the United States Olympic Committee,* p. 25.

90. Quoted in Scott, *The Athletic Revolution,* p. 89.

91. "Saturday's Hard-Pressed Heroes," *Forbes* (November 15, 1976), p. 80.

92. Quoted in Richard Kucner, "Higher Profits Produce More Winning Teams," *Baltimore News-American,* sports special (September 10, 1972), p. 6.

93. Leonard Koppett, "Colleges Question Old Views on Sports," *New York Times* (January 11, 1971).

94. *New York Times* (March 10, 1972), p. 52.

95. It is interesting to note, however, that in many instances sports dropped by a university administration as financially prohibitive are being reinstituted as student-initiated and student-run affairs, without any real institutional assistance, as had been the case in the formative years of American intercollegiate sports in the 19th century—thus moving full circle back to "the informal sport" level.

96. See James V. Koch, "A Troubled Cartel: The NCAA," *Law and Contemporary Problems* 38 (Winter-Spring, 1973), pp. 135-150.

97. James V. Koch, "The Economics of 'Big-Time' Intercollegiate Athletics," *Social Science Quarterly* 52 (September, 1971), p. 253.

98. Ibid., p. 254.

99. Ibid.

100. *Hearings,* p. 1059.

101. Larry Van Dyne, "College Baseball: The Majors' New Farm System?" *The Chronicle of Higher Education* (June 27, 1977), pp. 4 and 6.

102. *Hearings,* pp. 1098-1111.

103. See Joseph Durso, *The All American Dollar: The Big Business of Sports* (Boston: Houghton-Mifflin, 1971); Bill Surface, "In Pro Sports, the Dollar is King," *Reader's Digest* (March, 1972), pp. 146-149; Bob

Briner, "Making Sport of Us All," *Sports Illustrated* 39 (December 10, 1973), pp.36-42; "The Sports Boom Is Going Bust. . ." *Forbes* (February 15, 1975), pp. 24-28; Mark Stevens, "Are Salaries Ruining Pro Sports?" *Christian Science Monitor* News Service (November 4, 1975); and Howard L. Nixon II, *Sport and Social Organization* (Indianapolis: Bobbs-Merrill, 1976), pp. 56-63.

104. Angell, "The Sporting Scene," p. 107.

Sport, Social Stratification, and Social Mobility 8

Sport is generally assumed to be an egalitarian and meritocratic institution. It is accepted as egalitarian because it promotes interaction across social class and racial lines, and because interest in sport transcends class and social boundaries. Sport is believed to be meritocratic because persons with talent, regardless of social background, are upwardly mobile. The thrust of this chapter is that these two widely held assumptions are myths.

The empirical examination of the sports world demonstrates that sport, like the larger society, is highly stratified. Like all institutions, sport accommodates and reinforces the existing structure of social inequality. There are exceptions, as we will note, but as exceptions, they prove the rule.

For much of American history, sport was engaged in mainly by the affluent. Only the wealthy had time and money for such nonproductive activities. But in this century, the average work week has decreased from 60 to 37 hours. According to one estimate, in 1969 the American working class male had 1,200 hours a year more of leisure time than he did in 1880.[1] Innovations such as the four day work week (in 1972, some 500 companies had such a schedule), paid vacations, and the scheduling of many holidays to coincide with weekends have left the average person with time to devote to family activities, hobbies, recreation, and watching sports events. Moreover, because of the typical American's greater disposable income, sports equipment can be purchased more readily. From 1968 to 1971, disposable income rose on a per capita basis from $2,945 to $3,595. After allowing for inflation, this still amounts to an eight percent gain in money to spend on nonessentials. The result has been a high rate of participation in sports, as the data in table 8-1 on page 210 illustrates.

An obvious inference from the data in table 8-1 is that most Americans enjoy some form of sporting or recreational activity. Clearly, the majority of Americans have the time and the money to engage in these activities. Moreover, as cited in chapter 1, attendance figures at sports events from high school through the professional ranks show that most Americans also take the time and spend the money to watch gifted athletes perform. We also know that the most popular television programs are typically sports events. All of these facts suggest that Americans, regardless of socioeconomic status, enjoy sports, either as participants or as spectators.

But has this twentieth century phenomenon of increased interest and activity in sport across social class lines diminished the relationship between social class and sport?

Social Class and Sport

Americans enjoy playing and watching sports. But is what they do or prefer to do related to socioeconomic status or not? Let's look first at participation.

Table 8-1. Number of Participants by Sport or Recreational Activity, 1972.

Bicycling	60,000,000
Boating	43,000,000
Bowling	42,000,000
Camping	45,000,000
Fishing	30,000,000
Golf	12,000,000
Horseback Riding	12,000,000
Hunting	18,000,000
Scuba Diving	3,000,000
Skiing	6,000,000
Sky Diving	40,000
Swimming	70,000,000
Tennis	10,000,000

Source: Jurate Kazichas, "More Americans Work Harder in Extra Leisure Time," *Kansas City Times* (February 24, 1972), p. 16B.

Hodges, after reviewing the literature on the subject, made the following assertion:

> The evidence relating to social class differences in the passive-active sphere is fairly emphatic. It amounts, in essence, to this: the higher an American's social-class position, the likelier he is to be a sports "doer" than a sports "viewer."[2]

To support this conclusion, we will cite the evidence from two studies. The first was conducted for the President's Council on Physical Fitness and Sports and presents data from a national survey conducted in 1972 on the extent of physical activity by Americans. These data (see table 8-2) show, with the exception of walking, that the higher status individuals are more likely to engage in physical fitness activities than lower status persons.

This finding is buttressed by a study of the residents of Allegheny County, Pennsylvania (Pittsburgh is located in this county). Burdge divided the sample into four occupational prestige levels and found that the highest level was the most active in 57 of the 82 specific forms of leisure activity. The second, third, and fourth prestige levels were highest in 17, 11, and 3 activities, respectively.[3] The evidence from empirical studies, of which the two reported here are but a small sample, provide consistent support for the generalization: the higher the socioeconomic status of the individual, the more likely will that individual be actively engaged in leisure activities.

Table 8-2. Male Adult Participation in Exercise Activities by Socioeconomic Status (SES).

SES Level	Activity					
Education	**Walking**	**Swimming**	**Bicycling**	**Calisthenics**	**Jogging**	**Weight Training**
Less than High School	36%	7%	9%	6%	3%	2%
High School	34	16	15	11	8	5
Some College	47	30	28	23	16	10
Occupation						
Manual	31%	12%	13%	8%	5%	8%
Craftsmen	27	18	15	13	6	8
Managerial	38	24	23	19	6	9
Professional	53	33	30	25	12	18
Income						
Under $5,000	46%	7%	6%	5%	4%	4%
$7,000-9,999	30	16	14	11	7	5
$15,000 or over	44	27	29	19	13	6

Source: Adapted from *Physical Fitness Research Digest,* series 4, no. 2 (April, 1974), tables 3, 4, and 5.

Preference for Participation in Specific Sports by Socioeconomic Status

Research has shown the preference for type of sport to vary consistently by socioeconomic status. One difference is that members of the upper social classes tend to engage in individual sports such as golf and tennis while blue-collar workers tend to be more active in organized team sports: bowling, basketball, volleyball, softball, and baseball.[4] These teams may be sponsored by community recreation departments, churches, local businesses, and by unions and employers. Many industries, for example, have elaborate recreation facilities for their employees and schedule leagues and tournaments for the off-work hours.

There are four probable explanations for the participation of the affluent in individual sports. The most obvious is that many of the individual sports (e.g., sailing, golf, sports car racing) are too expensive for the less well-to-do. In addition to the money limitations, community facilities for golf and tennis are often limited unless one belongs to the local country club.

A second reason is that organizations for the affluent (country clubs) emphasize three individual sports: golf, tennis, and swimming. For youngsters growing up in such a milieu, interest in these sports is "natural," and they tend to develop the skills important to success in these sports. In addition to socialization factors, the affluent individual is attracted to individual sports because that is what his or her friends, relatives, and the "important" people in the community are doing.

An interesting speculation of why the affluent are disposed toward individual sports was presented by Thorstein Veblen in 1899. He argued that leisure activities are engaged in by the affluent to impress observers that they can afford expensive and wasteful activities. In other words, sport is used by these persons as a form of conspicuous consumption, to prove that they can devote great amounts of time away from work.[5] This rationale explains why the upper classes have held amateur sport as an ideal. For this reason, Olympic competition has traditionally been limited to the more well-to-do. As sociologist Howard Nixon has put it:

> One can thus detect a distinctly aristocratic flavor in the efforts of modern Olympic officials to deny amateur standing and Olympic eligibility of any athlete who has been shown to profit financially from sports participation.[6]

That the International Olympic Committee and the national Olympic committees are overrepresented by the affluent may explain why there has been a great reluctance to include team sports in the Olympics.

Another explanation is the difference by occupation in the amount of time one can devote to a rigid schedule of team practices and games. Lower level white collar workers, and skilled and semiskilled workers, unless they "moonlight," typically work forty hour weeks. They do not bring additional work home. When their daily work shift is over, they are free to engage in other activities. Businessmen, executives, and professionals, on the other hand, work at their jobs more hours per week and their work schedules fluctuate. Because it is more difficult for them to participate in scheduled sports activity, individual sports participation for this group is more practical than team sports. Sebastian de Grazia's study of leisure activities found, for example, that two thirds of all executives more or less regularly bring work home to do at night. Moreover, they often must entertain clients or associates. The result is that they work an average of 55 hours per week—and this does not include time spent commuting or business travel.[7] These persons are also more likely to participate in time-consuming civic affairs or leadership in voluntary associations.

At the lowest end of the stratification hierarchy—the unskilled and/or unemployed poor—participation in organized team sports is practically nonexistent. Their access to organized sports is severely limited by their lack of resources and the unavailability of teams or facilities. However, an interesting phenomenon, a variant of team sports, has become part of life in the urban ghetto—playground basketball. There are neither organized leagues nor teams, only individuals or groups of individuals challenging others. Axthelm has sensitively characterized it in this way:

> Basketball is the city game.
> Its battlegrounds are strips of asphalt between tattered wire fences or crumbling buildings; its rhythms grow from the uneven thump of a ball against hard surfaces. It demands no open spaces or lush backyards or elaborate equipment. It doesn't even require specified numbers of players; a one-on-one confrontation in a playground can be as memorable as a full-scale organized game.
>
> Basketball is the game for young athletes without cars or allowances—the game whose drama and action are intensified by its confined spaces and chaotic surroundings. . . .
>
> The game is simple, an act of one man challenging another, twisting, feinting, then perhaps breaking free to leap upward, directing a ball toward a target, a metal hoop ten feet above the ground. But its simple motions swirl into intricate patterns, its variations become almost endless, its brief soaring moments merge into a fascinating dance. To the uninitiated, the patterns may seem fleeting, elusive, even confusing; but on a city playground, a classic play is frozen in the minds of those who see it—a moment of order and achievement in a turbulent, frustrating existence. And a one-on-one challenge takes on wider meaning, defining identity and manhood in an urban society that breeds invisibility.[8]

Athletes also vary by socioeconomic status in their preference for contact or non-contact sports. Evidence from the United States,[9] Canada,[10] and Germany[11] confirm the generalization that athletes from lower social origins are much more likely to compete in contact sports.

Related to the inclination of the lower classes to engage in contact sports is the tendency of such persons to gravitate to sports that emphasize physical strength (weightlifting, arm wrestling) and physical toughness (boxing, wrestling).[12]

Spectator Preferences for Sport by Social Class

The mass media have been instrumental in generating interest in professional football, basketball, baseball, hockey, and track that transcends social class. Although lacking precise data, we may reasonably assume that since over 95 percent of all American homes have a television set, those tuning in the Superbowl or the World Series will not be disproportionately from one social class.

Nevertheless, there are particular sports that are favored by the various social classes. For the very rich, there are sports like polo, yachting, training horses for racing, and sports car racing. The middle classes enjoy watching or playing tennis, golf, sailing, and skiing. Since they are more likely to have attended college than those from the lower classes, they identify more closely with college sports events (in contrast to professional sports where the interest cuts across social class lines). Among the lower classes, there is a distinct preference for such sports as bowling,. pool, boxing, auto racing, arm wrestling, figure eight racing, motocross racing, demolition derbys, and such pseudo sports as professional wrestling and the roller derby.[13]

An excellent indicator of what type of audience will watch a sporting event on television is the type of sponsor who advertises during the time outs. Golf events generally advertise Cadillacs, Xerox copiers, and airlines, while the roller derby is typically sponsored by used-car dealers, beer distributors, and country and western record companies. Clearly, advertisers have researched sports audiences and discerned that for some sports activities, the audiences are disproportionately from certain social classes.

While simple logic suggests why the wealthy are interested in yachting, and why college graduates appreciate college sports, there is not a ready explanation for why the working classes gravitate toward their special sports (sometimes called "prole" sports, referring to Marx's term for the working class, "proletariat.") Let's now examine in greater detail why there are sports that especially attract the working classes.

Prole Sports

Why are blue-collar workers especially atttracted to particular kinds of sporting activities? On the surface, it would appear that these sports have several common attributes: speed, daring, physical strength, and violence. But let's examine several of these activities closer to see why these and other characteristics make them so appealing to this socioeconomic category. Before we proceed, however, it should be noted that the possible reasons are speculative, because no systematic research has yet been undertaken on the actual motivations of blue-collar fans.

The various forms of automobile and motorcycle racing appeal to working class members for several reasons. First, the artifacts of the sport (the machines, the necessary tools and equipment) are part of lower class life. The accessibility of the machines and the skills to drive them make it easy to identify with this sport. A second reason is that these machines and their drivers represent speed, excitement, and daring to persons whose work is dull and repetitive. Another possible symbolic reason is that cars and motorcycles are symbols of liberation to the working class person who otherwise feels trapped by his situation.[14] Closely related is the image of man and machine united in rebellion against a hostile environment.[15]

Two sociologists have suggested that motocross racing (motorcycle racing over a torturous course of jumps, sharp turns, water, and mud) is especially attractive to working class persons because it offers them a chance to prove their worth in aggressive, competitive situations. Such opportunities for the working class are not found in their work situations, so they seek it elsewhere.[16]

The demolition derby—one type of motor sports that especially appeals to the lower classes—is especially interesting because it is so blatantly violent. The contest is designed to encourage crashes among a hundred or so cars until one is left. Tom Wolfe has argued that this sport, because of its wanton aggression and destruction, is culturally the most important sport ever originated in the United States because of what it symbolizes.

> The unabashed, undisguised, quite purposeful sense of destruction of the demolition derby is its unique contribution. The aggression, the battering, the ruination are there to be enjoyed. The crowd at a demolition derby seldom gasps and often laughs. It enjoys the same full-throated participation as Romans at the Colosseum. After each trial or heat at a demolition derby two drivers go into the finals. One is the driver whose car was still going at the end. The other is the driver the crowd selects from among the 24 vanquished on the basis of his courage, showmanship or simply the awesomeness of his crashes.[17]

An apparent summit for demolition derby fans was the occasion in the Los Angeles Coliseum early in 1973. This event was billed as the "World's Richest Demolition Derby" since the cars to be demolished were all high-priced, late models (e.g., Lincoln Continental Mark IVs, Rolls Royce Silver Shadows, and Cadillac El Dorados). Twenty-four thousand thrill-seeking fans purchased tickets (at $8.00 for adults and $4.00 for children) for this ultimate in destructive acts. But why would there be interest in such an event? Judging by the kinds of movies they attend and the popularity of certain sports such as football and hockey, Americans appear to be fascinated by violence. This may be especially true of those persons who work at relatively low-paying and monotonous jobs (semiskilled workers). Their latent hostility toward the more well-to-do may explain why blue collar workers might be especially fascinated by the destruction of cars too expensive for them to ever own.

Roller derby and professional wrestling, which we have characterized as "pseudo sports" because the competition is contrived, depend in very large measure on the interest and attendance of blue collar workers and their families. These two types of shows have several common characteristics that may offer some clues as to why the lower classes are especially attracted to them. First, they emphasize strength, power, and violence rather than agility and finesse. Second, the actors are easy to identify with—some emphasize their ethnic or racial background; some are fat, while others are musclemen; some are heroes, while others are villains. Unlike other sports, these activities (especially the roller derby) give equal billing to female athletes, allowing women the possibility of someone with whom they can identify. Because of this propensity of spectators to identify with the players, the fans at wrestling matches and roller derbys usually are physically and emotionally involved in the events. They shout encouragement to their heroes, boo their villains, and occasionally throw things when they get upset with the officiating or the outcome of the event. The intensity they feel is also occasionally manifested in arguments or fights among themselves. The crowd behavior at these events is exactly the opposite of behavior found at upper middle class events such as golf or tennis. Unlike the passivity of fans at those sports, the fans at wrestling matches and roller derbys are intensely involved. One observer has characterized the typical crowd at a roller derby this way:

> You can't call the crowd of 10,000 an audience. It is an organized mob—near hysterical men and women writhing in great paroxysms of emotion, by turns ecstatic, argumentative, despairing and vindictive. But never silent. If the action on the rink is sport, the behavior is spectacle. The two spheres are at times competitive, leaving the spectators to choose between Aristotelian catharsis and just plain raising hell.[18]

Symbolically, wrestling matches are morality plays. As sociologist Gregory Stone has put it:

> There is always the "hero" who attempts to defeat the "villain" within the moral framework of the rules of the game. It is a case of law *versus* outlaw, cops and robbers, the "good guys" *versus* the "bad guys."[19]

Although not so pronounced, the roller derby scenario also has athletes who abide by the rules and those who flaunt them. In both pseudo sports, the fans tend to identify with the virtuous hero. When justice prevails and virtue triumphs, the fans' belief in law and order is reinforced. When the villains win, it is attributed to foul play, so when the rematch occurs, justice will finally reign. If it does not, then an alternate view of the world is reinforced. In this view, which Arthur Shostak posits as a major working class belief, the world operates so that some persons take advantage of others and get away with it.[20]

In summary, the prole sports and pseudo sports have several characteristics in common that make them especially attractive to the working classes.

1. The necessary equipment (such as automobiles or muscles) and skills (driving, mechanical aptitude, or self-defense) are part of working class life.
2. The sports emphasize physical prowess and manhood (*machismo*).
3. They are exciting and, therefore, serve as an emotional outlet.Some focus on the danger of high speed and powerful machines. Others stress violence to machines or human beings. Still others contrive events to excite the crowds (e.g., in wrestling events such as tag teams, Texas Death Matches, and the Battle Royales).
4. There is strong identification with heroes who are like the spectators in ethnicity, language, or behavior.
5. The sports are *not* school related.
6. With few exceptions, the sports they watch are individual rather than team-oriented (which is opposite their tendency to participate in team sports).

Segregation by Social Class

We have just noted that the different social strata have some unique preferences for sport. So, although they enjoy some sports in common (especially the mass media sports of professional football, basketball, and baseball), there is a self-selection process that segregates some sports by social class. But let's look beyond this process to ascertain whether there are any other mechanisms that operate to separate the social classes physically.

At the participatory level, some barriers serve to segregate social classes. In sports such as swimming, golf, and tennis, the affluent compete in private clubs or at the facilities limited to residents in an exclusive neighborhood or condominium (some of these are entirely fenced or walled, with gates where access is controlled by armed guards). The middle and lower classes may participate in these sports but only at public facilities. In a given city, then, there is often a dual system of competition, with tournaments or competitions for the wealthy and a separate set of events for the general public. The quality of play at these two levels varies, with the wealthy usually rated better because of their access to better facilities and private tutors. This difference in skill also serves to segregate the wealthy players from the less affluent players.

Spectators are often also segregated by social class at general-interest sporting events. This is accomplished in several ways. First, ticket prices often exclude the poor. The likelihood of this is increased, of course, when season tickets are considered. The common practice of differential prices by seating location also tends to segregate persons by socioeconomic status. The affluent rarely sit in the relatively low-cost bleacher seats, while the poor rarely purchase reserved seats or box seats.

The ultimate in differentially priced seating locations and segregation by social class has been reached in a relatively new practice—the purchase of very costly exclusive boxes. An example is the Texas Stadium, home of the Dallas Cowboys. The plan, as developed by owner Clint Murchison, sets up a unique stock-option plan for season's tickets. For $1,000, a person may buy a lifetime guarantee that he can *purchase* seats between the 30-yard lines (at the regular price). For the less wealthy, $250 buys the option to purchase seats from the 30-yard line into the end zone. For the very rich, however, the option costs $50,000.

> What you get for your $50,000 is a 16-foot-by-16-foot room, undecorated, and the right to purchase a dozen seats for every game at $10 a lick. Then the Inner Circle began to vibrate with the sound of costly decorations going up. A couple of construction men spent $34,000 on what has been described as "Texas Baroque" architecture. It is straight out of a private railroad car, circa 1888.

> "This is really the only way to watch football," said one oil baroness. "Our chauffer brings us out several hours before game time. We have dinner at the Texas Club, here on the Inner Circle level. There are cocktails served in our box. Afterwards, they show the highlights on closed circuit television and we sip champagne while the parking lot clears."[21]

This description illustrates segregation by wealth at sports events. It is also an example of conspicuous consumption—the purchase and display of expensive items to impress others of one's high status. This phenomenon is found among the wealthy, near wealthy, and those who fake wealth. Although all sports offer this opportunity, boxing—especially heavyweight boxing championship matches involving Muhammad Ali—are used by many status conscious persons to impress others. They buy the expensive seats, wear expensive jewelry and furs, and drive limousines to the arena.

> Again the curtain rises, revealing Ali. And he stands, as they cheer him, glistening in the light of their admiration. The status addicts, paying up to $200 each to breathe deeply his sweat. Pimps and politicians, who are closer than they admit. Expensive women and the men who have known them. Some have come from Paris on a junket that includes dinner and dancing at Regine's, a Park Avenue disco where the fashionable discuss the islands and the price of art. Some have come from the streets, where power grows from guns and the strong wear velvet. They have come because wherever Ali is, they must be. He is outrageous, compelling and important—everything they think they see in their mirrors.[22]

Public Arenas: Who Benefits?

In the chapter on economics, we considered the economic impact of a new stadium in an urban place. To recapitulate briefly, stadiums are very expensive (the New Orleans Superdome cost in excess of $163 million), but promoters argue that stadiums benefit the community by creating jobs and prosperity in the hotel, restaurant, transportation, construction, and related industries. Therefore, they are usually financed by a combination of user taxes (on the tickets sold, hotel rooms, restaurant bills), property tax (the owner of a house assessed at $20,000 in Seattle will pay about $1.38 a year for forty years to help pay for the King County Stadium), or by issuing revenue bonds (which, if not able to raise the needed money, become general obligation bonds paid through taxes).[23] The overall result is that these stadiums are financed by the general public at a huge cost. But does the community benefit more or less equally across social class lines? We would argue that the answer is no! for the following reasons:

1. The wealthy benefit disproportionately from the letting of building contracts, and through the feeding and housing of persons wishing to see games. Although more jobs may be created, the profits will accrue unequally to the capitalists, not the workers. This is especially true for team owners (and stockholders) who will profit from attendance *without* any investment in the land or construction. They cannot lose

financially because the burden is on the taxpayers. This is clearly a case of the wealthy receiving a public subsidy.

2. The price of individual and season tickets is usually too high for the lower classes. Ironically, bringing a major league team to an area (a primary reason for building a new stadium), usually means that the poor see fewer games than before, since home games would be blacked-out on television. By court order, however, this ban on televised home football games was lifted in 1973, if the game was sold out 48 hours before game time.

3. Often new stadiums are built in the suburbs or downtown rather than in residential areas. The old stadiums typically were in run-down neighborhoods and were abandoned with the completion of the new stadium. One consequence is that the poor living near the old stadiums are deprived of incomes previously derived from games (jobs as parking attendants, salesmen, janitors, cooks, etc.). They are also now deprived of easy access to games. Their lack of money and the generally insufficient system of mass transportation will make their attendance at games all the more improbable.

4. Publicly financed arenas are built for those sports that appeal more to the affluent—i.e., baseball, football, basketball, and hockey. Prole sports tend to occur in privately owned arenas.

Social Mobility and Sport

Typically, Americans believe that the United States is an "open" class system—i.e., positions of high pay and prestige are open to those with the requisite talents and aptitudes, regardless of social origin. The world of sport has done more than its share to give substance to this belief as poor boys from rural and urban America, whether white or black, have skyrocketed in fame and fortune through success in sports. Our task in this section is to investigate the extent to which social mobility actually operates in the sports world. Let's first examine the arguments and evidence supporting this belief.

Sport as a Mobility Escalator

The most obvious way in which sports participation facilitates upward social mobility is when a person from a low socioeconomic background becomes wealthy and famous because of his athletic ability.[24] This happens in almost all sports (except those more exclusively upper class such as polo, yachting, and, to a large extent, golf). Most typically, it occurs in boxing where the athletes are recruited almost exclusively from the lower socioeconomic levels—and some will earn millions of dollars during their careers.[25]

Successful athletes in some sports (football and basketball in particular) must also attend both high school and college. In this way, sports participation has the effect of encouraging, or, in some cases, forcing persons to attain more education than they might otherwise achieve. This, in turn, increases their opportunities for success outside of the sports world.

At the high school level, athletic participation requires that athletes stay out of trouble and maintain a minimum grade point to remain eligible. Schafer's research substantiates this but indicates it is most striking when comparing athletic and nonathletic sons of blue collar fathers. He found that athletes have the more desirable tendencies—to be nondelinquent and to achieve higher grades than their nonathletic colleagues.[27] Because the athletes are more successful, they will likely have a better self-concept and have higher aspirations than their nonathletic classmates of the same social class. Thus, boys who would be less academically oriented than sons of white collar fathers are encouraged to do well and even aspire to attain a college education. This is heightened by their inclusion in the school's "inner circle" (because of their athletic achievements) and subsequent association and identification with white-collar and college-bound members of the school's leading crowd.[28] Of course, the best high school athletes will probably go to college on athletic scholarships, thereby increasing their likelihood of upward social mobility. But the athletic experience, even for those not good enough to play in college, increases the probability that they, too, will attend college and have widened opportunities for attaining jobs of higher prestige than their parents. In concluding their research on this subject, Rehberg and Schafer said:

> [Our] data have shown that a greater proportion of athletes than non-athletes expect to enroll in a four-year college, even when the potentially confounding variables of status, academic performance, and parental encouragement are controlled. This relationship is especially marked among boys not otherwise disposed toward college, that is, those from working-class homes, those in the lower half of their graduating class, and those with low parental encouragement to go to college.[29]

The research of Emil Bend, who analyzed data from 18,500 persons in 1965 who had graduated from high school five years earlier, supports the contention that athletic participation fosters upward mobility.

Bend's data found in table 8-3 demonstrate that the greater the athletic prowess in high school, the greater the success as measured by salary, education, and expectations for the future. But this consistent relationship may be spurious—i.e., it may be accounted for by other factors—perhaps the better athletes come disproportionately from the middle and upper classes. Table 8-4 presents the same data controlling for parent's social class and respondent's IQ to determine if that is the case. In other words, nonathletes are now compared with superior athletes whose social class and IQ are relatively the same (i.e., in the same quartile of the distribution).

Table 8-3. High School Athletic Participation and Educational and Income Expectations.

	Athletic Performance Groups (High School)			
	I	II	III	IV
Variable	Nonathlete	Casual Athlete	Active Athlete	Superior
Median income expected in 1980	$8,467	$11,865	$12,307	$13,232
Median 1965 salary	$5,000	$ 5,157	$ 5,298	$ 5,327
Greatest amount of education expected:				
High School graduate only	23%	18%	14%	10%
Four year college graduate	24	32	37	43
Advanced degree	24	28	29	30
Percent with college degree (1965)	44	51	57	63

Source: Adapted from Emil Bend, *The Impact of Athletic Participation on Academic and Career Aspiration and Achievement* (Pittsburgh: American Institutes for Research, 1968).

Table 8-4. Income and Education by High and Low Endowment Levels.

	Low Endowment (Low SES, Low Aptitude)		High Endowment (High SES, High Aptitude)	
	Nonathlete	Superior Athlete	Nonathlete	Superior Athlete
Median 1965 salary	$ 4,548	$ 5,275	$ 5,023	$ 5,680
Income expectation in 1980	$ 8,436	$10,667	$14,622	$16,511
Percent graduating from college	5	7	81	86

Source: Adapted from Emil Bend, *The Impact of Athletic Participation on Academic and Career Aspiration and Achievement* (Pittsburgh: American Institutes for Research, 1968).

The data from table 8-4 show conclusively that high school athletes, when compared to nonathletes of the same social class and IQ range, have a greater likelihood of graduating from college and making more money. Clearly, superior athletes when compared to nonathletes are and will be more upwardly mobile.

Athletes at the college level, if from a family of low social status, will almost automatically surpass their parents due to their superior educational attainment. John

Loy's study of athletes at UCLA confirms this. He received questionnaires from 845 of the 1,021 former athletes in the sample who had engaged in college sports at least four years and had earned at least three letters. Table 8-5 provides his data comparing occupational status of the athletes with their father's (as measured by standard occupational prestige scales, the higher the score the higher the prestige).[30]

Table 8-5. A Comparison of Father's Occupational Status Scores and Education with Those of Son's Present Job and Education.

Sport	Father's Main Job	Son's Present Job	Percentage of Fathers Not Completing High School	Percentage of Sons with Advanced Degrees
Wrestling	43	77	50	50
Football	48	74	52	29
Baseball	49	75	50	37
Soccer	51	79	23	54
Track	53	77	44	46
Basketball	57	77	37	44
Gymnastics	58	80	38	62
Crew	62	78	24	30
Swimming	63	78	27	46
Tennis	64	75	26	41

Source: Adapted from tables 3, 4 and 5 of John W. Loy, Jr., "The Study of Sport and Social Mobility," *Aspects of Contemporary Sociology of Sport,* ed. Gerald S. Kenyon (Chicago: The Athletic Institute, 1969), pp. 114-116.

The data in table 8-5 suggest several interesting relationships. First, while the job prestige of former college athletes is fairly stable regardless of the sport played (a range of only six points), the occupational prestige of fathers by sport varies a good deal (a range of 21 points). Apparently, a college degree (remember, these athletes had played at least four years), makes the attainment of upper middle class jobs possible, regardless of social origin. Second, sons surpassed their fathers in occupational prestige regardless of the sport (the difference ranging from only ten points for basketball players to 34 points for wrestlers). Thus, these data show the degree of social mobility achieved by college athletes when compared to their fathers. This is buttressed further when one compares the last two columns in table 8-5, the percentage of fathers not completing high school and the percentage of sons with advanced degrees.[31]

We have seen that success in sports enhances the possibility of attending college. This, in turn, increases the probability of attaining a high status job, as the Loy study and several others have demonstrated. The 1963 fooball squad at the University of Pittsburgh, for example, had 71 players, 66 of whom earned degrees. Fifty percent of the squad also earned graduate degrees. Occupationally, three became doctors, 15 became lawyers, five are now engineers, seven are educators, two are ministers, and 28 are in business or industry.[32]

At the more elite colleges and universities, a college education is all the more advantageous. Table 8-6 shows the occupational distribution for lettermen at Yale University from 1872 to 1949.

Table 8-6. The Occupational Distribution of Yale Lettermen, 1872-1949.

Occupational Category	Number
Industry	288
Merchandising	237
Law	165
Finance	156
Education	59
Medicine	55
Insurance	55
Other Professional	43
Public Service	40
Ministry	14

Source: A.B. Crawford, ed., *Football Y Men*, Men of Yale series, vols. 1-3 (New Haven: Yale University Press, 1962-1963).

While these studies of UCLA, Pittsburgh, and Yale show that athletes tend to have high prestige occupations, they do *not* inform us as to whether or not athletes at colleges and universities fare better after their formal education than nonathletes from the same institutions. Two studies are instructive on this point, although they are limited to income. The first is a study of 1926 Dartmouth graduates conducted in 1946. The results showed that 20 years after graduation the average income of Dartmouth letter winners was $18,000 while the nonathlete graduates averaged $14,280.[33] The second study compared a sample of Minnesota letter winners with nonletter winners, and the athletes were found to have incomes that were $1,360 higher.[34]

Although these data are only from two schools, they lead to the tentative conclusion that athletes appear to do better (at least financially and we can infer from this, occupationally as well) than nonathletes. There are at least three possible reasons for this. First, athletic participation may lead to various forms of "occupational sponsorship.''[35] Because the college athlete is a popular hero, there is a greater likelihood that he will date and marry a girl who comes from a higher socioeconomic background than will the nonathlete. If this occurs, then the chances of the college athlete's father-in-law providing him with unusual benefits in the business world are much greater than for the average nonathlete. Another form of sponsorship may come from well-placed alumni who offer former athletes positions in their businesses after graduation. This may be done to help the firm's public relations, or it may be part of the pay-off in the recruiting wars that some alumni are willing to underwrite.

A second reason why athletes may fare better is because the selection process for many jobs requires that the applicant be ''well-rounded''—that is, that he have a number of successful experiences outside of the classroom. An extreme example of this is the selection of Rhodes Scholars, where demonstrated athletic ability is a requirement in addition to superior grades.

Finally, there is the possibility that sports participation in highly competitive situations may lead to the development of attitudes and behavior patterns highly valued in the larger occupational world. Valued attributes such as leadership, human relations skills, team work, compulsive-obsessive traits, and a highly developed competitive drive may be acquired in sports and thus may insure that athletes will succeed in other endeavors. Considerable debate surrounds this issue of whether sports builds character or whether only certain kinds of personalities survive (as we noted in chapter 4). There may be a self-fulfilling prophecy at work here, however, that may serve to make athletes unusually upwardly mobile—i.e., if employers assume that athletes possess these valued character traits, they will make their hiring and advancement decisions accordingly, giving athletes the advantage.

The Limitations of Social Mobility Through Sport

As we have noted, social mobility is accomplished through sport *indirectly* because of the educational attainment that is concomitant with school sports. Except for ''hardship'' cases in basketball, athletes in some sports must play college ball for four years (or at least wait until their class has graduated) before they are eligible for professional selection. This procedure should have the benefit of encouraging athletes to graduate, which will help their careers after sports. Unfortunately, though, there are barriers making graduation difficult for athletes. An obvious problem for athletes in school is the inordinate demands on their time and energy for practice, travel, and other sport-related activities. Because of these pressures many athletes are counseled into taking easy courses to maintain eligibility but that do not meet graduation requirements.[36] The result of such a practice is either to delay graduation or to make graduation an unrealistic goal.

Another barrier to graduation for many college athletes is a consequence of their being recruited for athletic prowess rather than academic skills and abilities. Athletes from the ghetto who attended inferior schools are generally not prepared for the intellectual demands of college.[37] A study by Harry Webb of persons who had graduated five years after initial enrollment at Michigan State University found that while the normal rate was 70 percent, only 49 percent of the team athletes and 60 percent of the individual sport athletes had received degrees there. Moreover, only 38 percent of the black athletes had graduated.[38]

When one examines only the percentage of football players who graduate, the picture is even more depressing. A study of athletes at the University of Colorado showed that football players had the worst graduation record (39 percent) among the athletes in ten varsity sports. This might be related to the social class of the athletes' parents. But, interestingly, only 40 percent of scholarship athletes in golf and skiing, both white middle class sports, graduated. And 55 percent of the basketball players graduated.[39] Table 8-7 shows the data on football players and graduation at seven major universities (four of which have a poorer graduation record than the University of Colorado).

Table 8-7. Football and the Prospect of Graduation from College.

	Total No. Football Seniors 1975 and 1976	No. of Graduates	Percentage	Total No. Former Players Active in NFL '76	No. of Graduates	Percentage
Brigham Young	20	5	25	5	1	20
Arizona State	18	5	28	17	6	35
Colorado State	38	11	29	7	1	14
Oklahoma State	31	10	32	5	2	40
University of Colorado	31	12	39	24	6	25
University of Oklahoma	36	20	56	16	4	25
University of Nebraska	39	27	69	19	11	58

Source: Adapted from Mike Madigan, "Graduation Academic to College Gridders," *Rocky Mountain News* (December 26, 1976), p. 96.

A final barrier to graduation for college athletes is that many perceive the college experience is only a preparation for their professional careers in sport. Study for them is necessary only to maintain eligibility. Such a view is unrealistic for all but the superstars, as we will see shortly. The view is also shortsighted because a professional athletic career, if one makes it to that level, is limited to but a few years. Few will be able to translate their success in athletics to success in their post-athletic careers.[40] Such a problem is especially true for blacks (as we will see in chapter 9).[41]

Forbes magazine asked the question several years ago: "Where does a young man go to get rich today? Wall Street? Law? Big Business?"[42] The answer provided was to enter professional sports. The argument was buttressed by the examples of the fantastic financial success of Arnold Palmer, Jack Nicklaus, and Joe Namath. This article, illustrative of a persistent media message, perpetuates the hope of upward mobility through sport for many youngsters and their parents.[43] And it would appear to make good sense. After all, the *average* salaries in the professional major leagues in 1976 were: hockey-$75,000, football-$42,000, baseball-$48,000, and basketball-$110,000.[44] Moreover, there are bonuses for signing, playoff checks, endorsements, and other financial benefits that accrue to the professional athlete.

But this dream of financial success through a sports career is just that—a dream—for all but an infinitesimal number. In 1974, for instance, 200,000 high school seniors played basketball for their schools, but there were only 5,700 college seniors playing basketball. The attrition process continued as only 211 of those college seniors were drafted by the pros in that year, and only 55 eventually signed with a professional team.[45] A government study reported (table 8-7) similar data for the three major sports in 1972.

The data from table 8-8 show clearly that a career in professional sports is nearly impossible to attain because of the fierce competition for major league positions. In baseball, for instance, the potential free agent pool of players (high school seniors, college seniors, collegians over 21, junior college graduates, and foreign players) is 120,000 persons each year. Only about 1,200 are actually drafted (one percent of the eligible pool), but most will never make it to the major leagues. Many will play in the minors for small salaries and hope to make it in the majors some day, but injuries and lack of talent deter most. In any one year, only about 100 new personnel are added to major league baseball rosters from the newly drafted players and minor leaguers. The

Table 8-8. Major League Career Opportunities by Type of Professional Sport, 1972.

	Baseball	Football	Basketball
Number of high school players	400,000	600,000	600,000*
Number of college players	25,000	40,000	17,000
Number of major league players	600	1,222	324
Number of rookies added per year	100	157	60
Average length of career (yrs.)	7-8	5	5

Source: Adapted from Harold Blitz, "The Drive to Win: Careers in Professional Sports," *Occupational Outlook Quarterly* 17 (Summer, 1973) pp. 3-16.

*This estimate is extrapolated from the data found in Steve Cady, "Sports Recruiting: For Every Winner, A Hundred Losers," *New York Times* (March 13, 1974), p. 46C.

irony is that although only a few gifted athletes ever make it, major league baseball sponsors television advertisements extolling the virtues of baseball as a career, explicitly suggesting that it is one for which youngsters should aspire.

The same rigorous "condensation process" occurs in football and basketball as well. In football, only three percent of those eligible are drafted and only three of ten drafted are actually added to team rosters. In basketball, the odds are even slimmer, since only one percent of the eligibles are drafted and only one of six draftees make it.

An additional factor from table 8-8 shows that even when major league status is attained, the probabilities of fame and fortune are limited. The average length of a career in professional sport is short, around five years, which means that even if the pay is relatively high, the employment does not last very long. Even those relatively few athletes with careers exceeding ten years face the reality that by their middle thirties they are no longer employable as competitors. Gilbert has characterized their plight in the following quote:

> Upon their retirement many athletes are faced with a humiliating reality. They can no longer perform in a specialty they have devoted their life to mastering. They are too young, and often not financially able, to spend the rest of their years in idleness. On the other hand, they are comparatively old to begin a meaningful second career—especially, as is often the case, if they have no training or experience in anything but competitive athletics.[46]

There is the possibility, however, of a sports-related career after one's playing days are over. Coaching, managing, scouting, sportscasting, public relations, are all possibilities for the ex-athlete but the opportunities are severely limited (even more so if the athlete is a minority group member).

We have focused on the limited possibilities in the major American sports of football, baseball, and basketball. Many persons in these sports, however, have attained a formal education, and this in the long run is the greatest contributor to upward social mobility. For those sports where education is not attained, the chances for mobility are minimal.[47] In boxing, for example, athletes are typically from a low socioeconomic background. For the few who succeed, the rise in status is abrupt, with some fighters getting in excess of several million dollars for a single fight. But the quick upward mobility experienced by the successful fighter is usually followed by a plummeting in social status.

> The successful boxers have a relatively quick economic ascent at a relatively young age in terms of earning power. But the punitive character of the sport, the boxers' dependence upon their managers, and their carefree spending during their boxing careers contribute to a quicker economic descent for many boxers. Their economic descent is accompanied by a drop in status and frequently by temporary or prolonged emotional difficulties in readjusting to their new roles.[48]

But most boxers do not achieve big-time status. Weinberg and Arond analyzed the careers of 127 fighters who had been professionals for at least eight years and found that 84 percent never had fights that were beyond the preliminary or semiwindup categories. Nine percent fought main events at the local level, and only seven percent ever achieved any national recognition (only one of whom was ever a champion).[49]

The Consequences of Accepting the Belief that Sport is a Mobility Escalator

We have shown that social mobility directly through sport is largely a myth. Despite the remoteness of mobility through sport for almost all participants, most Americans accept it as a viable method. For example, one variant of the myth has been stated by Frederick Rudolph:

> Eventually football would enable a whole generation of young men in the coal fields of Pennsylvania to turn their backs on the mines that had employed their fathers.[50]

To which Jack Scott replied:

> To put it politely, Rudolph is full of patriotic exaggeration. I make this statement as one who "escaped" an eastern Pennsylvania coal-mining town through the assistance of an athletic scholarship. My high school produced some of the finest athletic teams in the state, yet few of my teammates found athletics to be a means for social advancement. Yearly, close to two hundred athletes at my school would base their lives around varsity athletics, but at most only three or four individuals would be rewarded with athletic scholarships. . . . School boys who spend four years of high school dreaming of collegiate gridiron glory are suddenly confronted by reality on graduation day. For every Broadway Joe Namath there are hundreds of sad, disillusioned men standing on the street corners and sitting in the beer halls of Pennsylvania towns such as Scranton, Beaver Falls, and Altoona.[51]

This quote points to one negative consequence of believing that sport offers upward mobility—many boys work very hard to become great in sport, but only a very few will be successful. As we noted from the data in table 8-8, the number of boys who play high school baseball is 400,000 compared to 25,000 in college; the number in football dwindles from 600,000 to 40,000; and the number of varsity high school basketball players is 600,000 while the number in college is 17,000. In each case, only about one out of 16 high school players will play at the college level and not all of them will receive scholarships. But because the myth is so pervasive, many boys spend many hours per day developing their speed, strength, or "moves" to the virtual exclusion of those skills that have a greater likelihood of paying off in upward mobility—i.e., mathematical reasoning, and communication skills. While this is true for many lower class boys, it is especially damaging for blacks whose racial heroes are almost exclusively in music or sports. As Scott has put it:

> Gifted black athletes will usually make out all right, but what happens to the thousands of young unathletic black children whose only heroes are sports stars? How many brilliant doctors, lawyers, teachers, poets, and artists have been lost because intelligent but uncoordinated black youths had been led to believe by a racist society that their only chance for getting ahead was to develop a thirty foot jump shot or to run the hundred in 9.3?[52]

This futile pursuit of sports stardom by blacks is of serious consequence for their community, according to Harry Edwards. Blacks, by spending their energies and talents on athletic skills, are not pursuing occupations that will help themselves *and* that will help meet the political and material needs of blacks. Thus, because of belief in the sports myth, they remain dependent on whites and white institutions.[53] As Roscoe C. Brown, Jr., director of New York University's Institute for Afro-American Affairs, has said:

> We need more education. Black youngsters pour too much time and energy into sports. They're deluded and seduced by the athletic flesh-peddlers, used for public amusement—and discarded. . . . Most blacks find neither social mobility, educational fulfillment nor financial success through . . . "the mirage" of sports recruiting. For every Walt Frazier, posing next to his $30,000 Rolls-Royce, thousands of basketball prospects are rejected. Most of them are left without the skills needed for servicing or enriching the community . . . and that's the rip-off.[54]

Or, as argued by the black tennis star Arthur Ashe:

> Unfortunately, our most widely recognized role models are athletes and entertainers—"runnin' " and "jumpin' " and "singin' " and "dancin.' " While we are 60 percent of the National Basketball Association, we are less than 4 percent of the doctors and lawyers. While we are about 35 percent [sic] of major league baseball we are less than 2 percent of the engineers. While we are about 40 percent of the National Football League, we are less than 11 percent of construction workers such as carpenters and bricklayers.
>
> Our greatest heroes of the century have been athletes—Jack Johnson, Joe Louis and Muhammad Ali. Racial and economic discrimination forced us to channel our energies into athletics and entertainment. These were the ways out of the ghetto, the ways to get that Cadillac, those alligator shoes, that cashmere sport coat.
>
> Somehow, parents must instill a desire for learning alongside the desire to be a Walt Frazier. . . .
>
> We have been on the same roads—sports and entertainment—too long. We need to pull over, fill up at the library and speed away to Congress, and the Supreme Court, the unions and the business world.[55]

Summary

Two themes dominate this chapter. First, sport like the larger society is stratified. Socioeconomic status is related to the types of sports in which one participates and watches. The lower the status, the more inclined toward contact sports and pseudo sports such as professional wrestling and the roller derby. The socioeconomic strata are segregated in sport not only by preference but also by such barriers as entrance requirements and prohibitive costs.

The second theme is that sports participation has limited potential as a social mobility escalator. There is evidence that being a successful athlete enhances self confidence and the probability of attending college. Thus, social mobility is accomplished through sport indirectly because of the increased employment potential from educational attainment. Social mobility through sport is limited, however, if one is provided an inferior education, as is often the case. It is also limited by failure to graduate, and the *very* few number of positions in professional sport. Even for those who attain major league status, the probabilities of fame and fortune are small because of the fierce competition and injuries.

The myth that sport is a mobility escalator is especially dangerous for minority youth. Ghetto youngsters who devote their lives to the pursuit of athletic stardom are, except for the fortunate few, doomed to failure—failure in sport and in the real world where sports skills are essentially irrelevant to occupational placement and advancement.

Notes

1. Arthur B. Shostak, *Blue Collar Life* (New York: Random House, 1969), p. 187.
2. Harold M. Hodges, Jr., *Social Stratification: Class in America* (Cambridge, Mass.: Schenkman, 1964), p. 166.
3. Rabel J. Burdge, "Levels of Occupational Prestige and Leisure Activity," *Journal of Leisure Research* 1 (1969), pp. 262-274.
4. See John W. Loy, "The Study of Sport and Social Mobility," in *Aspects of Contemporary Sport Sociology,* ed. Gerald S. Kenyon (Chicago: The Athletic Institute, 1969), pp. 101-119; and John W. Loy, "Social Origins and Occupational Mobility Patterns of a Selected Sample of American Athletes," *International Review of Sport Sociology* 7 (1972), pp. 5-23.
5. Thorstein Veblen, *Theory of the Leisure Class* (New York: Macmillan, 1899).
6. Howard L. Nixon II, *Sport and Social Organization* (Indianapolis: Bobbs-Merrill, 1976), p. 35.
7. Sebastian de Grazia, *Of Time, Work, and Leisure* (Garden City, N.Y.: Doubleday Anchor Books, 1964), p. 127.
8. Pete Axthelm, *The City Game: Basketball in New York* (New York: Harper and Row, 1970), pp. ix-x.
9. See Loy, "The Study of Sport and Social Mobility," pp. 101-119; and Gregory Stone, "Some Meanings of American Sport: An Extended View," *Aspects of Contemporary Sport Sociology* pp. 5-16.
10. Richard S. Gruneau, "A Socioeconomic Analysis of the Competitors at the 1971 Canada Winter Games" (Master's thesis, University of Calgary, 1972).

11. Gunther Luschen, "Social Stratification and Social Mobility Among Young Sportsmen," in *Sport, Culture and Society,* eds. John W. Loy and Gerald S. Kenyon (New York: Macmillan, 1969), pp. 258-276.

12. See John M. Roberts and Brian Sutton-Smith, "Child Training and Game Involvement," *Sport, Culture and Society,* pp.116-136; and Walter A. Zelman, "The Sports People Play," *Parks & Recreation* 11 (February, 1976), pp. 27-38.

13. See Richard S. Gruneau, "Sport, Social Differentiation and Social Inequality," in *Sport and Social Order,* eds. Donald W. Ball and John W. Loy (Reading, Mass.: Addison-Wesley, 1975), pp. 121-184; and Doyle W. Bishop and Masaru Ikeda, "Status and Role Factors in the Leisure Behavior of Different Occupations," *Sociology and Social Research* 54 (January, 1970), pp. 190-208.

14. Lee Rainwater *et al., Workingman's Wife* (New York: Oceana, 1952), p. 192.

15. George H. Lewis, ed., *Side Saddle on the Golden Calf: Social Structure and Popular Culture in America* (Pacific Palisades, Cal.: Goodyear, 1972), pp. 35-36.

16. Thomas W. Martin and Kenneth J. Berry, "Competitive Sport in Post-Industrial Society: The Case of the Motocross Racer," *Journal of Popular Culture* 8 (Summer, 1974), pp. 107-120.

17. Tom Wolfe, "Clean Fun at Riverhead," *Side-Saddle on the Golden Calf,* p. 40.

18. Joan Grissim, "Nobody Loves Us But the Fans," *Rolling Stone* (March 15, 1969), p. 18.

19. Gregory P. Stone, "American Sports: Play and Display," in *Sport: Readings from a Sociological Perspective,* ed. Eric Dunning (Toronto: University of Toronto Press, 1972), p. 59.

20. Arthur B. Shostak, *Blue Collar Life*, p. 202.

21. Wells Twombly, "Life in Football's Half-Astrodome," *San Francisco Sunday Examiner & Chronicle* (January 2, 1972), p. 4C.

22. Tony Kornheiser, "Ali and the Status Addicts," *New York Times* (September 26, 1976), p. 3S.

23. Charles G. Burck, "It's Promoters vs. Taxpayers in the Superstadium Game," *Fortune* (March, 1973), p. 178.

24. Our consideration in this section will focus exclusively on males. Females in professional and college sport are found in golf, tennis, and track. Women in golf and tennis almost inevitably come from middle and upper class backgrounds. Lower class females, especially blacks, tend to be involved in track and field sports, which offer little direct chances for upward mobility. As Harry Edwards has put it, "We must also consider that to the extent that sport provides an escape route from the ghetto at all, it does so only for black *males* . . . and the escape of a few black men does not mean that an equal number of black women will go with them as their wives or girlfriends; consequently there is no guarantee that even a few black women will benefit from the success achieved by black male professional athletes." Harry Edwards, "The Black Athletes: 20th Century Gladiators for White Americans," *Psychology Today* 7 (November, 1973), p. 47.

25. The advanced student interested in the complexities of the relationship between sport and social mobility will want to read carefully: Emil Bend, "A Paradigm for Analyzing Some Relationships Between Sport and Social Mobility" (Paper presented at the Eighth World Congress of Sociology, Toronto (August, 1974).

26. Walter E. Schafer, "Some Social Sources and Consequences of Interscholastic Athletics: The Case of Participation and Delinquency," *Aspects of Contemporary Sport Sociology,* pp. 41-42.

27. Walter E. Schafer and J. Michael Armer, "Athletes Are Not Inferior Students," in *Games, Sport and Power,* ed. Gregory P. Stone (New Brunswick, N.J.: Transaction Books, 1972), p. 106-108.

28. Ibid., p. 109.

29. Richard A. Rehberg and Walter W. Schafer, "Participation in Interscholastic Athletics and College Expectation," *American Journal of Sociology* 73 (May, 1968), p. 739; see also Elmer Spreitzer and Meredith Pugh, "Interscholastic Athletics and Educational Expectations," *Sociology of Education* 46 (Spring, 1973), pp. 171-182.

30. Some examples of occupations by prestige scores as found in Peter M. Blau and O. Dudley Duncan, *The American Occupational Structure* (New York: John Wiley, 1967), pp. 122-123 are:
35-39 TV repairmen, firemen

40-44 Cashiers, clerks, policemen, construction foremen
45-49 Surveyors, telephone linemen
50-54 musicians, mail carriers, professional athletes
55-59 funeral directors, railroad conductors
60-64 postmasters, librarians, sports instructors and officials
65-69 artists, salesmen
70-74 teachers, stock brokers, department heads
75-79 accountants, chemists, veterinarians, insurance brokers
80-84 professors, editors, pharmacists
85-89 engineers, bankers
90-96 physicians, lawyers

31. This seemingly great mobility by college athletes compared to their fathers may be spurious. First, the comparison of college graduates with their fathers guarantees that the sons have exceeded the fathers (because not all of the fathers will have graduated but the sample is composed of sons who have). Second, there will always be a gap between fathers and sons because of the general trend to upgrade educational levels. The best method to determine whether athletes have more potential for social mobility, therefore, is to compare them with nonathletes.

32. Dean Billick, "Still Winners," *National Collegiate Sports Services Bulletin* (1973); see also the long-range analysis of athletes from Pittsburgh in Edward H. Litchfield and Myron Cope, "Saturday's Hero is Doing Fine," *Sports Illustrated* 17 (October 8, 1962), pp. 66-80.

33. R.W. Husband, "What do College Grades Predict?" *Fortune* 56 (1957), pp. 157-158.

34. M.H. Schrupp, "The Differential Effects of the Development of Athletic Ability of a High Order," *Research Quarterly* 24 (1952), pp. 218-222.

35. See Walter E. Schafer, "Athletic Success and Social Mobility" (Paper presented at the annual meeting of the American Association of Health, Physical Education, and Recreation, St. Louis, 1968).

36. See Dave Meggyesy, *Out of Their League* (Berkeley: Ramparts, 1970); Gary Shaw, *Meat on the Hoof* (New York: St. Martins, 1972); and John Underwood, "The Desperate Coach," *Sports Illustrated* 31 (August 25, September 1, 8, 1969).

37. See W.G. Spady, "Lament for the Letterman: Effects of Peer Status and Extracurricular Activities on Goals and Achievement," *American Journal of Sociology* 75 (January, 1970), pp. 680-702.

38. Harry Webb, "Success Patterns of College Athletes" (Paper presented at the annual meeting of the American Association of Health, Physical Education, and Recreation, St. Louis, 1968).

39. Mike Madigan, "Graduation Academic to College Gridders," *Rocky Mountain News* (December 26, 1976), p. 96.

40. Rudolf K. Haerle, Jr., "Education, Athletic Scholarships and the Occupational Career of the Professional Athlete," *Sociology of Work and Occupations* 2 (November, 1975), pp. 373-403.

41. See Paul E. Dubois, "Sport, Mobility, and the Black Athlete," *Sport Sociology Bulletin* 3 (Fall, 1974), pp. 40-61.

42. "Superstars! Supermoney!" *Forbes* (September 15, 1972), p. 25.

43. See Melvin L. Oliver, "Race, Class and the Family's Orientation to Mobility through Sports: An Analysis of the Social Meaning of Community Baseball" (Paper presented at the meetings of the Midwest Sociological Society, St. Louis, April, 1976).

44. Phil Elderkin, "Change of Pace," *Christian Science Monitor* (April 16, 1976), p. 10.

45. *New York Times* (March 13, 1974).

46. Bil Gilbert, "What Counselors Need to Know about College and Pro Sports," *Phil Delta Kappan* 61 (October, 1974), p. 122.

47. Rudolf K. Haerle, Jr., "Education, Athletic Scholarship, and the Occupational Career of the Professional Athlete," pp. 373-403.

48. S. Kirson Weinberg and Henry Arond, "The Occupational Culture of the Boxer," in *Sport, Culture and Society,* eds. John Loy Jr., and Gerald S. Kenyon (New York: Macmillan, 1969), p. 452.

49. Ibid., p. 447.

50. Frederick Rudolph, *The American College and University* (New York: Random House Vintage Books, 1962), p. 378.

51. Jack Scott, *The Athletic Revolution* (New York: The Free Press, 1971), pp. 178-179.

52. Ibid., p. 180; see also Robert Lipsyte, *Sportsworld: An American Dreamland* (New York: Quandrangle, 1975), p. 276.
53. Edwards, "The Black Athlete," pp. 43-52.
54. Quoted in Steve Cady, "Sports Recruiting: For Every Winner, a Hundred Losers," *New York Times* (March 13, 1974), p. 46C.
55. Arthur Ashe, "Send Your Children to the Libraries," *New York Times* (February 6, 1977), p. 2S.

USA

Racism in Sport 9

That there is a systematic and pervasive discrimination against blacks in American society is beyond doubt. But Americans commonly believe that sport is an oasis free of such problems and tensions. After all, the argument goes, sports are competitive; fans, coaches, and players want to win. Clearly, the color of the players involved is not a factor, only their performance. A further belief for the nonexistence of racism in sport is that the number of blacks in the major team sports far exceeds their proportion in the population.

The facts, however, lead to a very different conclusion. Rather than being immune from racism, sport is a microcosm of the larger society and reflects the same racial problems. The objective of this chapter is to document the historical and contemporary facts that support this claim. By showing that racism is prevalent in sport, we hope to bury the myth that sport is a meritocracy where skin color is disregarded and to alert the reader to this continuing societal problem.

This chapter will describe and explain the situation of one minority group in sport—blacks. This racial group has been selected because blacks are the most prominent minority in American sports. The modes of discrimination occurring for blacks, however, are not exclusive to them. Various racial and ethnic minorities such as American Indians, Chicanos, Puerto Ricans, Irish, and Poles have also experienced exclusion, low pay, derisive action, and other forms of abuse.

The History of Black Involvement in Sport

Until the end of World War II, sport was segregated by race, except for isolated instances.[1] Prior to the Emancipation Proclamation in 1863, most blacks were slaves and unable to participate in organized sports. After the Civil War, blacks made a few inroads in sport as boxers, jockeys, and baseball players (see table 9-1). But they were clearly exceptions because society and sport remained racially segregated by custom and in some places by law (e.g., Jim Crow laws). These discriminatory practices of society were most important in the development of black athletes after slavery. Because blacks were excluded from white organizations such as athletic clubs, they established their own. And because blacks were also excluded from white colleges for economic and social reasons, black colleges were established, allowing blacks the opportunity for organized athletic participation.

The History of Blacks in Professional Sport

The history of black involvement in white-dominated professional sport has been sporadic and for the most part nonexistent. In the 50 years following the Civil War, blacks made some breakthroughs—participating in boxing, horse racing, baseball, and

Table 9-1. Black Breakthroughs in American Professional Sports.

1800	Tom Molineaux, a slave, was America's first recognized heavyweight boxing champion.
1876	A black jockey rode in the Kentucky Derby.
1884	Moses and Weldy Walker (brothers) were the first blacks to play major league baseball.
1908	Jack Johnson won the heavyweight boxing championship.
1911	Henry McDonald was first black professional football player.
1922	First all-black pro basketball team (New York Renaissance) was formed.
1945	Los Angeles Rams broke the racial barrier in NFL by signing Kenny Washington and Woody Strode.
1946	Marion Motley was the first black in All-American Football Conference (Cleveland Browns).
1947	Branch Rickey brought Jackie Robinson to major league baseball.
1949	Jackie Robinson broke the racial barrier in major league baseball.
1950	Three blacks broke the racial barriers in NBA.
1959	Althea Gibson became the first black professional tennis player.
1962	Jackie Robinson elected to the Baseball Hall of Fame.
1966	Bill Russell was the first black head coach (Boston Celtics).
1968	American League hired the first black umpire, Emmit Ashford.
1971	Wayne Embry was the first black general manager (Milwaukee Bucks).
1975	Frank Robinson was the first black field manager (Cleveland Indians).
1975	James Harris was the first black starting quarterback for season.
1975	Lee Elder was the first black to play in the Master's Golf Tournament.

football. These were not much more than breakthroughs though because the participation by blacks was minimal. Early in the 1900s, blacks were totally excluded from professional sport, except in boxing, until after World War II. When blacks were barred from baseball, football, and basketball, they formed all-black teams and leagues.[2] The Harlem Globetrotters and the famous players of the black baseball leagues such as Satchel Paige and Josh Gibson emerged from this segregated situation. When Jackie Robinson broke the color barrier, first in 1946 in the minor leagues (the first black in the International League in 57 years), and then the next year in the majors, he received much verbal and physical abuse from players and fans who resented blacks playing on an equal level with whites. The great player Rogers Hornsby uttered the common attitude at the time about Robinson's entrance into white baseball: "They've been getting along all right playing together and should stay where they belong in their league."[3]

Boxing was the exception in professional sports. Blacks made early gains in that sport and increased their numbers over the years, even during the years when they were excluded from other professional sports. Perhaps boxing was the exception because it has typically been the sport of the most oppressed urban groups. At the turn of the century, the Irish dominated boxing, then the Jewish fighters, and by 1936, the Italians were the most numerous in boxing. During these times, blacks increased their numbers in boxing, and by 1948, coinciding with the huge migration of blacks to the urban North, blacks clearly became preeminent in that sport.[4] By 1971, more than 70 percent of American boxers were black.[5] Although blacks were allowed by the boxing establishment to participate continuously during the 1900s, they were still discriminated against. White boxers tended to receive more money than blacks. Because of the "great white hope" myth, the white promoters liked to match whites against blacks in the ring. But blacks often consented to lose just to obtain a match.[6]

With the exception of boxing, then, the history of black involvement in professional sport can be divided roughly into four stages: (1) almost total exclusion before the Civil War; (2) the initial breakthrough period following the Emancipation Proclamation; (3) racial segregation between the two World Wars; and (4) racial integration after World War II. This last period is especially interesting, and we will focus on it in this chapter. In the 30 years following World War II, blacks made tremendous strides in professional sport. The percentages of blacks in professional football went from zero to 42 and in basketball from zero to more than 60. Moreover, by the beginning of 1976, there was one manager in baseball and five head coaches in basketball. All football coaches were white, however, as were the owners of all professional teams in the major sports. As we will see in the final part of this chapter, the black athletes continued to experience discriminatory practices up to the present.

The History of Integration in Intercollegiate Sport

Blacks have been absent from big-time college sports for most of this century. A few Ivy League and other eastern schools had black athletes at an early time, but they were the exception. Perhaps the most famous black athlete at a white university was Paul Robeson, who made Walter Camp's All-American team in 1918 playing for Rutgers.[7] For the most part, though, blacks played at black colleges in black leagues. Although the system was segregated, it did provide many blacks with the opportunity to engage in organized sport.

Paralleling the situation in professional sports, college sports remained segregated, except for isolated instances, until after World War II. In 1948, for example, only 10 percent of college basketball teams had one or more blacks on their roster. This percentage increased to 45 percent of the teams in 1962 and 92 percent by 1975.[8] At the University of Michigan, for example, during the period from 1882 to 1945, there were only four black lettermen in football and none in basketball. From 1945 to 1972, however, the number of black lettermen swelled to 71 in football and 21 in basketball.[9]

The last major conference to integrate was the Southeastern (SEC). The University of Tennessee broke the barrier by signing a black defensive back in 1966. By 1968, there were 11 blacks on scholarships in that conference but Alabama, Auburn, Florida, Mississippi, Mississippi State, Louisiana State, and Georgia remained all-white.[10] Two years later, 41 blacks were on scholarships in the SEC (30 of them at three schools, Kentucky, Florida, and Tennessee). Two schools, LSU and Mississippi remained all-white athletically in 1970.[11] In 1972, there were about 100 blacks in football alone in the SEC, about 10 percent of the total blacks on athletic scholarships. Significantly, two schools, Tennessee and Mississippi, had black sophomores starting and starring at quarterback. By 1975, black athletes were common in the SEC, as they were in all the other athletic conferences. The transition from a segregated program to an integrated one is perhaps best illustrated by the University of Alabama. In 1968 that school had no blacks on athletic scholarship, but its 1975 basketball team had an all-black starting lineup.

That more and more schools were now searching for talented blacks to bolster their athletic programs had a detrimental effect on the all-black schools. Black schools once had a monopoly on black athletic talent, but this was watered down considerably as many of the best athletes were lured to integrated schools. The best black athletes found it advantageous to play at predominantly white schools because of the greater visibility, especially through television. This visibility would, for the best athletes, mean a better chance to sign a lucrative professional contract at the conclusion of their collegiate eligibility. The result was a depleted athletic program at black schools. This forced some black schools to drop their athletic programs, and some previously black leagues disbanded. Moreover, with a diminishing number of black teams, the black schools were no longer playing schedules that were exclusively black.[12]

The History of Black Political Activism Through Sport

The initial breakthroughs of blacks in white sports were, most fundamentally, political acts—political because they disturbed established customs. Most importantly, they called into question the existing unequal power relationships in society. But, for the most part, the pioneering black athletes were apolitical in their behaviors. Jackie Robinson, for example, was counseled by Branch Rickey to take the physical and verbal abuse passively. That advice was probably necessary if the black athletes were to be successful in breaking the racial barriers.

From Jackie Robinson's breakthrough in 1947 until the late 1960s, blacks generally kept a low political profile. But as society's oppressed segments tended toward increased militancy to correct social inequities in the 1960s, so too did many black athletes. For some, their activities involved a statement of black pride, such as wearing an Afro hairstyle. For others, it involved real attempts to change the distribution of power. The Olympic Games of 1968 provided the setting for one of the earliest organized attempts by blacks to dramatize the racism prevalent in America. Other instances of militancy by black athletes—e.g., the boycott of the New York Athletic Club's annual track meet because that club had segregationist membership policies; protest against the Mormon Church and Brigham Young University for alleged racist beliefs; and protest against racist coaches (see chapter 6)—were successful in raising the consciousness of previously apolitical black athletes and in changing some racist practices. The mood of black militancy was also instrumental in making the players' associations more aggressive in trying to change the power structure in professional sport.

Blacks in the past thirty years or so have not only changed the racial composition of American sport but also have shifted from passivity to activism. This latter trend has led to a dilemma for the contemporary black athlete; he is faced with contradictory demands.[13] The sports establishment expects him to be apolitical. To acquiesce to this expectation would probably benefit the black athlete at the personal level (salary, invitations to speak, endorsements, and the like). On the other hand, black leaders demand that he use his prestige and visibility as a prominent athlete to further the cause of black freedom and equality. Thus, black athletes experience the role conflict of being either a radical or an "Uncle Tom." The athletes' responses to this dilemma have been diverse.[14] Some have tried to ignore the pressures from one side and intensified their advocacy of the other. Of course, in doing so, they courted the rejection of one side. Others attempted to fulfill, at least partially, the demands of each side. This usually dissatisfied all concerned parties. Finally, for some athletes, the pressures became so great that they dropped out of sports permanently.

Black Dominance in Sport

We have seen that since World War II, blacks have dramatically increased their numbers in major team sports. The increase during the first 15 years or so, however, was relatively slow. The watershed year in professional sports (when the proportion of blacks approximated their proportion in the national population) for baseball was 1957; for basketball, 1958; and for football, 1960. Since then, however, the rate has virtually exploded. By 1975, as noted in the previous section, more than 60 percent of all professional basketball players were black, while they comprised more than 42 percent of all professional football and 21 percent of major league baseball players.

There are two possible explanations—genetic and social—for this disproportionate presence of blacks in American team sports. Let's examine the genetic hypothesis first.

Race-Linked Physical Differences

A common explanation for the overrepresentation of blacks in certain sports is that blacks are naturally better athletes than whites and their predominance in American sports is, therefore, attributed to their innate physical supremacy. The empirical evidence on black-white physical differences indicates that some differences may be related to athletic achievement.[15] Some problems with these studies, however, cloud the results. First, there is the issue of who is black. Racial categories in any society, but particularly in the United States where amalgamation of Africans, Caucasians, and Indians continues, are ill-defined and even socially defined.[16] Second, the studies that have found physical differences between the races have often used faulty methodology.[17] Since blacks, like whites, exhibit a wide range of physical builds and other physiological features, sampling becomes a problem. Does the scientist compare randomly selected whites with randomly selected blacks? Or, more logically to answer the question of athletic superiority, does the researcher compare a random selection of superior white and black athletes? Unfortunately, this has not been the case. Another methodological problem involves the use of averages to compare the two races. Edwards has summarized these methodological problems in the following statement:

> What physical characteristics does Kareem Abdul-Jabbar have in common with Elgin Baylor, or Wilt Chamberlain with Al Attles? The point is simply that Wilt Chamberlain and Kareem Abdul-Jabbar have more in common physically with Mel Counts and Hank Finkel, two seven-foot-tall white athletes, than with most of their fellow black athletes. Even aside from these hyperbolic illustrations, what emerges from objective analysis of supposed physical differences between so-called races is the fact that for a large number of phenotypes there are more differences among individual members of any one racial group than between any two groups as a whole. Thus, a fabricated "average" of the differences between racial groupings may serve certain heuristic purposes but provides a woefully inadequate basis for explaining specific cases of athletic excellence or superior ability. Black athletes (and the black population as a whole) manifest a wide range of physical builds, body proportions, and other highly diverse anatomical and physiological features—as do all other racial categories, including the so-called white race.[18]

Problems with existing empirical studies lead us to conclude that at present we do not know whether black athletes actually possess superior physical traits to whites or not.[19] Even if it is finally proven that blacks have genetic advantages over whites, we believe that they will likely be less important than the social reasons for black dominance in certain sports.

Race-Linked Cultural Differences

It may be that the overrepresentation of blacks in sport is the result of the uniqueness of the black subculture in America. James Green has argued that a positive emphasis in

the black subculture is placed on the importance of physical (and verbal) skill and dexterity. Athletic prowess in men is highly valued by both black women
athletically superior male is compara
something of a folk hero. He achie
peers, whether a publicly applauded
ample evidence of just such adulation
age, in the playgrounds of New York C

Cultural differences probably acc
performance between black Africans a
ferences are more or less controlled
however), we find great differences. In
in distance running but have won onl
(prior to the 1976 Olympics). Black Am
sprints and long jump with negligible su
other than physiology must explain this
ferences in history and geography doubtl

We must also consider cultural dif
and humor have emerged from the black
accounts for the blacks' interest and abili moves, speed, and aggression. The interest of other groups in particular sports is easily explained that way. For example, Japanese Americans, who constitute less than 0.3 percent of the total population, comprise over 20 percent of the top AAU judo competitors.[22] Although black culture might similarly contribute to black excellence in athletics and especially in certain sports, there is little systematic empirical evidence at present to substantiate the claim.

Social Structure

The most plausible reasons for black dominance in sport and in certain sports are found in the structural constraints on blacks in American society. These constraints can be divided into two types: (1) occupational discrimination, and (2) the sports opportunity structure.

Because opportunities for vertical mobility by blacks in American society are circumscribed, athletics may become perceived as one of the few means by which a black can succeed in a highly competitive American society; a young black male's primary role models are much more likely to be athletic heroes than a white's models. And the determination and motivation devoted to the pursuit of an athletic career may, therefore, be more intense than for the white adolescent, whose career options are greater. Jack Olsen, in *The Black Athlete,* quoting a prominent coach, made that point:

> People keep reminding me that there is a difference in physical ability between the races, but I think there isn't. The Negro boy practices longer and harder. The Negro

> has the keener desire to excel in sports because it is more mandatory for his future opportunitites than it is for a White boy. There are nine thousand different jobs available to a person if he is white.[23]

Or, as Harry Edwards has argued:

> Black society, as does the dominant white society, teaches its members to strive for that which is defined as the most desirable among potentially *achievable* goals—*among potentially achievable goals.* Since the onset of integrated, highly rewarding sports opportunities and the impact of television in communicating to all the ostensible influence . . . glamour, affluence, and so forth, of the successful black athlete, the talents of Afro-American males (and females, again, to a lesser extent) are disproportionately concentrated toward achievement in this one area. In high-prestige occupational positions outside of the sports realm, black role models are an all but insignificant few. These are not readily visible, and they seldom have contact or communications with the masses of blacks. . . . Thus, given the competition among athletic organizations for top-flight athletes, it is to be expected that a high proportion of the extremely gifted black individuals would be in sports. Whites, on the other hand, because they have visible alternative role models and greater potential access to alternative high-prestige positions, distribute their talents over a broader range of endeavors. Thus, the concentration of highly gifted whites in sports is proportionately less than the number of blacks. Under such circumstances, black athletes dominate sports in terms of excellence of performance, where both groups participate in numbers.[24]

Occupational limitations for blacks do not explain why they tend to gravitate toward some sports, such as boxing, basketball, football, track, and baseball, and why they are underrepresented in others, such as swimming, golf, skiing, tennis, and polo.*

Phillips has argued that the reason lies in what he has called the "sports opportunity structure."[26] Blacks tend to excel in those sports where facilities, coaching, and competition are available to them (i.e., in the schools and community recreation programs). Those sports where blacks are rarely found have facilities, coaching, and competition provided in private clubs. There are few excellent black golfers, for example, and they had to overcome the disadvantages of being self-taught and being limited to play at municipal courses.[27] Few blacks are competitive skiers for the obvious reasons that most blacks live far removed from snow and mountains, and because skiing is very expensive.[28]

*However, while blacks have been overrepresented in baseball, there is a recent trend for blacks to shun baseball in favor of football, track, and, especially, basketball. A study in 1976 revealed that the number of black baseball players had begun to dwindle on major league rosters but more so in the minor leagues and colleges.[25] The possible reasons for this shift in interest are: (1) blacks are increasingly living in inner cities where the space to play baseball is absent; (2) baseball requires a period of apprenticeship in the minors where the salaries are small and the publicity minimal, while football and basketball require playing in college where the benefits are an education, notoriety, and, when completed, major league status; and (3) most colleges offer football and basketball scholarships but comparatively few in baseball.

Blacks have been denied membership in private clubs (and the access to the best facilities and coaching in sports, such as golf and tennis) for economic and social reasons. The economic barrier to membership is the result of the discriminatory practices (in type of job, salaries/wages, and chances for promotion) prevalent in American society that deny most blacks affluence. The social barriers have occurred because of the discriminatory practices of many private clubs that exclude various racial and ethnic groups.[29]

But there is another type of discrimination implied in the sports opportunity structure. Poverty is not the only factor in the failure of blacks to engage in some sports; the powerful in some sports have denied access to blacks, even those with the requisite skills and financial support. Certain golf tournaments, the Masters', for instance, have been reluctant to permit blacks to play. Lee Elder became the first black to play the Masters' in 1975. Just as golf has allowed black caddies but not golfers, horse racing has allowed blacks as exercise boys but not jockeys. Automobile racing is another sport where blacks have found great difficulty in participating. The Indianapolis 500 still awaits its first black driver.[30]

The Consequences of Black Domination of Professional Team Sport

The paucity of blacks in some sports is balanced by their abundance in the team sports of football, basketball, and baseball. Their proportions in these sports, already large, continues to increase. Will this trend continue? Perhaps so, until the discrimination in society vanishes, and since this eventuality is a remote one in the near future at least, there is a real possibility of professional sports becoming virtually all black.

Frank Deford has speculated that this trend, if continued, will lead to the demise of these three professional sports.[31] Along with the trend toward more black players, concomitant trends converge to heighten the possibility that these sports will diminish—trends for new suburban stadiums to be built away from the central cities,[32] and for the cost of attending games to escalate so that only the affluent can afford to attend regularly. The result of these three trends is that the sports being played by blacks are being watched increasingly by affluent whites. Deford argues that these trends are creating a pattern of de facto segregation.

> Football, baseball, and basketball are approaching an identity crisis, the same one that all but destroyed boxing when it ran out of white boxers for the white ticket buyers to identify with. How long will white pride—white racism, if you will—support black athletics? . . . Thus most spectators are being asked to identify with a racial minority they have always rejected, even feared. The question is how long will the white American psyche tolerate this situation? Since whites have deserted their homes, neighborhoods, schools, stores, churches, cities, and city halls to escape association with black Americans, there is no reason to doubt that they will give up their sports, too.[33]

If Deford's prediction occurs, what will result? The possibilities are: (1) the rise of other, mostly white, sports, such as hockey, soccer, lacrosse, and car racing; (2) the declining revenues from attendance and television will force owners of football, basketball, and baseball teams to sell their franchises, perhaps to black interests; and (3) the demise of our present major sports.

Deford's dire forecast is predicated on the retention of the racism present in contemporary America.

> If white Americans persist in maintaining the attitudes that result in two separate societies, one price they will have to pay, it seems, will be the loss of the three games that have been such a large part of 20th-Century America.[34]

As of 1976, blacks have increased their numbers in the three major sports, but attendance has *not* declined as predicted. The next decade will likely be crucial in determining the future of these sports. Two related variables will account for the direction: (1) the degree of occupational discrimination in society; and (2) the degree of racial antipathy held by affluent whites.

Racial Discrimination in Sport

Sport seemingly is not free of racial discrimination.[35] But the dominant presence of blacks in the three major team sports would appear to belie the existence of racism in sport. Moreover, the prominence and huge salaries of black superstars such as Kareem Abdul-Jabbar and O.J. Simpson have led many Americans—black and white—to infer that collegiate and professional athletics have provided an avenue of mobility for blacks unavailable elsewhere in American society. Sport, thus, seems to have "done something for" black Americans.

Many commentators—social scientists, journalists, and black athletes themselves—have argued, however, that black visibility in collegiate and professional sports has merely served to mask the racism that pervades the entire sports establishment. According to these critics, the existence of racism in collegiate and professional sports is especially insidious because the promoters of, and commentators on, athletics have made sports sacred by projecting its image as the single institution in America relatively immune from racism.

In this section, we shall focus on three aspects of the athletic world that have been alleged to be racially biased—the assignment of playing positions, rewards and authority structures, and performance differentials. The analysis will be limited primarily to the three major professional team sports (baseball, basketball, and football) where blacks are found most prominently, and, therefore, slights the obvious dearth of blacks in other sports (e.g., hockey, tennis, golf, and swimming). In addition to describing and explaining the current situation in basketball, football, and baseball, we will attempt to determine whether any substantial changes have occurred or can be anticipated in the future.

Stacking

One of the best documented forms of discrimination in both college and professional ranks is popularly known as *stacking.* The term refers to situations in which minority group members are relegated to specific team positions and excluded from competing for others. The consequence is often that intrateam competition for starting positions is between members of the same race (e.g., those competing as running backs are black, while those competing as quarterbacks are white). For example, Rosenblatt noted that while there are twice as many pitchers on a baseball team as there are outfielders, in 1965, there were three times as many black outfielders as pitchers.[36]

Examination of the stacking phenomenon was first undertaken by Loy and McElvogue, who argued that racial segregation in sports is a function of centrality—that is, spatial location—in a team sports unit.[37] To explain positional racial segregation in sports, they combined organizational principles advanced by Hubert M. Blalock and Oscar Grusky. Blalock has argued that: (1) the lower the degree of purely social interaction on the job, the lower the degree of [racial] discrimination; and (2) to the extent that performance level is relatively independent of skill in interpersonal relations, the lower the degree of [racial] discrimination.[38] Grusky's notions about the formal structure of organizations are similar:

> All else being equal, the more central one's spatial location: (1) the greater the likelihood dependent or coordinative tasks will be performed and (2) the greater the rate of interaction with the occupants of other positions. Also, the performance of dependent tasks is positively related to frequency of interactions.[39]

Combining these propositions, Loy and McElvogue hypothesized that ". . . racial segregation in professional team sports is positively related to centrality."[40] Their analysis of football (where the central positions are quarterback, center, offensive guard, and linebacker) and baseball (where the central positions are the infield, catcher, and pitcher) demonstrated that the central positions were indeed overwhelmingly manned by whites, while blacks were overrepresented in the peripheral (noncentral) positions. Examining the data for baseball in 1967, they found that 83 percent of those listed as infielders were white, while 49 percent of the outfielders were black. The proportion of whites was greatest in the positions of catcher (96 percent) and pitcher (94 percent), the most central positions in baseball. The analysis of data from the 1975 major league baseball season showed little change from the situation described by Loy and McElvogue in 1967. By 1975, the percentage of infielders who were white had declined slightly to 76 percent, but the outfield was still disproportionately manned by blacks (49 percent). Moreover, the pitching (96 percent) and catching (95 percent) positions remained overwhelmingly white.

Table 9-2 compares the racial composition of positions in football for the 1960 and 1975 seasons. The conclusions drawn from these data are clear. While the proportion of blacks has increased dramatically during this fifteen year period, central positions continue to be disproportionately white. One difference between 1960 and 1975 is that blacks have increasingly supplanted whites at noncentral positions. In other words, as black entry into professional football has increased, they tend to occupy primarily noncentral positions. Blacks appear to have made some inroads in the central offensive positions, for example, a shift from 97 percent white to 87 percent white from 1960 to 1975. But when length of time in the league is controlled for, the overwhelming proportion of whites in these positions remains. Among those players in the league one to three years, 79 percent were white in 1975; four to six years, 80 percent white; seven to nine years, 80 percent white; and ten or more years, 96 percent white.[41]

Several explanations have been advanced to account for the stacking phenomenon. The Loy and McElvogue interpretation rested primarily on a position's spatial location in a team unit. However, Edwards has argued that the actual spatial location of a playing position is an incidental factor in the explanation of stacking. The crucial variable involved in positional segregation is the degree of outcome control or leadership responsibilities found in each position, according to him. For example, quarterbacks have greater team authority and ability to affect the outcome of the game than do individuals who occupy noncentral positions.[42]

Thus, the key is not the interaction potential of the playing position but the leadership and degree of responsibility for the game's outcome built into the position that account for the paucity of blacks at central positions. This is consonant with the stereotype hypothesis advanced by Brower (specifically for football but one that applies to other sports as well):

> The combined function of centrality in terms of responsibility and interaction provides a frame for exclusion of blacks and constitutes a definition of the situation for coaches and management. People in the world of professional football believe that various football positions require specific types of physically- and intellectually-endowed athletes. When these beliefs are combined with the stereotypes of blacks and whites, blacks are excluded from certain positions. Normal organizational processes when interlaced with racist conceptions of the world spell out an important consequence, namely, the racial basis of the division of labor in professional football.[43]

In this view, then, it is the racial stereotypes of blacks' abilities that lead to the view that they are more ideally suited for those positions labeled "noncentral." For example, Brower compared the requirements for the central and noncentral positions in football and found that the former required leadership, thinking ability, highly

Table 9-2. The Distribution of White and Black Players by Position in Major League Football: 1960 and 1975 (In Percentages).

Playing Position	1960* White	1960* Black	1960* Percent Black by Position**	1975 White	1975 Black	1975 Percent Black by Position
Kicker/Punter	1.2	0	0	9.0	0.2	1.3
Quarterback	6.3	0	0	9.7	0.5	3.5
Center	5.3	0	0	6.7	0.5	4.9
Linebacker	11.5	3.7	4.2	17.4	8.6	26.0
Offensive guard	8.0	1.8	3.1	8.7	4.5	26.9
Offensive tackle	8.3	24.1	28.3	8.6	5.7	31.8
Defensive front four	11.0	14.8	15.4	12.3	15.7	47.6
End/flanker	22.6	3.7	2.2	11.6	20.2	55.3
Running back	16.5	25.9	17.5	8.1	21.1	65.2
Defensive back	9.3	25.9	27.5	8.1	23.2	67.3
Totals	100.0	99.9		100.2	100.2	
N =	(199 1/2)	(27)	11.9	(870)	(620)	41.6

*The 1960 data are taken from Brower (1972), who obtained them from the media guides published annually by each team. Whenever a player was listed at two positions, Brower credited him as one-half at each position. 1975 data are taken from 1975 *Football Register* published annually by *The Sporting News.* Since both the media guides and the *Football Register* are published before each season, they include only information on veterans.

**Since blacks were 11.9 percent of the player population in 1960, those playing positions having less than 11.9 black percent were underrepresented. In 1975, those positions having less than 41.6 percent black were underrepresented.

refined techniques, stability under pressure, and responsibility for the outcome of the games. Noncentral positions, on the other hand, require athletes with speed, quickness, aggressiveness, "good hands," and "instinct."[44]

Evidence for the racial stereotype explanation for stacking is found in the paucity of blacks at the most important positions for outcome control in football (quarterback, kicker, and placekick holder). The data for 1975 show that: (1) of the 87 quarterbacks in the league, only three were black; (2) of the 70 punters and placekickers mentioned in the *Football Register,* only one was black; and (3) of the 26 placekick holders (and some were not quarterbacks), not one was black. It is inconceivable to us that blacks lack the ability to play these positions at the professional level. Placekick holders must, for example, have "good hands," an important quality for pass receivers, two-thirds of which were black, but not one was selected for the former role. Kicking requires a strong leg and the development of accuracy. Are blacks unable to develop strong legs or master the necessary technique? The conclusion seems inescapable. Blacks are precluded from occupying leadership positions (quarterback, defensive signal caller) because subtle but widely held stereotypes of black intellectual and leadership abilities still persist in the sports world. As a consequence, blacks are relegated to those positions where the requisite skills are speed, strength, and quick reactions, thinking or leadership ability positions are precluded.

Another explanation for stacking has been advanced by McPherson, who has argued that black youths may segregate themselves into specific sport roles because they wish to emulate black stars.[45] Contrary to the belief that "stacking" can be attributed to discriminatory acts by members of the majority group, this interpretation holds that the playing roles to which black youths aspire are those in which blacks have previously attained a high level of achievement. Since the first positions to be occupied by blacks in professional football were in the offensive and defensive backfield and the defensive line, subsequent imitation of their techniques by black youths has resulted in blacks being overrepresented in these positions today. Although the small sample makes his findings tentative, Brower has provided some support for this hypothesis.[46] He asked a sample of 23 white and 20 black high school football players which athletes they admired most and what position they would most like to play if they had the ability and opportunity. The overwhelming majority of blacks (70 percent) had only black heroes (role models), whereas whites chose heroes from both races. More important for our consideration is the finding that black high school athletes preferred to play at the "noncentral" positions now manned disproportionately by blacks in the pros. Brower concluded that "since the young blacks desire to perform at the 'standard' black positions, these findings make plain the impact and consequences of the present football position structure on succeeding generations of professional football players."[47] Although the role model orientation does not explain the initial discrimination, it helps to explain why, once established, the pattern of discrimination by player position tends to be maintained.

Since McPherson produced no empirical support for his explanation, Eitzen and Sanford sought to determine whether black athletes changed positions from central to noncentral more frequently than whites as they moved from high school to college to professional competition.[48] Their data from a sample of 387 professional football players indicated that there had been a statistically significant shift by blacks from central positions to noncentral ones.[49] That blacks in high school and college occupied positions held primarily by whites in professional football casts doubt on McPherson's model. Athletic role models or heroes will most likely have greater attraction for younger individuals in high school and college than for older athletes in professional sports, but professional players were found distributed at all positions during their high school playing days. The socialization model also assumes a high degree of irrationality on the part of the player—it assumes that as he becomes older and enters more keenly competitive playing conditions, he will more likely seek a position because of his identification with a black star rather than because of a rational assessment maximizing his ultimate athletic skills.

It is conceivable, however, that socialization variables do contribute to the racial stacking patterns in baseball and football, but in a negative sense. That is, given discrimination in the allocation of playing positions (or at least the belief in its existence), young black males will consciously avoid those positions for which opportunities are (or are believed to be) low (e.g., pitcher, quarterback) and will select instead those positions where they are most likely to succeed (e.g., the outfield, running and defensive backs). Gene Washington, all-pro wide receiver of the San Francisco 49ers, was a college quarterback at Stanford through his sophomore year, then switched to flanker. Washington requested the change himself. "It was strictly a matter of economics. I knew a black quarterback would have little chance in pro ball unless he was absolutely superb."[50]

Although social scientists have examined the stacking phenomenon in football and baseball, they have neglected basketball. They have tended to assume that it does not occur because, as Edwards has put it:

> In basketball there is no positional centrality as is the case in football and baseball because there are no fixed zones of role responsibility attached to specific position. . . . Nevertheless, one does find evidence of discrimination against black athletes on integrated basketball teams. Rather than stacking black athletes in positions involving relatively less control, *since this is a logistical impossibility,* [italics added] the number of black athletes directly involved in the action at any one time is simply limited.[51]

However, Eitzen and Tessendorf reasoned that positions in basketball do vary in responsibility, in leadership, in the mental qualities of good judgment, decision making, and recognition of opponents' tactics, and in outcome control.[52] To confirm this judgment, they undertook a content analysis of instructional books by prominent American basketball coaches to determine whether there were specific responsibilities or qualities attributed to the three playing positions—guard, forward, and center—in basketball. They discovered surprising unanimity among the authors on the attributes and responsibilities of the different positions. The guard was viewed as the team quarterback, its "floor general," and the most desired attributes for this position were the mental qualities of judgment, leadership, and dependability. The center was pictured as having the greatest amount of outcome control because that position is nearest the basket and because the offense revolves around it; the center was literally the pivot of the team's offense. Unlike the traits for other positions, the desired traits mentioned for forwards stressed physical attributes—speed, quickness, physical strength, and rebounding—even to the point of labeling the forward, the "animal."

Given this widespread agreement that there are varied zones of responsibility and different qualities expected of guards, forwards, and centers, Eitzen and Tessendorf hypothesized that blacks would be overrepresented—stacked—at the forward position, where the essential traits required are physical rather than mental, and under-represented at the guard and center positions, the most crucial positions for leadership and outcome control.[53] Using data from a sample of 274 NCAA basketball teams from the 1970-71 season, they found that blacks were, in fact, substantially overrepresented as forwards and underrepresented at the guard and center positions. Whereas 32 percent of their total sample of players were black, 41 percent of forwards were black; contrasted to 26 percent of guards and 25 percent of centers. This pattern held regardless of whether the players were starters or second-stringers, for college or university division teams.

Although racial stacking has occurred in collegiate basketball, it was not present in professional basketball, which is almost two-thirds black.[54] It would be interesting to see whether such a pattern may have occurred earlier in the history of professional basketball. Berghorn and Yetman,[55] utilizing data from the 1974-75 collegiate season, found that the races were relatively evenly distributed by position at that time, and that the pattern of stacking detected by Eitzen and Tessendorf for 1970-71 had not persisted. Thus, although stacking has remained in football and baseball, the situation in basketball, which, of the three major sports considered in this section, is most heavily black in racial composition, would appear to have undergone substantial change during the first half of the 1970s.

The effects of stacking in noncentral positions are far-reaching for blacks. In seventeen of the twenty-six pro football teams surveyed, approximately three-fourths of all 1971 advertising slots (radio, television, and newspapers) were allotted to players in central positions. Noncentral positions in football depend primarily on speed and quickness, which means in effect that playing careers are shortened for persons in those positions. For example, in 1975, only 4.1 percent of the players listed in the *Football Register* in the three predominantly black positions—defensive back, running back, and wide receiver (65 percent of all black players)—were in the pros for ten or more years, while 14.8 percent of players listed in the three predominantly white positions—quarterback, center, and offensive guard—remained that long. The shortened careers for noncentral players have two additional deleterious consequences—less lifetime earnings and limited benefits from the players' pension fund, which provides support on the basis of longevity.

Rewards and Authority

Discrimination in professional sports is explicit in the discrepancy between the salaries of white and black players. At first glance, such a charge appears to be unwarranted.

Black players rank among the highest paid in professional baseball (seven of ten superstars being paid more than $100,000 in 1970 were black), and the mean salaries of black outfielders, infielders, and pitchers exceed those of whites. Scully[56] reanalyzed data employed by Pascal and Rapping[57] and found substantial salary discrimination against blacks when performance levels were held constant. Blacks earned less than whites for equivalent performance. In addition, Dubois has noted that the central positions in football are those where the salaries are the greatest.[58]

An obvious case of monetary discrimination becomes apparent if one considers the total incomes of athletes (salary, endorsements, and off-season earnings). Pascal and Rapping, for instance, citing the Equal Opportunity Commission report of 1968, related that in the fall of 1966, black athletes appeared in only five percent of the 351 commercials associated with New York sports events.[59] The analysis of the advertising and media program slots featuring starting members of one professional football team in 1971 revealed that eight of eleven whites had such opportunities, while only two of thirteen blacks did. Blacks do not have the same opportunities as whites when their playing careers are finished. This is reflected in radio and television sportscasting, where no black person has had any job other than providing the "color."

Officiating is another area that is disproportionately white. Major League baseball has had only two black umpires in its history. Professional basketball has only recently broken the color line in officiating. Football officiating provides another case of racial stacking as blacks are typically head linesmen.

Although the percentage of black players in each of the three most prominent American professional sports greatly exceeds their percentage of the total population, there is ample evidence that few opportunities are available to them in managerial and entrepreneurial roles. For example, data from 1976 sources (*The Baseball Register, Football Register,* and *National Basketball Association Guide*) show that of the twenty-four major league baseball managers and twenty-six National Football League head coaches, only one was black. Five of the seventeen head coaches (29 percent) in the National Basketball Association (NBA) were black.

Assistant coaches and coaches or managers of minor league professional teams also are conspicuously white. In 1973, there were only two black managers among more than 100 minor league teams. During the same year, in the National Football League, which had a black player composition of 36 percent, there were only twelve blacks, or 6.7 percent, among the 180 assistant coaches. Finally, despite the disproportionate representation of blacks in major league baseball, only three coaches (less than three percent) were black. Moreover, black coaches are relegated to the less responsible coaching jobs. Baseball superstar Frank Robinson, who was appointed the first black major league field general after the conclusion of the regular 1974 season, has pointed out that blacks are excluded from the most important roles. "You hardly see any black third-base or pitching coaches. And those are the most important coaching jobs. The only place you see blacks coaching is at first base, where most anybody can do the job.''[60]

The dearth of black coaches in professional sports is paralleled at the college and high school levels. Although many predominantly white colleges and universities have, in response to pressures from angry black athletes, recently made frantic efforts to hire black coaches, blacks have been hired almost exclusively as assistant coaches, and seldom has a coaching staff included more than one black. As of this writing (1977), not a single major college has a black head football coach, and only a handful of major colleges (e.g., Arizona, Georgetown, Harvard, Illinois State, and Washington State) have head basketball or track coaches who are black.

Blacks, however, are increasingly found on the coaching staffs of college basketball teams. This phenomenon was noted by Leonard and Schmidt (1975), who reported that the number of black head coaches increased from two in 1970 to twenty-one in 1973.[61] However, their data are misleading since they failed to restrict their analysis to major (NCAA Division I) schools. Nevertheless, Berghorn and Yetman did detect an appreciable change between 1970 and 1975, during which time the percentage of black head basketball coaches at major colleges increased from 0.64 percent to 5.1 percent, while the percentage of major colleges with black members on their coaching staffs had increased from 20 percent in 1971 to 45 percent in 1975.[62]

The pattern of exclusion of blacks from coaching situations also has been found in American high schools. Blacks, historically, have held coaching jobs only in predominantly black high schools. And, although the precise figures are unavailable, it would appear that the movement toward integration of schools during the 1960s has had the effect of reducing the number of blacks in coaching positions, as it has reduced black principals and black teachers in general.[63] So anomalous is a black head coach at a predominantly white high school in the South that in 1970, when this barrier was broken, it was heralded by feature stories in the *New York Times* and *Sports Illustrated*.[64] And the situation appears to be little different outside the South, where head coaches are almost exclusively white.

The paucity of black coaches and managers could be the result of two forms of discrimination. Overt discrimination occurs when owners ignore competent blacks because of their prejudices or because they fear the negative reaction of fans to blacks in leadership position. The other form of discrimination is more subtle, however. Blacks are not considered for coaching positions because they did not, during their playing days, play at positions requiring leadership and decision making. For example, Scully has shown that in baseball, 68 percent of all the managers from 1871 to 1968 were former infielders.[65] Because blacks have tended to be ''stacked'' in the outfield, they do not possess the requisite infield experience that traditionally has provided access to the position of manager. The situation is similar in football. A study by

Massengale and Farrington revealed that 65 percent of head coaches at major universities played at the "central" positions of quarterback, offensive center and guard, and linebacker during their playing days. The researchers concluded that "about one-third of the playing positions are producing about two-thirds of the major college head football coaches."[66] Blacks rarely play at these positions, and, thus, they are almost automatically excluded from head coaching responsibilities.

Blacks are also excluded from executive positions in organizations that govern both amateur and professional sports. In 1977, only one major NCAA college had a black athletic director (Southern Illinois). On the professional level, there was no black representation in the principal ownership of a major league franchise. No black held a high executive capacity in any of baseball's twenty-four teams, although there was one black assistant to Baseball Commissioner Bowie Kuhn. Nor have there been any black general managers in pro football. Professional basketball's management structure is most progressive in this regard, although it must be recalled that ownership remains white. Two of seventeen NBA clubs had black general managers in 1973. However, it was a noteworthy event when, in 1970, former NBA star Wayne Embry was named general manager of the Milwaukee Bucks, thereby becoming the first black to occupy such a position in professional sports.

Ability and Opportunity

Another form of discrimination in sport is unequal opportunity for equal ability. This means that entrance requirements to the major leagues are more rigorous for blacks. Black players, therefore, must be better than white players to succeed in the sports world. Rosenblatt was one of the first to demonstrate this mode of discrimination. He found that in the period from 1953 to 1957, the mean batting average for blacks in the major leagues was 20.6 points above the average for whites. In the 1958-1961 period, the difference was 20.1 points, while from 1962 to 1965, it was 21.2 points. He concluded that:

> Discriminatory hiring practices are still in effect in the major leagues. The superior Negro is not subject to discrimination because he is more likely to help win games than fair to poor players. Discrimination is aimed, whether by design or not, against the substar Negro ball player. The findings clearly indicate that the undistinguished Negro player is less likely to play regularly in the major leagues than the equally undistinguished white players.[67]

Since Rosenblatt's analysis was only through 1965, Yetman and Eitzen extended it to include the years 1966-1970 and 1971-1975. The main difference between blacks and whites persisted; for those five-year periods, blacks batted an average of 20.8 and 21 points higher than whites, respectively.[68]

The existence of racial entry barriers in major league baseball was further supported by Pascal and Rapping, who extended Rosenblatt's research by including additional years and by examining the performance of the races in each separate position, including pitchers. They found, for instance, that the nineteen black pitchers in 1967 who appeared in at least ten games won a mean number of 10.2 games, while white pitchers won an average of 7.5. This, coupled with their findings that blacks were superior to whites in all other playing positions, led them to conclude that "on the average a black player must be better than a white player if he is to have an equal chance of transiting from the minor leagues to the major."[69] Moreover, Scully's elaborate analysis of baseball performance data led him to conclude that "not only do blacks have to out perform whites to get into baseball, but they must consistently outperform them over their playing careers in order to stay in baseball."[70] Similarly, Johnson and Marple's analysis of professional basketball revealed that black marginal players are less likely to continue to play after five years than are white marginal players.[71]

Brower found that the situation in professional football paralleled that in baseball and basketball.[72] "Black . . . players must be superior in athletic performance to their white counterparts if they are to be accepted into professional football."[73] His data revealed statistically significant differences in the percentages of black and white starters and nonstarters. Blacks were found disproportionately as starters, while second-string status was more readily accorded to whites. In 1970, 63 percent of black players were starters, contrasted with 51 percent of white players. Conversely, 49 percent of white players but only 37 percent of black players were not starters in that year. These findings led Brower to conclude that "mediocrity is a white luxury."[74]

Yetman and Eitzen have investigated whether black athletes are disproportionately overrepresented in the "star" category and underrepresented in the average, or journeyman, athletic category on collegiate and professional basketball teams.[75] Specifically, they wanted to determine whether blacks have been found disproportionately in the first five ranks (starters) and whether their average position ranking on the team has been higher than that of whites. Operationally defining the top players according to their offensive productivity as measured by their scoring average, they discovered the same situation of unequal opportunity for equal ability that Rosenblatt, Scully, and Pascal and Rapping found in professional baseball.[76] Using data from 1958, 1962, 1966 and 1970 professional and collegiate records, they found that during each year, the higher the scoring rank, the greater the likelihood that it would be occupied by a black player. This was most marked in the distribution of black players who were leading scorers and poorest point producers. While black players comprised no more than 29 percent of all the members of integrated teams during the years 1958-1970, in each of these years nearly half—and in some years, more than half—of the leading scorers were black. Conversely, black were disproportionately underrepresented in the lowest scoring position. Moreover, the data revealed that between 1958 and 1970, no less than two-thirds—and in some years as high as three-fourths—of all black players were starters.

By adding data from the 1975 season, however, to those previously obtained, Berghorn and Yetman found that although blacks continue to be overrepresented in starting positions, there has been a steady and substantial decline in this relationship from 1962, when 76 percent of all black college basketball players were starters, to 1975, when the figure had dropped to 61 percent.[77] In other words, black basketball recruits are no longer restricted to those likely to be starters. Thus, unlike the situations in professional baseball and football, which have demonstrated little change throughout the past two decades, collegiate basketball appears increasingly to provide equal opportunity for equal ability. Moreover, these changes parallel the decline in positional stacking and the increase in black coaches in collegiate basketball previously noted.

In professional basketball, where they have come to dominate the game, blacks were slightly overrepresented in starting roles until 1970, when equal numbers of blacks were starters and nonstarters. Following Rosenblatt's approach in comparing white and black batting averages, Eitzen and Yetman compared the scoring averages of black and white basketball players for five years (1957-58, 1961-62, 1965-66, 1969-70, 1974-75). Although scoring averages were identical for both races in 1957-58, blacks outscored whites in the remaining years by an average of 5.2, 3.3, 2.9, and 1.5 points, respectively.[78]

Summary

That black participation in the three major professional team sports continues to increase has led many observers incorrectly to conclude that sports participation is free of racial discrimination. As our analysis has demonstrated, stacking in football and baseball remains pronounced. Blacks are disproportionately found in those positions requiring physical rather than cognitive or leadership abilities. Moreover, the data indicate that although the patterns have been substantially altered in collegiate and professional basketball, black athletes in the two other major team sports have been and continue to be found disproportionately in starting roles and absent from journeymen positions.

Nearly as dramatic as the proportion of blacks in player roles is the dearth of blacks in administrative, managerial, and officiating positions. Although there have been significant advances for black athletes in the past quarter of a century, there has been no comparable access of blacks to decision-making positions. With the exception of professional basketball, the corporate and decision-making structure of professional sports is virtually as white as it was before Jackie Robinson entered major league baseball in 1947. The distribution of blacks in the sports world is, therefore, not unlike that in the larger society, where blacks are admitted to lower-level occupations but virtually excluded from positions of authority and power.

Despite some indications of change, discrimination against black athletes continues in American team sports; sport is not a meritocratic realm where race is ignored. Equality of opportunity is not the rule where one's race is a variable. These conclusions have implications that extend beyond the sports world. If discrimination occurs in so public an arena, one so generally acknowledged to be discrimination free, and one where a premium is placed on individual achievement rather than on ascription, how much more subtly pervasive must discrimination be in other areas of American life, where personal interaction is crucial and where the actions of power wielders are not subjected to public scrutiny.

Notes

1. The following is taken largely from E.B. Henderson, *The Negro in Sports* (Washington, D.C.: Associated Publishers, 1969); Harry Edwards, *The Revolt of The Black Athlete* (New York: The Free Press, 1969), pp. 1-29; Harry Edwards, *Sociology of Sport* (Homewood, Illinois: Dorsey Press, 1973), pp. 34-42; Ocania Chalk, *Pioneers of Black Sport* (New York: Dodd, Mead, 1975); Michael Govan, "The Emergence of the Black Athlete in America," *The Black Scholar* 3 (November, 1971), pp. 16-28; John P. Davis, "The Negro in Professional Football," *The American Negro Reference Book* (Englewood Cliffs, N.J.: Prentice-Hall, 1966), pp. 627-629; David Q. Voigt, *America Through Baseball* (Chicago: Nelson-Hall, 1976); and Barry D. McPherson, "Minority Group Involvement in Sport: The Black Athlete," in *Exercise and Sport Sciences Review* 2 (1974), especially pp. 72-73. For bibliographies on blacks in sports, see: Bruce Bennett, "Bibliography on the Negro in Sports," *JOHPER* 41 (January, 1970), pp. 77-78, and (September, 1970), p. 71; Grant G. Henry, "A Bibliography Concerning Negroes in Physical Education, Athletics, and Related Fields," *JOHPER* 44 (May, 1973), pp. 65-66.
2. See Art Rust, Jr., *Get That Nigger Off the Field!* (New York: Delacourte Press, 1976); Robert Peterson, *Only the Ball Was White* (Englewood Cliffs, N.J.: Prentice-Hall, 1970).
3. Quoted in Chalk, *Pioneers of Black Sport,* p. 78.
4. S. Kirson Weinberg and Henry Arond, "The Occupational Culture of the Boxer," *American Journal of Sociology* 57 (March, 1952), p. 460.
5. Nathan Hare, "A Study of the Black Fighter," *The Black Scholar* 3 (November, 1971), p. 2.
6. Robert H. Boyle, *Sports—Mirror of American Life* (Boston: Little, Brown, 1963), p. 103.
7. Stan Isaacs, "Football's Shrine Needs Paul Robeson," *Newsday* (July 30, 1971).
8. Forrest J. Berghorn and Norman R. Yetman, "Black Americans in Sport: The Changing Pattern of Collegiate Basketball" (Unpublished paper, University of Kansas, 1976).
9. John Behee, *Hail to the Victors: Black Athletes at the University of Michigan* (Ann Arbor, Mich.: Ulrich's Books, 1974), pp. 131-133.
10. "In Black and White," *Sports Illustrated* 28 (February 15, 1968), p. 10.
11. Frye Gaillard, "Crumbling Segregation in the Southeastern Conference," *The Black Athlete-1970* (Race Relations Information Center, August, 1970), pp. 19-40.
12. See Reginald Stuart, "All-Black Sports World Changing," *Race Relations Reporter* 2 (April 19, 1971), pp. 8-10; and Larry Van

Dyne, "The South's Black Colleges Lose a Football Monopoly," *The Chronicle of Higher Education* (November 15, 1976), pp. 1, 8.

13. See Barry D. McPherson, "The Black Athlete: An Overview and Analysis," in *Social Problems in Athletics,* ed. Daniel M. Landers (Urbana, Ill.: University of Illinois Press, 1976), pp. 142-144.

14. Edwards, *Sociology of Sport,* p. 180.

15. See Marshall Smith, "Giving the Olympics an Anthropological Once-Over," *Life* (October 23, 1964), pp. 81-84; James Jordan, "Physiological and Anthropometrical Comparisons of Negroes and Whites," *JOHPER* 40 (November-December, 1969), pp. 93-99; and Martin Kane, "An Assessment of 'Black is Best,' " *Sports Illustrated* 34 (January 18, 1971), pp. 72-83.

16. Curt Stern, "The Biology of the Negro," *Scientific American* 191 (October, 1954), pp. 81-84.

17. Edwards, *Sociology of Sport,* p. 193.

18. Ibid., pp. 194-195.

19. For a critique of the "racial superiority" interpretation, see Edwards, *Sociology of Sport,* pp. 193-196; and Harry Edwards, "The Myth of the Racially Superior Athlete," *Intellectual Digest* 2 (March, 1972), pp. 58-60.

20. James Green, personal communication to Norman R. Yetman and D. Stanley Eitzen, 1971.

21. Pete Axthelm, *The City Game* (New York: Simon and Schuster Pocketbooks, 1971).

22. John C. Phillips, "Toward an Explanation of Racial Variations in Top-Level Sports Participation," *International Review of Sport Sociology* (November 3, 1976), pp. 39-55.

23. Jack Olsen, *The Black Athlete* (New York: Time-Life Books, 1968), p. 41.

24. Edwards, *Sociology of Sport,* pp. 201-202; see also, Terry Bledsoe, "Black Dominance of Sports: Strictly from Hunger," *The Progressive* 37 (June, 1973), pp. 16-19.

25. C.C. Johnson Spink, "Black Supply Turns from Torrent to Trickle," *The Sporting News* (February 19, 1977), pp. 39, 43.

26. Phillips, "Toward an Explanation of Racial Variations in Top-Level Sports Participation."

27. Dick Mackey, "Blacks Find Golf a Tough Game," *Kansas City Star* (May 28, 1972).

28. The first black to attempt professional skiing was Larry Vinson in 1973; "Larry Vinson, First Black on White," Associated Press release (December 23, 1973).

29. See D. Stanley Eitzen, *Social Structure and Social Problems* (Boston: Allyn and Bacon, 1974), pp. 184-190.

30. See Jim Murray, "Racing's Black Chauffeur," *Rockey Mountain News* (May 22, 1975).

31. The following speculative section is taken largely from Frank Deford, "The Big Game Is Over: This Way to the Exit, Bwana," *Oui* (Spring, 1973), pp. 51, 132, 134.

32. The exceptions are the new parks in Pittsburgh, Cincinnati, New Orleans, St. Louis, and Washington. These are offset by the Texans playing in Arlington, the Twins in Bloomington, the Patriots in Foxboro, the Angels in Orange County, the New York Giants football team leaving the Bronx for suburban New Jersey, the Bullets in Largo, Maryland, the Cavaliers in suburban Cleveland, and the Kansas City Chiefs in the suburbs.

33. Deford, "The Big Game is Over," p. 132.

34. Ibid., p. 134.

35. This section is largely taken from D. Stanley Eitzen and Norman R. Yetman, "Immune from Racism?" *Civil Rights Digest* 9 (Winter, 1977), pp. 2-13. Two other papers by these authors also made important contributions to this section: Norman R. Yetman and D. Stanley Eitzen, "Black Athletes on Intercollegiate Basketball Teams: An Empirical Test of Discrimination," in *Majority and Minority: The Dynamics of Racial and Ethnic Relations,* eds. Norman R. Yetman and C. Hoy Steele (Boston: Allyn and Bacon, 1971), pp. 509-517; and Norman R. Yetman and D. Stanley Eitzen, "Black Americans in Sports: Unequal Opportunity for Equal Ability," *Civil Rights Digest* 5 (August, 1972), pp. 20-34.

36. Aaron Rosenblatt, "Negroes in Baseball: The Failure of Success," *Trans-Action* 4 (September, 1967), pp. 51-53.

37. John W. Loy and Joseph F. McElvogue, "Racial Segregation in American Sport," *International Review of Sport Sociology* 5 (1970), pp. 5-24.

38. H.M. Blalock, Jr., "Occupational Discrimination: Some Theoretical Propositions," *Social Problems* 9 (Winter, 1962), p. 246.
39. Oscar Grusky, "The Effects of Formal Structure on Managerial Recruitment: A Study of Baseball Organization," *Sociometry* 26 (September, 1963), pp. 345-353.
40. Loy and McElvogue, "Racial Segregation in American Sport."
41. This may be a consequence of the league's having a small proportion of black players in the past.
42. Edwards, *Sociology of Sport,* p. 209.
43. Jonathan J. Brower, "The Racial Basis of the Division of Labor Among Players in the National Football League as a Function of Stereotypes" (Paper presented at the annual meetings of the Pacific Sociological Association, Portland, 1972), p. 27.
44. Ibid., pp. 3-27.
45. Barry D. McPherson, "The Segregation by Playing Position Hypothesis in Sport: An Alternative Hypothesis," *Social Science Quarterly* 55 (March, 1975), pp. 960-966. This was presented as a paper in 1971 and served as a catalyst for the studies by Brower and Eitzen and Sanford.
46. Brower, "The Racial Basis of the Division of Labor Among Players."
47. Ibid., p. 28.
48. D. Stanley Eitzen and David C. Sanford, "The Segregation of Blacks by Playing Position in Football: Accident or Design?" *Social Science Quarterly* 55 (March, 1975), pp. 948-959.
49. A similar study was conducted by Donna R. Madison and Daniel M. Landers, "Racial Discrimination in Football: A Test of the 'Stacking' of Playing Positions Hypothesis," in *Social Problems in Athletics,* ed. Daniel M. Landers (Urbana: University of Illinois Press, 1976), pp. 151-156. As in the Eitzen and Sanford study, these researchers found blacks were much more likely than whites to have been shifted from central to noncentral positions as they moved from the college to the professional level.
50. Quoted in Jack Olsen, "The Black Athlete—A Shameful Story," *Sports Illustrated* 29 (July 22, 1968), p. 29.
51. Edwards, *Sociology of Sport,* p. 213.
52. D. Stanley Eitzen and Irl Tessendorf, "Racial Segregation by Position in Sports: The Special Case of Basketball," *Review of Sport and Leisure* (in press).
53. Ibid.
54. Ibid.
55. Berghorn and Yetman, "Black Americans in Sports."
56. Gerald W. Scully, "Discrimination: The Case of Baseball," in *Government and the Sports Business,* ed. Roger G. Noll (Washington, D.C.: The Brookings Institution, 1974), pp. 221-273.
57. Anthony M. Pascal and Leonard A. Rapping, *Racial Discrimination in Organized Baseball* (Santa Monica, Calif.: The Rand Corporation, 1970).
58. Paul E. Dubois, "Sport, Mobility and the Black Athlete," *Sport Sociology Bulletin* 3 (Fall, 1974), pp. 55-56.
59. Pascal and Rapping, *Racial Discrimination in Organized Baseball,* p. 40.
60. Quoted in Pete Axthelm, "Black Out," *Newsweek* (July 15, 1974), p. 57.
61. Wilbert M. Leonard II and Susan Schmidt, "Observations on the Changing Social Organization of Collegiate and Professional Basketball," *Sport Sociology Bulletin* 4 (Fall, 1975), pp. 13-35.
62. Berghorn and Yetman, "Black Americans in Sports."
63. In Alabama, for example, the number of black principals decreased from 646 in 1966 to 284 in 1971. In 1954, Kentucky had 350 black principals, but by 1970, only 36 were left, a drop of 90 percent. See Melvin I. Evans, "The Vanishing Americans," *JOHPER* 44 (October, 1973), pp. 55-57; and V. Evans and C.D. Henry, "The Black High School Coach—Will He Become Extinct?" *The Physical Educator* 30 (1973), pp. 152-153.
64. See Pat Jordan, "The Man Who Was Cut Out for the Job," *Sports Illustrated* 35 (October 11, 1971), pp. 90-102.
65. Scully, "Discrimination: The Case of Baseball," p. 246.
66. John D. Massengale and Steven R. Farrington, "The Influence of Playing Posi-

tion Centrality on the Careers of College Football Coaches,'' *Review of Sport and Leisure* 2 (June, 1977), pp. 107-115.

67. Rosenblatt, ''Negroes in Baseball,'' p. 53.
68. Eitzen and Yetman, ''Immune from Racism?''; and Yetman and Eitzen, ''Black Americans in Sports.''
69. Pascal and Rapping, *Racial Discrimination in Organized Baseball,* p. 36.
70. Scully, ''Discrimination: The Case of Baseball,'' p. 263.
71. Norris R. Johnson and David P. Marple, ''Racial Discrimination in Professional Basketball,'' *Sociological Focus* 6 (Fall, 1973), pp. 6-18.
72. Jonathan J. Brower, ''The Quota System: The White Gatekeeper's Regulation of Professional Football's Black Community'' (Paper presented at the annual meetings of the American Sociological Association, New York, August, 1973).
73. Ibid.
74. Ibid., p. 3.
75. Yetman and Eitzen, ''Black Athletes on Intercollegiate Basketball Teams''; Yetman and Eitzen, ''Black Americans in Sports.''
76. Yetman and Eitzen, ''Black Americans in Sports.''
77. Berghorn and Yetman, ''Black Americans in Sports: The Changing Pattern of Collegiate Basketball.''
78. Eitzen and Yetman, ''Immune from Racism?''

Females in American Sport: Continuity and Change

17

"Sports may be good for people, but they are considered a lot gooder for male people than for female people."[1]

You may be asking, "Why a separate chapter on females and sport?" The answer is that until very recently sport was male turf; females who participated were considered intruders. Indeed, most of the content in all of the previous chapters has been about males, as you may have observed. Because the role of women in American sport has been so radically different from that of men, and because this role is changing so rapidly, we believe that a separate chapter on women is warranted.

The most persistent and widespread prejudice and discrimination in American sport has been imposed on females. Not only have women's opportunities and rewards been unequal, but their facilities and sport organizations have been segregated from and inferior to men's. Gilbert and Williamson have succinctly characterized this state of affairs:

> There may be worse (more socially serious) forms of prejudice in the United States, but there is no sharper example of discrimination today than that which operates against girls and women who take part in competitive sports, wish to take part, or might wish to if society did not scorn such endeavors.[2]

American society prides itself on its concern for the fullest development of each person's human potential, but as a nation we have been quite insensitive to the social handicaps imposed by sex—in sport, as well as in other aspects of life.

The world of sport has pretty much been the exclusive domain of males until quite recently. In Jack Scott's words, there has been "a stag party atmosphere . . . [in] American athletics."[3] Men typically have engaged more often in sports and have manifested greater interest and achievement. Sports heroes and "superstars" are mostly male, and male dominance has also been notable in administrative and leadership branches of sports, where men have clearly overshadowed women in power and numbers.

The combined role of woman and successful athlete was virtually impossible in the United States until the past few years. Women who wished to participate in competitive sports and remain "feminine" faced almost certain social isolation and censure. By choosing the physically active life, the female was repudiating the traditional female sex-role expectations. Female athletes did not fit the American ideology of femininity, and those who persisted in sport suffered for it.

In the past decade, women have turned to the unfinished business of their equality and America has witnessed a new revolution—women's liberation. As one dimension of this movement, women have begun to respond to inequalities in organized sports by demanding their rightful place as equals. They are no longer content to be the cheerleaders and pom pon girls, urging on their male counterparts to glory, prestige, and power. Targets for change vary from the kinds of legal and extralegal restrictions that prevent females from having equal access to sport opportunities to attempts to elevate the social and political consciousness of women as a group. Coming under special attack are stereotypes of the ways males and females are supposed to behave, including the anachronistic idea that participation in intensive competitive sports masculinizes females.

Females have taken up tennis rackets, golf clubs, and donned swimsuits, gymnastic slippers, and ice skates, and demonstrated that they are willing and capable of outstanding physical performance. Not only have they become highly skilled in sports requiring rhythm, balance, grace, and aesthetic form, but they have shown that they can become quite good at throwing the javelin and discus as well as high jumping and even tackling and blocking in football—all while remaining feminine. Indeed, the concept of femininity has undergone a much needed redefinition under the auspices of female athletes who are no longer embarrassed about being labeled "jocks."

Sports opportunities for girls and women have increased tremendously in recent years—mainly because of court decisions and federal laws—and sport for females is a fast-growing, fast-changing element in American society. Although there is a great deal of ambiguity about what constitutes equality and discrimination of sports opportunity, conditions are unquestionably improving for females. But prejudices are not altered by courts and legislation, and culturally conditioned responses to sex-role ideology are ubiquitous and resistent to sudden changes. Therefore, while laws may force compliance with equality of opportunity for females in the world of sport, sexism in sport will probably continue, albeit in more subtle and insidious forms, as has been the case with racism in sport.

The subject of the role of women in American sport is sociologically significant from the standpoint of the social structure and processes that have excluded females from this form of social behavior. It is also significant from the standpoint of the social change that has occurred in the past few years and is likely to continue in the future. The following sections of this chapter will examine the social bases for the prejudice and discrimination that has traditionally confronted the would-be female athlete, the consequences of the processes, and the current developments in this subject. Unfortunately, while race relations have generated substantial sociological interest among sport sociologists, the issue of female sport involvement has generated little research interest, perhaps reflecting social attitudes toward females and their place in sports.

Social Sources of Sexism in Sport

Sexism is an unfavorable attitude toward and the unequal treatment of persons of one sex, based on an elaborate series of negative traits assumed to be distributed among this sex. The sexism imposed on females in the world of sport will be the subject of this chapter. The ultimate basis of sexism in American sport is embedded in the socio-cultural milieu of this society, and the cultural traditions of Western civilization are foundational to American society.

Western Culture

Whether sports participation is considered feminine depends mostly on cultural definitions of appropriate feminine behavior. During the past 2,500 years, Western culture has taught that females are by nature different from men—inferior and dependent. Broom and Selznick have noted that in Western society the difference in masculine and feminine roles is associated with sharp and contrasting differences in temperament. The female is seen as naturally nonaggressive and passive, while the male is seen as naturally aggressive and active. This contrasting of temperaments of males and females has been associated with the dominance of one and the submission of the other. Thus, the more dominant a man, the more masculine he is considered to be; the more passive and submissive a woman, the more feminine.[4]

Women have been defined as biologically and physically limited—to be given, at best, a place of protection or benign neglect. Throughout the centuries, this notion has been passed on uncritically and has permeated every sphere of life so thoroughly that it has become one of the "laws of nature." Intellectuals and common persons have accepted this idea and have based on it various behavioral expectations to the disadvantage of women. One of these is the cultural norm that either denies women the opportunity to achieve their own physical optimum or stigmatizes such development as unfeminine. Thus, stereotypes, prejudices, and misconceptions have limited females sports participation in vigorous, competitive physical activities for centuries. Another factor that accounts for the traditionally insignificant position of women in sport is the fact that in most Western societies, the woman's culturally prescribed tasks have been child rearing and "homemaking;" these tasks left little time for participation in sports.

Much of Western cultural traditions originated with the ancient Greeks. These people were polytheists,[5] and they assigned to male gods all the traits appropriate to their own image of masculinity, while the traits of femininity were assigned to female gods, or goddesses. Male gods were seen as leaders, powerful, rational, athletic, and intellectual. In contrast, goddesses were almost completely lacking in any physical strength or quality of athletic ability; they were helpmates, beautiful, and sexually desirable creatures. Goddesses who were physically active, such as Artemis and Athena, were not desired by men, nor did they desire male companionship. Greek men considered any woman who was physically or intellectually superior to them unfeminine, and called her an "Amazon," which literally means "without breasts," since the mythological female warriors reputedly cut off one breast to facilitate archery. These are the elements out of which Western culture developed prototypes of masculinity and femininity, and notions about appropriate physical activity for males and females.

Western societies also inherited from the Greeks the philosophy that woman is the weaker, passive, inferior sex. Greek women were little more than servants in a marriage. They performed the daily domestic tasks and otherwise remained apart from the males of the family, spending their idle hours spinning, weaving, and sewing. Plutarch agreed with Thucydides: "The name of a decent woman, like her person, should be shut up in the house."[6] They had little legal status, since they could not make contracts nor incur debts beyond a trifling sum; they could not bring actions at law—indeed, anything done under the influence of women had no validity of law. Women were literally excluded from sports in ancient Greece. They were strictly barred from even viewing the Olympic Games, and punishments were prescribed for any woman caught at the Games.[7]

Rome was, of course, a most influential contributor to Western culture. The most basic Roman institution was the patriarchal family; the power of the husband was nearly absolute. Of the family, he alone had any rights before the law in the early Republic; he alone could negotiate property or make contracts. If his wife was accused of a crime, she was committed to him for judgment and punishment; he could condemn her to death for infidelity or for stealing the keys to his wine. At every age of life, the female was under the tutelage of a man—her father, her brother, her husband, her son, or a guardian.[8] Physically active amusements and sports were strictly for male participants, and women were only allowed to be spectators and admirers of the chariot racers, gladiators, and athletes.

The status of women was not much improved in the early Christian church. Women were admitted to congregations, but the church required them to live lives of modest submission and retirement. St. Paul instructed that: "Let the woman learn in silence with all subjection. But I suffer not a woman to teach, nor to usurp authority over the man, but to be in silence."[9] As a reaction to the paganism and brutality of Roman sports, the early Christians did not encourage sport either for males or females.

During the Middle Ages, as the strength of the Church grew and spread throughout Europe, the theories of churchmen were generally hostile to women, and many laws of the Church enhanced her subjection. To priests and theologians, she was the favorite instrument of Satan in leading men to hell, and, according to St. Thomas Aquinas, she was in some ways below a slave:

> The woman is subject to the man on account of the weakness of her nature, both of mind and body . . . Woman is subjection according to the law of nature, but a slave is not. . . . Children ought to love their father more than their mother.[10]

Andreas Capellanus' book *The Art of Courtly Love* ushered in a new image of women and men.[11] In this manual for upper-class romantics, he glorified women as objects of romance and assigned males the duty to love protect, and watch over the lovely, frail creatures. This chivalric ideal emphasized the passivity and dependence of women and glorified them as sex objects. Women found themselves placed on pedestals and literally worshipped as models of spiritual and physical beauty. The knightly sports provided a symbolic expression of this female-male ideal, as the knights fought jousts and tournaments under the admiring eyes of women. Women were almost completely excluded from sports activity of any kind.

Women's place—or lack of it—received little enlightened support from the "enlightened" writers. From Shakespeare, we learn that "frailty thy name is woman." The social customs—manners, dress, language—all conspired to restrict female physical activity. Even into the nineteenth century, females were deliberately socialized away from sports. Herbert Spencer, after having observed the activities of a school for girls for several months, noted: "It appears . . . that at [the school for young ladies] noisy play like that daily indulged in by boys, is a punishable offense; and it is to be inferred that this noisy play is forbidden, lest unladylike habits should be formed."[12]

The traditions of Western civilization have been perpetuated in America, with respect to the status of women. When the framers of the Declaration of Independence wrote that "all men are created equal" (excluding black men, of course) that is literally what they meant, and it was not until 144 years later that women were even considered worthy of the right to vote. A woman's place was in the home, and those who did enter the world of work found that female occupations were limited to those involving nurturing, helping, and empathizing, such as nursing, teaching, and social work; occupations requiring characteristics such as detachment, independence, assertiveness, such as law, medicine, science, were not considered appropriate for women. In describing the ideal woman of 1900, Margaret Coffey says: "Her role was childbearer, childrearer, housekeeper, and cook. A woman's body was meant not only to be useful, but to be beautiful."[13]

Western cultural ideology has defined females as inferior and dependent on men, whose primary role prescriptions were childbearer, childrearer, homemaker, and sex object. These cultural definitions of female expectations served to legitimize the exclusion of females from organized competitive sports. Thus, the sexism rampant in American sports is merely a reflection of the sexism fundamental to Western culture. The overemphasis of protecting females from achievement and success experiences and the underemphasis on developing physical skills fits nicely into the socialization pattern of preparing women for the adult role of being passive helpmates of men, standing on the sidelines of history cheering men on to their achievements and successes.

Parental Child-Rearing Practices

Sexual identity is the core of personal identity; it is a fundamental aspect of total personality development and adjustment. A male or female identity is a product of both direct and indirect teaching. In the former, children are taught to call and perceive themselves as male or female. In the latter, they are responded to or taught to behave in sex-specific ways, and thus, come to respond to themselves as others respond to them.

The teaching of sex-role ideology comes from a range of cultural sources—peers, teachers, ministers, mass media, etc.—but the earliest and most persistent instruction comes from parents. Parents make a major contribution to the shaping of sex-role ideology by acting differently toward boys and girls as early as their first exposure to them and throughout the remaining years of child rearing. Summarizing his observations of parental behavior, Lewis notes that from infancy, there are both marked and subtle differences in the way parents speak to sons and daughters, the way they are dressed, the toys they are given, the activities they are encouraged and permitted to engage in. A certain level of aggression is not only permitted to boys, it is enjoined. Much less is approved in the case of girls. Techniques of control tend to differ also, with praise and withdrawal of love used more often with girls; physical punishment used relatively more often with boys.[14]

Children rapidly learn differences in parental expectations concerning sex-appropriate behavior, and they differ in the degree to which they perform and value these behaviors. The typical parental message is that desirable qualities for males are aggressiveness, independence, and achievement-orientation, while desirable qualities for females are passivity, affiliation, nurturance, and dependence. Sports and vigorous physical pursuits are positively identified with the male sex role and negatively associated with the female sex role in our society.[15]

Gender identity becomes established in rudimentary form well before three years of age and becomes elaborated into well-defined perceptions of appropriate behavior for males and females, including preference in toys and games.[16]

The School

The school serves to reinforce and extend the sex-role stereotyping that begins in the home. Schools tend to be dominated by women—especially elementary schools where women constitute about 85 percent of the teaching force. The presence of female teachers molds the traditional sex role differences both directly and indirectly.[17] Serbin and O'Leary found that teachers foster an environment in which children learn that boys are aggressive and physically capable, while girls are submissive and passive. They do this by reacting much more frequently to a boy's behavior, bad or good, than to a girl's.[18]

An indirect means by which the school reinforces traditional sex roles is through its own authority structure. While 85 percent of all elementary school teachers are women, 79 percent of the elementary school principals are men, and about 95 percent of secondary school principals are men even though some 50 percent of the teachers at this educational level are women. Thus, schoolchildren learn the differential status of men and women simply by attending school.[19]

Another mechanism of sex-role reinforcement is segregated classes and activities. Many elementary schools have experimented with all-boy classes, which emphasize the traditionally active masculine activities. Classes that teach cooking, sewing, and other homemaking skills are encouraged primarily for girls, while classes in woodworking or "shop" are encouraged primarily for boys. In high school, certain subjects, such as math and science, are viewed as male subjects, while English and fine arts are regarded as female subjects. And, of course, physical education has traditionally been sex-segregated after elementary school.[20]

One of the basic sources for learning in schools—the textbooks—perpetuate sex-role ideologies. The kind of history they purvey, the kinds of suggestions they present for adult occupational choices, the leisure time pursuits, all suggest a negative image of women—as unimportant and unable.[21] In a study of the treatment of sex roles in the "very best" children's books, Weitzman and colleagues found that women are excluded from the world of sports, politics, and science. Their future is presented as consisting primarily of glamour and service.[22] Another study found that children's readers presented boys as active and competent and girls as passive, docile, and dependent. Boys, in fact, were the subjects of stories five times more often than girls.[23] Finally, Duquin analyzed elementary textbooks for the "amplitude appropriation" found in them (the size of that portion of the environment a child envisions as appropriate for his or her activity and the degree of movement he or she perceives as possible in that environment), and reported that children are 13 times more likely to see a vigorously active man than a vigorously active woman. The ratio of vigorously active boys to girls was 3.5 to 1.[24]

Interschool sports programs are eloquent testimony to the importance of boys and men and the neglect of girls and women. Traditionally, the boys' athletic program has received more money, a larger coaching staff, greater use of the facilities, and more time than the girls' program. Of all the aspects of the American school system in which females are shortchanged, none is more glaring or more damaging than the area of interschool sports.

The Mass Media

Social contexts and descriptions of women in the mass media—newspapers, magazine, radio, and television—generally reinforce the sex-role stereotypes with messages portraying women as sex objects, housekeepers, mothers, and menial workers. Women are shown waxing floors, feeding children, spraying their hair, or otherwise using toiletries designed to trap a man. According to Komisar, advertisers:

> . . . legitimize the idealized, stereotyped roles of woman as temptress, wife, mother, and sex object, and portray women as less than intelligent and more dependent than

> men. It makes women believe that their chief role is to please men and their fulfillment will be as wives, mothers, and homemakers. It makes women feel unfeminine if they are not pretty and guilty if they do not spend most of their time in desperate attempts to imitate gourmet cooks. . . . It makes women believe that their own lives, talents, and interests ought to be secondary to the needs of their husbands and families.[25]

Hennessee and Nicholson report that in a study of 1,241 commercials, 42.6 percent showed women involved in household tasks; 37.5 percent showed them as domestic helpers to men, and 16.7 percent depicted them as sex objects. Almost all of them showed women inside the home.[26] Dominick and Rauch reported similar results in a study of 986 prime-time television commercials, in that 75 percent used females for kitchen and bathroom products.[27]

Motion pictures have also been a powerful influence in keeping women in their place. An independent woman has usually been depicted on a screen as an unattractive crusader, while the career girl is a frigid, fussbudget. Movie producers have tended to project two identities for women: as a sex object or as a wife-mother figure; never as a physically active athlete. There have been numerous movies about male athletes, none about female athletes. But, of course, there have been very few famous female athletes about whom to make a movie.[28] American enculturization had effectively driven them out of sport.

In newspapers and magazines, stories about female athletes have been traditionally sparse and, when they did appear, were centered largely on a discussion of figures and fashions of the women. Two separate studies of popular magazine advertisements showing women revealed that the women were rarely shown in sport settings.[29] While male professional athletes have been principal figures for the promotion of a bewildering array of products in all of the media, only in the past few years have female athletes been employed to peddle goods and services.

Sportswriters have done little to enhance an attitude of respect for the female athlete because their emphasis has been typically on women athletes as attractive objects rather than as skillful performers. In a content analysis of the presentation of the female athlete by *Sports Illustrated,* Corrigan found that every article analyzed contained one or more descriptions of physical appearance, with most of the comments directed to the women's hair color, eye color, height, and weight.[30] For example, one *Sports Illustrated* article about a woman's golf tournament, had this to say about one of the participants:

> A cool, braided California blond named Laura Baugh made quite a splash . . . her perfectly tanned, well-formed legs swinging jauntily. The hair on her tapered arms was bleached absolutely white against a milk-chocolate tan. Her platinum hair was pulled smartly back in a Viking-maiden braid.[31]

After watching a woman's Olympic track team work out a few years ago, a noted sportswriter said: "Girls are for laughs, no? Not for sports."[32]

Recently created magazines, such as *Sportswoman* and *WomenSports,* have attempted to redress the distorted and inadequate coverage by the traditional sports magazines of female athletes and their sports achievements. These new magazines present a more complete and a fairer portrayal of women in sport.

Role Models

An individual or group of individuals whose behavior in a particular role provides a standard or model for other persons for determining appropriate attitudes and actions is said to be a role model. There are few feminine counterparts to Frank Merriwell, Jack Armstrong, Joe Palooka, or the real-to-life Johnny Bench, Hank Aaron, Rick Barry, and Jack Nicklaus. While boys are bombarded with daily accounts about high school, college, and professional athletes, the feats of outstanding female athletes have seldom been reported, or if they have been, the story was brief and was filled with references to physical appearance rather than performance feats.

In an informal survey taken in 1973 for their *Sports Illustrated* series on women in sports, Gilbert and Williamson reported that "nearly all of some 100 high school girls scattered across the country could name 10 male athletes in college or professional sports whom they admired—or at least whose names they knew. But not a single girl to whom the question was put could name 10 prominent women athletes."[33] This should not be surprising because the entire socialization milieu is organized to provide a model of the typical girl as a frilly thing with a smile on her face, having a passive attitude toward life, and admiring the achievements of boys, while the typical adult woman is a wife, mother, and, perhaps, a sexy bed partner. Until very recently female athletes were omitted almost entirely from newspapers, magazines, and television—the media which are the most effective in creating and displaying role models. As recently as 1973, CBS televised some 260 hours of men's sports and 10 hours of women's sports in a year.[34]

Consequences of Sexism for Females in Sport

Sexism directed against females, like prejudice and discrimination of any kind, is insidious and denigrating. It takes many forms. There is first the perpetuation of a folklore of myths about the biological and psychological characteristics of females, and, thus, stereotyping of what is appropriate and inappropriate behavior. Unequal opportunity for participation in many activities is another form. Finally, there is unequal access to the authority and power structure. Each of these forms of prejudice and discrimination has been used to socialize females out of sports participation and deny them equal access to the rewards sport has to offer.

Negative Stereotypes

A number of myths prevalent in American society support sport as an exclusively masculine activity.

Myth 1: Athletic Participation Masculinizes Females

One of the oldest and most persistent folklores salient throughout sport, and a main deterrent to female sports participation, is the notion that vigorous physical activity tends to masculinize the physique and behavior of girls and women.[35] For centuries, women of physical competence have been stigmatized as masculine by persons who believed that women who have excellent physical ability were unfeminine. As Robert Lipsyte said: "Sports is a male sanctuary, therefore any woman who tries to invade it is not really a woman."[36] Thus, consciously or unconsciously, the female has equated athletic achievement with loss of femininity.

The impression that physical activity *produces* "masculine" body types is undoubtedly a result of the fact that some female athletes are indeed muscular and exhibit movement characteristics more commonly seen in men. But their muscularity and movement patterns probably led them to enter sports, instead of it being a consequence of their participation. In other words, if a larger proportion of "masculine" females are in sport, it may be a function of the physical, behavioral, and psychological characteristics that make one more proficient in motor activity.

There is also another dimension of this issue. Until very recently, the top-level athletes in most sports were males. To become highly proficient in these sports, males learned to employ the most effective and efficient movement patterns to execute the skills. As females began to engage in these same sports, behavioral patterns necessary for high-skill proficiency often corresponded to that employed by skilled male performers. Thus, the female who was seen using movement patterns that were traditionally associated with male performers was labeled "masculine." For example, the skillful execution of the overhand throw requires the use of a cross-lateral pattern (in throwing with the right hand, the upper body is rotated to the right and as the ball is thrown the performer steps forward with the left foot and quickly rotates the upper body to the left). Since few females learned to be effective overhand throwers, they typically stepped forward with the right foot and used no upper-body rotation, and this pattern was recognized by everyone as "the way a girl throws." When females began training to become skilled overhand throwers for sports such as softball, they were accused of "throwing like a boy," and movement patterns of this nature labeled them as masculine. In fact, the movement pattern has nothing to do with masculinity or feminity, but is concerned with the most efficient use of the body to accomplish a task.

The threat of masculization was sufficiently terrifying to scare many females from attempting to become physically active. As a result, the process of sex-role socialization has reinforced existing patterns of sex discrimination in sport insofar as sport has been seen as an undesirable, unfeminine pursuit by females. Thus, many females simply avoided sports completely. Others tried to compromise, accommodating their athletic aspirations to the cultural attitudes. Many female athletes have attempted to maintain a "ladylike" appearance. Harris has articulately described this phenomenon:

> . . . the blond, bouffant, sprayed hairdos of female track teams, the ruffles on the tennis outfits, the mod apparel worn by many women golfers; the ski togs that flatter the feminine figure, the fancy swim caps and suits, etc. All of these artifacts of femininity assist in reducing the threat of sports participation to the revered feminine image.[37]

Little evidence exists to support the notion that vigorous physical activity alters the biological constitution of a female and makes her more masculine. Indeed, several exercise physiologists have noted that excessive muscular development is not a concomitant of female sports participation. Klafs and Arnheim have said: "Contrary to lay opinion, participation in sports does not masculinize women. Within a sex, the secretion of testosterone, androgen, and estrogen varies considerably, accounting for marked variation in terms of muscularity and general morphology among males and females."[38]

The above statements should not suggest that there are no physical or psychological differences between female athletes and nonathletes. Prolonged physical training in a sport alters female physique, physiological support systems, and psychosocial characteristics, just as it does with males. Indeed, athletes, as a group, seem to have somewhat unique physical and psychological characteristics, but, as was noted earlier, these characteristics may have existed before the individuals became involved in sports—perhaps these characteristics attracted them to sports in the first place. However, when changes in the physique of females do result from sport involvement, they tend to be less marked than changes in males.[39]

The definition of feminine and masculine behavior is culturally determined, but contemporary women are no longer willing to have traditional definitions imposed on them, particularly when these definitions prevent females from experiencing highly valued social activities. In this view, the notion that women become masculinized from sports participation is a hoax used to enforce cultural traditions, and women are increasingly rejecting it.

Myth 2: Sports Participation is Harmful to the Health of Females

Another well-entrenched folklore concerning women's participation in sports is that sports are harmful to their health. This claim is principally concerned with physical injury to the reproductive organs and the breasts, effects on the menstrual cycle and pregnancy, and on the psychological well-being of females.

The literature of the past 100 years is laden with opinions of how competitive sports are harmful to females. At one time, physicians and other professionals made a convincing case that females' pregnancy and reproductive capabilities would be hampered by stressful physical activity. In the 1920s, Ernest Herman Arnold, a well-respected physical educator, reported that athletic sports caused a diminution in the number, extent, and flow of menstruation, and according to him, any reduction in menses results in a reduction in fertility.[40] Another famous physical educator of that same period claimed: "Natural feminine health and attractiveness . . . are impaired if not destroyed by the belligerent attitudes and competitive spirit and development of which intense athletics inevitably fosters."[41]

Women themselves have cooperated to reinforce the notion that women's health is harmed by competitive sports. The height of women's objection to stressful competition for females came in the 1920s and '30s, but its effects were felt into the early 1970s. Ethel Perrin, chairperson of the Executive Committee of the Women's Division of the National Amateur Athletic Federation, voiced her opposition to Olympic participation of women in this way:

> Girls are not suited for the same athletic programs as boys. The difference between them cannot be ignored. . . . Under prolonged and intense physical strain a girl goes to pieces nervously. . . . The fact that a girl's nervous resistence cannot hold out under intensive physical strain is nature's warning. A little more strain and she will be in danger both physically and nervously.[42]

In 1933, Agnes Wayman, President of the American Physical Education Association, echoed Ms. Perrin:

> External stimuli such as cheering audiences, bands, lights, etc., cause a great response in girls and are apt to upset the endocrine balance. Under emotional stress a girl may easily overdo. There is widespread agreement that girls should not be exposed to extremes of fatigue or strain either emotional or physical.[43]

Surveys undertaken in 1923 and 1930 by Mabel Lee, a leading woman physical educator and first woman president of the American Alliance for Health, Physical Education, and Recreation (AAHPER), showed the extent to which women physical educators were opposed to athletics because of the suspected health dangers. In 1924, Lee reported that 60 percent of those women surveyed felt that intercollegiate athletics for women were harmful physically to the participants. In the 1931 report, two of the disadvantages of intercollegiate sports listed were: (1) the emotional strain of such competition would be injurious, and (2) participation during the menstrual period would be encouraged, and, therefore, harmful.[44] Not until the early 1960s did the Division of Girls' and Women's Sports (DWGS) of the AAHPER begin active promotion of interschool sports programs.

While physicians and educators were able to convince the public of the health dangers of sports for females, no substantial evidence supported the claims, and research, when it has been done, suggests that the health hazards are imaginary. The internal reproductive organs have a most effective shock-resistent system. The external genitalia of females is less exposed than those of men, and can be easily protected with safety equipment. Strenuous competitive activities do not delay the onset or regularity of menstruation, and, indeed, females may participate in sports during menstruation. In fact, menstruating athletes have set national and world records.[45] Allan Ryan concluded his exhaustive review of the gynecological effects of sports in this way: "There is no evidence that sports of themselves invoke any significant changes in the menstrual cycle . . . for the majority of women.[46]

Obstetrical data indicate physical activity may actually prove beneficial to both mother and infant. The combined data of Erdelyi and Zaharieva on over 740 female athletes show that the athletes actually had shorter labor periods than the average, and 50 percent fewer Caesarean sections occurred in the athletic sample than in "normal" populations.[47] One of the world's most esteemed exercise physiologists, Per-Olof Astrand, reported that the obstetric and gynecological history of a group of 84 former champion swimmers was normal[48]

The idea that emotional excitement engendered by competitive sport is psychologically damaging is no more convincing for females than it is for males. As a matter of fact, little empirical support exists for this opinion, and experienced female athletes are able to control their emotional state about as well as males.

Dr. Clayton Thomas, formerly a member of the U.S. Olympic Medical and Training Services Committee, summarizes the research on the health aspects of sport for females in this way:

> I do not believe there is evidence available to support the view that it is possible for healthy women of any age to indulge in a sport which is too strenuous for them. Although the literature contains many opinions stating that competitive events are harmful for women, there are no supporting data.[49]

The Committee on the Medical Aspects of Sports reiterated the beneficial aspects of sports and exercise for girls and women. According to this group, "physiological and social benefits are to be gained by girls and women through physical activity and sports competition. In many cases, vigorous physical activity improves the distinctive biological functions of the female."[50]

Myth 3: Women Are Not Interested in Sports and They Do Not Play Well Enough to Be Taken Seriously

Contempt for the female athlete has been shown by the contention that women are not really interested in nor very good at sports. Those who make this claim point out the paucity of women in sports, and that their best performances are inferior to those of men.

Such arguments are common; but they are faulty because they ignore the systematic socialization of females. Beginning in infancy when they are dressed differently from boy babies to emphasize their "prettiness," the socialization continues in childhood when they get dolls, dishes, stoves, and pretty dresses as presents, and is firmly established in adolescence when they realize that attracting men, and eventually a husband, is their life's business. It also ignores the fact that strength and structural limitations mitigate against females matching the achievements of males in many sports.

Actually, the physical performance of girls from infancy up to the time of menarche is equal to that of boys; however, there are not significant sex-related differences in total size or muscle mass during these years.[51] Moreover, the physically active preadolescent girl may achieve some encouragement and recognition through motor-skill achievement, but later, in adolescence, when teenagers are cruel in their demands for stereotyped conformity, the active girl traditionally undergoes a deep crisis that ordinarily results in a withdrawal from sports. Girls drop the pursuit of sport, not because of physical inability or innate lack of predisposition for sports, but because of societal pressures that produce the internalization of the norm—physical inactivity and passivity.

With respect to females' inability to perform up to male standards, one must acknowledge that this is true of many sports, when records are considered. Eleanor Metheny argued persuasively that while women's performances as a group may be less spectacular than those of men, some top-level female athletes individually excel average male athletes in certain sports—we have only to recall the Billie Jean King-Bobby Riggs tennis match to have this fact confirmed—and women seem to be competent as men to fulfill even the most strenuous sport roles.[52] For example, the 400-meter free-style world swimming record set by Don Schollander in the 1964 Olympics was surpassed by almost 3 full seconds by a 15-year-old East German girl at the 1976 Montreal Olympics.

Men have been unimpressed by women athletes, particularly because they have evaluated women's performances in relation to men's, which is, of course, a nonsensical comparison—just as comparing elephants and men on feats of strength is meaningless. Perhaps Simone de Beauvoir, one of the most esteemed writers in the world, best described the absurdity of comparing male and female sports performances:

> In sports the end in view is not success independent of physical equipment; it is rather the attainment of perfection within the limitations of each physical type; the featherweight boxing champion is as much a champion as is the heavyweight; the

> woman skiing champion is not the inferior of the faster male champion; they belong to two different classes.[53]

Attitudes Toward Female Athletes

Societies that accept myths develop attitudes toward the objects or persons that have been the subject of the myths. Attitudes involve what people think about, feel about, and how they would like to behave toward other people or objects. Those attitudes are learned rather than innate, and are enduring but changeable. Attitudes are the end products of the socialization process, significantly influencing human responses to other persons and to groups of persons.

Sex-role stereotyping is clearly responsible for attitudes about appropriate male and female behavior, and, once established, these attitudes are resistant to change. Given the social conditioning about female role expectations described in earlier sections of this chapter, we may expect that an underlying negative attitude toward female participation in sports would exist, and so there has been. Perhaps the statement of a male athlete most succinctly captures this attitude: "If a woman is really grunting and groaning and sweating, how can she be feminine?"[54] Woody Hayes, one of the most exalted intercollegiate football coaches, noted:

> I hear they're even letting w-o-m-e-n in their sports program now [referring to Oberlin College]. That's your Women's Liberation, boy—bunch of goddamn lesbians. . . . You can bet your ass that if you have women around—and I've talked to psychiatrists about this— you aren't gonna be worth a damn. No sir! Man has to dominate . . . the best way to treat a woman, . . . is to knock her up and hide her shoes.[55]

That sex role stereotyping is difficult to change can be seen from this comment of one high school athletic director:

> We tried to organize a girls' sports program but it hasn't worked out very well. . . . Unfortunately, the girls didn't show a lot of interest. Only 12 came out for the team. There were two big tomboyish girls who remained quite enthused, but the others have not been faithful about practice. I'm not blaming them because I think a normal girl at that age is going to be more interested in catching a boy than catching a basketball.[56]

Fundamental attitudes toward appropriate female behaviors have implications for sport involvement for females. Patricia Griffith assessed college students' perceptions of women's roles in terms of three factors: evaluative, potency, and activity. The women's roles studied were: housewife, woman athlete, girl friend, woman professor, mother, and ideal woman. She found that women's roles perceived as highly associated with activity and potency were not highly evaluated roles, and, therefore, were less socially desirable. On the other hand, roles perceived as more desirable for women were seen as extremely low in potency and activity. Since "woman athlete" and ''woman professor'' were perceived to have active and potent roles, which is inconsistent with the accepted behavioral norms for women, their's were nonpreferred roles.[57]

Even professional persons have beliefs about sex-role behaviors that can be viewed as derogatory toward female athletes. Broverman and her colleagues asked male and female clinical psychologists to list behavior traits that they felt characterized the healthy female, healthy male, and healthy adult (no sex indicated). The healthy adult male and healthy adult were characterized as independent, logical, self-confident, and aggressive. The healthy adult female was described as dependent, emotional, intuitive, nonagressive, noncompetitive, and passive.[58] It is clear that the qualities necessary for excellence in sports are almost the opposite of those descriptive of females. According to these findings, a female athlete is a social deviant.

Americans have generally accepted sports for women that emphasized grace and beauty over bravery and strength. More than 10 years ago Metheney classified acceptable female sports from data on attitudes expressed by college women. The most acceptable ones involved projecting the body through space in aesthetically pleasing patterns, using force through a light implement, or overcoming the resistance of a light object, with skill and manipulation. Unacceptable sports involved body contact, application of force to a heavy object, and projecting the body through space over long distances.[59] But the speed of social change in sport over the past decade or so can be seen in the fact that women now commonly participate in some of the sport forms that Metheny suggested were inappropriate.

A consistent finding about attitudes toward female athletic participation is that individual sports are more acceptable than team sports.[60] Table 10-1 shows that respondents in Sherriff's study consider individual sports more desirable than team sports. Garman reported that her respondents described gymnasts as the most feminine female athletes, while softball players were identified as the least feminine.

Undoubtedly, attitudes toward female athletes have changed since these studies were completed. Within the past few years, feminist efforts have resulted in women being given a greater share in American life in many ways. Many of the myths about inabilities of women and the dangers inherent in certain activities have been destroyed, and enlightened males and females now recognize that females need not be limited in the physical activities they undertake. Female participation in an ever-increasing variety of sports is dramatically increasing, and it has become evident that negative attitudes toward female athletic participation is incongruent with the realities of female potential. Moreover, many are realizing that the ideology of equal opportunity is ill-served when half the population is either kept on the sidelines or allowed to play only part of the time.

Table 10-1. Rank Order of Sports Believed to Be the Most and Least Desirable for Female Competitors.

Most Desirable		Least Desirable	
Male	**Female**	**Male**	**Female**
		Parents (N=36)	
Swimming	Swimming	Soccer	Field hockey
Tennis	Tennis	Field hockey	Soccer
Gymnastics	Gymnastics	Track and field	Basketball
Bowling	Golf	Fencing	Track and field
Golf	Bowling	Bowling	Fencing
Softball	Diving	Basketball	Field games
			Gymnastics
			Archery
			Softball
		Peers (N=175)	
Swimming	Swimming	Soccer	Field hockey
Gymnastics	Gymnastics	Basketball	Soccer
Tennis	Tennis	Field hockey	Track and field
Diving	Diving	Fencing	Fencing
Bowling	Badminton	Track and field	Basketball
Volleyball	Volleyball	Softball	Softball

Source: Marie Christine Sherrif, "The Status of Female Athletes as Viewed by Selected Peers and Parents in Certain High Schools of Central California" (Master's thesis, Chico, California State College, 1969). Reprinted by permission.

The Opportunity and Reward Structure

Denial of equal access to various sports opportunities and unequal rewards for sports achievements are the two most ubiquitous consequences of sexism in sport. Although the opportunity and reward structure for female sports participants have improved drastically in the past five years (there are more females involved in sports and receiving more rewards for their achievements than ever before), this is a relatively recent phenomenon. It would take an entire book to catalog the numerous ways in which females have been deprived of equal opportunity for sport involvement and received inferior rewards for their sports achievements. Only brief mention can be made of these forms of discrimination here.

Youth sports programs introduce most American children to the experience of organized sports. Little League, Babe Ruth, Connie Mack baseball are three of the most popular baseball programs; Pop Warner football and Biddie Basketball initiate youngsters to tackling, blocking, and jump shooting. Age-group programs in swimming, track and field, and gymnastics are only a few of the over-25 youth programs that involve more than 15 million children annually in sports. Until very recently, all but a very small percentage of the participants were males, and many of the organizations had formal policies excluding females.

Lacking organized outlets for sports, girls with the support of their parents began to go out for all-boy teams. The reaction of the sports organizations and their leaders was predictable; the girls were prohibited from playing on the teams. Several law suits were initiated on behalf of the girls who wanted to play. At first, there was a reluctance by judges to acknowledge female's rights to equal opportunity, reflecting the cultural definitions of "appropriate" female behaviors. A judge in a 1971 Connecticut court case denied girls the right to participate on a cross-country team, saying:

> The present generation of our younger male population has not become so decadent that boys will experience a thrill in defeating girls in running contests, whether the girls be members of their own team or an adversary team. . . . Athletic competition builds character in our boys. We do not need that kind of character in girls, the women of tomorrow.[61]

The sport organization which has come under the severest attack for its sex discrimination is Little League, a baseball organization that operates 9,100 leagues in 31 countries for 2.5 million boys 8 to 12 years of age. Until 1974, Little League had an all-male policy as part of its federal charter, which prevented girls from playing on its teams. But this policy was challenged by several girls or their representatives, and it was reluctantly rescinded by Little League officers. The outlines of a couple of these cases will be described to illustrate the battle that had to be waged by girls to have an opportunity to play baseball.

In 1973, a girl in Ypsilanti, Michigan went out for a Little League team and qualified for a position. Little League headquarters threatened to withdraw the league charter. The city council responded by threatening to withdraw city support for the league and bar it from using the city-owned ball field. The local team allowed the girl to play, and Little League national headquarters promptly withdrew the local charter. Just as promptly, the city council filed a suit in federal court charging violation of the U.S. Constitution.[62] Although the local group did not win an outright approval for the girl's participation, it did serve to weaken the Little League policy excluding girls.

In New Jersey, a Hoboken girl was rejected from a Little League team whose charter had been threatened by national headquarters. A complaint on behalf of the girl was brought to the state civil rights division, which ordered the league to allow the girl to play. When this judgment was upheld by the appellate division of the state superior court, the majority of leagues throughout the state voted to suspend play—benching 150,000 boys rather than allowing them to play on teams with girls. Eventually, though, they capitulated and decided that they would operate an integrated baseball program after all.[63]

To resolve cases like the ones in Michigan and New Jersey, Little League changed its policy in June, 1974, to permit girls to play on its teams. Precedents seemed to be on the girls' side, as courts in several states handed down decisions banning sex discrimination in athletics. Moreover, the mounting number of lawsuits by girls, prompted by their desire to play sports, threatened Little League with financial disaster.[64] Nevertheless, prejudices die hard and in the summer of 1975, a local Little League organization in a small city in Michigan made what appeared to be a veiled attempt to circumvent court rulings and national Little League policy. The league established a policy requiring every player—girls as well as boys—to wear athletic supporters and protective cups, and coaches made "cup" inspections before each game. One girl's parents tried to ridicule the rule by pinning a toy teacup to their 8-year-old daughter's jersey. But the coach benched her and said that she "won't play until she wears a cup like the other kids."[65] The situation was finally resolved in favor of the girls when a lawsuit was threatened.

Discrimination in sports opportunities for females in American high schools and colleges has been scandalous. Some states have actually had legislation prohibiting interscholastic sports for girls, and, until recently, boys' interscholastic sports teams in Illinois could be declared ineligible from state competition if the girls played any inter-school sports contests.

As part of the demand for social equality, high school and college girls have challenged the discrimination in school sports programs and through legal and legislative action have won a great many concessions. Beginning in the early 1970s, a number of lawsuits were brought by girls against school districts or state high school athletic regulatory bodies. In general, the cases fell into one of two categories: (1) a girl desired to participate on the boys' team when a girls' team was not provided at her school; or (2) a girl wished to be on the boys' team even though her school provided a girls' team. In the first type of case, the courts have generally ruled in favor of the girls, even though some of these suits required appeals. In the second type of case, the girls were not successful, since the court reasoned that equal protection had not been denied the girl.[66]

Perhaps a more important issue than whether females can play on school teams with males is the provision of greater opportunities for girls to have teams of their own. Only a decade ago, it was not unusual for a high school or college with ten to twelve teams for boys to have no teams or perhaps a couple of teams for girls. Moreover, the season for a boys' sport might run three months, with fifteen or twenty contests; the girls' typically might extend three to four weeks, with two or three contests. Title IX of the Educational Amendments Act of 1972 has changed all that. Now, schools receiving federal funds (about 16,000 school districts and 2,700 colleges) must provide equal opportunities for both males and females.

The differences in financing male and female school sports programs have also been disgraceful in the past. In high schools and colleges with a female enrollment nearly equal to male's, it has not been unusual for females to receive less than one percent of the money the institution spent on sports. While females needed bake sales, bazaar nights, and Christmas tree sales to finance their athletic programs, male programs in the same schools provided new and expensive uniforms and equipment and generous per diem travel expenses, with never a request for the athletes to help raise money or spend some of their own. Conditions have improved for women, but there remains an undercurrent of feeling that they do not deserve parity with programs for males. In an otherwise sympathetic treatment of the plight of women in sport, novelist James Michener in his book, *Sports in America,* says that if he had his way, he would divide up a college athletic department budget by allocating 77 percent of the budget to the men's program and 23 percent to the women's in an institution that he expects to be composed of 50 percent men and 50 percent women students.[67]

Athletic scholarships are an integral part of intercollegiate sports, and until the past several years, they were given almost exclusively to male athletes. In 1974, the Colorado state legislature appropriated $956,000 for men's collegiate athletic scholarships and $15,000 for women's.[68] A full athletic scholarship, as approved by the National Collegiate Athletic Association (NCAA) provides payment of tuition, fees, room, meals, and, until 1976, $15 per month for "laundry expenses." In 1973, five major college conferences—Southeast, Big Ten, Big Eight, Southwest, and PAC-8—had approximately 5,000 students on football scholarships alone, while women athletes had scarcely a handful. However, by 1976 of the 843 member college and universities in the Association of Intercollegiate Athletics for Women (AIAW), the number of schools offering financial aid to women for specific sports had more than tripled between 1974 and 1976, and some 5,000 to 8,000 female athletic scholarships were available. Although women have begun to obtain athletic scholarships, there has been a strong objection to this trend by many male coaches and athletic directors who have claimed that men's programs will be destroyed if athletic revenues must be diluted to support women athletes.[69]

Facilities for female high school and college programs have customarily been second-rate. The newer and larger gym routinely went to the men, while the older gym was routinely given to the women. When facilities existed, the women were expected to use them in the off-hours—during meals, before sunrise, late at night. The girls got cheaper equipment and were expected to keep it. This sort of routine relegation of the women's program to second-class status is now illegal according to Title IX.

The contrast in male and female professional athletic programs is stark testimoney to the differential opportunity and reward system of sport. Earning inequities between salaries, often for the same types of performances, illustrate the status of female athletes. Salaries in excess of $100,000 per year have been rather common for male professional athletes for over 15 years, but the first female to win that much money in one year was Billie Jean King, who accomplished the feat in 1971, while her male counterpart in tennis, Rod Laver, earned $290,000 the same year. At the U.S. Open Tennis tournament in 1972, Ms. King, the winner of the women's competition, received $10,000 for her victory, while the men's winner, Ilie Nastase, collected $25,000. In golf, Kathy Whitworth won $65,000 as the leading women's professional golfer in 1972, and Jack Nicklaus collected $320,542, while playing in ten fewer tournaments.[69] In the summer of 1976, Judy Rankin became the first woman golfer to win $100,000 in tournament money; Arnold Palmer accomplished this feat for male golfers in 1963.[71]

The discrepancy in salaries and prize money between men and women professionals is even more marked among the lesser competitors. Salaries below the top-money earners in most professional sports are better for men than for women, and, of course, there are far more professional sports opportunities for males.

Television is professional sports and professional sports is television; thus, televised events are the heart and soul of professional athletics. Until quite recently, professional women's athletic events rarely appeared on television. For example, between August 1972 and September 1973, NBC televised 366 hours of "live" sport, one hour of which was devoted to women. A television executive at ABC was quoted as saying: "Women don't play sports."[72]

Many male professional athletes earn more money through commercial endorsements than from actually playing their sport. It has been an American tradition for everything from breakfast cereal to panty hose to be promoted by male sports stars. Female athletes are only now beginning to share in this bonanza.

The world of sport has not only discriminated against females as sport participants, it has until recently excluded them as sports reporters. Newswomen were not assigned to sports, partly because when they were given a sports assignment, they were frequently barred from press boxes and locker rooms. But it was also believed that the public would not accept sports reporting by women. After all, it was reasoned, what could a woman possibly know about sports. Despite the addition of women sports reporters by TV networks and newspapers, there are still relatively few women in the field.[73]

Women's Liberation Movement and Sport

American women have resented discrimination for decades, and have occasionally organized in an effort to acquire greater equality, i.e., the suffragettes secured passage of the 19th amendment of the U.S. Constitution, granting women the right to vote. But it was not until the mid-1960s that a full-scale women's liberation movement was launched, designed to comprehensively redress sexism throughout American Society. The original impetus for the new feminism was the publication of Betty Friedan's book, *The Feminine Mystique,* in 1963. But it was not until effective organizations began to appear, such as the Women's Action Group (WAG), the National Organization of Women (NOW), and others, that a concerted effort was made to eliminate sexism and force America to practice its avowed values of civil rights and equal opportunity. According to Shulamith Firestone:

> The new feminism is not just the revival of a serious political movement for social equality. It is the second wave of the most important revolution in history. Its aim: overthrow the oldest, most rigid caste-class system in existence, the class system based on sex—a system consolidated over thousands of years, lending the archetypal male and female roles an undeserved legitimacy and seeming permanence.[74]

Over the past decade, the National Organization for Women (NOW) has been the most active and most visible organization for the promotion of the women's liberation movement. In the organizing conference in Washington, D.C. in 1966, the purpose of the organization was codified:

> We men and women hereby constitute ourselves as the National Organization for Women, believe that the time has come for a new movement toward true equality for all women in America and toward a fully equal partnership of the sexes as part of the worldwide revolution of human rights now taking place within and beyond our national borders. The purpose of NOW is to take action to bring women into full participation in the mainstream of American society now, exercise all the privileges and responsibilities thereof in truly equal partnership with men.[75]

The feminist movement was slow to recognize the importance of sport as a domain of sexual prejudice and discrimination, but at its sixth annual conference in 1973, NOW passed a resolution stating that it "opposes and actively works to eliminate all forms of discrimination against women and girls in recreation and sports, including school, (college) community physical education, and recreation programs and facilities," and a task force was created to implement sports policies. Locally, NOW has been extremely active and successful in obtaining increased athletic opportunities for girls and women, and has supported girls in several court cases involving discrimination in sports programs.

As significant as the various feminist groups have been in dismantling barriers to equal access to the world of sport for females, undoubtedly the most formidable ally females have in their drive for equitable athletic programs is Title IX of the Educational Amendments Act of 1972, a key regulation of which reads:

> No person shall, on the basis of sex, be excluded from participation in, be denied the benefits of, be treated differently from another person or otherwise be discriminated against in any interscholastic, intercollegiate, club or intramural athletics offered by a recipient, and no recipient shall provide any such athletics separately on such basis.[76]

The word "recipient" refers to educational institutions and activities receiving or benefiting from federal financial assistance. Title IX constitutes a considerable weapon against sex discrimination in the nation's public school and collegiate sports programs, since some 16,000 public school districts and 2,700 colleges and universities benefit from federal funds.

It took three years to work out the implementing regulations for enforcing Title IX, which went into effect in July 1975. High schools and colleges were given three years to bring their programs into compliance with the law. Rumors about the provisions of Title IX are legion; many are false. Spending for men's and women's athletics does not have to be exactly the same. Separate teams for males and females are allowed under certain circumstances. Male and female students do not have to share shower rooms. The basis of Title IX—forbidding sex discrimination in educational institutions receiving federal funds—is easy to grasp, but the finer points are elusive, and only the events of the next few years will clarify some of the issues raised by this legislation.[77]

Making discrimination illegal does not eliminate it, as the previous experiences with civil rights legislation so clearly illustrates. Socially conditioned attitudes are slow to change—in some individual cases, they cannot be changed. Stereotypes are persistent, and feed on the inevitable examples that confirm them. Nevertheless, attitudes and behavior have changed in remarkably significant ways in the past 10 years in response to feminist challenges and demands, and as Jan Felshin noted, there "is no end to the contemporary chronicle of change in both the individual participation of women in sport and the collective phenomenon of women's sports.[78]

Summary

Because the traditional female role in American sport had been so markedly different from that of males, and because this role is now changing rapidly, we felt that a separate chapter on females in sports was justified. In this chapter, we examined the social bases for the prejudice and discrimination that has traditionally confronted the would-be female athlete, the consequences of the processes, and the current developments in this topic.

For the past 2,500 years, Western culture has taught that females are biologically and physically limited, and this notion has permeated the sex role ideology about females. In addition, culturally prescribed tasks for females have been child rearing and homemaking. Thus, much of Western cultural tradition discouraged sports activities for females, and the sexism that has been present in American sports is merely a reflection of sexism in the precepts of Western culture.

Prejudice and discrimination against females in sport have taken many forms. First, a number of myths about the biological and psychological effects of competitive sports on women have effectively discouraged their participation. Second, there has been unequal opportunity for participation in sports. Finally, females have had unequal access to the authority and power structure of sport. Sexism has been employed to socialize females out of sports and deny them equal access to the rewards of sport.

Recent legislation and court decisions have made it more difficult for discrimination to be imposed on females in sports. Greater opportunities are now available for women who wish to compete in sports.

Notes

1. Bil Gilbert and Nancy Williamson, "Sport is Unfair to Women," *Sports Illustrated* 38 (May 28, 1973), p. 90.
2. Ibid., p. 88.
3. Jack Scott, "The Masculine Obsession in Sports," in *Women's Athletics: Coping with Controversy,* ed. B.J. Hoepner (Washington, D.C.: American Association for Health, Physical Education, and Recreation, 1974), p. 83.
4. Leonard Broom and Philip Selznick, *Sociology,* 5th ed. (New York: Harper and Row, 1973), pp. 113-123.
5. Polytheists believe in many gods.
6. P. Lacroix, *History of Prostitution,* vol. 1, trans. Samuel Putnam (New York: Covici, Friede, 1931), p. 143.
7. H.A. Harris, *Sport in Greece and Rome* (Ithaca, N.Y.: Cornell University Press, 1972).
8. Will Durant, *Caesar and Christ* (New York: Simon and Schuster, 1944).
9. I Tim. 2:11-12.
10. St. Thomas Aquinas, *Summa Theologica,* trans. Fathers of the English Dominican Province (London: Burns, Oates, and Washbourne, 1914-42).
11. Andreas Capellanus, *The Art of Courtly Love,* trans. John Jay Parry (New York: Columbia University Press, 1941).
12. Herbert Spencer, *Education: Intellectual, Moral, and Physical* (New York: Hurst, 1900), p. 277.
13. Margaret A. Coffey, "The Sportswoman," *Journal of Health, Physical Education, and Recreation* 36 (February, 1965), p. 38.
14. Michael Lewis, "There's No Unisex in the Nursery," *Psychology Today* 5 (May, 1972), pp. 54-57.
15. Ibid.; see also L.B. Fauls and W.D. Smith, "Sex-Role Learning of Five-Year-Olds," *Journal Genetic Psychology* 89 (September, 1956), pp. 105-117.
16. See J. Money, "Sexual Dimorphism and Homosexual Gender Identity," *Psychological Bulletin* 74 (December, 1970), pp. 425-440; R.E. Hartley and F.P. Hardesty, "Children's Perceptions of Sex Rules in Childhood," *Journal Genetic Psychology* 105 (September, 1964), pp. 43-51; B. Sutton-Smith, B.G. Rosenberg, and E.F. Morgan, Jr. "Development of Sex Differences in Play Choices During Preadolescence," *Child Development* 34 (March, 1963), pp. 119-126.
17. Citizens Advisory Council on the Status of Women, *Women in 1972* (Washington, D.C.: U.S. Government Printing Office, May, 1973).
18. L.A. Serbin and K.D. O'Leary, "How Nursery Schools Teach Girls to Shut Up," *Psychology Today* 9 (December, 1975), pp. 57-58.

19. National Education Association, *Sex Role Stereotyping in the Schools* (Washington, D.C.: National Education Association, 1973).

20. Ibid.

21. Marjorie B. See, "The Image of Women in Textbooks," in *Woman in Sexist Society,* eds. Vivian Gornick and Barbara K. Moran (New York: Basic Books, 1971), pp. 218-225.

22. D.E. Weitzman, D. Eifler, E. Hokada, and C. Ross, "Sex-Role Socialization in Picture Books for Preschool Children," *American Journal of Sociology* 77 (May, 1972), pp. 1125-1150.

23. Women on Words and Images, *Dick and Jane as Victims: Sex Stereotyping in Children's Readers* (A task force of Central New Jersey NOW, ERIC, 1972).

24. Mary E. Duquin, "Differential Sex Role Socialization Toward Amplitude Appropriation" *Research Quarterly* 48 (May, 1977), pp. 288-292.

25. Lucy Komisar, "The Image of Woman in Advertising," in Gornick and Moran, *Woman in Sexist Society,* pp. 211-212.

26. J.A. Hennessee and J. Nickolson, "NOW says TV Commericals Insult Women," *New York Times Magazine* (May 28, 1972), pp. 12-13, 48- 51.

27. J.R. Dominick and G.E. Rauch, "The Image of Women in Network TV Commercials," *Journal of Broadcasting* 16 (Summer, 1972), pp. 259-265.

28. In 1975, there was a special TV program on the life of "Babe" Didrickson Zaharias, the most famous female athlete of the 1930-1955 era.

29. Y. Lab. Slatton, "The Role of Women in Sport as Depicted Through Advertising in Selected Magazines, 1900-1968" (Ph.D. diss., University of Iowa, 1970). Alison Poe, "Active Women in Ads," *Journal of Communication,* 26 (Autumn, 1976), pp. 185-192.

30. M. Corrigan, "Societal Acceptance of the Female Athletes as Seen Through the Analysis of Content of a Sports Magazine" (Unpublished paper, May 11, 1972), cited in E.R. Gerber, J. Felshin, P. Berlin, and W. Wyrick *The American Woman in Sport* (Reading, Mass.: Addison-Wesley, 1974), pp. 263-264.

31. Harold Peterson, "Formful Win in a Most Formful Affair," *Sports Illustrated* 35 (August 23, 1971), p. 48.

32. Quoted in Dorothy V. Harris, "The Sportswoman in Our Society," in *DGWS Research Reports: Women in Sports,* ed. Dorothy V. Harris (Washington, D.C.: American Association for Health, Physical Education, and Recreation, 1971), p. 3.

33. Gilbert and Williamson, "Sport is Unfair to Women," p. 96.

34. Ibid.

35. "Masculine" used in this sense refers to body structure and behavioral pattern, not to biological considerations. Every culture defines what is appropriate and inappropriate ideal male and female appearance and behavior (and this varies from culture to culture), and establishes severe negative sanctions for those who do not meet cultural standards of masculinity and femininity.

36. Robert Lipsyte, *Sports World: An American Dreamland,* (New York: Quadrangle Books, 1975), p. 217.

37. Dorothy V. Harris, *Women in Sports,* p. 1.

38. C.E. Klafs and D.D. Arnheim, *Modern Principles of Athletic Training,* (St. Louis: C.V. Mosby, 1969), p. 128.

39. See Harmon Brown and Jack H. Wilmore, "The Effects of Maximum Resistance Training on the Strength and Body Composition of Women Athletes," *Medicine and Science in Sports* 6 (Fall, 1974), pp. 174-177; Jack H. Wilmore and C. Harmon Brown, "Physiological Profiles of Women Distance Runners," *Medicine and Science in Sports* 6 (Fall, 1974), p. 180; Jack H. Wilmore, "Inferiority of the Female Athlete: Myth or Reality?" *Sports Medicine Bulletin* 10 (April, 1975), p. 7; Jack Wilmore, "Body Composition and Strength Development," *Journal of Physical Education and Recreation,* 46 (January, 1974), p. 29.

40. Ernst H. Arnold, "Athletics for Women," *American Physical Education Review,* 29 (October, 1924), pp. 452-457.

41. Frederick R. Rogers, "Olympics for Girls," *School and Society* 30 (August 10, 1929) p. 191.

42. Ethel Perrin, "A Crisis in Girls Athletics," *Sportsmanship* 1 (December, 1928), pp. 10-12.

43. Agnes Wayman, quoted in Marjorie S. Loggia, "On the Playing Fields of History," *Ms* (July, 1973), p. 64.

44. Mabel Lee, "The Case for and Against Intercollegiate Athletics for Women and the Situation as it Stands Today," *American Physical Education Review* 29 (January, 1924), pp. 13-19; Mabel Lee, "The Case for and Against Intercollegiate Athletics for Women and the Situation Since 1923," *Research Quarterly* 2 (May, 1931), pp. 93-127.

45. Clayton L. Thomas, "The Female Sports Participant: Some Physiological Questions," in Harris, *Women in Sports,* pp. 37-44.

46. Allan J. Ryan, "Gynecological Considerations," *Journal of Health, Physical Education, and Recreation* 46 (January, 1975), p. 41.

47. G.J. Erdelyi, "Women in Athletics," *Proceedings of the Second National Conference on the Medical Aspects of Sports,* (Chicago: American Medical Association, 1961); E. Zaharieva, "Survey of Sportswomen at the Tokyo Olympics," *Journal of Sports Medicine and Physical Fitness* 5 (December, 1965), pp. 215-219.

48. Per-Olof Astrand, L. Engstrom, B.O. Erickson, P. Karlberg, I. Nylander, B. Saltin, and C. Thoren, "Girl Swimmers With Special Reference to Respiratory and Circulatory Adaptation and Gynaecological and Psychiatric Aspects," *Acta Paediat. Scand.,* supp. 147, 1963.

49. Thomas, "The Female Sports Participant," p. 38.

50. Committee on the Medical Aspects of Sports of the American Medical Association, "Female Athletics," *Journal of Physical Education and Recreation* 46 (January, 1975), p. 45.

51. Anna S. Espenschade and Helen M. Eckert, *Motor Development* (Columbus, Ohio: Charles E. Merrill, 1967), see especially, chapters 7 and 8.

52. Eleanor Metheny, "Symbolic Forms of Movement: The Feminine Image in Sports," in *Sport and American Society,* 2nd ed., George H. Sage (Reading, Mass.: Addison-Wesley, 1974), pp. 289-301.

53. Simone de Beauvoir, *The Second Sex* (New York: Bantam Books, 1952), p. 311.

54. Quoted in Harris, *Women in Sports,* p. 3.

55. Quoted from Robert Vare, *Buckeye: A Study of Coach Woody Hayes and the Ohio State Football Machine* (New York: Harper Magazine Publishers, 1974), p. 38.

56. Bil Gilbert and Nancy Williamson, "Are You Being Two-Faced?" *Sports Illustrated* 38 (June 4, 1973), p. 47.

57. Patricia S. Griffith, "What's a Nice Girl Like You Doing in a Profession Like This?" *Quest* 19 (January, 1973), pp. 96-101.

58. I.K. Broverman, D.M. Broverman, F.E. Clarkson, P.S. Rosenkrantz, and S.R. Vogel, "Sex Role Stereotypes and Clinical Judgments of Mental Health," *Journal of Consulting Clinical Psychology* 34 (February, 1970), pp. 1-7.

59. Eleanor Metheny, *Connotations of Movement in Sport and Dance.* (Dubuque, Iowa: W.C. Brown, 1965).

60. Bea Harres, "Attitudes of Students Toward Women's Athletic Competition," *Research Quarterly* 39 (May, 1966), pp. 278-284; Marie C. Sherrif, "The Status of Female Athletes as Viewed by Selected Peers and Parents in Certain High Schools of Central California" (Master's thesis, Chico State College, 1969); E.W. Garman, "A Study of Attitudes Toward Softball Competition for Women" (Master's thesis, University of California, Santa Barbara, 1969); Diane L. Debacy, Ree Spaeth, and Roxanne Busch, "What Do Men Really Think About Athletic Competition for Women?" *Journal of Health, Physical Education, and Recreation* 41 (November-December, 1970), pp. 28-29.

61. Quoted in Margaret C. Dunkle, "Equal Rights for Women in Sports," in Hoepner, *Women's Athletics: Coping with Controversy,* p. 9.

62. *Time* (June 4, 1973), p. 48.

63. *New York Times* (February 28, 1974).

64. *The Kansas City Times* (June 13, 1974), p. 70.

65. *Rocky Mountain News* (June 14, 1975), p. 148.

66. Ellen W. Gerber, Jan Felshin, Pearl Berlin, and Waneen Wyrick, *The American Woman in Sport*, pp. 221-228.

67. James A. Michener, *Sports in America* (New York: Random House, 1976), pp. 139-140.

68. "More Collegiate Sports Money Available," *Rocky Mountain News* (September 27, 1976), p. 6.

69. See "College Recruiting of Women Athletes Is Increasing Rapidly," *New York Times* (November 14, 1976), p. 10. "Number of Colleges Providing Aid to Female Athletes Triples

in Year," *President's Council on Physical Fitness and Sport Newsletter* (May, 1977), p. 4.

70. Ibid.

71. "The Lady is a Champ," *Sports Illustrated* 45 (July 26, 1976), p. 12.

72. Gilbert and Williamson, "Sport is Unfair to Women," p. 96.

73. Daniel Rapoport, "Help Wanted: Women Sportswriters," *Rocky Mountain News—Parade* section (December 5, 1976), pp. 17-19.

74. Shulamith Firestone, "The Dialectic of Sex: The Case for Feminist Revolution," in Gornick and Moran, *Woman in Sexist Society,* p. 485.

75. The National Organization for Women, *Statement of Purpose* (Washington, D.C.: 1966), p. 1.

76. *Federal Register* 40 (June 4, 1975), part II, (Washington, D.C.: Department of Health, Education, and Welfare), p. 24142.

77. George R. LaNoue, "Athletics and Equality: How to Comply with Title IX without Tearing Down the Stadium," *Change* 8 (November, 1976), pp. 27-30, 63-64. Also see "Compliance with Title IX in Secondary School Physical Education," *Journal of Physical Education and Recreation* 48 (January, 1977), pp. 19-22.

78. Jan Felshin, "The Social View," in Gerber et al., *The American Woman in Sport,* p. 220.

Gulf
Gulf

Contemporary Trends and the Future of Sport in America 11

"We live in a changing society" is an often heard cliche. It is voguish to depict our society as dynamic and progressive, where the pace of life is fast, growth and change the only constants, and the accelerating rate of change likely to inflict "future shock" on many of us. These ideas are buttressed by an apparent obsession with the future; several of the most popular books of the past generation have been futuristic.[1] George Orwell's *1984* has fascinated and terrified a generation, while Alvin Toffler's recent best seller, *Future Shock,* describes how the accelerating rate of technological change may be impossible for many people to cope with psychologically. Meanwhile, groups of social forecasters—social scientists who are actively involved with forecasting societal activity—have also been busy with futuristic studies. The American Academy of Arts and Science has created the Commission of the Year 2000, and the Hudson Institute and Rand Corporation have plunged full-scale into studies of the future.[2]

Notwithstanding the cliches, change in America is a ubiquitous fact. The social and physical environment is vastly different from that of only a generation ago, to say nothing of three or four generations. The changes over the past three decades have been in direction as well as in rate, and the total amount of change has been so vast and thorough that it can only be conceptualized as a social and cultural revolution. Therefore, we will conclude this volume with a chapter that examines the future of sport in America for, as we have frequently argued, sports reflects American society, and as the society changes sport will also undoubtedly undergo some transformation. As William Johnson noted in his article "From Here to 2000," "In searching out the future of sport . . . there is really only one point of certitude: As it always has, sport will continue to reflect the society in which it occurs."[3]

Trends in Population

Population Growth

One of the most significant trends in American society is the changing nature of its population—total numbers, composition, and location. Futurists are much concerned about population trends. Some 80 million Americans were born between 1945 and 1965, an annual birth rate of 23.3 per thousand, but this has now dropped to about 14.9 per thousand. While improved birth control measures and a social commitment to zero population growth will partially control the numbers of newborns in the next two decades, a continued increase is expected in U.S. population. Estimates are that by 2000 the population of the United States will increase from its present 220 million to some 290 million.[4]

Population Composition

Throughout the twentieth century, the United States has had a young population because the birth rate remained high for an expanding number of people of child-bearing age. This condition is now changing rapidly because the long-term trend for birth and death rates is expected to decline. Thus, the proportion of young people will diminish and the proportion of older people will increase. This will markedly affect population composition because the average age in the United States will rise dramatically from 28 in 1970 to about 35 in 2000.[5]

Location of Population

People will probably congregate into at least three gargantuan "megalopolises" that Kahn and Wiener have labeled "Boswash," "Chipitts," and "Sansan." Boswash will extend between Boston and Washington, with Chicago and Pittsburgh as the centers for the second metropolitan giant, and Sansan will stretch from San Francisco to San Diego. These megalopolises seem likely to "contain roughly one-half of the total United States population, including the overwhelming majority of the most technologically and scientifically advanced, prosperous, intellectual, and creative elements."[6] The growth of these giant centers of population will be accompanied by the continuing trend toward urbanization, which began in the nineteenth century, accelerated in the early twentieth century, and will result in an urban population of between 80 and 90 percent of the total population in the next two decades.

Population Trends and Sport

The giant metropolitan areas stretched out over hundreds of miles, and engulfing many small communities as well as large cities may very well require the basing of professional sports organizations on some feature other than city name. Mike Palmer of the Institute for the Future contends "it is irrational to attach pro teams to cities; no one has loyalty to a city in these days of suburbs and transiency." He goes on to suggest that teams might be organized on the basis of ethnic or ideological loyalties to maintain interest, such as "games featuring the Steelworkers vs. the Executives, the Hippies vs. the Straights, Hunters vs. Animal Lovers."[7]

Whether such team arrangements as prophesized by Palmer will come to pass is still an open question, but professional sports managements are preparing for a future where regional considerations will take precedence over single-city loyalties. Within the past few years, the naming of professional sport franchises and the location of playing arenas demonstrate that owners are aware of the outmoded practice of single-city affiliation. Regionalistic team names have been adopted by several owners: the California Angels and Texas Rangers in major league baseball, the New England Patriots of the NFL, the Colorado Rockies of the NHL, the Golden State Warriors of the NBA. All are names that give evidence of the transcendence of city boundries. Newly built football stadiums by the Patriots and the Dallas Cowboys, and the sports areas built in Richfield, Ohio, by the owner of the NBA Cleveland Cavaliers, have been constructed with a view towards the anticipated future of urban development, since they are all removed from what are now highly urbanized areas.

Professional sport has been one of the most financially successful and growing industries during the 1960s and '70s, seemingly riding the crest of a huge population of young people. Consumer-spectator interest has seemed to have no limit—new franchises have sprung up all over the United States to be greeted with sell-out crowds. The NFL is still expanding, adding two teams in 1976, making a total of 28, with expectations of exceeding 30, and perhaps adding European or Asian franchises. Major league baseball has plans for further expansion in the next few years, and professional soccer team owners anticipate that the growing popularity of soccer at the amateur level will ultimately justify expansion. In addition, new professional sports, such as volleyball, are attempting to gain a foothold. But the rapid growth years are probably over for pro sports, and the changing composition of the population over the next two decades may produce some significant changes. Figures compiled by various sources have begun to show that spectator interest in many sports has not increased in recent years, and season ticket sales have stabilized. Some sports have actually experienced declining attendance.[8] According to Leonard Koppett of the *New York Times,* a shakeout is coming: "The easy-money, apparently endless expansion era is over and the major league scene, which has doubled in size during the last 15 years, is now headed for contraction."[9]

Another potential economic problem for the professional sports of the future is the stabilizing pool of new athletes. Current athletes are part of the "baby boom" of the 1940s and '50s, but within a few years that pool will not increase. In fact, it is estimated that the number of people in the population between 20 and 30 years of age in 2000 will be slightly less than it was in 1975.[10]

Trends of Industry and Technology

From an Industrial to a Postindustrial Society

Industrialization and technology not only changed the way products were produced, but they also changed the conditions under which they were produced. At first, factories brought large groups of primarily women and children into "sweatshops" to toil literally from sunrise to sunset; later, as steel and other large industries grew, men were attracted to the plants by the prospect of steady work and a livable wage. Hours were long, but, until the emergence of labor union power, there was little workers could do if they wished to remain employed. However, beginning near the turn of the century, there has been a gradual reduction in the average work week from about 65 hours to

40 hours for nonagricultural workers. Some futurists are predicting that the average work week in industry will decline to between 30 and 32 hours by the year 2000.[11]

One promise of industry and technology, at least covertly if not overtly, has been that industrialization and technological advances will ultimately free the ties that bind workers to their jobs. Accompanying this has been the prediction that "there will be a great flowering of leisure-time activities for the common man."[12] Despite impressive statistics about the diminishing work week and laborsaving devices to accomplish domestic duties, the "flowering of leisure" has not yet materialized, and there are some who question whether it will in the immediate future. We will say more about this later in the chapter.

Industrialization has undergone numerous refinements since its beginnings in England, when water and steam power were first used in manufacture, and the factory began to replace the family-run shop. The introduction of electric power in the latter nineteenth century and the changes in production, especially the assembly line and scientific management procedures in the early twentieth century, and more recently the use of nuclear power and other new energy sources have transformed all areas of occupational as well as social life. Accompanying and supporting industrial trends over the past century have been remarkable technological developments and the growth of bureaucratic organization. Combined, these forces form the most salient feature of American institutional life. But additional changes are expected. The way in which the economy is being transformed and the occupational system reworked, and with the new relations between theory (science) and empiricism (technology), the present and future of American society suggests that we have entered what sociologist Daniel Bell has called a "postindustrial society."[13] This stage of society is one in which the organization of theoretical knowledge becomes paramount for innovation in the society, and in which intellectual institutions become central in the social structure. More specifically, Bell has identified five dimensions, or components, of the postindustrial society:

1. Economic sector: the change from a goods producing to a service economy;
2. Occupational distribution: the preeminence of the professional and technical class;
3. Axial principle: the centrality of theoretical knowledge as the source of innovation and of policy formulation for the society;
4. Future orientation: the control of technology and technological assessment;
5. Decision-making: the creation of a new "intellectual technology."[14]

While Bell claims that we will increasingly take on the characteristics of a postindustrial society, Theodore Roszak envisions, and fears, a technocracy, a "social form in which an industrial society reaches the peak of its organizational integration . . . and . . . in which those who govern justify themselves by appeal to scientific forms of knowledge. And beyond the authority of science, there is no appeal."[15]

The Reaction Against Postindustrial Society and Technocracy

The ubiquitousness of technology is captured by Sykes:

> Our lives are becoming drastically transformed not by any self-conscious plan or the machinations of a few, but by the unanticipated consequences of economic and technological development in which we are all implicated. It is the man of business and industry, especially his goal of productivity and his skillful allocation of resources, who has been the great revolutionary of our era. He has remade our existence far more than any ideologist, smashing institutions, shifting the landscape, stuffing some regions with people and depopulating others—all without a policy or overall purpose."[16]

Technological developments have been characterized by an ever-increasing scale of giant organizations, the depersonalization of social relationships, and the eclipse of polity and community. American business is now organized into huge corporate bureaucracies. Of the almost 2 million corporations in the United States, a mere 1/10 of 1 percent control 55 percent of total corporate assets; and only 1.1 percent control 82 percent of the assets. At the other end of the spectrum, 94 percent of the corporations own only 9 percent of the total assets.[17] Concurrent with this trend in business has been the bureaucratization of organizations in all other social institutions of American life.[18] The outcome of these technological and bureaucratic trends has produced, according to several social scientists, the typical American—an organization man, a bureaucratic hack, a conformist, a status seeker, and an adaptable role player.[19]

While most Americans would not wish to give up many of the products of technocracy—television, central heating, air conditioning, automobiles, etc.—there is, nevertheless, an accelerating disaffection with the dehumanization that accompanies it. Theodore Roszak described the opposition to technocracy that has surfaced among many of the nation's youth:

> It is the American young, with their undeveloped radical background who seem to have grasped most clearly the fact that, while such immediate emergencies as the Vietnam war, racial injustice, and hard-core poverty demand a good deal of old-style politicking, the paramount struggle of our day is against a far more formidable, far less obvious, opponent, . . . "the technocracy"—a social form more highly developed in American than in any other society.[20]

A major stimulus to the emergence of social criticism is the recognition that the bureaucratic machine is dehumanizing; according to Thomas Kando, "the general point being that modern technological civilization fragments human personality, forces man to repress essential needs, deprives him of the experiential gestalt enjoyed by primitive man, and thus, reduces him to a mechanized and dehumanized entity."[21] The major tenet of this new social criticism is a hostility to all forms of technological innovation and bureaucratic organization, and an affirmation of a wide range of spontaneous, activist, and democratic methods of participation. In short, the critics respond to images of a technocracy and a bureaucratic society by rebelling against large-scale organizations.[22]

Postindustrial Society and Leisure Activities

The amount and type of sport involvement in the future will depend to a great extent on the leisure time available to Americans. Some rather exotic forecasts for the future of leisure have been sketched recently. Most are optimistic that postindustrial society will reduce work time and that a new leisure consciousness will emerge in which leisure will take a more central and valued place in our lives. In *The Year 2000,* the prediction is that workers will spend only about 32 hours per week on the job, and they will work only 20 weeks per year, conjuring up visions of a nation blessed with vast amounts of time to enjoy leisure.[23]

To a great extent, the prediction of a "leisure society" is based on a misperception of the amount of leisure time at present. While the work-nonwork cycle created by industrialization has been altered over the past century so that there now appears to be more time away from work, there is little evidence that nonwork time has increased appreciably since World War II. As a matter of fact, since 1945 the percentage of people working more than 48 hours per week has risen from 13 percent to 20 percent of the labor force, with some 5 percent of the labor force actually holding two full-time jobs in the mid-1970s.[24]

Sebastian deGrazia has shown that, at least up to the present, Americans have not been able to translate time off-the-job into leisure activities. More importantly, while the statistics of the length of the workweek show a gradual reduction (see table 11-1), they are misleading because when allowance is made for such things as commuting, moonlighting, etc., most of the alleged gain in nonwork time disappears. The weekly gain in free time since 1850, demonstrated by deGrazia, is actually only about 8.5 hours per week. He concluded that "comparisons in our favor are delusive. Since 1850, free time has not appreciably increased."[25] Similarly, Harvard economist John Kenneth Galbraith pointed out that "the notion of a new era of greatly expanded leisure is, in fact, a conventional conversation piece. Nor will it serve much longer to convey an impression of social vision. The tendency of the industrial system is not in this direction."[26]

Even conceding that technology has given workers some additional free time, what do they do with it? Such time has often been used for busywork or second jobs. "When Americans are asked why they would like more free time, they answer typically that they could then get the shopping done, or take the children to the dentist, or replace that worn-out weather stripping on the back door." In other words, according to deGrazia, "they mention such unfree things because they assume 'free' means off-the-

Table 11-1. Length of the Average Workweek in Agriculture and Nonagricultural Industries—1850 to 1972*.

Years	All Industries	Agriculture	Nonagricultural Industries
1850	69.7	72.0	65.7
1860	67.8	71.0	63.3
1870	65.3	70.0	60.0
1880	63.8	69.0	58.8
1890	61.7	68.0	57.1
1900	60.1	67.0	55.9
1910	54.9	65.0	50.3
1920	49.4	60.0	45.5
1930	45.7	55.0	43.2
1940	43.8	54.6	41.1
1950	39.9	47.2	38.8
1951	40.4	47.9	39.4
1952	40.5	47.4	39.6
1953	40.0	47.9	39.2
1954	38.9	47.0	37.9
1955	39.7	46.5	38.9
1956	39.5	44.9	38.8
1957	39.1	44.2	38.6
1958	38.6	43.7	38.1
1959	38.5	43.8	38.0
1960	38.5	44.0	38.0
1961	38.6	41.1	38.3
1962	38.8	42.0	38.5
1963	38.4	43.9	37.9
1964	38.7	42.5	38.5
1965	38.0	42.1	37.7
1966	38.7	42.3	38.5
1967	38.5	43.3	38.2
1968	37.1	43.1	36.7
1969	38.0	41.8	37.8
1970	37.7	42.1	37.4
1971	37.5	43.7	37.1
1972	37.6	42.8	37.4

*Sources: (1850-1960): Sebastian de Grazia, *Of Time, Work, and Leisure* ©1962 by The Twentieth Century Fund, New York. First published in 1962; First Anchor Book paperback edition, 1964, p. 419. (1961-1972): Bureau of Labor Statistics (1961-1972). The averages published by the bureau were adjusted downward, as had been done by de Grazia up to 1960, to reflect zero hours of work for those "with a job but not at work." Also, we continued to use each year's May figures, as did de Grazia, to avoid problems of seasonal fluctuation.

job."[27] Moreover, that technology may perhaps give us free time but not leisure is one of the central arguments of deGrazia and his followers.

> Machines give us free time, perhaps, but not leisure. We must create leisure ourselves. Leisure requires a sacrifice. Anybody can have free time. Not everybody can have leisure. Free time is a realizable idea of democracy. Leisure is not fully realizable, and hence an ideal, not alone an idea. . . . Leisure refers to a state of being, a condition of man, which few desire and fewer achieve.[28]

Ignoring for the moment the conceptual distinctions between free time and leisure, and recognizing that the alleged greater free time that technology has provided is basically a myth, how can we account for the fact that participation rates in leisure activities and expenditures on leisure pursuits are at an all-time high? Several writers have suggested that people now undertake a number of activities concurrently—a phenomenon sometimes called "time deepening." According to one twelve-nation study of people's use of time:

> The more a person is part of an industrial society with a very high density of communication, and the more educated a person, the more likely he is to do a number of activities simultaneously. While it is generally true that everyone—regardless of status or nationality—has the same 24 hours at his disposal, there is actually something like "time deepening": . . . if a person develops the ability to do several things simultaneously, he can crowd a greater number of activities into the same 24 hours.[29]

Meyersohn has referred to this idea as "the more, the more," suggesting that under the pressure of expanding interest and motivations, the more people do, the more they wish to do, and vice versa.[30] This may be one plausible explanation for recreational trends of the past 20 years.

The Four-Day Workweek

Many private and public organizations have experimented with the four-day workweek in recent years; it has been hailed as one of the most important steps toward creating a leisure society. In addition, since futurists predict something like a 30-hour workweek by the year 2000, a four-day workweek appears to be a tangible step in that direction. But under all four-day workweek schemes tried so far, the workweek remains a 40-hour workweek; thus, this trend has nothing to do with a reduction in working hours, it is merely a rescheduling of the workload. It "fails to even touch upon the more important issue of the desirability of a reduction in the overall length of the workweek."[31]

Although the hours of the workweek remain the same under the various four-day workweek plans, several potential benefits accrue with respect to leisure time. The extra long weekends make travel and other extended leisure time activities possible, and commuting time may be reduced by as much as 20 percent, some of which might be used for leisure activities. On the other hand, the extra time afforded by the four-day week may be a mixed blessing. There is, for example, no guarantee that the time will not be spent working at a second job; indeed, this is a distinct possibility, since the continuing inflation tends to drive up the standard of living, requiring more money to maintain one's current living standard. Moreover, there is the question of how people will spend large amounts of free time. Unless radical changes in attitude toward constructive use of leisure occur, people might actually be reluctant victims of too much leisure. James Rue described the potential problems of a four-day workweek:

> Too many families are ill-prepared to cope with that much leisure time. . . . Thousands can't get along on two days off. Of all the adjustments in marriage, recreation and use of leisure time are among the most difficult. For families who enjoy things together— camping, the desert, the beach, active sports—the four-day workweek is fine. But we are a nation of spectators—movies, TV, spectator sports—and I'm afraid we'd just be watching more TV. I'm fully convinced the four-day workweek is coming—and that it could be disaster unless we are fully prepared for it.[32]

Experience with reduction in the workweek and with manipulation of work schedules to provide greater free time suggests that future increases in nonwork time will, in all likelihood, continue to be used primarily as an opportunity to perform extra work of some kind. Kando has argued:

> Workers—blue collar as well as white collar—simply do not and cannot opt for leisure. Despite the lip service paid to leisure by unions and management, the truth of the matter is that our lives and our attitudes are not geared to it until some fundamental social changes occur.[33]

It appears, then, that the emergence of a true leisure society will require a respiritualization of our society and the rise of a fundamentally different valuation of work and leisure. According to Kando, "much of what passes for leisure [today] is really increased buying power."[34]

Sports of Postindustrial Society

Postindustrial society is expected to become increasingly more of a "learning society." In part, this will be a function of the "information explosion," but it will be mostly because of the rapid change. According to Daniel Bell: "The postindustrial society . . . is a knowledge society. . . . The chief resource of the postindustrial society is its scientific personnel."[35] Thus, information—its acquisition and use—will become extremely important. The major problem will be adequate numbers of educated persons of professional and technical competence, so Bell expects education, especially college and graduate education, to be acquired by a much greater proportion of the population than at present.

Intellectual or Violent Sports?

What are the implications for sport for a "cerebral" population? Two diametrically opposed predications have been advanced in recent years. The first suggests that there will be a trend away from violent forms of sport, with a greater emphasis upon "intellectual" sports; the other suggests that violent sports will increase.

Johnson has proposed that as we become more cerebral our choices will tend away from the violent sports such as football, hockey, and auto racing and toward such activities as volleyball, bicycling, sailing, and mountain climbing. In addition, greater attention might be paid to the technical competence of the performers rather than just the outcome of the contest. In projecting this notion to an extreme, Johnson fantasized:

> A football game of the future may consist of no more than four plays, each replayed over and over, dissected, and analyzed and criticized from a dozen different angles of slow-motion replays, with each player's performance judged and scored for its nearness to perfection (like figure skating). The winner of the game will not be the team that scores the most touchdowns but the team that executes its four plays perfectly. Such might be the content of Monday Night Football for a nation of intellectuals in the year 2000.[36]

At least two sociologists believe that there will be a reduction in the appeal of violence in sport. John Loy argued: "I don't see any great demand for blood sport in the future. The growth of sport in the United States actually parallels increasing controls over violence." And Fred Crawford noted: "Our value system is actually moving in the opposite direction and in the future I think that an Evel Knievel would have to prove that he is *not* going to be killed before they allow him to do it."[37]

In contrast, there is the possibility of continued or even increased violence in sports. There are those who believe, as William James once said, that "sports are the moral equivalent of war." More recently, scholars such as Konrad Lorenz have argued that sport provides a "cathartic discharge of aggressive urge," and, therefore, violence done under the auspices of sports will "keep the cap on social violence."[38] Similarily, Elias and Dunning have proposed that the meaning of sport may be in the "quest for excitement in an unexciting society," and vigorous and violent sport may serve as a restoration of tension and excitement.[39] One of the executives of an NHL team believes that violent sports meet the needs of a future society:

> I think the sports that will claim the big on-site crowds are the violent sports, where there is the chance of injury. People who enjoy that kind of sport won't be able to get the true experience without being on the site to see the blood, hear the smack of the fist on the head or witness the crash of an automobile. . . . I think hockey and football will be more violent in the year 2000 because we may be such a sedentary society that we need some release for our emotions.[40]

The popularity of such sports as football, hockey, boxing, and auto racing validates the current public interest in violent sports. The public image projected through TV commercials and specials about these sports promotes the idea of violence, although the escalating violent nature of these games may have reached its peak as lawsuits in hockey brought against aggressors and increasing penalties by commissioners of pro football and hockey show signs of controlling the violence of these sports.[41]

The recent movie *Rollerball* satirizes the ultimate incarnation of sport. It postulates a society of the future in which war has been abolished by a world government of paternalistic corporations. The society demands a war substitute, and this is provided by a deadly sport called Rollerball, a game in which the dead and maimed are posted on the scoreboard along with the score. A fantasy that will never come to pass? Perhaps, but it remains to be seen whether a "knowledge society" will opt for intelligent sports or for violent sports.

Technosports or Ecosports?

The world of sports has made tremendous use of technology, and much in current sport is the product of technological innovation. But sport has also always had an affinity for the outdoors, the natural relationship between humanity and the environment. The type of sport that emerges from technological advances has sometimes been called "technosport," while the environmental relationship with sport has been referred to as "ecosport." Will one or the other become the dominant form of sports in the future? The answer is that each form will probably have its followers. A number of futurists agree that a dominant characteristic of our future will probably be pluralism, which will allow nearly everything to exist with nearly everything else.[42]

The Future of Technosport To a great extent, the emergence of superior athletic performance is a consequence of technological innovation. One of the prerequisites of a technological society is a pool of specialized experts who perform specialized, fragmented tasks. Assuming that sport continues to adopt the procedures and techniques of the technological society, the sports world will probably attempt to select personnel more deliberately and rationally. At perhaps the most futuristic extreme, this might take the form of "genetic engineering"—that is, breeding superior athletes—but this possibility is not likely within the next generation or so due to moral as well as biotechnical problems.

We may expect, however, that the deliberate selection of future athletes during their early childhood on the basis of their physical and psychological attributes will become a reality. Once the potential athletes have been identified, they will receive special training in preparation for their ultimate careers in athletics. Eastern European countries already have programs of this type fully underway, and their successes during the past two Olympiads are publicly attributed to these "early selection" procedures.[43] Talk of implementing similar programs in the United States has already begun.

The technological ethos will probably lead to increased specialization in sports. Two-platoon football, adopted in the 1940s, led the way in specialization of playing positions. Other sports have been gradually following suit. The recent adoption of the designated hitter rule by the American League signifies that baseball is moving toward specialization. Indeed, there has been talk of separate offensive and defensive teams in baseball—one group of players will serve as batters, a different group will play in the field.

Technosport will be evident in the playing arenas of the future. The domed stadiums at Houston, Detroit, New Orleans, and Seattle are miniature prototypes of the giant arenas on the drawing boards. These new edifices will be equipped with many spectacular accoutrements, from push-button vending machines at each seat to individual TV consoles for instant replays. In addition, according to Johnson, spectators "will be able to listen in to press-box scouts giving advice to the bench, to miked-and-wired conversations at the pitching mounds, to quarterbacks' calls in the huddle, to halftime pep talks."[44]

Because postindustrial society will be an information-based society, the computer will be a central object. Computers will be a staple for technosport, just as they will be for technoindustry. Coaches and athletes will be able to receive instant information on their own teams and opponents. The Dallas Cowboys have used computers for several years for the selection of athletes and as an aid in scouting opponents. Computer use will undoubtedly proliferate; Johnson predicts that "every sideline bench will have one to pop out sheets of probability tables to help call each play, each pitch, each infield shift."[45]

Computer simulation models will be used for everything from building a better mouse trap to supersonic aircraft design. Sport has already experimented with computer simulation, but this technique will be used more in the future. Several years ago, simulated boxing matches between former champions were tried by programming a computer with pertinent information such as "the punching power . . . general physical condition, stamina, power behind a left hook, power behind a straight right," with the computer then printing out a blow-by-blow account of various champions of the past matched against each other.[46] The more sophisticated computers of the future presumably could be used to simulate sports contests of all types.

The Future of Ecosport Ecosports involve natural play and unstructured games, usually out-of-doors, without boundaries, often without codified rules, and frequently emphasizing cooperation rather than competition, the struggle rather than the triumph. The main point of ecosport is to play, to enjoy, to exist. Some view this form of sport as a reaction not only to the technocorporate form of organization characteristic of our social institutions but also to the organized and corporate levels of sport described in chapter 1, where the outcome supersedes the process. Ecosport has its affinities with informal sport, where process—participating—has top priority.

The ecosport movement is well underway and is manifested in activities such as hiking, orienteering, rock climbing, scuba diving, rafting, sailing, hang gliding, skydiving, Frisbee throwing, and many others. Postindustrial society confronts us with a congested urban life-style—houses jammed tightly against each other, apartments stacked story on story, offices and factories made up of steel and concrete, and jobs forcing us to work around multitudes of our fellow human beings. Thus, many Americans yearn for the out-of-doors, away from the crush of people—the mountains, oceans, lakes, rivers, and the sky itself beckon. In the past decade, the number of Americans participating in ecosport activities has grown dramatically. Cross-country skiers increased from some 2,000 in 1964 to 500,000 in 1974. Hikers more than doubled in the past ten years, and now some 20 million persons hike. At the national parks, backpacking has increased 100 percent between 1967 and 1977. The number of mountaineers in Grand Teton National Park doubled between 1965 and 1972. Colleges and universities have begun to offer courses in scuba diving, sport parachuting, hang gliding, and many other nontraditional activities.[47]

Several of the oriental martial arts, such as aikido, karate, judo, and ti-kwon-do are offsprings of ecosport, since they do not require elaborate equipment and organization, and competition is not important to mastery of the arts (indeed, in aikido, competition is forbidden). The movements are frequently like a dance and the performers achieve a transcendent beauty in the whirling, throwing, kicking, and jumping common to these activities.

Ecosports may not attract the publicity of the technosports, and most of them certainly will not attract masses of spectators. But the essence of ecosports is participation, so the fanfare and hoopla associated with technosports will not be missed.

The American Economy

It is beyond the scope of this book to examine the U.S. economy in any detail; moreover, an earlier chapter was devoted to sport and the economy. Therefore, we will include only limited aspects of trends in the economic system.

The American economic system is a complex mixture of capitalism and socialism. A trend throughout this century has been steadily away from laissez-faire (virtually unregulated) capitalism and toward managerial capitalism and the adoption of many socialistic features, causing some observers to predict that capitalism will die out in the United States. This view is not shared by Daniel Bell, who said, "barring the breakdown of the political shell . . . the social forms of managerial capitalism—the corporate business enterprise, private decision on investment, the differential privileges based on control of property—are likely to remain for a long time.[48]

Given the enormous influence of the corporate rich and the tendency for most Americans to accept the present economic structure as proper, a commitment to capitalism will undoubtedly remain a pillar of American society. At the same time, there is increasing dissatisfaction on the part of many people concerning the privilege and power conferred on a select few under capitalism, there is increasing governmental control over certain aspects of the economy, i.e., a ceiling on wages imposed by President Nixon in 1971, as well as a general mood by many Americans that national priorities must be reordered to provide greater assistance to the average citizen, all of which point to a trend toward increased socialism.[49]

The future economy—barring nuclear holocaust, unforeseen energy problems, or other catastrophic events—will probably continue to go through its cycles of prosperity, recession, and prosperity. Kahn and Wiener have estimate an average annual growth rate of the gross national product from 3.5 up to 5.0 percent between now and the year 2000.[50]

Sport and the Economy

Professional spectator sport in the United States has grown at an unprecedented rate in the past 20 years, and it is now a sprawling multibillion-a-year industry that is clearly Big Business and in which "winning, losing, and playing the game, all count far less than counting the money,"[51] Talamini and Page have noted: "as it has emerged as a major part of mass entertainment, sport has become big business, marked by the principal features of such enterprise: long-range planning, large capital investment, such efficiency practices as cost accounting and market forecasting, and formalization of employee-management relationships."[52]

Professional sports franchise owners once generally had a deep emotional commitment to the sport and believed that the administration and financial operations were merely necessary adjuncts to owning a team. The current owners think primarily of maximizing profit through rational business procedures. The spectacle of sport is only a secondary consideration."[53] In this respect, Shecter has written:

> There is no other business in this country which operates so cynically to make enormous profits on the one hand, while demanding to be favored as a public service on the other. Municipalities are badgered out of valuable property, coerced into building multimillion- dollar stadiums with public funds only to be deserted by carpet-bagging owners who have found a new town to strip-mine.[54]

In the early 1950s, professional sports owners were beset with decreasing attendance and the prospect of failure until television rescued the industry. The importance of television and radio markets has been a salient factor in the growth and expansion of all professional sports, and at the present time, professional sports and television enjoy a reciprocal relationship. As one pro sports executive said, "If sports lost those [TV] revenues, we'd all go out of business."[55] Therefore, for professional sports to maintain their current entertainment status or continue to expand, they will have to depend on the benevolence of television. As long as the TV networks consider pro sports an asset—a moneymaker—sports will prosper, but should television executives decide that sports are not good business, the pro sports industry could crumble.

What could cause such a change of interest on the part of the TV networks? First, declining interest in televised sports, a real possibility, could force such a change. Hours scheduled for network sports increased from 679 in 1960 to nearly 1,500 in 1977, and with this increasing amount of televised coverage of sports, the prospect of TV saturation looms. Whether this will occur is problematic at the present, but if it does, there is little doubt that television will adapt to the changing viewer interests, perhaps at the expense of the sports industry. Another possibility is that technosport and/or ecosport innovations will reduce TV viewing. Finally, perhaps as professional sports turns into show business, the heavy monetary outlay will destroy the meaning, and, therefore, interest in the game. Signs indicate that this is already happening. John Sterling, a New York radio personality, has reported:

> Something has definitely happened to fans. There is an absence of love and loyalty. With it has come an anger and a new kind of violence. . . . The fan gets up every morning, shaves, earns a hard day's pay, and drags himself home. He watches and reads about athletes working maybe three to four days a week for six months a year at $100,000 plus. The athlete may deserve what he's getting, but it doesn't matter. The constant exposure has made fans aware that this is not sports, that there aren't any sports heroes anymore.[56]

Again, if and when these trends unfold, pro sports will suffer as television reduces its expenditures for sports.

One of the most dynamic economic dimensions of pro sports is player salaries and conditions of employment. Million-dollar contracts are becoming almost commonplace; the top athletes are earning more in a year than many Americans will make in a lifetime. However, pro athletes did not create the high salary structure. Rampant inflation over the past decade, competing conferences, such as the AFL, ABA, World Football League, and World Hockey League, and increased TV revenues for the owners are three of the main factors in escalating player salaries.

Another factor is the recent abolishment of the "reserve clause" and its variations. Until very recently, the standard pro contract bound the athlete for one year and gave his employer a reservation on his services for the next year. The rules provided that if the athlete refused to sign a new contract—which would include a built-in "reserve clause" for still another year—the employer could renew the old one with all its terms for a period of one year. The club owners contended that the terms renewed included another reserve clause that could be exercised a year later, when there would be still another reserve clause, and so on throughout the player's career. Unless he was sold to another team, the athlete was bound to the original one—in essence, the athlete either accepted the owner's salary terms or he found a new way of making a living. Variations in some sports allowed the athlete to play a year without a signed contract—"play out his option"—and he then became a "free agent." However, if he were then signed by another team, that team had to compensate his previous team in some way (usually decided by the commissioner of the sport). Thus, the option arrangement was merely an elaborate fiction by which athletes appeared free to better themselves.

A series of judicial rulings, out-of-court settlements, and arbitrators' decisions have struck down the reserve clause and its variations, and has changed the one-sided relationship between owner and athlete, permitting athletes to play out their contract and then become free to negotiate a new contract with a team of their choice (twenty-four major leaguers fell into this category at the end of the 1976 season). The net effect is that athletes have been able to secure some very lucrative pacts, and pro salaries, at least for the few who have negotiated as free agents, have risen considerably.[57]

Most professional team owners are very disturbed by this new turn of events because they believe that in a completely open market, where athletes can pick and choose where to play, the wealthiest owners will be able to hire the best athletes, thus dominating the sport, and ultimately driving out the others. Unless labor contracts are developed between player unions and the owners to regulate free agency status in some way, we will have an opportunity to see whether the owners' predictions are correct. Actually, both owners and athletes are aware of the need for a system that maintains order and competitive balance, and some compromise arrangements have already been negotiated between the owners and the player unions. Economist Roger Noll has predicted: "In the long run pro games will appear much as they have, except that players will be making much of the money that once went to owners."[58]

Intercollegiate Athletics

Professional sports is not limited to privately owned sports franchises. "Big time" collegiate sports constitute a professional industry in every sense of the word. The eleven football bowls that climaxed the 1976 football season paid the twenty-two teams involved (or their conferences) a total of $9.8 million—an average of nearly half a million dollars each. Many of the top colleges spend over $3 million a year on sports and as much as $700,000 on athletic scholarships alone. The NCAA contract with ABC in 1976 called for $18 million to be paid to the NCAA and individual colleges.[59] These "big time" collegiate programs are every bit as dependent on economic considerations as pro sports franchises, and as television goes, so will go these collegiate programs.

Even with the bonanza of TV money, intercollegiate athletic programs have had increasing problems in recent years. The major problem is money, or lack of it. Growth in attendance—ticket sales are the main source of revenue—has drastically slowed, as competition, both from the professional sports and other distractions, has increased. Meanwhile, inflation has taken a brutal toll on athletic budgets of many colleges. One college president said, "Intercollegiate athletics across the nation are in financial difficulty. The inflationary spiral of increasing costs is having a devastating effect."[60] Adding an eleventh game to the traditional ten-game football schedule, permitting freshmen to play on varsity teams, expanding play-off schedules in basketball and bowl games in football, limiting the size of coaching staffs and de-emphasizing or dropping "nonrevenue" sports have all been recently adopted economic measures to add revenue or reduce expenses in intercollegiate athletics.

But still all is not well on the campuses. For example, many state-supported universities receive substantial support for collegiate athletics from tax funds, and there is growing public opposition to this. Legislatures are weighing the athletic appropriations against, for example, faculty salaries and state aid for disadvantaged students; other educational considerations are being weighed, including more spending for community colleges and expansion of vocational education. Also, needs are being considered in other fields, such as mental health, welfare, law enforcement and general administrattion of government. As one state legislator said: "It is one thing to have intercollegiate athletics on an amateur basis but it is another thing to spend money to buy a team to beat another college which is also spending taxpayer money to buy a team."[61]

The revenue-generating resources of most collegiate athletic departments appear to be fully exploited without any readily available sources of new revenue, but still the programs operate in the red, for the most part. In an effort to resolve the depressed economic situation in which athletic departments find themselves, the NCAA held a convention in August, 1975, to develop money-saving policies for the institutions. Frank Deford reported: "The results of the meeting were dubious. . . . The accomplishments were predictable and conservative. The substantive issues were never joined."[62] Recommended changes have not received full support, and, indeed, have resulted in several law suits when they have been implemented. Moreover, dissatisfaction with the NCAA by the major universities has resulted in threats to bolt the NCAA and create a "super conference," an overall governing body for the top college teams in the country. Basically, the super conference idea is concerned with money, big-time football and basketball money.[63]

What does the future hold for intercollegiate athletics? A polarization is possible whereby a few major universities sponsor a "professional-entertainment" type of athletic program, while most of the other colleges return to an amateur approach in which teams are student-run and in which the coaches coach as an avocation. More than one hundred colleges have dropped football within the past two decades, while other colleges have adopted student-centered programs as recreational outlets.[64]

Secondary School Athletics

The 1970s have not been prosperous years for secondary school athletics either. Inflation, the increasing reluctance of taxpayers to support education, and the hesitancy of many state legislatures to raise taxes have combined to force many school systems to curtail or even abolish some of their sports programs. In a period of austerity, school administrators invariably look to the extracurricular activities as a source of revenue savings, and since athletics is typically the most expensive extracurricular function, it is an obvious target.

This issue first surfaced in the early 1970s, when Philadelphia's school board, faced with an immense deficit in its budget, voted to discontinue all extracurricular activities, including athletics.[65] While the board's action was later reversed, the trend has continued throughout the decade, and school systems in San Francisco and Denver have seriously considered abolishing athletics. In each case, so far, money has come forth to maintain the sports programs. But if financial difficulties continue to plague the public schools, modifications, or even abolishment of the sports programs, will probably occur. There is serious talk in some communities of having the municipal recreation department assume the sponsorship of sports programs for all age groups and of phasing sports out of the school entirely.

Gambling and Sports

With the enormous increase in interest in spectator sports over the past two decades, there has been a corresponding explosion in gambling on sports. Recently, pollster Louis Harris reported that "almost one in four football fans in the country . . . report they 'regularly bet on pro football games.' "[66] Bookies and betting syndicates handle an estimated $15 billion a year.[67] As a result, gambling now stands as a major U.S. industry. There are several reasons for this increase in betting: weakening of the social stigma against betting, more extensive and sophisticated communications systems for transacting the bets, and many more sports events on which bookmakers will take bets. But perhaps the most important reason is that it is managed and manipulated by a national crime syndicate. Indeed, gambling experts have estimated that for every dollar bet legally, five to seven dollars are wagered illegally.[68] As Norman Levy, head of the rackets bureau of the New York district attorney's office for suburban Nassau County, told the *Wall Street Journal:*

> The purpose of the crime syndicate—its very reason for existence—is to run and protect bookmaking. Gambling money finances all of the gangs' other enterprises and they are

extremely jealous of it. There may be a barber somewhere who takes a few dollars a day in bets without the gangs' knowing it, but if the word gets out, he won't do it for long.[69]

Because its schedule offers the most games, major league baseball is estimated to lead in bets handled each year, but pro basketball is not far behind, and pro football generates by far the most action. Football is perhaps the best example of a perfect marriage of sports, gambling, and television. The game itself is perfectly suited for the medium, and the use of point spreads equalizes teams enough to make all games competitive from a betting standpoint. So, armchair sports fans regularly combine watching and betting, with results that have been quite satisfactory for all concerned.

The legalization of gambling and the use of the profits as a source of income to help support sport organizations and state and federal governments has been proposed in a number of states in recent years. In the early 1960s, outside of Nevada, state-sanctioned gambling was almost entirely confined to track betting. Today, over 40 states have some form of legalized gambling, and the kinds are growing. Legislation to permit new and expanded types of wagering—from jai alai to dog racing—is pending in over 30 states.[70] Delaware recently became the first state to start a football lottery; it's called Touchdown. It takes into account the point spread between opposing teams, just as the bookies do. This form of wagering can make the most lackluster game exciting for those who have money on it. It has been predicted that legalized gambling on all sports is in the near future. Bill Veeck, owner of the Chicago White Sox, said: "There will be off-park betting . . . and eventually there will be mutuals in our stadiums."[71]

In general, those who foresee legalized betting argue that people are always going to bet on games, but at the present time, since most sports wagering is done illegally, the bookies and crime syndicates are the major beneficiaries, which is not in the public good. If betting is legalized, a percentage of the exchange could go back into the sport itself and/or to state and federal governments. "Not only could the economy of sports be revitalized, gambling might add enthusiasm to spectatorship in general," according to Johnson.[72] Moreover, it is argued that legalized betting would eliminate, or at least greatly reduce, illegal gambling activities and, thus, put many bookies and underworld characters out of business.

Given the economic crisis in sports and in government, the prospect of the enormous windfall that could be generated from legalized betting is very attractive to some sports owners and politicians. But there are also fears about legalizing betting on sports events. Some feel that it will stimulate excessive betting; the fear is that persons will bet money that they can ill afford to lose. Second, there is the prospect of corruption of athletes and coaches. The "point-shaving" scandals of collegiate basketball come easily to mind. And what of the heightened pressures on athletes resulting from the inevitable dropped pass, strike out, or missed free-throw? A suspicion that perhaps the action was deliberate and charges of "dumping" the game or "shaving points" will follow. However, Edwards has predicted that these fears of legalized betting will not prevent its development:

> Nonetheless, it should be expected that coming decades will bring the legalization of OTB [off-track betting]. The economic crises faced today by the nation's educational institutions and by the sports world, coupled with a growing dissatisfaction with skyrocketing property and sales taxes will likely make OTB inevitable.[73]

Future Trends for Minorities in American Sport

Recent Liberation Movements

While official documents of American government imply equality for all and the national folklore proclaims that this is a land of "equal opportunity" and "freedom for all," the mosaic of different social categories and the unequal power, resources, and prestige of different groups has resulted in discrimination against numerous American minorities throughout our history. Historically, the largest social groups to suffer the most persistent and consistent discrimination have been blacks and females. Conditions for both of these groups are changing rapidly because of "liberation movements" over the past two decades, first by blacks and more recently by women. Federal and state laws now make it illegal to discriminate on the basis of race, nationality, religion, and sex in most private and public sectors of American life. Several of the most significant of these laws are recent, and implementation is just now getting underway.

Laws prohibiting discrimination do not, of course, directly affect attitudes, so while blacks and women must be given equal consideration for employment when a job is open, there is no guarantee that they will get equal treatment because prejudiced persons can still subtly manipulate organizational arrangements to their own ends.[74] In other words, saying that members of a minority cannot be kept out does not mean that they will get in. Nevertheless, the change toward greater equality for minority groups and women is one of the most salient trends at the present, and it will undoubtedly continue in the coming years.

Minorities and Sports

There is no question that organized sports, from the youth programs to the professional level, have made great strides toward equalitarianism in the past decade, but the goal has not yet been achieved. In chapter 8, we described how overt discrimination against blacks, such as denying them access to sports teams, has been gradually eliminated but that discrimination remains in subtler forms, such as excluding them from central positions and leadership positions on teams. But even these subtle forms of discrimination are giving way, as more and more blacks are gaining access to positions of prestige, power, and leadership within sports. There are still sports in which there are few blacks, such as hockey, swimming, golf, tennis, and gymnastics, to name a few, but each year blacks make new inroads into more and more sports. Moreover, they are now taking their rightful place among teammates in central positions in football and baseball, and they now hold coaching and management positions in a number of sports programs. The future of blacks in American sports appears to be quite secure.

Title IX of the Educational Amendments of 1972 was the single most significant legislation for females in sports. The legislation has helped to reduce discriminatory practices in educational institutions, and female participation in interscholastic sports has increased from 294,000 in 1971 to 1,645,000 in 1976.[75] It has also brought with it the potential for forcing women into the male model of interscholastic and intercollegiate athletics, a model which has been riddled with conflict and corruption, a model that often dehumanizes the athletes.

The women's sports movement and the passage of Title IX was accompanied by an excitement and an anticipation that women were not only going to move into greater sport involvement but that they were going to develop a new model for interscholastic and intercollegiate sports, a model that would contain the best features of the male programs but that would exclude the worst features, a model that would add new, exciting, humane features. It was reasoned that for more than 50 years, women had the opportunity to observe, sometimes with horror, as male high school and collegiate athletics, in the process of fostering healthful, educational sports, entered the field of professional entertainment. For the male coaches, marketplace criteria became virtually the only measure of coaching ability, and "win" became synonymous with success and "lose" became associated with failure. Prestige in coaching was based on won-loss records. This system tended to emphasize the treatment of athletes for what they could do for the coach—win—rather than the treatment of athletes based on what coaches could do for the personal-social growth of athletes as persons.

Surely, many thought, leaders of female interschool sports programs would, in their wisdom and with their years of observing male sports programs, advance an alternative educational sports model. It appears, though, that the main thrust of the women's sports movement is to mirror the men's programs in virtually every respect in the name of equal opportunity. For example, a new recruiting game has developed in the past few years on many campuses, and an estimated 5,000 to 8,000 female athletic scholarships are available and the number is growing every week.[76] While there are some differences between the agencies that control men's and women's intercollegiate athletic programs (National Collegiate Athletic Association and the National Association of Intercollegiate Athletics control men's programs and the Association of Intercollegiate Athletics for Women control women's) with regard to regulations governing recruiting and awarding of scholarships, the scholarships are based solely on athletic ability by both groups. The opportunity to observe the strengths and weaknesses of male programs over the past half century and to select the strengths for emulation and reject the weaknesses as unwanted seems to have been sacrificed in the quest for equality, regardless of the consequences. Women coaches and athletes appear to be fighting merely to be exploited on an equal basis with their male counterparts.

It may be too much to expect that women will be able to develop an ideal sports model in the first decade of intensive interschool sports involvement. But we can hope for better things because an alternative sports structure that stresses cooperation, participation, expressiveness, fun, intrinsic motivation, and self-actualization would be a refreshing substitute for the current emphasis in interscholastic and intercollegiate programs.

Notwithstanding the mandate of Title IX and regardless of the sports model that women adopt, male athletic programs still receive a far greater share of the total athletic budgets, and female athletes are not receiving equal treatment in many educational institutions.[77] Maybe complete equality in the programs will never be achieved, but laws, changes in values, and what Herbert Gans calls the "equalitarian revolution" will combine to promote greater opportunities in sports for those girls and women who wish to participate. But eventually schools may have to restructure the "business" of interschool sports altogether, to provide *all* students with fair and equal opportunities to participate in recreational and organized sports.

Many concrete gains in women's professional sports have spurred hopes for further advances. Increased sponsorship has meant the richest tournaments ever for women in golf, tennis, and bowling. Prize money on the Ladies Professional Golf Association tour has soared from a few thousand dollars to over $2.5 million in the past decade. Breakthroughs for professional female athletes proliferate. In 1976, a 10-team women's professional softball league was formed, and professional tennis player, Chris Evert, was selected as Sportswoman of the Year by *Sports Illustrated,* the first time this publication awarded the honor solely to a female; moreover, six other finalists in the voting were women.[78] In 1977, Janet Guthrie became the first woman to race in the Indianapolis 500.

Trends in American Values

The Equality Revolution

The decades of the 1960s and '70s have witnessed a great deal of social unrest, and protests ranging from demonstrations to violent uprisings have been a part of the American scene. Instead of protests directed against social and working conditions, as had frequently been the case in the past, the protests of the '60s and early '70s were typically aimed at the pervasive inequalities remaining in American life. As we noted in a previous section, the two major demands for greater equality have come from blacks and women, and black liberation and women's liberation have been the two most salient social movements of the past 15 years. These two movements have spawned several others, and Gans has predicted that America will face a demand for more equality—a demand that will become widespread enough to be described as an "equality revolution."[79] He has argued that Americans are demanding more autonomy, democracy, and greater participation in their places of work and their government. All these demands, according to Gans, add up to a quest for more control over one's life, and requiring the reduction of economic, political, and social inequalities that now prevent people from determining their own destinies.[80] Supporting this notion, James Murphy has noted: "There are increasing demands on all American institutions to participate more actively in social, cultural, and political programs to improve the *quality* of life."[81]

Other Value Changes

In addition to a greater valuation of equality, other traditional American values are being modified. In chapter 3, we identified the dominant values salient in American society. These mainstream values include an entire constellation of beliefs involving the importance of individual personal effort and accomplishment in defining one's status and worth, both economic and social, and one's relation to social institutions. Success through personal achievement, achievement through hard work, continued striving, deferred gratification, and competition were identified as core values. These values are buttressed by a belief in progress, especially material progress, and an emphasis on conformity to group and institutional norms. We cautioned that the pluralistic orientation and diversity of American society precludes the universal holding of values and that values are not always consistent with behavior. However, despite inconsistencies and ambiguities, there are certain basic values that underlie social relationships and institutional life in America.

These values, like other aspects of American life, have been undergoing rather radical change; indeed, it could be argued that we are on the verge of a cultural crisis that will ultimately revolutionize American values and institutions. The roots of this movement reside in a strong disillusionment with traditional values. The essence of these changes is related to new ideas about humanity and methods of interpersonal relations. There is a more optimistic, democratic, humanistic conception of human nature. These newly emerging values have already had an impact on social institutions, such as education, politics, and religion, and they are making their presence felt in the business world.

The actual beginnings of a social movement are always difficult to trace, and so it is with the contemporary changes in value orientation. The roots of the contemporary ideology may be found in the thinking of such persons as Thoreau, but only in the 1960s did the ideas appear on a large-scale. The massive youth movement thrust on America in the mid-1960s was the most significant force opposing traditional American values and priorities, so the redefinition of values was supported primarily by the youth culture, and in the early 1970s became popularly known as the "counterculture." More recently, the themes running through the counterculture position have been subsumed under what is termed "humanism," and social groups across a broad spectrum of American society—hippies, blacks, American Indians, even professional groups, such as lawyers and teachers—have played a part in the emerging ideology of values. The key concerns of humanism are with liberation and expressiveness, and Spates and Levin have articulately contrasted these new values with the old:

> The middle-class value system, by its overbearing emphasis on all forms of achievement (which produces persons enslaved to a "rat race"), rational behavior (which qualified anything not specifically directed toward the attainment of sanctioned goals as being "irrational"), and economic endeavor (which produces a system of continually expanding "exploitation") has now developed to the point where it continually denies or represses other, more vital, human values and needs: the most important of these being the need of each person to develop his own humanness through his own personalized life style; the need to be personally and meaningfully concerned for the welfare of others; the need to be affective, loving and trustful with other people; and the need for self-realization and spiritual development through religious and/or philosophical inquiry.[82]

The vanguard of the new humanism was the youth groups who protested the denial of freedom of speech and assembly on university campuses, the continuation of the Vietnam War, and the insensitivity of educational, religious, political, and business organizations to the personal human needs of those whom they were intended to serve. The early protests took the form of sit-ins, boycotts, confrontations, and even riots. As the Vietnam War came to an end, blatant discrimination attenuated, organizational conditions improved, the overt impact of the new humanism declined, but the modification in values and priorities has continued in more subtle forms, not directly through activism, but indirectly through changes in the consciousness of great numbers of people. Moreover, it has ceased to be only a youth movement, as mainstream America has begun to accept some of the values originally espoused by the youth groups. The result has been a shift in consciousness—personal goals, value priorities, ways of perceiving and ordering the world outside the person. Thus, the value themes running through the humanistic ideology have been subsumed under what may be viewed as a more humane, expressive, and equalitarian pattern of values. These values promise to produce profound changes in the objective social, political, and economic structures of American society, if they in fact become internalized by a substantial portion of American people. According to James Murphy:

> The American cultural revolution: appears to be characterized by the need to move away from fragmented, standardized, and uniform approaches to living toward more destandardized, decentralized, and diverse ways of living. There seems to be a growing emphasis on self fulfillment and self actualization through the fusion of work and leisure. . . . Such a humanistic or anti-industrial form of relationships attempts to view the whole person and the interrelationships of the human experience.[83]

We are not suggesting that the revolution in values envisioned by the counter-culturalists in the early 1970s has actually occurred—the "greening of America" did not happen—at least not yet—but there has been a trend towards new value priorities among many persons.

Trends in Sports Values

Since many traditional American values have come under attack in the past decade, and since sport is a social institution, it is no surprise that it too has been affected by the emerging values. Institutions are based on traditional norms and values, and are, therefore, vulnerable to the effects of value changes among significant segments of the society. In accord with the new equalitarian emphasis, athletes are demanding changes in sports at all levels; they are especially pressing for greater participation in the decisions that affect their athletic lives and for a greater responsiveness on the part of coaches and athletic administrators. They have also pressed for more autonomy, for the freedom to be what they want to be and to choose how they will live. The rigid authoritarian structure of traditional sport is being repudiated to allow more humane qualities to emerge. Though the mass media have paid most attention to the more radical advocates of athletic change, equality and democracy are sought by an ever-increasing number of liberal and even conservative athletes.

Several years ago, in his book, *The Athletic Revolution,* Jack Scott claimed that "athletics as we enter the 1970s is facing its most severe crisis."[84] Student dissent on campuses throughout the United States, the black liberation movement, and the emerging counterculturalists all had an impact on school sports during the late 1960s, leading to numerous clashes between athletes and those who controlled athletic programs—coaches, athletic directors, principals, school boards, the NCAA, etc. Until the late 1960s, critics of sports had come almost entirely from outside the athletic community—university professors and presidents, journalists—but between 1968 and 1973 attacks on organized sports began to come from within and were indigenous to the sports world. More than one hundred colleges and universities experienced athletic disturbances of some kind between 1967 and 1971, and Jack Scott prophesied that an athletic revolution was mounting.[85] Rehberg and Cohen concurred:

> The past decade has seen a historically unprecedented rise of political and social awareness, involvement, and protest among athletes, in the United States. The actions of black trackmen in 1968, the writings of former football pro, Dave Meggysey, and the protests of athletes from Berkeley to the Ivy League are selected instances of the growing political and social conscience of those who participate in sports, whether it be on the playing fields of the local high school or the stadium of the metropolis.[86]

Although a few professional and collegiate athletes have recently called for a change toward greater humanism within the structure and functioning of sport, they have been a minority, and it is unlikely that athletes will be in the vanguard of social change in the future. The world of sports generates a fundamental acceptance of the established norms and values. American physical education faculties and coaches—the two most powerful socializing agents of the sports world—are conservative and usually accept traditional values.[87] The influence of these persons on the social consciousness of athletes is bound to be powerful, and, in fact, during the volatile years of the late 1960s and early 1970s, athletes did not take part in the various protest movements; indeed, "during the times of campus turmoil, it was common to see various references in the mass and underground media to the identification of athletic groups with antagonism toward radical or liberal social action. . . . To be a "jock" on many campuses is to be regarded as out of step with the new politics, the humanism, and the youth culture."[88]

But while athletes as a group may not catalyze much change, nevertheless, they are members of their own youth culture, a culture that is pressing for greater humanism. Professional and collegiate athletes, today, are more likely to challenge the management establishment. The old athlete tended to confront authority less frequently than the current athletes. This attitude is displayed by the recent strikes by both pro baseball and football athletes. Current directions in sport suggest increased equalitarianism, democracy, and humanism, but these are trends that will only occur gradually, and only as they become a part of the American society.

To the extent that societal values change in the future, sport will undoubtedly be a battleground for the clash of colliding value orientations. Thus, it may be useful to review some of the criticisms of traditional sports and examine alternatives advanced by the "new humanism."

The most critical problem in contemporary sport, according to its critics, is its "corporate" nature. In this respect, sport merely reflects one larger societal trend, namely, the trend toward mass society, technocracy, rationalization, and away from community and primary relations. Leadership practices traditionally employed by coaches in American sport are firmly based on bureaucratic organizational ideology.

Corporate organization and traditional values have made sport an element for the promotion of these systems. There is a societal acceptance of the priority of institutions and organizations and a belief that individuals must subordinate their will to them. Consider the recent public outcry against Portland Trailblazer basketball player, Bill Walton, because he was outspoken in defense of personal freedoms and individual rights. Meanwhile, this same public has reacted to violations of NCAA policies and unethical coaching behavior with a shoulder shrug and a response that "after all one has to win to have a successful program, and besides everyone else is doing it." The organization must be served. The moral stance of the University of Minnesota basketball coach, Bill Musselman, who left the university for the pros just before the NCAA levied formal charges at him, is symptomatic of this value orientation. When he was asked how he felt about the charges against Minnesota, Musselman replied, "I'm not a member of the university staff anymore, so my conscience is clear."[89]

Corporate sport is an authoritarian, product-oriented enterprise. The basic concern is with athletes subjecting themselves to the will of the coach, whose primary concern often becomes winning athletic contests. Jack Scott succinctly summarized this sports ethic:

> The American ethic sustains a product-oriented system that has turned out an excellent product. The system has demanded and received the sacrifices and hard work of many dedicated men. One of the ways excellence in sport has been developed is by believing winning isn't everything, it's the only thing. Not surprising, the opponent at best is viewed as an obstacle and at worst as an enemy to be overcome in achieving victory. Needless to say, the entire struggle takes place in a rigidly authoritarian structure. Taken together, these elements form the traditional ethic of American sport.[90]

The days of unquestioning support for traditional athletic priorities and practices have begun to be replaced by a new set of standards, many of which are related to changes occurring in the larger society. The emerging humanistic value orientation renounces much of the traditional ideas about leadership. The new ideology of leadership emphasizes an empathetic identification with others, an openness to experience, and a commitment to help develop a positive self-concept in others. In this approach, the leader is viewed as one who releases, facilitates, and assists, not one who manipulates, coerces, and appeases to "shape" appropriate behavior. Leadership behavior is flexible and open to revision in view of long-term issues and consequences rather than focused on immediate goals and short-term, current consequences. Finally, the leader's task is perceived as beginning from a clear acceptance of other persons and their current ways of thinking, feeling, and behaving. These ideas of leadership are already being successfully implemented in the world of business.[91] The importance of these viewpoints for sport is particularly related to coaching and management methods, which most effectively facilitate these goals.

With regard to school sports programs, the new value perspective starts with the basic premise that the sports are for the athletes, not the coaches. Accordingly, coaches will be expected to become resource persons rather than authority figures. They will be expected to help make individuals of their players—self-reliant athletes able to make their own decisions and responsible for their own actions.[92] Individual expression will be placed above group conformity, self-discipline above authority, independence above dependence.

Acknowledging that contemporary society requires self-directing, responsible adults capable of independent behavior, the new humanism believes that athletes learn to control themselves through opportunities to make their own decisions. Self-discipline comes from practice in disciplining oneself, not by being obedient to others' demands. If choice is a basic fact of human existence, then athletes should be given the opportunity to make choices. They cannot be expected to develop the ability to choose widely if all choices are made for them. Freedom is the opportunity for self-control. The traditional sports pattern of training for self-discipline is exposed as hypocritical by former All-Pro football player, George Sauer, who said:

> It's interesting to go back and listen to the people on the high school level talk about sport programs and how they develop a kid's self-discipline and responsibility. I think the giveaway, that most of this stuff being preached on the lower levels is a lie, is when you get to college and professional levels, the coaches still treat you as an adolescent. They know damn well that you were never given a chance to become responsible or self-disciplined. Even in the pros you are told when to go to bed, when to turn your lights off, when to wake up, when to eat, and what to eat.[93]

Those who have been exposed to traditional sports practices the longest—the pros—are ironically held in virtual bondage. Note that "freedom" for the players has been a key issue in the negotiations between professional players association and the owners. That is, professional athletes are asking for freedom from curfews, fines, and other silly rules. These are grown men asking for their individual freedom, not adolescents!

The new ideology argues that if sports helps build character, as coaches claim, then players need a chance to make their own choices. In a way, character is composed of the choices one makes. So, if coaches make all the decisions, they are stunting character development, not nurturing it. Moreover, coaches are not military leaders, fashion designers, or judges, and the preoccupation with rigid standards of personal appearance, political beliefs, interests, and private behavior is misplaced. Coaches should realize that clothes, hair cuts, and personal likes and dislikes are not valid criteria for judging the societal worth of people.[94]

Many high school and college coaches and physical educators have already experimented with interesting humanistic approaches. High school football coach,

George Davis, permits his players to vote on the starting line-up before each game. What does the vote achieve? According to Davis:

> It takes the problems of discipline and responsibility and puts them where they belong, with the players. The coach becomes a teacher, what he is being paid to do, a resource unit. My job is to teach, to help athletes reach a level of independence. At any level this is how democracy works and why it succeeds.[95]

Coaches in other sports have experimented with giving athletes a greater share in team decision making. Jerry Krause, basketball coach at Eastern Washington University, has introduced what he calls "a complete program of shared responsibility," which begins with the players establishing the basic rules regarding training, conduct, and appearance, and how they will be enforced. The players vote each week on the starting line-up for the upcoming games. The basketball coaches at the University of Northern Colorado also employ the vote, and they agree that this technique gets players involved and committed to responsibility and self-discipline.

These are only a few examples of coaches who are turning to techniques of coaching congruent with humanistic ideology. There are undoubtedly hundreds of others who are using innovative methods with the same purpose. A growing literature in physical education describes such humanistic practices.[96]

Another target of the new humanism is the "winning is the only thing" ideology. Traditional sports programs have emphasized the utilitarian and competitive aspects of athletic activities rather than their spontaneity and fun. The new value perspective is repelled by the extreme competitiveness of the Lombardian ethic ("winning isn't everything, it's the only thing"). The new humanism "looks at the myopic product-orientation of the Lombardian ethic and demands that we stop being so product oriented and focus instead on the process."[97] With the rise of increasingly organized and codified sports, the characteristics of the enterprise has closely modeled traditional American value perspectives, with an emphasis on intensive competition and the idea that we must struggle against others to get ahead. If one has to be ruthless and unscrupulous in accomplishing the objective, well too bad, the important thing was beating the opposition.

Cooperation replaces competition, process replaces the emphasis on product in the new view. While cooperation is given preference over competition, competition is not rejected in a sport context. Within the limits of sport, competition is accepted for its own pleasure. But, except when carried out as fun, there is a belief that intensive competition has the danger of generating conditional self-worth, role-specific relationships, excellence based on competitive merit, self as a means, and subjection of self to external control.[98] In this respect, William Spady has said:

> The athlete needs to accept a new set of standards for evaluating his engagement by replacing winning (which is inherently extrinsic and comparative) with a more intrinsic

> form of reward for competent performance in its own right. Until then, he will remain dependent on dominating others for gratification and on the limitations of conditional self-acceptance which it implies.[99]

Perhaps Leonard best summarizes this perspective with regard to competition. He says, "There is nothing wrong with competition in the proper perspective. Like a little salt, it adds zest to the game and to life itself. But when the seasoning is mistaken for the substance, only sickness can follow. Similarly, when winning becomes 'the only thing,' it can lead only to eventual emptiness and anomie."[100] One does not have to search far for examples of the consequences of the "win at any cost" mentality: basketball scandals of the 1950s and '60s; recruiting violations in the recent years by Michigan State, Oklahoma, Southwest Louisiana, Long Beach State, Minnesota, and numerous others; the 1973 Ohio State-Minnesota basketball game, and even the Watergate scandal in politics.

Invariably, when anyone criticizes the "winning is the only thing" ethic, traditionalists smugly counter with: "If winning is not important, why keep score?" For the humanist, it is not a question of whether a score is kept; of course, a score is kept in sport competition, and it is important. It measures one's quality of performance; it is a means of ascertaining the skill displayed during competition. But it is not an end; it is a means! The end in sport is the joy, exhilaration, and self-fulfillment that one obtains from movement; it is the display of skill, the challenge of matching tactical wits with competitors, and the sensual feelings that arise in competition. Using victory as the only end, the goal of sport competition is too limiting, confining, too shallow, too short- sighted for humanism. One reason winning is so overvalued in America is that we haven't been taught to enjoy the doing—the process—of whatever we are attempting.

Miller suggests that individuals who play games to win are actually not "playing" games, they are working at them. Thus, they do not win anything of value. In a program that is end-oriented, the game is for winning; in the means-oriented program, the game is the game—it is for playing. In the first program, the player cannot be happy unless he is winning, is successful; whereas, in the second, if one is satisfied and happy with the play, he is successful. In this second program, the expressive nature of sport is emphasized, and, as Ingham and Loy have said: "sport needs no other justification than that it provides a setting for sociability and fun."[101] So, it goes without saying that the "winning is the only thing" ethic is rejected by humanism because it so severely restricts the rich potential for human growth, development of a positive self-concept, and opportunity for peak experiences through competition.

A growing trend in youth sports programs is the structuring of play to foster participation, cooperation, and sportsmanship rather than competitiveness. For example, such rules as every child who registers is assigned to a team and every child on a team plays in every game are becoming more common. Some leagues feature no-win games, where no points are awarded for a win or loss and no records are kept of league standings or of leading scorers. Those who conduct such programs claim that the youngsters seem to have a lot of fun.[102]

The humanistic orientation basically attempts to recreate community and primary relationships, and reject the institutionalization and technocratization of many facets of contemporary society. It has, therefore, been associated with a rejection of conventional sport activities—those kinds of sports that consist of passive recreation, consumption, and spectatorship. In its place is active sport for fun, fitness, and recreation. Team sports taught in the typical school and youth athletic programs practically demand that adults turn into spectators. But the humanistic orientation is being manifested in several trends. Throughout the United States, physical education programs are finally breaking the traditional mold of offering the same limited set of team sports year after year. Individual and lifetime sports are increasingly being taught. In one California high school, 45 courses, ranging from yoga to yachting, from rock climbing to kayaking, are being offered.[103]

Today's college students are increasingly rejecting the traditional offerings of campus intramural programs and demanding other, more innovative programs with greater potential to satisfy their immediate and long-term needs. As a consequence, intramural programs have had to adjust and adopt new and different activities, to de-emphasize championships, to eliminate trophies, to sponsor sports clubs, to include equal sports opportunities for women, and to provide for more "open recreation" facility use.[104] At one college, all consideration for extrinsic rewards has been abolished; no point systems nor awards of any kind are employed. The importance of victory has been de-emphasized by doing away with championships and limiting protests to on-the-spot, right-or-wrong final decisions by activity supervisors. Any combination of undergraduate and graduate students and faculty may form teams. Women may participate on teams that compete in the men's division.[105] At Emporia State University in Kansas, the intramural department has been abolished, at least in name, and replaced by a "play factory" that sponsors a wide variety of games and sports emphasizing fun, spontaneity, and participation and de-emphasizing such traditional customs as trophies, championships, and eligibility requirements.[106]

People of all ages are beginning to experiment with unusual physical activity forms for fun and excitement. In his book *The Ultimate Athlete,* George Leonard describes a variety of "new games" that emphasize cooperation rather than competition and that can be played by large groups and all ages. According to him, these games provide new modes for expressing the spirit of sports.[107] If the humanistic orientation should eventually prevail, we might see the demise of corporate and highly organized sports and a return of informal sports.

Edwards has claimed that "America would gain far more than she would lose through initiation of . . . an alternative sport structure . . . in which the younger generation can be socialized with values stressing cooperation rather than antagonism, participation and self-actualization rather than confrontation and domination."[108] But how incongruous can the actual institution of sport become in relation to the dominant social norms and values? Edwards says that "without some massive change in the value prescriptions of American society as a whole—and not merely among some significant segments thereof—the institution of sport cannot alter its structure and functioning and still survive."[109]

Summary

This is an era of rapid change in American Society, and sport, like other social institutions, is undergoing changes in its forms and content—changes related to those of the larger society. We have identified a number of the more salient social changes and speculated about how current and future trends may affect sport.

Trends in population suggest that rapid expansion of professional sports is over and that these organizations may soon organize along regional rather than single-city lines. Industrialization and technology have reduced the average workweek, but other conditions have arisen that have nullified the actual leisure time of adults. The leisure time available in the future may be used either in sports of a more "intellectual" nature or of a more violent nature; moreover, technological developments will probably result in "technosport" forms, while those who rebel against technology will engage in "ecosports."

Professional and big-time intercollegiate sports have become successful business enterprises, mainly because of TV involvement. Their future rests heavily upon the directions dictated by television. Gambling will probably become more prominent in sports, as it becomes legalized.

Minorities have gained greater opportunities in the world of sport, and the equalitarian trend suggests that sports opportunities will increase in the years ahead for all persons.

Changes in value orientations over the past decade have emphasized equality and humanism, and the world of sport has experienced protest and even violent revolt, as athletes have rebelled against traditional authoritarian leadership and the "win" ethic. A new humanism has begun to make inroads into sport, and innovative programs and practices are beginning to incorporate this new value-orientation.

Notes

1. George Orwell, *1984* (New York: Harcourt, Brace, and World, 1949); Alvin Toffler, *Future Shock* (New York: Bantam Books, 1970).
2. See Herman Kahn and Anthony J. Wiener, *The Year 2000* (New York: Macmillan, 1967); Herman Kahn, William Brown, and Leon Martel, *The Next 200 Years: A Scenario for America and the World* (New York: William Morrow, 1976); both books are from the Hudson Institute's continuing study of the future.
3. William O. Johnson, "From Here to 2000," *Sports Illustrated* 41 (December 23, 1974), p. 73.
4. *Statistical Abstracts of the United States (1975).* (Washington, D.C.: U.S. Government Printing Office, 1976), p. 6.
5. Ibid, pp. 6-7. Also see William Paterson, *Population* (New York: Macmillan, 1975); and "The Graying of America," *Newsweek* (February 28, 1977), pp. 50-53.
6. Kahn and Wiener, *The Year 2000,* pp. 61-62.
7. Johnson, "From Here to 2000," p. 73.
8. Peter Gammons, "A Matter of Dollars and Sense," *Sports Illustrated* 45 (November 29, 1976), pp. 28-29.
9. Quoted in Randall Poe, "The Angry Fan," *Harpers* (November, 1975), p. 90.
10. *Statistical Abstracts (1975),* p. 6.
11. Kahn and Wiener, *The Year 2000,* p. 175.
12. Arnold M. Rose and Caroline B. Rose, *Sociology—The Study of Human Relations,* 3rd ed. (New York: Alfred A. Knopf, 1969), p. 515.
13. Daniel Bell, *The Coming of Post-Industrial Society* (New York: Basic Books, 1973), p. 14.
14. Ibid.
15. Theodore Roszak, *The Making of a Counter Culture* (Garden City, N.Y.: Doubleday, 1969), pp. 5, 8.
16. Gresham M. Sykes, *Social Problems in America* (Glenview, Ill.: Scott, Foresman, 1971), p. 30.
17. *Statistical Abstracts of the United States (1971).* (Washington, D.C.: U.S. Government Printing Office, 1972), table 727.
18. Joseph Bensman and Arthur Vidich, *The New American Society* (Chicago: Quadrangle Books, 1971) pp. 21-25.
19. See David Riesman, Nathan Glazer, and Denny Reuel, *The Lonely Crowd* (New Haven, Conn.: Yale University Press, 1950); William H. Whyte, Jr., *The Organization Man* (Garden City: Anchor Books, 1956); Vance Parkard, *The Status Seekers* (New York: David McKay, 1959); Charles A. Reich, *The Greening of America* (New York: Random House, 1970); Theodore Roszak, *Politics and Transcendence in Post-Industrial Society* (New York: Anchor Books, 1973).
20. Roszak, *The Making of a Counter Culture,* p. 4.
21. Thomas M. Kando, *Leisure and Popular Culture in Transition* (St. Louis: C.V. Mosby, 1975), p. 67. For an alternative point of view about the consequences of technology, see Samuel C. Florman, "In Praise of Technology," *Harpers Magazine* (November, 1975), pp. 53-72.
22. See Jaques Ellul, *The Technological Society* (New York: Alfred A. Knopf, 1964); Herbert Marcuse, *One-Dimensional Man: Studies in the Ideology of Advanced Industrial Society* (Boston: Beacon Press, 1964); Toffler, *Future Shock;* Anton C. Zijderveld, *The Abstract Society—A Cultural Analysis of Our Time* (New York: Anchor Books, 1971); Reich, *The Greening of America.*
23. Kahn and Wiener, *The Year 2000,* pp. 175, 195.
24. *Statistical Abstracts (1975),* p. 352.
25. Sebastian de Grazia, *Of Time, Work and Leisure* (New York: Anchor Books, 1964), p. 83.
26. John Kenneth Galbraith, *The New Industrial State* (Boston: Houghton Mifflin, 1967), pp. 363-364. In "The 40-Hour Week is a Myth for Millions," *U.S. News and World Report* (May 24, 1976), pp. 76-77, evidence is cited to show that professional, technical, managerial, and administrative positions have the largest proportions of people working 50 or more hours per week.

27. Sebastian de Grazia, *Of Time, Work and Leisure* (New York: Twentieth Century Fund, 1962), p. 87.
28. de Grazia, *Of Time, Work and Leisure* (1964), p. 5.
29. Erwin K. Scheuch, "The Time Budget Interview," in *The Use of Time-Daily Activities of Urban and Suburban Populations in Twelve Countries,* ed. Alexander Szalai (The Hague, Netherlands: Mouton, 1972), p. 77.
30. Rolf Meyersohn, "Television and the Best of Leisure," *PUBLIC Opinion Quarterly* 1 (1968), pp. 111-112.
31. Kando, *Leisure and Popular Culture in Transition,* p. 84.
32. Quoted in Ursula Vils, "Four-day Work Week—Boom or Bust," *Los Angeles Times* (June, 1971), p. 18.
33. Kando, *Leisure and Popular Culture in Transition,* p. 96.
34. Ibid., p. 97.
35. Bell, *The Coming of Post-Industrial Society,* pp. 212, 221.
36. Johnson, "From Here to 2000," p. 74.
37. Ibid., pp. 74, 77.
38. Konrad Lorenz, *On Aggression* (New York: Harcourt, Brace, and World, 1963), p. 280.
39. Norbert Elias and Eric Dunning, "The Quest for Excitement in Unexciting Societies," in *The Cross-Cultural Analysis of Sport and Games,* ed. Gunther Luschen (Champaign, Ill.: Stipes, 1970), pp. 31-51.
40. Quoted in Johnson, "From Here to 2000," p. 77.
41. J.D. Reed, "Week of Disgrace on the Ice," *Sports Illustrated* 44 (April 26, 1976), pp. 22-25. Even a sport such as baseball has experienced an escalation of violent outbreaks in recent years; see Larry Keith, "Yankee Doodle Series Was a Dandy," *Sports Illustrated* 44 (May 31, 1976), pp. 18-21.
42. Toffler, *Future Shock.*
43. For a discussion of the East German sports system, see Jerry Kirshenbaum, "Assembly Line for Champions," *Sports Illustrated* 45 (July 12, 1976), pp. 56-65. For a discussion of the Soviet Union's system, see "The Soviet Union Views Sports Strength as a Power Tool," *The New York Times* (Olympic section, July 11, 1976), p. 15.
44. Johnson, "From Here to 2000," p. 80.
45. Ibid.
46. D. Daniel, "The Ring Computer Series Gets Top Rating With Few Booboos," *The Ring* 48 (February, 1968), p. 18.
47. Wayne Wilson, "Social Discontent and the Growth of Wilderness Sport in America: 1965-1974," *Quest* 27 (Winter, 1977), pp. 54-60; Peter Donnelly, "Vertigo in America: A Social Comment," *Quest* 27 (Winter, 1977), pp. 106-113.
48. Bell, *The Coming of Post-Industrial Society,* p. 372. For an alternative interpretation of the future of capitalism, see Douglas F. Dowd, "Structural Instability," *Society* (January- February, 1974), pp. 15-18, and Robert Heilbroner, "The Human Prospect," *New York Review of Books* (January 24, 1974), pp. 21-34.
49. For a fuller discussion of these trends, see D. Stanley Eitzen, *Social Structure and Social Problems* (Boston: Allyn and Bacon, 1974), pp. 373-377.
50. Kahn and Wiener, *The Year 2000,* p. 167.
51. Leonard Shecter, *The Jocks* (New York: Paperback Library, 1970), p. 8.
52. John T. Talamini and Charles H. Page, *Sport and Society: An Anthology* (Boston: Little, Brown, 1973), p. 27.
53. R. Terry Furst, "Social Change and the Commercialization of Professional Sports," *International Review of the Sociology of Sport* 6 (1971), p. 161. For a discussion of the financial difficulties of professional team owners, see "The Sports Boom in Going Bust," *Forbes* (February 15, 1975), pp. 24-28; for a discussion of the profitability of professional sports, see Roger G. Noll, "The U.S. Team Sports Industry: An Introduction," in *Government and the Sports Business* ed. Roger G. Noll (Washington, D.C.: The Brookings Institution, 1974), pp. 10-29.
54. Schecter, *The Jocks,* p. 8.
55. "The Sports Boom in Going Bust," *Forbes,* p. 25.
56. Quoted in Randell Poe, "The Angry Fan," p. 94.

57. "Baseball's Money Madness," *Newsweek* (June 28, 1976), pp. 62-66; Peter Gammons, "Cashing in Their Tickets," *Sports Illustrated* 45 (November 22, 1976), pp. 82, 87; Ron Reid, "He's Free, But Not Cheap," *Sports Illustrated* 44 (June 7, 1976), pp. 69-72; Larry Keith, "After the Free-For-All Was Over," *Sports Illustrated* 45 (December 13, 1976), pp. 29-34.
58. Quoted in "Baseball's Money Madness," *Newsweek* (June 28, 1976), p. 66.
59. Joseph Durso, "The Sports Factory" (New York: Quadrangle, 1975); "Saturday's Hard-Pressed Heroes," *Forbes* (November, 1976), pp. 77-80; "Behind Those Saturday Football Telecasts," *Chronicle of Higher Education* (October 20, 1975), p. 3.
60. "Inflation Takes Toll on Organized Athletic Programs," *Greeley Tribune* (April 24, 1975), p. 4-A.
61. *Rocky Mountain News* (June 3, 1973), p. 76; (June 16, 1973), p. 20.
62. Frank Deford, "Same Old Song: 'Football uber Alles,' " *Sports Illustrated* 43 (August 25, 1975), p. 40; see also "Holding the Line on Sports Budgets," *Chronicle of Higher Education* (September 2, 1975), p. 8.
63. "Scorecard," *Sports Illustrated* 45 (September 27, 1976), p. 9.
64. "The Budget Crunch and City U. Sports." *New York Times* (June 20, 1976), p. 25; "At Hampshire the Players Are in Charge," *New York Times* (October 17, 1976), p. 25; John Underwood, "Beating Their Brains Out," *Sports Illustrated* 44 (May 26, 1976), pp. 63-96; George H. Hanford, *An Inquiry Into the Need for and Feasibility of Intercollegiate Sports* (Washington, D.C.: American Council on Education, 1974), appendix I.
65. Ron Fimrite, "We Expect Them to Storm the Gates," *Sports Illustrated* 35 (September 6, 1971), pp. 20-25.
66. Louis Harris, "One in Four Bets on Football Games," *Rocky Mountain News* (January 1, 1973), p. 10.
67. "The Betting Bowl," *Time* (January 14, 1974), p. 35.
68. Ibid.
69. Quoted in Bernie Parrish, *They Call It a Game* (New York: New American Library, 1971), p. 186.
70. "Gambling Goes Legit," *Time* (December 6, 1976), p. 54.
71. Quoted in Johnson, "From Here to 2000," p. 77.
72. Ibid.
73. Harry Edwards, *Sociology of Sport,* (Homewood, Ill.: Dorsey, 1973), p. 360.
74. See Jerome H. Skolnick, *The Politics of Protest, A Staff Report to the National Commission on the Causes and Prevention of Violence* (New York: Ballantine Books, 1969); California Survey Research Center, Charles Y. Glock, Robert Wuthnow, J. Piliavin, and M. Spencer, *Adolescent Prejudice* (New York: Harper and Row, 1975).
75. "Sports Participation Survey" (National Federation of State High School Associations, December 3, 1976), p. 1.
76. "College Recruiting of Women Athletes is Increasing Rapidly," *New York Times* (November 14, 1976), p. S10.
77. Candonce Lyle Hogan, "Fair Shake or Shakesdown?" *WomenSports* 3 (September, 1976), pp. 50-54.
78. Sarah Pileggi, "Sportswoman of the Year," *Sports Illustrated* 45 (December 20, 1976), pp. 42-50.
79. Herbert J. Gans, *More Equality* (New York: Pantheon Books, 1973), p. 8.
80. Ibid., pp. 7-32. Also see Ronald Inglehart, *The Silent Revolution: Changing Values and Political Styles* (Princeton, N.J.: Princeton University Press, 1977).
81. James J. Murphy, "Leisure Dialetic: An Exploration of Socio-Cultural Processes and Changing American National Character," *Journal of Physical Education and Recreation* 47 (October, 1976), p. 32.
82. J.L. Spates and J. Levin, "Beats, Hippies, the Hip Generation, and the American Middle Class: An Analysis of Values," *International Social Science Journal* 24 (No. 2, 1972), p. 330. For a comprehensive treatment of this movement, see John F. Glass and John R. Staude, eds., *Humanistic Society* (Pacific Palisades, Calif.: Goodyear, 1972).
83. Murphy, "Leisure Dialectic," p. 1.
84. Jack Scott, *The Athletic Revolution* (New York: The Free Press, 1971), p. v.

85. Ibid.
86. Richard A. Rehberg and Michael Cohen, "Political Attitudes and Participation in Extracurricular Activities," in *Social Problems in Athletics,* ed. Daniel M. Landers (Urbana: University of Illinois Press, 1976), p. 201.
87. George H. Sage, "The Coach as Management: Organizational Leadership in American Sport," *Quest* 19 (January, 1973), pp. 35-40; George H. Sage, "Socialization of Coaches: Antecedents to Coaches' Beliefs and Behaviors," *78th Proceedings of the National College Physical Education Association for Men* (1975), pp. 124-132.
88. Brian M. Petrie, "The Athletic Group as an Emerging Deviant Subculture," in *Social Problems in Athletics,* p. 225.
89. "Scorecard," *Sports Illustrated* 43 (August 11, 1975), p. 8.
90. Jack Scott, "Sport and the Radical Ethic," *Quest* 19 (January, 1973), p. 73.
91. See Edward M. Glaser, *Productivity Gains Through Worklife Improvement* (New York: The Psychological Corporation, 1976); H. Meltzer and Frederic R. Wickert, *Humanizing Organizational Behavior* (Springfield, Ill.: Charles C. Thomas, 1976).
92. N.T. Laughlin, "Existentialism, Education, and Sport," in *Issues in Physical Education and Sport,* ed. G.H. McGlynn (Palo Alto, Calif.: National Press Books, 1974), pp. 169-180.
93. "The Souring of George Sauer," *Intellectual Digest* 2 (December, 1971, p. 55.
94. M. Mosston and R. Mueller, "Mission, Omission, and Submission in Physical Education," in *Issues in Physical Education and Sport,* pp. 97-106.
95. Neil Amdur, *The Fifth Down* (New York: Coward, McCann, and Geoghegan, 1971), p. 218.
96. See Donald R. Hellison, *Humanistic Physical Education* (Englewood Cliffs, N.J.: Prentice-Hall, 1973); Helen M. Heitman and Marian E. Kneer, *Physical Education Instructional Techniques: An Individualized Humanistic Approach* (Englewood Cliffs, N.J.: Prentice-Hall, 1976). Frank Rosato, "The Group Process: Some Suggestions for Athletics," *The Physical Educator* 31 (May, 1974), pp. 87-89; Vern Dickinson, "Modernization and Sport," *Quest* 24 (Summer, 1975), pp. 48-58.
97. Scott, "Sport and the Radical Ethic," p. 73.
98. Walter E. Schafer, "Sport and Youth Counter-Culture: Contrasting Socialization Themes," in *Social Problems in Athletics,* pp. 183-200.
99. William G. Spady, "A Commentary on Sport and the New Left," in *Social Problems in Athletics,* p. 221.
100. George B. Leonard, "Winning Isn't Everything, It's Nothing,"*Intellectual Digest* 4 (October, 1973), p. 47.
101. D.L. Miller, *Gods and Games: Toward a Theology of Play* (New York: World, 1970); Alan G. Ingham and John W. Loy, Jr. "The Social System of Sport: A Humanistic Perspective," *Quest* 19 (January, 1973), p. 7.
102. Thomas Tutko and William Bruns, *Winning is Everything and Other American Myths,* (New York: Macmillan, 1976). pp. 222-229.
103. Jim Kaplan, "Jim Dandy Gym," *Sports Illustrated* 45 (November 15, 1976), pp. 44-46; see also Lee Johnson, "Coed Sports in High School," *Journal of Physical Education and Recreation* 48 (January, 1977), pp. 23-25.
104. "Coeducational Recreational Activities," *Journal of Physical Education and Recreation* 47 (May, 1976), pp. 16-21; Lloyd A. Heywood and Rodney B. Warnick, "Campus Recreation: The Intramural Revolution," *Journal of Physical Education and Recreation* 47 (October, 1976), pp. 52-54.
105. Francis M. Rokosz, "Looking Good," *Journal of Physical Education and Recreation* 48 (February, 1977), p. 31.
106. Bil Gilbert, "Imagine Going to School to Learn to Play," *Sports Illustrated* 43 (October 13, 1975), pp. 84-87.
107. George Leonard, *The Ultimate Athlete* (New York: Viking Press, 1975).
108. Harry Edwards, "Desegregating Sexist Sport," *Intellectual Digest* 3 (November, 1972), p. 83.
109. Edwards, *Sociology of Sport,* p. 354.

Index

Aaron, Hank, 63, 73, 150, 269
Abdul-Jabbar, Kareem, 191, 240, 244
Adelbert College, 156
Africa, 146
Agnew, Spiro, 150-53, 161
Alabama, University of, 96, 238
Albany, New York, 31
Ali, Muhammad, 73, 162, 218
Alienation, 5, 65
All-American Conference, 191
Allen, George, 67, 120
Alumni, 94, 122
Amateur Athletic Union (AAU), 15, 19, 143, 161, 197
Amateur, ideal, 197
Amateur Softball Association, 45
American Academy of Arts and Science, 289
American Basketball Association, 19, 137, 143, 175, 177, 190, 192, 202, 303
American Broadcasting Company (ABC), 147, 161, 181, 281, 304
American Football League, 175, 303
American history, sport and religion, 116-20
American Physical Education Association, 272
American Sabbath Union, 118
American Way of Life, 75
Amherst College, 51
Angell, Robert, 195, 203
Ann Arbor, Michigan, 135
Antitrust, 15
  laws, 188, 191
  and Monopoly Subcommittee, 169, 189
Apollo, 115
Arizona, University of, 252
Arledge, Roone, 181
Armer, J.M., 83
Armstrong, Jack, 269
Arnheim, D.D., 271
Arnold, Ernest Herman, 272
Arond, Henry, 228
Asch, Solomon, 6
Ashe, Arthur, 146, 229
Ashford, Emmit, 236
Association of Intercollegiate Athletics for Women (AIAW), 280, 309
Astrand, Per-Olof, 273
Astrodome, 111
Athletes
  collegiate
    big-time, 201, 304
    farm teams for pros, 201
    political attitudes, 155, 159-62
  high school, 306
    compared to nonathletes, 6, 83, 90-91
    educational expectations, 221
    income expectations, 221
    popularity of, 151
  professional, 176-77
    average length of career, 227
    salaries, 196, 226
Athletes in Action, 123-24, 127
Athletic Institute, 84
Athletic Revolution, 75, 100
Athletic Revolution, The, 313
Athletic scholarship, 177, 198, 199, 220, 280, 304
Atkinson, George, 53
Atlantic Coast Conference (ACC), 175
Attendance, 16-17, 30
Attles, Al, 240
Auburn, University of, 238
Australia, Melbourne, 144
Automobile racing, 33-34
Autry, Gene, 193
Axthelm, Pete, 212, 241

Babe Ruth Baseball, 78
Baltimore, 34
Banham, Charles, 90
Barry, Rick, 190, 269
Baseball Register, The, 251
Bayh, Birch, 150
Baylor, Don, 193
Baylor, Elgin, 190, 240
Becker, Judy, 136
Beecher, Catherine, 51
Bell, Daniel, 292, 297, 301
Bench, Johnny, 196
Bend, Emil, 220
Benedict, Ruth, 69
Benton, Illinois, 84
Berger, Bennett, 83
Berger, Peter, 5
Bette, John R., 31-32
Biddie Basketball, 278
Big Eight, 161
Biology, 1
Black Athlete, The, 241
Black colleges, 238
Blacks
  baseball, 239
  basketball, 239
  boxing, 237
  dominance in sport, 243-44

football, 239
physical differences, 240
political activism, 238-39
Blalock, Herbert, 8, 245
Blaming the victim, 63
Blue-collar fans, 214
Boston, 43
Boston Celtics, 180, 190
"Boswash," 290
Boyle, Robert H., 16, 25
Bradley, Bill, 149
Brailsford, Dennis, 116
Brazil, 148
Brigham Young University, 154, 239
Brooklyn College, 100
Brooklyn Dodgers, 183, 190
Broom, Leonard, 263
Broverman, I.K., 276
Brower, Jonathan J., 246-48, 254
Brown, Jim, 150
Brown, Roscoe C., Jr., 229
Bryant, Paul "Bear," 96, 120, 150
Buffalo, University of, 147, 161
Bulgaria, 145
Burdge, Rabel J., 210
Bureaucratization, 13-15, 46-49, 65-66, 292-93
Burke, Michael, 180, 183
Byers, Walter, 161, 201

California, 130, 145
California Angels, 290
Calvin, John, 116, 125-26
Camp, Walter, 237
Campus Crusade for Christ, 123
Canada, 133, 144
Canadian Athletes, and political attitudes, 160
Canadian League, 188
Capellanus, Andreas, 264
Capitalism, 125-28
Carey, Bob, 173
Carlos, John, 146
Carnegie Commission on Higher Education, 157
Carnegie Foundation, 94
Carnegie Tech University, 98, 156
Carpentier, George, 36
Carter, Jimmy, 150
Castro, Premier, 145
Catholic Youth Organization (CYO), 119, 121
Catlett, Gale, 135
Centrality, 8
and stacking, 245-50
Chamberlain, Wilt, 63, 73, 150, 190, 201, 240
Character building through sport, 90-91
Charisma, 8
Charleston, South Carolina, 43
Chataway, Christopher, 143, 198
Cheating, 94-95
Chemistry, 5
Chicago, 42-43
Chicago Bears, 45
Chicago Times-Herald, 33
Chicago, University of, 52
Chicago White Sox, 307
Child-rearing, 265-66
China
Peoples Republic, 144
sport in, 153
Republic of, 144
"Chipitts," 290
Chivalric ideal, 265
Christian Church, early,
sexism, 264
sport, 115-16
Chrysler Corporation, 171
Cincinnati, University of, 135
Civil War, 28, 31, 235, 237
Clarenback, Kathryn, 93
Cleaver, Eldridge, 53
Cleveland Cavaliers, 291
Coaches
authoritarian, 13, 48-49, 73-74, 97-98, 103
political attitudes of, 74, 155-59
pressure on, 67, 98, 100
Coffey, Margaret, 265
Cohen, Michael, 314
Coleman, James, 81-85, 87
Collett, Wayne, 148
Collins, Doug, 190
Colonial period, sport in, 25-27
Colorado Rockies, 290
Colorado, University of, 225
Columbia Broadcasting System, 180, 181, 269
Columbia University, 37
Law school, 188
Commission of the Year 2000, 289
Committee on the Medical Aspects of Sports, 273
Communication innovations and sport
radio, 36
telegraph, 34-36
telephone, 35-36
television, 37
trans-atlantic cable, 35
Communists, 145, 146

Competition
  in American society, 14
  characteristic of sport, 18
  value of, 60-63, 66-71
Conformity, value of, 65, 73-74
Connie Mack Baseball, 278
Contraculture, 82
Corrigan, M., 268
Counterculture, 84
Counts, Mel, 240
Cousins, Norman, 99
Cousy, Bob, 91
Cozens, Frederick, 33, 37, 39, 120
Crain, Mike, 122
Cratsley, Melvin, 98, 156
Crawford, Fred, 298
Csonka, Larry, 194
Cub Scouts, 62
Cuba, 145
Cultural agents, 3
Culture, 2, 8-12, 66
Culture pattern model, 70-71
Currie, Elliott, 12
Czechoslovakia, 145

Dallas Cowboys, 124, 127, 217, 291, 300
Daniels, Bob, 135
Dartmouth College, 223
Davis, Angela, 154
Davis, George, 103, 317
de Beauvoir, Simone, 274
Declaration of Independence, 12, 265
Deford, Frank, III, 124-25, 243, 244, 305
de Grazia, Sebastian, 212, 294-96
Dehumanization of athletes, 96-97
Delaware, 307
Delaware, University of, 156
Democracy in sport, 103-4
Demolition derby, 214, 215
Dempsey, Jack, 29, 36
Denver Nuggets, 121, 137
Des Moines, Iowa, 41
Detroit Lions, 175
Detroit News, 36
DeWitt Clinton High School, 89
Discrimination in sports
  against blacks, 235-56
  against females, 261-84
Division of Girl's and Women's Sports (DGWS), 272
Dominick, J.R., 268

Drive discharge model, 70-71
Drugs
  amphetamines, 95
  anabolic steroids, 95
Dubois, Paul E., 251
Duguin, Mary E., 267
Dulles, Foster Rhea, 26-28
Dunning, Eric, 298

Eastern Washington University, 317
Eastman Kodak, 39
Ecology crisis, 63
Economy
  American, 301-8
  institution, 10
  and sport, 302-8
Ecosports, 299-301, 303, 320
Edison, Thomas A., 40
Education
  benefits of sport for, 79-80, 101
  dysfunction of sport for, 79, 90-92
  enculturation through sport, 92-93
  functions of, 92-93
  as an institution, 10
  positive consequences of sport for, 86-90
  role of sport in secondary, 80-86
  sports problem in higher education, 93-100
  sports problem in secondary education, 100-4
Education Policies Commission for Schools, 101-3
Edwards, Harry, 11, 104, 111, 127-28, 153, 159, 161, 229, 240, 242, 246, 249, 308, 320
Eitzen, D. Stanley, 7, 84-85, 248-50, 253-55
Elder, Lee, 236, 243
Electricity, impact on sport, 40-41
Elias, Norbert, 298
El Salvador, 144
Emancipation Proclamation, 235, 237
Embry, Wayne, 236, 253
Emerson, Ralph Waldo, 51, 117
Emporia State University, 319
Emprise, 178
Engineering, 5
Equal Opportunity Commission, 251
Equality revolution, 310-11
Erasmus, Desiderius, 115
Erdelyl, G.J., 273
Erving, Julius, 190
Eskimo, 114
Ethos, 60
Etzioni, Amitai, 62
Evangelism through sport, 122-24

Evans, Tom, 181
Evert, Chris, 150, 310
Ewing, William, 26
Executive Committee of the Women's Division of the National Amateur Athletic Federation, 272

Failure, 91
Family
  influence of, 2-3
  institution of, 10
Farrington, Steven R., 253
Fellowship of Christian Athletes, 123-25
Felshin, Jan, 283
Female athletes
  attitudes toward, 275-77
  role models, 269-70
  in sport, 261-83
Feminine ideology, 261
Feminine Mystique, The, 282
Fetishes, 134-35
Field, Cyrus, 35
Finkel, Hank, 240
Firestone, Shulamith, 282
Fleming, Peggy, 150
Flood, Curt, 192
Florida, University of, 238
Football, 28-29, 34
  Monday night, 173, 187, 298
  professional, 174
Football Register, 247, 250-51
Forbes, 180, 226
Ford, Gerald, 149-50
Ford, Henry, 33
Ford Motor Company, 33, 68
Ford, William C., 175
Fort Riley, Kansas, 146-47
Foster, Stephen, 27
Four-day workweek, 296-97
Foyt, A.J., 171
Franchise shifts, 72
Free enterprise system, 4
Freedom from social constraints, 3, 5
Friedan, Betty, 282
Friedenberg, Edgar, 90
Friedrichs, Robert W., 13
Future Shock, 289

Galbraith, John Kenneth, 294
Gallup poll, 16
Gambling, 50, 116-17, 178
  legalized betting, 179
  and sports, 306
Gans, Herbert, 310-11
Garagiola, Joe, 150
Garman, E.W., 276
Gender identity, 266
General Motors, 46, 180
Georgetown University, 252
Georgia, University of, 238
Germany
  East, 145
  West, 145
Gibson, Althea, 63, 236
Gibson, Josh, 236
Gilbert, Bil, 18, 171, 227, 261, 269
Gipp, George, 111
Gmelch, George, 133, 135-36
Goal attainment research, 7-8
Golden State Warriors, 290
Goodhart, Phillip, 143
Goodyear, Charles, 41
Goodyear Wingfoots, 45
Gouldner, Alvin, 7
Graham, Billy, 122
Gratification, deferred, 64
Greeks, ancient
  and sexism, 263-64
  sport and religion, 114-15
Green, James, 240
Green Bay Packers, 45, 66, 68, 75, 121, 135, 190
Green Bay, Wisconsin, 45
Green Berets, 147
Gregory, C. Jane, 133-34
Grich, Bobby, 193
Griffith, Patricia, 275
Groups
  characteristics of, 1
  imperfect nature of, 4
  inertia of, 4
  as products of interaction, 4
Grusky, Oscar, 7-8, 245
Guthrie, Janet, 310

Habermas, J., 49
Hampshire College, 100
Harlem Globetrotters, 23, 236
Harper, William Rainey, 52
Harris, Dorothy, 271
Harris, H.A., 197
Harris, James, 236

Harris, Louis, 306
Harvard University, 28, 32, 35, 80, 252, 294
Hayes, Woody, 120, 125, 150
Hearst, William Randolph, 38
Hennessee, J.A., 268
Hill, Jesse, 60
Hitchcock, Edward, 51
Hitler, Adolph, 145
Hoch, Paul, 48
Hodges, Harold M., 210
Holmes, Oliver Wendell, 51, 117, 188
Holy Cross College, 161
Homer, 129
Honduras, 144
Hornsby, Roger, 236
Howe, Elias, 41
Hudson Institute, 289
Hughes, Thomas, 39
Humanism, and sport, 313-20
Humans, as puppets, 3-4
Hungarian revolt, 144
Hungary, 145
Hunter, Catfish, 193
Hypocrisy in sport, 95-96

Identity, 3
Illinois State University, 252
Immigrants, impact on sport, 49-50
Indiana Pacers, 137
Indianapolis 500, 178, 243, 310
Individuals, social nature of, 2-4
Industrialization, impact on sport, 27, 30, 41-45, 117
Ingham, Alan G., 318
Institute for Athletic Perfection, 123
Institute for the Future, 290
Institutions, 9-12, 47
  change of, 12
  conservative nature of, 11
  defined, 9-10
  inertia of, 11-12
  societal problems and institutions, 10-11
  sport as, 11, 14, 49, 111
Integration (cohesion) of groups, 8
Interaction, 1
  and formation of human groups, 4
  forms of, 8
Intercollegiate athletics
  authoritarian coaches, 97-98
  big business, 98-99
  cheating, 94-95
  dehumanization of athletes, 96-97
  history of, 28, 51-52
  hypocrisy in, 95-96
Internal combustion engine, impact on sport, 33-34
Internal Revenue Service, 62
International Olympic Committee, 19, 154, 198, 212
International Student Congress on Evangelism, 124
International Telephone and Telegraph, 62
Intramural sports, 101
Isenberg, Jerry, 147
Israeli, athletes, 154

Jackson, Reggie, 196
James, William, 298
Jeansonne, John, 91
Jim Crow laws, 235
Johnson, Jack, 236
Johnson, Norris R., 254
Johnson, William, 153, 174, 176, 289, 298, 300, 307
Jones, Bobby, 29
Jones, Frank, 84
Journalism, sports, 35, 38-39

Kahn, Herman, 290, 302
Kando, Thomas, 30, 293
Kansas City, 42
Kansas City Athletics, 175
Kansas State University, 97
Kansas, University of, 156
Kapp, Joe, 194
Kayser, B.D., 83
Kehoe, Jim, 198
Kellerman, Bob, 191, 192
Kemp, Jack, 149, 150
Kempton, Murray, 90
Kent State University, 87
Kentucky Derby, 178
Kentucky, University of, 97, 238
Khan, Genghis, 156
King, Billie Jean, 274, 281
Klafs, C.E., 271
Knickerbockers, 28
Knight, Bobby, 125
Koch, James V., 200
Kohlsaat, H.H., 33
Komisar, Lucy, 267
Koppett, Leonard, 291

Korbut, Olga, 197
Krause, Jerry, 317
Kuhn, Bowie, 253

Labor unions, 45
Ladies Professional Golf Association, 310
Lambert, Paul, 135
Landry, Tom, 150
Laver, Rod, 281
Lawrence, Kansas, 67
Leadership, 7-8
Lee, Mabel, 272
Leisure, 30, 43, 66, 119
Leonard, George, 318-19
Leonard, Wilbert M., 252
Levin, J., 312
Levy, Norman, 306
Lewis, Guy, 32, 51, 118
Lewis, Michael, 266
Liberation movements, 308
Lincoln, Abraham, 60
Lindsay, John, 184
Lipsyte, Robert, 270
Little League Baseball, 278
  and sex discrimination, 278-79
Locker room slogans, 67, 71, 74, 120
Lombardi, Vince, 54, 62, 66, 68, 74-75, 111, 120, 135
Lombardian ethic, 317
Long Beach State University, 95, 318
Long, Bob, 68
Lord's Day Alliance, 118
Lorenz, Konrad, 298
Los Angeles Coliseum, 215
Los Angeles Dodgers, 183
Los Angeles Lakers, 73, 190
Louisiana State University, 238
Louisville, Kentucky, 43
Loy, John W., 8, 222, 245-46, 298, 318
Lude, Mike, 87
Lueptow, L.B., 83
Luther, Martin, 116

MacArthur, Douglas, 71
Macauley, Thomas B., 116
McDonald, Henry, 236
McElvague, Joseph F., 8, 245
McGee, Reece, 3
McGinnis, George, 190
McGovern, George, 63, 150
Mack, Connie, 38
McNally, Dave, 193
McPherson, Barry, 248
Macro level, 8-12
Macy's Department Store, 44
Madison Square Garden, 40-41, 147
Magical practices, 129, 131-37
Malinowski, Bronislaw, 129, 131-32, 136
Managerial change, effects of, 7-8
Mandell, Richard, 145
Manning, William T., 119
Marbeto, Joseph A., Jr., 130-31
Marple, David P., 254
Marshall University, 135
Martin, Billy, 150
Maryland, University of, 175, 198
Masculinization of females, 262, 270-71
Massachusetts Institute of Technology, 100
Massengale, John D., 253
Materialism
  in American society, 14
  value of, 64, 72-73
Mathias, Bob, 149
Matthews, Vince, 148
Matza, David, 88
Mears, Ray, 74
Medicine
  as an institution, 11
Meggyesy, Dave, 155, 314
Merchant, Larry, 130
Mergers, 19
Merriwell, Frank, 39, 269
Meschery, Tom, 72-73, 102
Messersmith, Andy, 193
Metcalfe, Ralph, 149
Metheny, Eleanor, 274, 276
Meyersohn, Rolf, 296
Miami Dolphins, 174
Miami, Florida, 127
  Department of Publicity and Tourism, 178
Michener, James, 280
Michigan State University, 95, 225
Michigan, University of, 135, 150, 154, 198, 237, 318
Micro level, 6-8
Middle Ages, and sexism, 264
Miller, D.L., 318
Miller, Marvin, 193
Milwaukee Braves, 175, 183
Milwaukee Bucks, 253

Minnesota, University of, 95, 223, 315, 318
Mississippi State University, 238
Mississippi, University of, 238
Mitchell, Jack, 156
Mitchell, John, 63
Mizell, "Vinegar Bend," 149
Mobility escalator function of sport, 5, 7, 219-24
  myth of, 224-29
Molineaux, Tom, 236
Monopoly, 19, 45
Montague, Susan P., 72
Morais, Robert, 72
Morford, W.R., 48
Mormon Church, 154, 239
Morse, Samuel F.D., 34
Motion pictures and impact on sport, 40
Motley, Marion, 236
Motocross racing, 214
Murchison, Clint, 217
Murphy, James, 311
Murray, Jim, 94
Muscular Christianity Movement, 50-51, 118
Musselman, Bill, 315
Muybridge, Eadweard, 40

Namath, Joe, 60, 73, 226
Nastase, Ilie, 281
Natchez, Mississippi, 31
National anthem, 130, 146, 147, 148, 162
National Association of Basketball Coaches, 95, 202
National Association of Intercollegiate Athletics (NAIA), 309
National Baseball Congress, 45
National Basketball Association, 18-19, 143, 177, 180, 189, 190, 192, 202, 251, 253, 290-91
National Basketball Association Guide, 251
National Broadcasting Company (NBC), 175, 281
National Collegiate Athletic Association (NCAA), 15, 19, 63, 96, 123, 143, 161, 198, 199, 200, 203, 250, 252-53, 280, 304-5, 309, 313, 315
National Football League (NFL), 45, 67, 143, 150, 162, 169, 171, 173-74, 194, 251, 290-91
  player-management agreement, 176
  player salaries, 192
  Player's Association, 194
  playoffs, 191
  stadiums, 186
National Hockey League, 290, 298
National Industrial Basketball League, 45
National Organization of Women (NOW), 282
Nazi Olympics, The, 145
NCAA News, 161
Neilsen survey, 16
Nelson, David, 156
New England, 26, 33, 42, 116
New England Patriots, 194, 290
New Hampshire, 32
New Jersey, East Rutherford, 184
New Mexico, 114
New Orleans, Louisiana, 31, 43
New Orleans Superdome, 184, 185, 218
New York Athletic Club, 154, 239
New York Business Bureau, 178
New York City, 31, 40, 43, 81, 89, 119, 178, 179
  high schools, 160
  playgrounds, 241
  renovation of Yankee stadium, 183
New York City Council, 147
New York Convention and Business Bureau, 187
New York Giants, 190
New York Herald, 35, 38
New York Jets, 73, 194
New York Journal, 38
New York Knicks, 203
New York Mets, 162
New York Renaissance Pro basketball team, 236
New York Sun, 38
New York Times, 37, 148, 178, 252, 291
New York Tribune, 35
New York Yankees, 121, 178, 180, 181, 183, 187, 189, 190, 193
New Zealand, 154
Nicholson, J., 268
Nicklaus, Jack, 226, 269, 281
1984, 289
Nineteenth century, and growth of sport, 28
Nixon, Howard, 212
Nixon, Richard, 62, 149, 150, 302
Nobis, Tommy, 150
Noll, Roger, 180, 304
Norms, 8-9, 47
North Carolina State University, 94, 175
Notre Dame University, 29, 87, 122, 130

Oakland Athletics, 38
Oakland Raiders, 53
Of Time, Work, and Leisure, 295
Ogilvie, Bruce, 157
Ohio State University, 94, 203, 318

Oklahoma, University of, 95, 318
Okner, Benjamin A., 185, 187
Oldfield, Barney, 33
O'Leary, K.D., 266
Olsen, Jack, 241
Olympic Games
ancient, 115, 264
modern, 144-46, 198, 239, 241, 300
Oral Roberts University, 122, 127
Oregon State University, 161
Organization, power of, 15
Orr, Johnny, 135
Orwell, George, 289
Outing Publishing Company, 39
Owners
professional sports teams, 162, 179, 194, 244
relationship with athletes, 187-96
and taxes, 182
Oxford University, 35

Page, Charles, 47, 302
Paige, Satchel, 236
Palestinian guerrilla, 154
Palmer, Arnold, 177, 226, 281
Palmer, Jim, 196
Palmer, Mike, 290
Palooka, Joe, 269
Pan American Games, 145
Parrish, Bernie, 155, 184
Participation, 16-17, 29-30, 79
Pascal, Anthony M., 251, 254
Patten, Gilbert, 39
Paul, the Apostle, 115
Pele, 148
Peoria Caterpillers, 45
Perrin, Ethel, 272
Petrie, Brian M., 133-34, 160
Philadelphia, 35
Phillips, John C., 242
Phillips Petroleum, 68
Phillips 66ers, 45
Photography and impact on sport, 39-40
Physical education
introduced into schools, 51
political attitudes of teachers of, 157
Physical fitness
and lower-class status, 210
and upper-class status, 210
Pitch, Hit, and Throw Contest, 68
Pittsburgh, 36
Pittsburgh Pirates, 178
Pittsburgh, University of, 97
Plessner, H., 49
Plumb, Joseph Charles, Jr., 147
Plutarch, 264
Poland, 145
Polity, 10
Pollution, 4, 63
Polyphasic Values Inventory, 157
Pop Warner Football, 278
Population
composition, 290
growth, 289-91
and sport, 290-91
Portland Trailblazers, 315
Poseidon, 115
Postindustrial society, 291-92
and leisure activities, 294-301
reaction against, 293-94
sports of, 297-301
Prayer, 129-31
Prescott, Arizona, 123
President's Council on Youth Fitness, 210
Pretty Prairie (Kansas) High School, 6
Primitive societies, sport and religion, 114
Princeton University, 32, 37
Pro Athletes Outreach, 123
Professional athlete player associations, 192-96
Progress, value of, 64, 72
Prole sports, 214, 216, 219
Protestant (work) ethic, 119, 125-28
Pseudosports, 23, 69, 215, 216, 230
Psychology, 1
Public sports arenas, 218-19
Punt, Pass, and Kick Contest, 68
Purdue University, 150
Puritans, attitude toward sport, 26, 50, 63, 116-18

Racism, 3, 5, 8, 13, 15, 63, 125, 153, 235-55
Radio, impact on sport, 36
Railroads, impact on sport, 31-33
Rainwater, Clarence E., 118
Rand Corporation, 289
Rankin, Judy, 281
Rapping, Leonard A., 251, 254
Rauch, G.E., 268
Recreation, company sponsored, 44-45
Recruiting
illegal, 13, 63, 125
Redford, Robert, 196

Redmond, Gerald, 120
Reformation, sport and religion, 116
Rehberg, Richard A., 220, 314
Reid, Elizabeth L., 160
Religion
  ceremonies, 112-13
  defined, 112
  encouragement of sport, 118-20
  functions of, 112-14
  history of sport and, 114-20
  as institution, 11, 112-14
  sport as, 111, 120-21
  sport, interrelationship, 111-37
  sport's use of, 111, 128-31
  use of sport by, 111, 121-25
Religious organization for athletes, 122-24
Republic, early, sports in, 27-28
Research perspectives
  muckraking, 13-14
  nonnormative, 13-14
  normative, 12-13
  value neutrality, 13
Reserve clause, 188-96, 199, 303-4
Reston, James, 89, 150
Retirement from sport, 91-92
Rhodes Scholars, 224
Rhodesia, 154
Richards, Bob, 122
Rickey, Branch, 236, 238
Riesman, David, 65
Riggins, John, 194
Riggs, Bobby, 274
Roberts, Oral, 122, 127
Robeson, Paul, 237
Robinson, Frank, 236, 251
Robinson, Jackie, 238, 256
Rockefeller, John D., 60
Rockne, Knute, 29, 111, 120
Rogers, Cornish, 120
Role, 9
Roller derby, 23, 215, 216, 230
Rollerball, 299
Rome, ancient, and sexism, 264
Rose Bowl, 154
Rosenblatt, Aaron, 245, 253-55
Roszak, Theodore, 292-93
Royal, Darrell, 144
Rozelle, Pete, 162, 171, 188
Rozelle Rule, 188, 194-95
Rubber, vulcanization of, impact on sport, 41
Rudi, Joe, 193
Rudolph, Frederick, 228
Rumania, 145
Russell, Bill, 236
Rutgers University, 32, 237
Ruth, Babe, 29, 73, 120, 196
Ryan, Allan, 273
Ryun, Jim, 72

Sabbath, sports on, 26, 111, 116, 118
Sage, George, 87, 157
St. Bernard, 115
St. Helena High School, 103
St. John the Divine Cathedral, 119
St. Louis Cardinals, 190, 192
St. Louis, Missouri, 43
St. Paul, 264
St. Thomas Aquinas, 264
Salaries, average in major leagues, 226
Sample, Johnny, 68
Sanders, Thomas G., 148
San Diego Conquistadores, 73
San Diego Rockets, 180
Sanford, David C., 248
San Francisco, 35
San Francisco 49ers, 249
San Jose State College, 154
"Sansan," 290
Sauer, George, 53, 70, 155, 316
Scapegoating, ritual, 7
Schafer, Walter, 83, 92, 103, 159, 160, 220
Schmidt, Susan, 252
Schoenke, Ray, 150
Schollander, Don, 274
Science, as an institution, 11
Scientific management, 46-47
Scott, Jack, 13, 100, 161, 197, 229, 313-15
Scully, Gerald W., 251-52, 254
Sears, Roebuck, 44
Segregation of spectators, 217-18
Selznick, Philip, 263
Serbin, L.A., 266
Sexism, 3, 13, 125, 262
  consequences of, 269-81
  myths, 270-75
  social sources for, 262-69
Sex role ideology, 262, 266-67
Sex role stereotyping
  of female athletes, 275
  freedom from, 5
  in mass media, 267-69

reinforcement of, through sport, 93
in school, 266-67
Seymour, Harold, 28
Shakespeare, 265
Shaw, Gary, 96
Shecter, Leonard, 162, 302
Sherman Antitrust Act, 152
Sherriff, Marie C., 276-77
Shoemaker, Willie, 150
Shostak, Arthur, 216
Shula, Don, 67
Simpson, O.J., 63, 172, 244
Simpson, Tony, 156
Sinatra, Frank, 196
Ski Retailer Council, 176
Skolnick, Jerome, 12
Slavery, 4, 28
Smelser, Neil, 114-15
Smith, Red, 196
Smith, Tommie, 147
Snyder, Eldon, 104-5
Soap Box Derby, 68
Social change, 4-5, 47
Social control, 8, 113
through sport in school, 88-89
Social Darwinism and sport, 52-54, 68-69
Social determinism, 4
Social forces, 3-4
Social life, complexity of, 5
Social location, 2-3
Social organization, 1-2
characteristics of, 1
imperfect nature of, 4
inertia of, 4
positive and negative consequences of, 4
as products of interaction, 4
Social psychological approach, 6
Social status through sport, 81-86, 88
Social structuration, 114
Social structure, 8-12
Socialization, 14, 59, 65-67, 70, 92-93, 97
anticipatory, 158
Society, 3-4, 113
inconsistencies in, 5
Sociobiology, 1
Sociological analysis, units of, 6-12
Sociological perspective
assumptions of, 2-5
problems with, 4-5
Sociology
assumptions of, 2-5
defined, 1
functions of, 3
problems with, 4-5
as a science, 12-14
use of history, 25
Sociology of sport
bibliographies of, 21
journals of, 22
research perspectives of, 12-14
South Africa, 154
apartheid policies, 144
Southeastern Conference (SEC), 238
Southern California, University of, 60
Southern Illinois, University of, 135, 253
Southwest Louisiana University, 95, 318
Sovern, Michael I., 188, 189
Soviet Union, 144-45
Spady, Williams, 317
Spates, J.L., 312
Spaulding, Albert G., 44
Spectators, 27
norms of, 9
reinforcement of values for, 72
sportmania, 15
Spencer, Herbert, 52, 265
Spitz, Mark, 73, 172
Sport
black, dominance in, 239-43
change, 153
corporate, 18-19, 169, 179-83, 319
defined, 16, 18
economics
amateur, 196
antitrust laws, 144
beneficiaries, 176-79
big business, 179
capitalistic values, 170-72
collegiate, 198-202
and corporation, 171-72
facilities, 183-87
as egalitarian, 209
functions for society, 11
history of black involvement in, 235-39
intercollegiate sport, 237-38
professional sport, 235-37
impact of federal government in, 144
informal, 18-19, 169, 319
institution, 11, 14, 49
intellectuals and, 298
media, 173
microcosm of society, 14-16, 25, 49, 55, 68-69, 104, 235
model of law and order, 144

opiate of the masses, 87, 148-49
organized, 18-19, 169, 319
participation, preference for, by social class, 211-13
pervasiveness of, 15-18, 29-30, 126-27
polity, 143-63
nationalism, 146-48
political uses of, 145-55
politicians, 149-51
propaganda vehicle, 145-46
pseudo, 23, 69, 215-16, 230
social class, 209-11
socialization agent, 151
social mobility, 219-29
consequences of accepting belief, 228-29
limitations of, 224-28
social stratification, 209-30
values, 59-75, 313-20
violence, 69-71, 298
Sportianity, 124-25, 127
Sporting News, The, 247
Sports in America, 280
Sportservice, 178
Sports Illustrated, 39, 97, 111, 124, 252, 268-69, 310
Spreitzer, Elmer, 104-5
Springfield College, 119
Sprong, Senator William B., 169
Stacking, as a form of discrimination, 245-50
Stadiums, 34, 183-87
Busch, 171
King County, 218
Mile High, 185
Rich, 171
Robert F. Kennedy, 183
Texas, 217
Yankee, 111, 183-84
Stagg, Amos Alonzo, 52
Standard Oil Company, 42
Stanford, Leland, 40
Stanford University, 249
Status (position), 9
Staub, Rusty, 196
Staubach, Roger, 124, 127
Steam engine, impact on sport, 31
Sterling, John, 303
Stockbridge, Michigan, 84
Stone, Gregory, 216
Strode, Woody, 236
Stumpf, Florence, 33, 37, 39, 120
Subculture, adolescent, 82-83
Success, value of, 60-61, 66-71
Sullivan, John L., 32
Sumner, William Graham, 53
Sunday League of America, 118
Superbowl, 67, 127, 162, 171, 173, 174, 178, 213
Superstition, 133-35
Supreme Court, and the reserve clause, 193
Sutton, Eddie, 135

Taboos, 134-35
Talamini, John T., 101, 302
Tangerine Bowl, 87
Tangu (of New Guinea), 69
Tannenbaum, Abraham J., 181
Taylor, Charlie, 68
Taylor, Frederick W., 46-47
Teams
effects of managerial change on, 7-8
goal attainment of, 7-8
homogeneity of members, 7-8
majority-minority relations in, 8
research settings, 6
social structure of, 7
Technology
impact on sport, 27, 30-41
value of progress, 64
Technosports, 299-300, 303, 320
Telegraph, impact on sport, 34-36
Telephone, impact on sport, 35-36
Television, 15, 25, 30, 37, 66, 72
Tennessee, University of, 74, 97, 238
Tessendorf, Irl, 249-50
Texas Rangers, 290
Texas, University of, 96-97
Theodosius, 115
Thomas, Clayton, 273
Thorpe, Jim, 111
Thucydides, 264
Tilden, Bill, 29
Title IX of the Educational Amendments Act of 1972, 280, 282-83, 309-10
Toffler, Alvin, 289
Touchdown Club, Birmingham, Alabama, 152
Tracy, California, 84
Tradition, sanctity of, 4
Transportation innovations and sport
internal combustion engine, 33-34
airplanes, 33-34
automobiles, 33-34
railroads, 31-33, 42
steam engine, 31
Tunney, Gene, 36

Tutko, Thomas, 157
Twentieth century, growth of sport, 29-30

Udall, Morris, 150
Ultimate Athlete, The, 319
Uni-Managers International, 177
United Automobile Workers, 45
United Nations, 146
United States Information Agency, 146
United States Naval Reserve, 147
United States Olympic Committee (USOC), 14-15, 143, 147, 197-98
United States Olympic Medical Training Services Committee, 273
U.S. Steel Corporation, 42
Unity, through sport, 87-90
University of California at Los Angeles, 222, 223
Urbanization, impact on sport, 27, 41-45, 117, 290
  and spectator sports, 43

Valued means to achieve, 63-64, 71-72
Values, 14, 47, 54
  American, 59-69, 311-13
    sport, 65-74, 88-89, 313-20
    sports creed, 127
  defined, 9, 59
  inconsistency with behavior, 59-60
  socialization through sport, 92-93
  value diversity, 59
Veblen, Thorstein, 79, 212
Veeck, Bill, 307
Vicksburg, Mississippi, 31
Violence, 8
  minimized through sport, 89
  sport, 69-71
Virginia, 116
Virginia, University of, 96

Wagner, Berny, 161
Walker, Moses, 236
Walker, Weldy, 236
Wall Street Journal, 306
Wall, William L., 202
Walker, Willard, 88, 102
Wallace, George, 150
Walton, Bill, 191, 315
Washington, D.C., 34
Washington, Gene, 249
Washington, Kenny, 236
Washington Monument, 149
Washington Redskins, 150, 174, 183
Washington Senators, 183
Washington State University, 252
Watergate, 62-63, 318
Wayman, Agnes, 272
Webb, Harry, 225
Weber, Max, 46, 125-26
Weinberg, S. Kirson, 228
Weiss, George, 162
Weitzman, D.E., 268
Werblin, Sonny, 73
Western culture, and sexism, 263, 265
Western Union, 35
White, Ray, 196
White, "Whizzer," 149
Whitworth, Kathy, 281
Whyte, William H., 65
Wichita, Kansas, 41
Wicker, Tom, 148
Wiener, Anthony J., 290, 302
Williams, Robin, 60
Williamson, Nancy, 261, 269
Wilson, Edward, 1
Wisconsin, University of, 93
Witchcraft, 136-37
Wolfe, Tom, 214
Woman's Action Group (WAG), 282
Women's Liberation, and sport, 281
WomenSports, 269
Wooden, John, 60-61
Worcester Polytechnic Institute, 100
World Cup, 148
World Football League, 175, 192, 303
World Hockey Association, 130, 303
World Series, 36, 173, 178, 213
World War II, 237, 239, 294
Wrestling, professional, 23
Wright, Oliver, 34
Wright, Wilbur, 34
Wrigley, Phillip K., 41
Wyoming, University of, 154

Yale University, 28, 32, 53, 80, 136
Yates Center, Kansas, 84
Year 2000, The, 294
Yetman, Norman R., 7, 252-55
Yinger, Milton, 82, 112
YMCA, 16, 18, 121

YMHA, 16
YWCA, 16, 121
Youth sports, 16, 22-23, 30, 67-68
Yugoslavia, 145
Zaharieva, E., 273
Zeioli, Billy, 124
Zeus, 115
Zuni Indians, 69, 114